In-Yer-Face Theatre

Aleks Sierz is theatre critic of *Tribune*, and also reviews for *The Stage*. He works as a freelance journalist and teaches at Goldsmiths College, University of London. He has written extensively about theatre.

in the same series

IN-YER-FACE THEATRE
British Drama Today

ALEKS SIERZ

faber and faber

First published in 2001
by Faber and Faber Limited
3 Queen Square London WC1N 3AU

Typeset by Faber and Faber Limited
Printed in England by Clays Ltd, St Ives plc

A CIP record for this book
is available from the British Library

ISBN 0–571–20049–4

10 9 8 7 6 5 4 3 2 1

For Lia Ghilardi and Krystyna Sierz

Contents

Acknowledgements

First, I would like to thank all the writers who answered my questions and generously gave of their time and energy to help me understand their work: Simon Block, David Eldridge, Harry Gibson, Nick Grosso, Sarah Kane, Tracy Letts, Patrick Marber, Phyllis Nagy, Anthony Neilson, Joe Penhall, Rebecca Prichard, Mark Ravenhill, Philip Ridley, Peter Rose, Che Walker, Naomi Wallace and Richard Zajdlic. I am also indebted to other theatre workers: Jack Bradley (National Theatre), Mike Bradwell (Bush), Ian Brown (Traverse), Stephen Daldry (Royal Court), Dominic Dromgoole (Bush), Sue Higginson (National Studio), Ben Jancovich (Hampstead), James Macdonald (Royal Court), Anne Mayer (Royal Court), Jonathan Meth (New Playwrights Trust/Writernet), Nick Philippou (Actors Touring Company), Simon Reade (Royal Shakespeare Company), Ian Rickson (Royal Court), Phil Setren (London New Play Festival), Paul Sirett (Soho Theatre Company), Jenny Topper (Hampstead), Graham Whybrow (Royal Court) and Phil Willmott (The Steam Industry).

Second, I am indebted to all those who read parts of the book, especially John Elsom, Lia Ghilardi, Simon Kane, Mel Kenyon, Dan Rebellato and David Tushingham.

Third, I would like to thank Danielle Ausrotas (William Morris Agency), Clare Barker (Rod Hall), Andreas Beck (Stuttgart), Guido Belli (Varese), Nicole Boireau (Metz University), John Bull (Reading University), Isobel Campbell, Catherine Cooper (*The Stage*), John Deeney (Ulster University), William Dixon, Cameron Duncan, Matthew Dunster, Michael Earley (Methuen), David Edgar, Jane Edwardes (*Time Out*), Alex Gammie (Bush), Giselle Glasman (Royal Court), Manny Goldstein, Amanda Hill (Bush), Marie-Louise Hogan (Casarotto Ramsay), Ian Herbert (*Theatre Record*), Nadine Holdsworth (De Montfort University), Stephanie Howard (Steppenwolf Theatre), Malcolm Jones (Theatre Museum), Eleanor Knight (Methuen), Jonathan Lewis, Mary Luckhurst (York University), Sally Ann Lycett (Royal Court), Jan McTaggart (Traverse), Samantha Marlowe (*What's On*), Louise Mulvey, John Richard Parker (MBA), Philip Patterson (Curtis Brown), Enrico Pitozzi (Bologna), Anna Reading (South Bank University), Caroline

Rees (*Tribune*), Guy Rose (Vernon Futerman), Jemima Rhys-Evans (Nick Hern), Alexa Sanzone (*New Yorker*), Emma Schad, Marieke Spencer, Ian Spring (Luton University), Nils Tabert (Hamburg), Peter Thomson (Exeter University), Simon Trussler (*New Theatre Quarterly*), Julia Tyrrell (Hamilton Asper), Emma Waghorn, Colin Watkeys and Carole Woddis. Without their aid, this book would have been much poorer. Any mistakes or misunderstandings are solely my responsibility.

Introduction

This is a personal and polemical history of British theatre in the
nineties, the most exciting decade for new writing since the heady days
sparked off by John Osborne's *Look Back in Anger* in 1956. Unlike most
accounts of contemporary British theatre – which focus on the work of
older writers such as Edward Bond, Howard Barker and Caryl Churchill
– this book looks at young writers such as Anthony Neilson, Sarah Kane
and Mark Ravenhill, as well as a host of other talents.

It puts writers, as opposed to directors, designers or performers, centre stage, not only because the writer is central to the process of play-
making but also because they have a wider significance: the writer
defines the Britishness of British theatre. What characterizes British
theatre during its golden ages of creativity – Elizabethan and Jacobean,
Restoration, Edwardian, and postwar – is not its actors, nor its directors,
nor its theorists, but its writers. The people you remember are Shakespeare and Webster, Congreve and Wycherley, Wilde and Shaw,
Osborne, Pinter, Bond and Stoppard. Not for nothing has the spoken
word in live performance had an importance in Britain that it lacks in
other theatre traditions. In fact, since the fifties and the media hype
about Angry Young Men, writers have become something of a tradition
in British theatre: they have held public conversations not only with
their audiences, but also with each other and with their precursors.

This book is based on the experience of going to the theatre. So, as
well as assessing the literary value of plays as texts, it also stresses the
contribution of directors, designers, actors and publicists in the creation
of a play's meaning. It is not just a literary critique of a body of writing,
but a series of frontline reports about what was happening on the public stage. It is mainly concerned with conveying what plays are like when
you see them in performance, what it feels like to see a whole rash of new
work, how the shock of the new is discussed and how meaning is created
from the experience of theatregoing.

One of this book's main sources is interviews with writers, as well as
with other theatre workers. It is mainly about writers who first came to
prominence in the nineties; although many were then in their twenties,

their age matters less than the fact that their theatre debuts took place at that time. Because it focuses on plays performed at the main London venues, it is less a guide to new writing than a personal selection of those writers and those plays that have had the most impact during an exciting decade.

Central to the story of new writing is Sarah Kane's *Blasted*, which opened at London's Royal Court theatre in January 1995. With its explicit scenes of sexual abuse and cannibalism, its blatant language and the rawness of its emotions, *Blasted* was both shockingly radical in form and deeply unsettling in content. It was attacked by critics with unprecedented fury and the resulting uproar demonstrated that, far from being irrelevant, theatre could be highly provocative and controversial. About six months later, Jez Butterworth's *Mojo* and the stage version of Irvine Welsh's *Trainspotting* began alerting audiences to an exciting new frankness of tone. Soon after, Mark Ravenhill's *Shopping and Fucking* and Patrick Marber's *Closer* were seen and discussed by people who ten years previously wouldn't have bothered to go to see a new play. In the wake of such successes, scores of young writers emerged and contributed to the renaissance in new writing. Stories about them appeared in the media; people with only a passing interest in drama became aware of the phenomenon. As a buzz developed, theatre was counted among the glories of British culture in that brief but highly hyped moment of cultural confidence known as Cool Britannia. New writing had rediscovered the angry, oppositional and questioning spirit of 1956, the year of the original Angry Young Men.

While writers once again became a valued cultural asset, it was one type of writer that had the most influence. The most important new writers, the ones that really changed the sensibility of British theatre in the nineties, were a small group of provocative in-yer-face antagonists. An avant-garde that explored theatrical possibility, they pioneered a new aesthetic – more blatant, aggressive and confrontational – that opened up new possibilities for British drama. In doing so, they helped revive playwriting, exploring new areas of expression and suggesting daring new experiments. Without them, writing for the stage might have stagnated and become increasingly irrelevant. In the nineties, British drama was in trouble; it was in-yer-face writers that saved British theatre.

The most provocative new writers of the decade – Anthony Neilson, Sarah Kane and Mark Ravenhill – had an influence that far outweighed the number of plays they wrote at the time, and that remained strong despite the uneven quality of some of their work. What they did was to transform the language of theatre, making it more direct, raw and explicit. They not only introduced a new dramatic vocabulary, they also pushed theatre into being more experiential, more aggressively aimed at making audiences feel and respond. Of course, all theatre has designs on the feelings of its audience – what characterized in-yer-face theatre was its intensity, its deliberate relentlessness and its ruthless commitment to extremes. As well as Neilson, Kane and Ravenhill, many other writers emerged during the decade, and, within a couple of years, their work was put on all over Europe and exported to the wider world. Since then, many have gone on to make film versions of their plays, introducing audiences outside the narrow ambit of theatre to their highly individual accounts of the new sensibility. In this way, theatre has been an image factory, producing ways of seeing that affect the wider culture. In the nineties, provocative theatre helped redefine what it meant to be British.

As far as that decade was concerned, contemporary theatre was in-yer-face theatre. But although it was new, it was not completely unprecedented. Chapter 1 defines its characteristics and discusses its historical antecedents. Chapter 2 looks at two writers (Philip Ridley and Phyllis Nagy) and two plays (*Trainspotting* and *Killer Joe*) that did much to popularize the new aesthetic. The next three chapters analyse the work of Neilson, Kane and Ravenhill, and a further three chapters take a thematic look at the characteristic aspects of the new theatrical style: men, sex and violence. The first looks at the crisis of masculinity as expressed in Jez Butterworth's *Mojo*, Naomi Wallace's *The War Boys*, Simon Block's *Not a Game for Boys* and David Eldridge's *Serving It Up*. The second examines contemporary views of sexual relationships by focusing on Patrick Marber's *Closer*, Nick Grosso's *Peaches* and *Sweetheart*, Che Walker's *Been So Long* and Richard Zajdlic's *Dogs Barking*, while the third analyses the problem of violence in the work of Martin McDonagh (*The Beauty Queen of Leenane*), Joe Penhall (*Some Voices*), Judy Upton (*Ashes and Sand* and *Bruises*) and Rebecca Prichard (*Yard Gal*). Amid the clamour of these diverse voices, an unforgettable picture emerges of contemporary British society that may be initially shocking but is ultimately a testament to the vision, creativity and resilience of this country's theatre.

January, 2000

IN-YER-FACE THEATRE

1 What is in-yer-face theatre?

It offends today, but we look harder and we know,
it will not offend tomorrow.

(Urgentino in Howard Barker's *Scenes from an Execution*)

On 4 November 1998, a small but lively audience filled the Pleasance theatre in north London for the opening night of *Snatch*, a seventy-five-minute play by twenty-one-year-old Peter Rose. Put on by the Soho Theatre Company, it kicked off a four-week season of new drama. As the programme explained, to make the most of the excitement generated when the 'text is lifted off the page and, for the very first time, acquires a life of its own', each play was given only one week of rehearsal. This both saved money and meant that the work was seen in its 'most raw and energetic state'.

Set in an untidy flat, *Snatch* begins with two students, Paul and Simon, boasting about a girl they've picked up and raped during the night. As dawn breaks, a huddled figure lying at the back of the stage begins to move. When she gets up, Beth is trembling and covered in bruises. 'It could be worse,' she says, 'I could be you.' 'There's a draught,' says one of the blokes. 'Shut your legs.' Simon goes out and Beth curls up in a foetal position. Paul, who claims to be a real 'ladykiller', tries to rape her again. Suddenly, there is a red flash and Beth and Paul swap bodies. Now Beth strides around the room showing off 'her' muscles and Paul cowers, defenceless in a woman's body. Beth gags and ties him up. When Simon returns, she invites him to abuse 'Beth', and he does so, unaware that he is having sex with his mate. Beth returns with a tattoo on 'her' forehead. It reads RAPIST. Simon is appalled. Then Beth cuts off 'her' penis. As the blood spreads, there is another flash and Beth and Paul swap bodies again. Beth blinds Simon and leaves, shouting: 'I'll get over this – I will.'

With a full-on play such as this, you expect an emotional reaction from the audience. When Beth mutilated 'her' manhood, there were gasps. Some people hid their eyes. Next to me, two young women squirmed. Men instinctively squeezed their thighs together. There were groans. When the play was over, and the audience began to leave, some people complained about the play's viciousness, others hated its brutal images, but a few were excited by its emotional punch. Rose's youth was

3

mentioned, his writing praised, his imagination attacked. It was pointed out that even when Beth had become a bloke, it was a woman's body that bore the brunt of male attack; others noted that, compared to the laddish banter, the woman's voice was muted. Most tried to come to grips with the anger and agony shown onstage. But, above all, what was striking was the buzz of discussion – this audience had gone to the theatre and emerged shaken, talking, arguing, feeling.

Watching *Snatch*, I was reminded of the gut rage of Sarah Kane's *Blasted*, the gender issues of Mark Ravenhill's *Shopping and Fucking* and the fearsome violence of Anthony Neilson's *Penetrator*. It was neither the first play of its kind nor the last, but it was one of those moments when you feel that a new sensibility has become the norm in British theatre. In-yer-face theatre had not only arrived, it had become the dominant theatrical style of the decade.

The widest definition of in-yer-face theatre is any drama that takes the audience by the scruff of the neck and shakes it until it gets the message. It is a theatre of sensation: it jolts both actors and spectators out of conventional responses, touching nerves and provoking alarm. Often such drama employs shock tactics, or is shocking because it is new in tone or structure, or because it is bolder or more experimental than what audiences are used to. Questioning moral norms, it affronts the ruling ideas of what can or should be shown onstage; it also taps into more primitive feelings, smashing taboos, mentioning the forbidden, creating discomfort. Crucially, it tells us more about who we really are. Unlike the type of theatre that allows us to sit back and contemplate what we see in detachment, the best in-yer-face theatre takes us on an emotional journey, getting under our skin. In other words, it is experiential, not speculative.

The phrase 'in-your-face' is defined by the *New Oxford English Dictionary* (1998) as something 'blatantly aggressive or provocative, impossible to ignore or avoid'. The *Collins English Dictionary* (1998) adds the adjective 'confrontational'. The phrase originated in American sports journalism during the mid-seventies, and gradually seeped into more mainstream slang over the following decade. It implies that you are being forced to see something close up, that your personal space has been invaded. It suggests the crossing of normal boundaries. In short, it describes perfectly the kind of theatre that puts audiences in just such a situation.

How can you tell if a play is in-yer-face? It really isn't difficult: the language is usually filthy, characters talk about unmentionable subjects, take their clothes off, have sex, humiliate each another, experience unpleasant emotions, become suddenly violent. At its best, this kind of theatre is so powerful, so visceral, that it forces audiences to react: either they feel like fleeing the building or they are suddenly convinced that it is the best thing they have ever seen, and want all their friends to see it too. It is the kind of theatre that inspires us to use superlatives, whether in praise or condemnation.

Usually, when writers use shock tactics, it is because they have something urgent to say. If they are dealing with disturbing subjects, or want to explore difficult feelings, shock is one way of waking up the audience. Writers who provoke audiences or try to confront them are usually trying to push the boundaries of what is acceptable – often because they want to question current ideas of what is normal, what it means to be human, what is natural or what is real. In other words, the use of shock is part of a search for deeper meaning, part of a rediscovery of theatrical possibility – an attempt by writers to see just how far they can go.

Provocation in performance can range from a new tone of voice being heard for the first time, a question of sensibility, to deliberate attacks on an audience's prejudices. The most successful plays are often those that seduce the audience with a naturalistic mood and then hit it with intense emotional material, or those where an experiment in form encourages people to question their assumptions. In such cases, what is being renegotiated is the relationship between audience and performers – shock disturbs the spectator's habitual gaze.

Controversy may often be sought, but usually only takes off by chance. For a play to be controversial, it needs to touch raw nerves. Often, although the audience's feelings of discomfort and outrage are real enough, the form that controversy takes is itself a performance: walkouts, letters to the press, leader articles denouncing a 'waste of public money', calls for bans or cuts in funding, mocking cartoons, questions in parliament, or even prosecution on charges of obscenity or blasphemy.

A useful distinction can be made between the hot and cool versions of in-yer-face theatre. The hot version – often performed in small studio theatres with audiences of between fifty and 200 people – uses the aesthetics of extremism. The language is blatant, the actions explicit, the emotions heightened. Here, the aggression is open and the intention is to make the experience unforgettable. Cooler versions mediate the disturbing power of extreme emotions by using a number of distancing devices: larger auditoriums, a more naturalistic style or a more traditional structure. Comedy is the most effective distancing device and can sometimes completely defuse an emotionally fraught situation. After all, a common reaction to terror is either to ignore it or to laugh at it.

But whether hot or cool, this kind of theatre should always have an unusual power to trouble the audience emotionally, to contain material that questions our ideas about who we are. For this reason, what outraged audiences say is often revealing: the vocabulary of disgust nearly always involves ideas about what is dirty, what is natural, what is human, what is right and proper. Most in-yer-face theatre challenges the distinctions we use to define who we are: human/animal; clean/dirty; healthy/unhealthy; normal/abnormal; good/evil; true/untrue; real/unreal; right/wrong; just/unjust; art/life. These binary oppositions are central to our world-view; questioning them can be unsettling. But the terms in which a play is attacked says as much about the attackers as about the play. Often, some members of the audience are blinded by their own outrage – they remember words or scenes that never occurred onstage. Such incidents show just how malleable memory can be.

In-yer-face theatre always forces us to look at ideas and feelings we would normally avoid because they are too painful, too frightening, too unpleasant or too acute. We avoid them for good reason – what they have to tell us is bad news: they remind us of the awful things human beings are capable of, and of the limits of our self-control. They summon up ancient fears about the power of the irrational and the fragility of our sense of the world. At the same time, theatre is similar to other cultural forms in that it provides a comparatively safe place in which to explore such emotions. Experiential theatre is potent precisely when it threatens to violate that sense of safety.

A play's content can be provocative because it is expressed in blatant or confrontational language or stage images, but its power as drama also depends greatly on its form. The further a play departs from the conventions of naturalism, especially those of the well-made three-act drama, the more difficult it is for many audiences to accept. On the other hand, some shocking emotional material may be made more acceptable by being placed within a theatrical frame that is traditional, either in its tone or form. Naturalistic representations of disturbing subjects are usually much easier to handle than emotionally fraught situations that are presented in a unfamiliar theatrical style.

How can theatre be so shocking? The main reason is that it is live. Taboos are broken not in individual seclusion but out in the open. When you're watching a play, which is mostly in real time with real people acting just a few feet away from you, not only do you find yourself reacting but you also know that others are reacting and are aware of your reaction. Subjects that might be bearable when you read about them in private suddenly seem electrifying when shown in public. Situations that are essentially private, such as sex, seem embarrassingly intimate onstage. Compared with the rather detached feeling of reading a playtext, sitting in the dark surrounded by a body of people while watching an explicit performance can be an overwhelming experience. When taboos are broken in public, the spectators often become complicit witnesses.

Because every performance is different, there is always the risk that something unexpected might happen. In a provocative play, this feeds into the tension of what is happening onstage. For such reasons, theatre can be a place that conveys a strong sense of territorial threat and of the vulnerability of the audience's personal space. Live performance heightens awareness, increases potential embarrassment, and can make the representation of private pain on a public stage almost unendurable. But theatre depends not only on willing suspension of disbelief but also on empathy. For while no one believes literally in what is shown onstage – no actual atrocity is actually being committed – many spectators will invest emotionally in it. Although what is shown is make-believe, they take it close to their hearts. And because the actors are always real people breathing the same air as the audience, the public tends to empathize strongly with them.

For these reasons, in-yer-face theatre has the potential to be much more visceral, more shocking than other art forms. It can sometimes be an emotional journey that gives you a startling feeling of having lived through the experience being represented. This can tell you more about an extreme state of mind than just reading about it. And since censorship in Britain was abolished in 1968, theatre has been a much freer cultural space than film or television. But if provocative theatre is a search for a deeper knowledge of ourselves, what does it tell us?

Because humans are language animals, words often seem to cause more offence than the acts to which they refer. Taboo words, such as 'fuck' and 'cunt', work because we give them a magic power, which makes them more than simple signs that describe a real-life event or thing. Like all taboos, they are a way of guarding against imagined infections, a way

7

of drawing a line that must not be crossed. In every case, the words tell us all we need to know about what a culture is embarrassed by, afraid of or resentful about. The violent impact of sexual swearwords in British culture says much about what we feel about sex or women. Because they refer to sex, but are violent in intent, those words pack a double punch. Unlike euphemism, which is a way of defusing difficult subjects, of circling around a meaning, the swearword aims to compact more than one hatred, becoming a verbal act of aggression, a slap in the mouth. In theatre, 'bad language' seems even stronger because it is used openly.

Staging private and intimate situations in public generates a strong emotional charge which can feel more unsettling than the same experience in real life. Theatre is a deliberate act, and can cause offence because the representation of real life is invested with more power than real life itself. When it comes to showing sex onstage, its public performance immediately raises questions about privacy, voyeurism and 'realistic' acting. We may suspend disbelief about many emotions in theatre, but we know that most sex acts in public are not the real thing. Nevertheless, showing sex in public is often unsettling because it is a reminder of many of our most intimate feelings, and of what we most desire to keep secret. Images of sex cause anxiety because they refer to powerful and uncontrollable feelings. When sex is coupled with emotions such as neediness or loneliness, the effect can be immensely disturbing.

Nudity onstage is more powerful than nudity in films, paintings or sculpture for the simple reason that a real person is actually present. Unable to hide behind camera angles or fig leaves, the nudity of the actor can expose human frailty as well as the body beautiful, our mortality as well as our resilience. A naked body's inherent vulnerability can be heavy with metaphorical significance: it can be morally 'exposed', or 'stripped' of illusions. At other times, removing your clothes can be an act of political power, of liberation from convention, a statement of transgression that can expose a spectator's mixed feelings about being naked. As always, responses to a natural fact, nudity, imply a cultural act, nakedness in all the many meanings of the word.

Violence becomes impossible to ignore when it confronts you by showing pain, humiliation and degradation. Sometimes this is a question of showing violent acts literally; at other times, the suggestion of extreme mental cruelty is enough to disturb. Violent actions are shocking because they break the rules of debate; they go beyond words and thus can get out of control. Violence feels primitive, irrational and destructive. Violence onstage also disturbs when we feel the emotion behind the acting, or catch ourselves enjoying the violence vicariously.

Provocative theatre is controversial because, although most people assume that mere titillation is bad and that gratuitous violence is irresponsible, no one can agree which plays fall into which category.

What most affronts us can sometimes be what most fascinates us. It is as if we want to know more about ourselves, but are too afraid to find out. Because in-yer-face theatre is about intimate subjects, it touches what is both most central to our humanity and most often hidden in our daily behaviour. The public staging of secret desires and monstrous acts both repels us and draws us in. And there is always the possibility that what we enjoy watching might tell us unwelcome truths about who we really are.

Shock is an essential part of a confrontational sensibility. Depending as it does on audience expectations, it is usually relative. What startles us the first time may merely amuse us the second time. Small shocks may gradually make us immune to bigger ones. Shock is relative not only in terms of time and experience but also in terms of geography. While in Britain most metropolitan audiences are unshockable, or want to appear to be so, small-town audiences may react with greater disgust, or perhaps greater candour.

Often shock comes from demolishing the simple binary oppositions that hold society together. In this way, modernism's 'shock of the new' has a political agenda. It asks profound questions about social mores and moral norms. Sensation spawns many tactics: from startling audiences by attacking them to refusing to provide easily digestible meanings. Even when newness itself becomes an established tradition – the avant-garde writers of one decade become the school syllabus fodder of the next – shock can still force spectators to reassess their responses. It can educate the senses as well as stimulating curiosity. And because it often sells shows, shock can also be a marketing tool.

Just because something is shocking does not mean it is automatically good or praiseworthy. Just because a work is openly aggressive does not mean that it is profound, or excellent, or ethical. The wish to disgust may be politically motivated, but it can also be puerile. Since almost any theatrical image can be used either in a way that conveys moral outrage or in a way that is voyeuristic and reactionary, a negative reaction to sensation is not necessarily philistine. For these reasons, confrontational theatre is a constantly contested territory.

In the nineties, in-yer-face theatre injected a dose of blatant extremism into British theatre and changed theatrical sensibility. But although it was a new phenomenon, it also had firm roots in tradition.

A brief history of provocation

In-yer-face drama is a theatrical space with a distinctive geography that has attracted explorers for centuries. On the cover of the playtext of Sarah Kane's *Blasted* is a photograph of a man's face with both eyes gouged out: it could be Oedipus, Gloucester or Hamm. The programme of *Trainspotting* shows men in skull masks, a reminder of T. S. Eliot's image of Jacobean theatre: 'The skull beneath the skin.' Sex and violence are scarcely new in theatre.

The greatest of the ancient Greek tragedies deal with extreme states of mind: brutal deaths and terrible suicides, agonizing pain and dreadful suffering, human sacrifice and cannibalism, rape and incest, mutilations and humiliations. Thanks to Freud, Oedipus now symbolizes the most familiar taboo – even to people who never go to the theatre. And think of the crimes and emotions, from child murder to incestuous passion, evoked by the names Medea, Phaedra and Agamemnon. The content of tragedy is a meeting between the waywardness of fate and some of our most intimate fears, and the Greeks were well aware of the mixture of heroism and hopelessness involved in taking a stand against the inexorable and inexplicable. But of all the theories about the purpose of tragedy, the most suggestive is the idea that it was meant to purge the bad feelings of the audience. The idea of putting yourself through hell in order to exorcize your inner demons is at the root of experiential theatre. Yet Greek drama was probably intended not to attack but to heal the audience, to make it better able to face its time. This argues for a kind of utilitarian role for theatre, making it a form of shock therapy.

The heightened emotions of Greek tragedy must have battered audience sensibilities. Plutarch, for example, records that, at one performance of a lost play by Euripides, the audience rose to its feet in horror when, in ignorance, a mother was about to kill her son. In an anonymous *Life of Aeschylus*, it says that at the beginning of his *Eumenides*, spectators were so shocked by the fearful appearance of the Furies that children fainted and women miscarried. (So much for the notion that women and children weren't allowed into the theatre.)

True or not, such stories remind us that tragedy should churn up the emotions; they also challenge writers to reinvent the genre.

Helped by Renaissance translations of Seneca, the Jacobean version of tragedy delighted in horrible murder, painful torture, wanton acts of cruelty and vicious vengeance. Not for nothing is the revenge tragedy called the 'tragedy of blood'. Consider the ingredients of Horatio's closing speech in *Hamlet*: 'Of carnal, bloody, and unnatural acts,/ Of accidental judgements, casual slaughters'. In other plays, murder is depicted in bloody detail, with poisoned pictures and skulls (*The White Devil* and *The Revenger's Tragedy*), mutilation (*The Changeling*) and even incest ('*Tis Pity She's a Whore*). You can see why George Bernard Shaw saw in John Webster's work only gratuitous shocks, and christened him 'Tussaud Laureate'. Because they occur in so many plays – from *Titus Andronicus* to *King Lear* – such effects were obviously popular. Audiences were delighted by horrific stage images and thrilled by depictions of evil, but what tended to disturb them was the upsetting of the Christian moral universe that such acts implied. Only the expectation that morality would be finally restored gave them permission to guiltlessly enjoy such poetic inflammations of sensation, such orgies of feeling.

Long after the Jacobean age, the thrill and chill of gore lived on, like an impoverished vampire feeding off a richer host, in gothic fantasy, melodrama, Grand Guignol ('great punch') and the horror story. No one could bury the lush language of violence, the shock of forbidden desire or the fun of transgression. Small wonder that critics label some violent contemporary plays 'Jacobean'.

But uncontrolled emotions were often seen as dangerous, and the best way of making theatre safe for audiences was censorship. Introduced in Britain in 1737, modified in 1843 and, from 1909, governed by parliamentary guidelines, strict rules controlled the nation's stages. The Lord Chamberlain read and licensed all plays, forbidding the showing of material that was indecent, blasphemous or otherwise offensive: from explicit stagings of sex and violence to suggestions of 'perversion'. The list of things routinely banned included swearwords; nudity; risqué stage business; representations of God, the Royal family or anyone living; and homosexuality. Profanity was forbidden and political radicalism discouraged. An actor and actress could not appear together in bed under the same sheet. Until its abolition, theatrical censorship was a fair index not of what the Establishment thought was offensive but of what it thought would be too much for the general public. But if in theory the censor was authoritarian, unaccountable and undemocratic, in practice the process was one of negotiation: his edicts were contested by writers, and a compromise reached.

The effects of censorship were paradoxical: on the one hand, it aimed to inhibit even suggestions of sex and violence; on the other, it drew attention to them, often publicizing a play more effectively than any advertising. Censorship aimed to make theatre safe, but by doing so it provoked writers to examine subjects simply because they were forbidden. It also tended to make writers give moral justifications for plays that were confrontational or subversive.

Victorian and Edwardian theatre belongs to an age when strict ideas of decorum policed the public stage. George Bernard Shaw and Harley Granville-Barker were censored more than once. As late as 1909, Edward Garnett couldn't describe the condition of the heroine of his play, *The Breaking Point*, as 'pregnant' because it was considered vulgar and likely to inflame lascivious thoughts. He had to use the French '*enceinte*'. If you were classy enough to speak French, presumably you were immune to sudden lust.

Foreign imports were often regarded with dread. Several adaptations of Dumas's *La Dame aux camélias* were banned. When Henrik Ibsen's *Ghosts* had its London premiere in 1891, critics were shocked by its allusions to syphilis. The *Telegraph* called it an 'open drain; a loathsome sore unbandaged' and the *Standard* said it was 'unutterably offensive'. The outrage of the critics may seem exaggerated, yet their expressions of a sense of defilement and dirt clearly show how a naturalistic play could cross the imaginary boundary between the decent and the dirty. This feeling is satirized in Act III of Noel Coward's *Private Lives* (1930), when Sibyl complains: 'I feel smirched and unclean as though slimy horrible things have been crawling all over me.'

Sometimes one word was enough to set off an explosion. A celebrated breach of stage decorum occurs in Shaw's *Pygmalion*, when Eliza, a cockney who has been taught to speak 'proper', makes a humorous lapse:

LIZA [*perfectly elegant diction*] Walk! Not bloody likely.
[*Sensation*]. I am going in a taxi.

The sensation this caused when the play was first put on in London in April 1914 was not confined to the stage. On Eliza's exit line, the audience gasped, then burst out laughing, paused, then laughed again – this time for so long that Shaw felt 'really doubtful' whether the play could go on.

What made Eliza's expletive explosive was the fact that it was uttered by a woman. In the following days, despite the threat of world war, a moral panic built up. Bishops wanted to ban the play, one even claiming to be saddened that such a vulgar word had to be uttered by a married actress who had children. The Women's Purity League protested to the prime minister. The *Daily Express* found a real Covent Garden flower girl called Eliza, took her to the show and reported that she'd been shocked. The Eton debating society attacked the 'debasement' of the commercial theatre, while the Oxford Union voted in favour of the 'sanguinary expletive' as 'a liberating influence on the English language'.

The clever thing about Shaw's play is that after Eliza's exit the rest of the scene is used to defuse the shock of her line. 'Old-fashioned' Mrs Eynsford Hill says that although her daughter Clara calls everything 'filthy and beastly', 'bloody' is too much; Pickering claims ignorance – he has been in India for so long that manners have changed. Working-class vocabulary is dismissed as the 'new small talk'. Eventually, Clara sums up: 'It's all a matter of habit. Nobody means anything by it.' Such words simply give 'such a smart emphasis to things that are not in themselves witty'.

No better example of a word's trajectory from sensational to mundane can be found than Shaw's 'bloody'. By 1956, when *My Fair Lady*, the musical version of *Pygmalion*, was put on at London's Drury Lane, 'bloody' was deemed too banal to have the right effect. Instead, during the Ascot scene, Eliza urges on her horse by shouting: 'Move your ruddy arse!' The adjective had at first been 'blooming' but had been changed because audiences had been found to be more responsive to 'ruddy'. By the time *My Fair Lady* was made into a film, in 1964, the phrase had reverted to: 'Move yer bloomin' arse!' Gauging the power of words – even euphemisms – is clearly a matter of fine tuning.

Even in private houses, select audiences were not safe from embarrassment. Intimate scenes always caused disquiet. A clear example occurred in 1923, when a performance of Arthur Schnitzler's *Reigen* (*La Ronde*) was given at a private party in London. Members of the Bloomsbury Group were there and Virginia Woolf complained that 'the audience felt simply as if a real copulation were going on in the room and tried to talk down the very realistic groans made by [Ralph] Partridge! It was a great relief when Marjorie sang hymns.'

Outside such coteries, Continental modernism was often perceived as dangerous. Imports that fell foul of the censor include Strindberg's

Miss Julie, Pirandello's *Six Characters in Search of an Author* and Wedekind's *Spring Awakening*. If British theatre guarded itself against shock, it soon found experimental theatre creeping in, despite rigorous border controls. Although the earliest London production of Georg Büchner's *Woyzeck* – the first working-class tragedy – was delayed until 1948, other writers didn't have to wait so long. Gradually, small groups of enthusiasts learnt the lessons of Zola and Ibsen, Strindberg and Chekhov, Jarry and Tzara, Wedekind and Brecht, Ionesco and Genet, Grotowski and Artaud. Especially Artaud. Not surprisingly, his radical ideas about a Theatre of Cruelty were derived from the Greeks and Jacobeans. One of transgressive theatre's greatest theorists, he was also the least performed. But his writings proved inspirational:

> The theatre will never find itself again except by furnishing the spectator with the truthful precipitates of dreams, in which his taste for crime, his erotic obsessions, his savagery, his chimeras, his utopian sense of life and matter, even his cannibalism, pour out on a level not counterfeit and illusory, but interior.

(Antonin Artaud, 'The Theatre of Cruelty: First Manifesto')

This was written during the thirties, and even though Artaud was not immediately translated into English, his ideas rapidly crossed the Channel.

Equally suspect was traffic across the Atlantic. Naturalism was provocative when it crossed those imaginary boundaries between the 'done thing' and the unthinkable. Middle-class audiences, described by Terence Rattigan as 'Aunt Ednas', were often allergic to depictions of the rougher side of life. In 1949, Tennessee Williams's *A Streetcar Named Desire*, which opened in the West End, was shocking because audiences were not used to seeing life in the raw: domestic brawls, a rape scene and even the sound of a lavatory flushing offstage troubled the public.

Yet naturalism was preferable to the Absurd. Joan Plowright remembers director George Devine's pleasure when their 1957 production of Ionesco's *The Chairs* – at London's Royal Court theatre – was greeted with walkouts and cries of 'surrealist rubbish'. 'When people went out shouting and grumbling into Sloane Square,' she recalls, 'George would watch through his window and smoke his pipe and think: "That's what I'm here for."' At the Court, scandal soon became a tradition.

In the postwar period, censorship was increasingly seen as a trivial nuisance and writers began to enjoy provoking the Lord Chamberlain. The way to avoid censorship was to form the theatre into a private club, which sold tickets only to members in advance. Club performances were allowed on the assumption that the audience was select and that innocent members of the public couldn't just wander in. Once again, a largely imaginary distinction allowed uncensored club theatres to exist side-by-side with a rigorously controlled mainstream.

The absurdities of censorship were exemplified by the case of Samuel Beckett. Here was an internationally renowned literary figure who was treated as if he were a smutty schoolboy. When *Endgame* was submitted to the Lord Chamberlain in 1958, it was rejected because Hamm's line about God – 'The bastard! He doesn't exist!' – was judged to 'do violence to the sentiment of religious reverence'. A French version of the play had been performed the year before without any problems, so one suggestion was to say the line in French. As the Court's George Devine pointed out: 'You can get away with much more in French.' Beckett refused on principle, but later changed 'bastard' to 'swine'. This was accepted. Yet the censor always looked suspiciously at Beckett's work: he was not allowed to have an ambiguous line such as 'Let me in' said on tape in *Krapp's Last Tape* because the 'Lord Chamberpot' imagined it referred to a man 'rogering' a woman.

Homosexuality was both illegal and seen by some as 'unnatural', so blatant representations of it were banned. Some writers, often pioneering Americans, challenged this. Robert Anderson's *Tea and Sympathy* (1953) or one kiss in Arthur Miller's *A View from the Bridge* (1956) were daring enough to upset audiences. When the Lord Chamberlain considered Tennessee Williams's *Suddenly Last Summer* in 1958, he was more worried about its references to homosexuality than about its account of cannibalism. But the censor wasn't as oppressive as liberal myths have it. After he relaxed the rules in December 1958, allowing homosexuality to be shown, there was no great rush of gay plays.

Although most shocks were due to taboo subjects and deliberate transgressions, sometimes offence was caused by the arrival of a new sensibility. At the legendary first night of John Osborne's *Look Back in Anger* on 8 May 1956 at the Royal Court, what offended the critics was not only the shabby setting (a Nottingham bedsit rather than a Home Counties living room) but also the hectoring tone of the play, and especially the language used by its antihero, Jimmy Porter. When Lord Harewood, a member of the board, showed the text to a friend, the response was: 'Well, it's very excitingly written, but you can't put that on in a theatre! People won't stand for being shouted at like that, it's not what they go to the theatre for.' If, in the year of Suez, Britain was complacently snoozing, Osborne wanted to shake it awake, to teach audiences to feel. To do so, he showed how class war can be fought through sexual conquest. Many critics resented this. One hated *Look Back in Anger*'s 'laborious shock tactics', another 'felt bruised' by its 'verbal artillery'. But while the play became notorious, it was not the only shock to hit theatre in 1956. Nigel Dennis's *Cards of Identity*, also at the Court, aroused even more hostility. In it, the Rev Golden Orfe delivers a ten-minute sermon, which begins: 'I stink, therefore I am.' This was regularly interrupted by shouts of 'Get off!' or 'Rubbish!', and, occasionally, by the slamming of vacated seats.

One of the ways in which sensibility became increasingly in-yer-face was when dramatists searched for new social landscapes to explore. At the Theatre Royal Stratford East, Joan Littlewood introduced new themes in Irish and working-class accents by writers such as Brendan Behan and Shelagh Delaney. At the Court, John Arden, Arnold Wesker, Edward Bond and David Mercer (joined by Barrie Keeffe at the Soho Poly) began to depict the working classes, the poor and disadvantaged, as well as people who lived outside the Home Counties. This could shock, annoy or confuse those used to cut-glass accents and French windows. Gangs, rituals and hooligan violence burst onto the scene in Ann Jellicoe's fiercely unorthodox 1958 street-gang saga, *The Sport of My Mad Mother*. Later, Jellicoe's *The Knack* shocked some sixties audiences not because it was suggestive but because its characters were working class.

Under the rules of censorship, nudity on the British stage was only allowed if the figure did not move. Hence Osborne's *The Entertainer* in 1957 featured a motionless female nude 'in Britannia's helmet and holding a bulldog and trident', her tackiness an apt symbol of lost empire. But equally powerful could be the suggestion of violence. Two years later, Arden's *Serjeant Musgrave's Dance* featured a machine gun trained on the audience, a potent image of war. As always, what happens in front of the spectators' eyes is less important than what happens inside their minds.

In 1961, Tom Murphy's debut, *A Whistle in the Dark*, at Stratford East, struck critic Kenneth Tynan as 'the most uninhibited display of brutality that the London theatre has ever witnessed'. Interestingly enough, the violence onstage is swift and sharp. The troubling sense of brutalization comes from the language that Dada uses to control his sons, and from scenes we hear about but do not witness. Fintan O'Toole writes that 'the most violent image of the play is not to do with knives and knuckle dusters and chains. It is Harry's memory of a teacher searching his hair for lice and fleas, a memory of cruelty and degradation.'

The repellent and unremitting savagery in David Rudkin's work aimed to exorcize unconscious demons by assaulting audience sensibilities. In *Afore Night Come*, he got around the censor by substituting 'firk' for 'fuck' – which looks different in print but, when said onstage in a Worcestershire accent, sounds the same. When it was first put on by the Royal Shakespeare Company in 1962, the *Sunday Telegraph*'s Alan Brien reported that one spectator fainted when the severed head of the ritually sacrificed old tramp 'was slowly rolled in a furry ball towards the footlights'. Like other reviewers, Brien then aptly quotes Artaud on drama being the 'truthful precipitate of dreams'. Rudkin's work is a nightmare of animal copulations, guards sodomizing prisoners, dismemberment, demented and deformed characters, werewolves; in one case, a baby is eaten; in another, a womb is burnt, yet the meaning always involves purgation and, ultimately, regeneration. Despite the fact that Rudkin's shock tactics are critical of social norms and his ideas about sexuality ally him with some feminists, his work has been marginalized by its own extremism.

The censor was suspicious of more than just bad language. The abortion scene in *Alfie* (1963) was not allowed to happen onstage; the hanging scene at the end of Arden's *Armstrong's Last Goodnight* (1964) was not allowed to be too graphic, or too political – hanging had not yet been abolished. The disturbing infantilism of David Mercer's *Ride a Cock Horse* (1965) was closely scrutinized. Peter Terson's football saga *Zigger Zagger* (1967), a rowdy, youthful play, was one of the last to get the blue-pencil treatment. Among other things, the censor wanted Terson to change 'spring up your arse' to 'spring in your arse'. But the play's aggression came not from graphic violence (there was none), but from the mighty roar of football chants coming from a cast of eighty.

The early sixties saw the first steps in the emergence of a truly confrontational theatre in Britain. When Charles Marowitz and Ken Dewey staged a Happening at the Edinburgh Theatre Conference in 1963, they caused a sensation when a nude woman appeared. But because she was wheeled in on a trolley, Dewey could evade censorship by arguing that she wasn't moving. Still, the Lord Chamberlain wasn't always dogmatic: in the same year, he allowed a glimpse of Honor Klein's breasts in J. B. Priestley and Iris Murdoch's *A Severed Head*.

One of the foremost champions of Artaud's ideas was Peter Brook. In the 1964 'Theatre of Cruelty' season, he used Artaud's theories in a series of experiments that sparked the 'dirty plays' controversy. When he put on Peter Weiss's *The Marat/Sade*, Brook wrote one of the classic manifestos of provocative theatre: the intention was to 'crack the spectator on the jaw, then douse him with ice-cold water, then force him to assess intelligently what has happened to him, then give him a kick in the balls, then bring him back to his senses again'. Reviewing the play, Charles Marowitz commented on its 'genuine feel of violence and hostility'. Brook used the season to smash taboos left, right and centre. Glenda Jackson, playing Jackie Kennedy and Christine Keeler, stripped off in the bath. As Keeler, she whipped a client. In Genet's *The Screens*, actors mimed defecation. In Artaud's *Spurt of Blood*, a woman lifted her skirt to reveal a nest of scorpions. The 'dirty plays' controversy – in which libertarians took on conservatives, and reckless youth thumbed its nose at venerable age – filled the correspondence columns of *The Times*. Theatre suddenly seemed to matter again.

By the mid-sixties, liberals were becoming increasingly provocative. On 13 November 1965, during a live BBC late-night discussion about showing sex onstage, Kenneth Tynan said 'fuck' for the first time on television. 'The result,' says Kathleen Tynan, his widow, 'was to set off an explosion, to produce a national fit of apoplexy.' The discussion, chaired by Robert Robinson, was about censorship, and Tynan's offending sentence was: 'I doubt if there are very many rational people in this world to whom the word "fuck" is particularly diabolical or revolting or totally forbidden.' Was he being deliberately provocative? Certainly – he was meant to be answering a question about whether sex acts should be allowed onstage. But he didn't use the word in anger. In fact, he later explained, 'I used an old English word in a completely neutral way to illustrate a serious point.' The public disagreed. The BBC switchboard was jammed and, over the next few days, as Tynan's collection of more than a thousand newspaper cuttings shows, the story took off all over the world. The *Daily Express*'s political correspondent, William Barkley, wrote that Tynan's use of the four-letter word was 'the bloodiest outrage I have ever known'. The *Sunday Times* quoted a history of colloquial English that claimed that the word 'chills the blood and raises gooseflesh'. Mrs Mary Whitehouse, leader of the 1964 Clean Up TV Campaign, wrote to the Queen. Four motions were set down in parliament. Robinson now says that breaking the taboo felt like defying a 'magic prohibition'.

The night after the incident, Tynan was on a panel at the Royal Court theatre discussing the censorship of Edward Bond's play *Saved*. In it, the scene where a baby in a pram is stoned to death by a gang of youths unsettled many in the audience – even though the pram was empty, without even a doll in it. Reactions to the play were passionate and diverse: some attacked this 'unmotivated and unexplained', 'muddled and muddling play', or felt 'cold disgust at being asked to sit through such a scene', while others defended it as 'a study of personality that makes no excuses', 'a clear demonstration of what is permissible' and praised its 'honesty' and its social criticism. *Saved* was attacked and defended with all the heat a cultural event can generate. As reactionaries moralized, progressives pontificated and liberals exaggerated the play's virtues, it became a symbol in the argument for and against censorship. One of the reasons it provoked such extreme emotions was that it was seen as part of a wider trend, which included plays such as Fred Watson's *Infanticide in the House of Fred Ginger* and Giles Cooper's *Everything in the Garden*. But what disturbed *Saved*'s first audiences was not just the violence but its callousness, the indifference of the characters to their own viciousness, the fact that they were lower class, alienated and didn't care.

Theatre director Mike Alfreds remembers *Saved* as 'one of the few occasions that I have actually really been shaken by theatre', not so much by the pram scene as by 'the absolutely truthful and simple way the play showed how people who cannot express themselves resort to the physical'. As Bond noted: 'I write about violence as naturally as Jane Austen wrote about manners. Violence shapes and obsesses our society . . .' In a letter to the *Observer*, Laurence Olivier defended the play because he saw theatre as a place that could show us how to comprehend cruelty, 'teaching the human heart the knowledge of itself'. But the main reason for *Saved*'s impact was, as Tynan wrote in the *New Statesman*, that 'the image of violence' confronts us with 'our own complicity', making 'us face the fact that something in us responds to it', forcing us 'to admit that violence is not foreign to our nature'.

Many years later, in 1979, Bond called such shock tactics the 'aggro-effect'. The reason for putting audiences through such ordeals, he argued, 'must be because you feel you have something desperately important to tell them'. But why use shock tactics? 'Shock is justified by the desperation of the situation or as a way of forcing the audience to search for reasons in the rest of the play.'

But breaking taboos also raises expectations. Playwright Alun Owen appeared with Tynan at an arts symposium in Liverpool soon after the infamous broadcast: 'Every time he hesitated, the audience would tense and wait for a word. Would he say "cunt" this time?' He didn't, but the year 1965 was an *annus mirabilis* for other theatrical provocations. For example, after the first half of Harold Pinter's *The Homecoming*, which opened in June, one 'indignant lady stalked into the foyer' exclaiming: 'They're exactly like animals!' Another playwright claimed that the play was degrading: like 'masturbating in public'. Today, the aggression of the image seems more disturbing than the content of the play.

In the same year, seven years after relaxing the rules about homosexuality, the censor refused a licence to Osborne's *A Patriot for Me* – which featured a drag ball – and a *cause célèbre* ensued. Put on as a club performance, the play provoked no letters of complaint. Other plays, such as Noel Coward's *A Song at Twilight*, made subjects such as homosexuality seem theatrically exciting. But when, also in 1965, Frank Marcus put lesbianism on a West End stage in *The Killing of Sister George*, he broached a completely taboo subject, and the play was often booed. At a matinee, Joe Orton saw some women walk out when George makes her lover drink bath water, a moment that – according to Marcus's agent, Peggy Ramsay – was one of the play's 'little claws'. What was shocking was not so much the sexuality as the sadism of the relationship.

In 'Swinging London', Orton was a merry prankster who not only wrote provocative plays but also scripted his audience's outraged reaction, sending letters to the press from 'Edna Welthorpe' denouncing his own work. With their swirling currents of sex, incest, violence and death, his plays mixed anarchic morality with manic frivolity. The reaction of the seventy-four-year-old *Telegraph* critic to *Entertaining Mr Sloane* in May 1964 was typical: he felt 'as if snakes had been writhing' around his feet. When Orton's *Loot* hit the West End two years later, the Lord Chamberlain received complaints: 'It breaks every canon of decent behaviour and is a shocking example to young people.' In Bournemouth, one woman called it a 'filthy' play about Jesus 'being a queer', when, in fact, *Loot* doesn't even imply that Christ was homosexual. Other reactions compared the play to a 'sickness'. If taboos aim to inhibit thought by drawing sharp boundaries, Orton asserted the individual's right to shout the unsayable. But as social norms changed, so the shock of his work wore off. If its sparkling wit is still delightful, it never really explores the dark emotions it so frantically drags into view.

More lastingly problematic is work that gives insights into the mentality of violence. In 1966, the West End production of David Halliwell's *Little Malcolm and His Struggle Against the Eunuchs* amused audiences with its satire on political fanaticism, then undercut the laughter by showing a vicious attack on a woman. Its account of how violence results when empty blokeish rhetoric is exposed by a woman's sense of reality remains troubling to this day, as evidenced by the frequency of the play's revival in the nineties.

The case of Peter Nichols's *A Day in the Death of Joe Egg* (1967) shows that not all the things we want to avoid are necessarily violent. Here, the taboo was on showing a handicapped child. However unsettling the origins of this mental blind spot, what the censor objected to in the play was the sex. Although Joe Egg's parents are married, they were not allowed to discuss their sex lives in front of her. So every night during the first production, Joe Egg had to be wheeled off in the middle of a scene before sex could be talked about.

Changes in public mores meant that deliberate provocations, such as Bond's *Early Morning* (1968), gained some support. This strange and poetic play pushed the boundaries of the acceptable by including not only cannibalism but also a lesbian relationship between Queen Victoria and Florence Nightingale. It was refused a licence during the last year of theatre censorship.

By then the climate was changing. The first full-frontal female nude is usually credited to *Harold Muggins Is a Martyr*, which was put on at the lefty Unity theatre in Spring 1968. During this satire on Harold Wilson's Labour government by the Cartoon Archetypical Slogan Theatre (CAST), one scene involved a striptease that ridiculed both the commercial exploitation of the female body and the fashion for sexual liberation. It was John Arden's idea: he thought nudity would 'confront the audience'. In this he may have been a victim of the generation gap. Roland Muldoon of CAST said that younger people didn't need to make a 'big point of nudity'. Arden got his way, and this time it was not Tory greyhairs but some of the straighter leftists who were shocked. The Communist old guard had a positively Presbyterian prudery about sex.

The end of theatre censorship in Britain was celebrated when *Hair*, an American musical that advocated draft evasion and heralded the 'dawning of the age of Aquarius', opened at the Shaftesbury theatre on 28 September 1968. Provocative both in name (evoking hippie 'longhairs') and in its nudity (which argued that we are all one under the skin) the 'tribal rock musical' was a big commercial hit. But at first the new freedoms allowed by the demise of censorship were treated with considerable caution. Dim lighting was used to cover any nudity, whether in *Hair* or in Ronald Millar's *Abelard and Héloise* (1970).

In 1969, Tynan's *Oh! Calcutta!* boasted sketches that included simulated sex for the first time on a commercial London stage. In the programme, Tynan reminded audiences that to titillate means 'to tickle, to excite pleasantly', and the play ran for a decade, eventually being seen by some 85 million people in productions all around the world. When it opened, Milton Shulman wrote that '*Oh! Calcutta!* will certainly shock some people – it will deprave and corrupt nobody.' Other critics thought its content was simply too weak to disturb.

The late sixties were particularly rich in assaults on audience sensibilities. In *Do It!* – a recreation of the American Yippies assault on the Pentagon – Pip Simmons created a 'madhouse', with actors running into the audience and urging people to take sides: 'Come on! You can't all be pigs!' In *The George Jackson Black and White Minstrel Show*, three-quarters of an hour of sneering racism culminated in an auction in which audience members 'bought' slaves and remained chained to them during the interval. In this way, the master and slave relationship was recreated and questioned in the minds of the spectators. Some found the show's racism searingly explicit and nasty. It was meant to be.

As so often before, confrontational extremism came from abroad. Early visits by America's Café La Mama, the Open Theatre and the Living Theatre raised conservative hackles, but inspired radicals. The Living Theatre's 1961 tour of Jack Gelber's unbearably naturalistic *The Connection* even lead to booing and fights outside the theatre. Later visits by the group, with shows such as *Paradise Now* (1969), gave nakedness a political slant – it meant rejecting the 'system' and discarding the 'uniform' of society. 'Ritual' meant getting the spectators to strip. But if the Living Theatre seduced audiences by images of free sex, it also insulted them, with Julian Beck screaming 'motherfucking bourgeois intellectuals' in their faces. Other provocations – such as Andy Warhol's *Pork*, Les Tréteaux Libres's *Requiem for Romeo and Juliet*, Michael McClure's *The Beard* and Fernando Arrabal's *The Labyrinth* – suggested similarly extreme forms of theatrical transgression. In comparison, Britain's The People Show theatre group seemed rather tame, although some of its images (for example, a man masturbating and then disgorging raw meat from his stomach) left an indelible imprint.

Provocative new British writers included Howard Brenton, whose *Christie in Love* (1969) was intended to give audiences a 'sense of moral vertigo'. It began with a policeman reciting a limerick: 'There was a young girl called Heather/ Whose cunt was made out of leather . . .' By portraying the murderer Christie as 'normal' and the police as 'surreal', Brenton questioned social norms and asked what sexual needs were 'natural'. But he also turned the policemen into Brechtian presenters, playing tricks with audience expectations. As he said in 1975, 'Theatre's a real bear pit. It's not the place for reasoned discussion. It is the place for really savage insights.'

By 1970, audiences were rapidly acclimatizing to the new countercultural insights. John Hopkins's *Find Your Way Home*, which featured sado-masochism, caused no scandal. In Chris Wilkinson's touring shows, *I Was Hitler's Maid* (1971) and *Plays for Rubber Go-Go Girls* (1972), the pornographic fantasies were less disturbing than the bleakness of his vision of life, where sex had more to do with darkness than with liberation. Similarly, Portable Theatre's *Lay-By* (1971), a collectively written confrontational piece, was about a particularly nasty rape and showed mortuary attendants playing sex games with the body of an addict. For David Hare, one of its authors, the piece captured 'something about the ugliness and perverse excitement of pornography'. In John Osborne's *A Sense of Detachment* (1972), readings from pornography were juxtaposed with love poetry – and the play provoked boos as well as cheers. Heathcote Williams's Artaudian *AC/DC* (1970) caused a sensation at the Royal Court because of its rawness and verbal extravagance. In the first half, five characters rant about sex and energy in a celebration of psychic anarchy. Near the end of the second, a woman masturbates with rolled-up celebrity photos and finally drills a hole in a man's head. With its startling vision of 'psychic capitalism', *AC/DC* attacked straight society and foretold disaster. When revived as part of the 'Come Together' festival, it showed how the fringe could redraw the boundaries between alternative and mainstream culture. Meanwhile, in the regions, groups such as Hull Truck featured characters who swore, smoked dope and talked frankly about sex.

By this time, feminism had become the cutting edge of a radical new sensibility, which challenged not only the mainstream but alternative theatre as well. Once again, what were questioned were assumptions about the 'natural' role of women and what could or should be shown in public. Whatever its tone, women's drama argued against the marginalization of the female. One of its earliest and most powerful statements came from Jane Arden's *Vagina Rex and the Gas Oven* (1969). This lived

23

up to its provocative title by using music, a slide show and strobe lights to create a cacophony of sensations: the violence that Arden saw as imposed on women was reflected in the violence of the stage images imposed on the audience. In Maureen Duffy's *Rites* (1969), women broke taboos by speaking, perhaps for the first time, with an earthy frankness about sex. Set in a women's lavatory, one scene shows a girl using sanitary towels to bandage her cut wrists; another features a murderous attack on a lesbian. By 1971, Jane Arden and Sheila Allen's *A New Communion for Freaks, Prophets and Witches* annoyed spectators with its half-naked woman in top hat and cane simulating a rape on another woman.

Some depictions of sexual violence were even more politically explicit. For example, in *Occupations*, Trevor Griffiths's 1971 play, Kabak, a Communist revolutionary, is callous in regard to his dying wife and crude in his attempts to seduce his maid. When ordered to strip, she does so with resentment. In the Royal Shakespeare Company's original staging, the image of her – vulnerable, angry and almost aggressively naked – left a haunting sense of violation that words cannot adequately express. In *The Party* (1973), the politically impotent TV producer masturbates while images of May '68 are projected behind him. In 1975, Griffiths broke the taboo on writing about breast cancer in *Through the Night*; and – three years later – so did Louise Page, in a more personal way, with *Tissue*.

Women continued to speak the unspoken. Early shows by the Women's Theatre group in 1975, such as *My Mother Says*, examined underage sex and other taboos. But in this era, the left could be as outraged as the right. Monstrous Regiment's 1978 cabaret, *Time Gentlemen Please*, irritated radical feminists and gay activists because it was seen as promoting a glossy, middle-class view of sexual liberation. By the end of the seventies, the subversive idea that feminists could have fun led to the formation of groups such as Cunning Stunts (1977), whose spoonerism of a title advertised their absurdist style and self-irony, and the Sadista Sisters, whose chaotic approach – wearing messy clothes, throwing food around and disembowelling a doll – up-ended traditional ideas of domesticity.

Nor was feminist sensibility a stranger for long to the West End. One of its first commercial successes was Mary O'Malley's *Once a Catholic* in 1977. Set in a convent school, it satirized sexual repression. But when a nun waves a packet of Tampax or when one of the girls sticks a long Plasticine penis onto a statue of Jesus, it also mischievously touched on taboos. Other commercial successes were more problematic. After its

1981 run at Stratford East, Nell Dunn's *Steaming* transferred to the West End, but the play's subversive notion of showing a women-only space and older women's bodies was undercut by a production that some critics condemned as titillating.

Militant gay theatre has often been deliberately in-yer-face, with the intention of confronting audiences with their prejudices and rallying the gay community with assertions of pride in its identity. For example, the taboo-smashing *Mr X*, staged by Gay Sweatshop in 1975, begins with four actors miming masturbation. A piece of agitprop, it aimed not to charm but to provoke. Gay Sweatshop's attitude proved widely influential.

The seventies also witnessed plays that rewrote sensibility in other ways. In *Comedians* (1975), Griffiths stages a debate between veteran comedian Eddie Waters and youngblood Gethin Price about a 'joke that hates women'. Later, Price performs a 'repulsive' stand-up routine: instead of the usual sexist and racist jokes, he plays the part of a football hooligan and uses two stuffed dummies dressed in evening dress as foils for an aggressive attack. Here class antagonism was as confrontational as sexual explicitness. At the Nottingham Playhouse production, directed by Richard Eyre, reviewers were as shocked as the play's imaginary audience. One called Jonathan Pryce's Price 'the one clown who rebels, breaks taboos', and commented, 'I didn't like his act much either.' Another called him the most interesting antihero 'since Jimmy Porter hit us between the eyes'.

Steven Berkoff remembers that in the same year, at the Edinburgh Traverse production of his *East*, he had 'great trouble' with 'the "cunt" speech'. In a work that he describes as a 'scream or a shout of pain', and that uses exuberant mock-Shakespearean language to describe the bodily functions and sentimental nostalgia of the East End working class, this carnivalesque speech is intended to be a 'a loving appreciation' of the 'female form'. 'Mike's Cunt Speech' begins:

> We always found good cunt at the Lyceum. Friendly cunt, clean cunt, spare cunt, jeans and knicker stuffed full of nice juicy hairy cunt, handfuls of cunt, palmful grabbing the cunt by the stem, or the root – infantile memories of cunt – backrow slides – slithery oily cunt, the cunt that breathes – the cunt that's neatly wrapped in cotton, in silk, in nylon, that announces, that speaks or thrusts, that winks, that's squeezed in a triangle of furtive cloth backed by an arse that's creamy springy billowy cushiony tight . . .

And carries on like this for another fifteen or so lines. Berkoff, a pioneer of in-yer-face theatre, says he 'wanted to break the taboo barrier'.

> In those days it was a formidable hurdle to say this word in front
> of a mixed audience and not just say it, but say it over and over
> again until the word is pummelled to death and the shock has
> worn off and by a process of overkill the taboo power is reduced.

What made it easier is that Berkoff 'tried to endow each "cunt" with a character and act it out'. As he developed this on successive nights, it made the audience 'giggle'. Gradually, by adding mime, he 'took the sting out of the cunt speech and made it silly, farcical, astonished and without offence'. In the programme of Berkoff's 1999 revival of the play, the producers coyly renamed the scene 'the pudenda speech'. Berkoff remains highly influential: when Debbie Isitt, who remembered *East* as being 'full of fury', set up her own theatre company in 1986, she called it Snarling Beasties, one of Berkoff's terms for male genitals.

Using jokes in 'bad taste' is a way of testing taboos. But some stage images, such as the gigantic golden penis that emerged from Carlos II's embroidered gown in Peter Barnes's *The Bewitched* (1974), were more amusing than shocking. By contrast, Barnes's *Laughter!*, a 1978 double bill of black farces – one set in Ivan the Terrible's Russia, the other in Auschwitz – was seen as going too far even by the liberal standards of the Royal Court. Joking about gas chambers was judged to be in irredeemable bad taste and defined the limits of what could be shown onstage for a generation. Although Barnes deliberately uses material from 'the outer limits of farce where everything is pushed to extremes of pain and cruelty', his visceral assaults on audience sensibilities resulted in people avoiding his plays, not because they were in bad taste but because they were seen as trivializing their subjects. As Barnes said: 'If there is a certain way of achieving absolute unpopularity it is by writing against prevailing modes and pieties.'

More commercially successful was Martin Sherman's moving and metaphorical *Bent* (1979). Inspired by Gay Sweatshop's *As Time Goes By*, it features a scene in which two men, Max and Horst, make love simply by using words, without touching or looking at each other, symbolizing a love that is forbidden. Here, fantasy is integral to gay desire. But the play's images of cruelty were shocking at the time. Critic Nicholas de Jongh says: 'I still remember the unique sense of raw shock and disgust that *Bent* engendered. It returned the electricity of surprise to the stage and a physical sense of revulsion and horror.' But Sherman's most premeditated shock tactic didn't survive the play's fame: the first fifteen minutes are set in an ordinary living room and it is only when the Nazis storm in that the first audiences realized that the play is about Hitler's Germany.

By 1979, some plays, such as Caryl Churchill's *Cloud Nine*, could talk about sex frankly and amusingly while experimenting with structure; there were others that wanted to go further. In its version of Dacia Maraini's *Dialogue Between a Prostitute and Her Client* (1980), Monstrous Regiment challenged the separation between performers and spectators by interrupting the action and asking the audience to discuss the play with them. But as far as writing goes, it was Churchill who had the most innovative and thrilling theatrical voice. In *Top Girls* (1982), her prophetic play about women and Thatcherism, she used overlapping dialogue, shifting timescales and emotional truth in a unique combination that revitalized theatrical language.

But it was sexual violence that caused the most public controversy. In Scene 3 of Howard Brenton's *The Romans in Britain* (1980), an attempted homosexual rape of a young Celt by a Roman soldier became the focus of moral panic. 'What is so hard to take,' explained Brenton, 'is the flippancy of the soldiers.' In a letter to the *Guardian*, Milton Shulman said the play was 'far closer to the sado-masochistic, pornographic literature of Soho' than to any 'classic' play. One performance was interrupted when members of the South London Action Group, claiming to uphold 'moral standards', threw eggs, flour and fireworks at the stage. More serious was a prosecution initiated by Mrs Mary Whitehouse and the National Viewers and Listeners Association, which argued that a simulation of what she saw as an act of 'gross indecency' was itself such an act – and therefore an offence under the 1956 Sexual Offences Act, a law usually used against those caught having sex in public toilets. What is interesting is that the moralists argued that the law makes no distinction between a sex act onstage and a real act, which was either desperately naive or pure bad faith. But before the trial got very far, the prosecution withdrew its case and the press, deprived of a spectacle, attacked Whitehouse for wasting public money.

With the use of 'fuck' increasingly common, 'cunt' became the most explosive expletive. At the climax of David Mamet's *Glengarry Glen Ross* (1983), Williamson spoils salesman Roma's pitch by speaking out of turn. When the client leaves, Roma turns on Williamson – the speech begins 'You stupid fucking cunt' and ends with: 'You stupid fucking *cunt*.

You *idiot*. Whoever told you you could work with *men*?' Onstage, it can sound like a whiplash, with all of Roma's frustrated ambition and hatred packed into these insults. And, as Mamet's emphases make clear, what is at stake is masculinity itself. That is what gives this testosterone-fuelled play its desperate charge and this speech its electric impact. As other plays – such as G. F. Newman's *Operation Bad Apple* (1982) – show, in an all-male play sexual swearing indicates emotional desperation. Power and sexuality are intimately intertwined.

With the growth of the fringe, small theatre spaces could be used to intensify the shock of a sex scene. *Coming Clean*, Kevin Elyot's 1982 debut at the tiny Bush pub theatre, had, he says, 'a charged intimacy' because of the 'close-range eroticism of certain scenes'. The local paper's response was the headline: 'Male nudes bring blush to the Bush'. At the same venue, in 1985, Richard Zajdlic remembers a two-hander called *Through the Leaves*, by Franz Xaver Kroetz, which had 'simulated sex on a kitchen table, a blow job to orgasm and some of the best acting I'd ever seen'. The spectators at the Bush are so closely packed together that an emotional charge can quickly build up. Sex onstage seems almost within the audience's grasp.

While some feminists were accepted by the mainstream, others were not. Labelled a man-hating 'feminazi', Sarah Daniels explored the explosive subject of power relations between the sexes. Often attacked as 'embittered', 'shrill' and 'fanatical', Daniels's theatrical methods have always excited controversy. In *Ripen Our Darkness* (1981), she used a mix of despair and hilarity. Mary kills herself after her husband threatens to commit her to an asylum, and her farewell note reads: 'Dear David, your dinner and my head are in the oven.' *Masterpieces*, Daniels's 1983 polemic against porn and snuff movies, is typically impassioned and exaggerated. It opens with a scene in a restaurant where three couples are having a meal. The men tell misogynist jokes, mainly about rape. When the play transferred to the Royal Court in 1984, audiences joined in the laughter until Yvonne, one of the women, tells an anti-male joke: 'How many men does it take to tile a bathroom? (*Pause.*) Three, but you have to slice them thinly.' Yvonne's friend, Rowena, eventually kills a man because he is harassing her, and the play ends with an uncomfortably explicit description of a snuff movie.

Other eighties plays dramatized the brutality of life for women under Thatcher. While Debbie Horsfield's *Red Devils* (1983) tackled jobless teenage girls, Kay Adshead's *Thatcher's Women* (1987) was about northern women coming down to London to work as prostitutes in order to keep their families. Clare McIntyre's *Low Level Panic* (1988) explored female attitudes to pornography and came up with a disturbing picture of mixed feelings. Above all, Andrea Dunbar's *Rita, Sue and Bob Too* (1982) and *Shirley* (1986) were so stark that her work was dubbed 'new brutalism', a term revived a decade later to describe other provocative authors.

Of course, the history of outrage is not a simple narrative of progress from repression to liberation. Instead, taboos are broken, reform and are broken yet again. And sometimes it takes the hammer of high art to smash them. For almost three decades, Howard Barker has tried to change the habitual complicity between spectators and actors by putting on complex texts that refuse simple explanations. In a world where moral expectations are systematically subverted, Barker's characters often go mad or sink into despair. Always, there is so much going on. In his *Victory* (1983), for example, the dim shadows of Eros and Thanatos lurk behind the verbal obscenities. The short opening scene contains nine 'cunts' in less than a page of text, and, soon after, Charles II, fresh from his coronation, is masturbated by his mistress, the Duchess of Devonshire. Afterwards, he tells her to lick her hand clean. But, in the end, it is the savage opulence of Barker's imagination, his crazy and audacious images – rather than any obscenity – that leaves you dizzy.

In his *Arguments for a Theatre*, Barker presents a highly charged manifesto for a 'Theatre of Catastrophe', a form of tragedy that offers no comfort. He attacks the conventions of naturalistic theatre and defends his own theatrical excesses. Aiming to create offence 'even among the already offended', he points out that it 'is not for nothing that the word "cunt" operates both as the most extreme notation of abuse and also the farthest reach of desire, and not only in male speech' – the attempt to censor language is 'an attack on the body itself'. With Barker, the body is never safe. It is hard to forget, for example, how in *The Europeans* (1987) Katrin gives birth, a scene that, argues Barker, is deeply unsettling not because 'childbirth is rarely enacted onstage', but rather because 'the catastrophic enterprise of the heroine at her most assertive and irrational exposes the false content of the values that are being imposed on her'. Certainly, the play's literary denseness deranges the senses through the relentless lushness of its language.

However influential, Barker is a less immediate precursor of the new sensibility of the nineties than Jim Cartwright, whose *Road* (1986) painted a poetic and lurid picture of the squalor, agony and confusion of a Lancashire town hit by poverty and joblessness. The play's promenade performance at the Court broke down barriers between actors and audiences, just as the play's rawness aimed to subvert complacency. Blatant in its language and confrontational in its attitude, *Road* christened the world 'a fat toilet', and glumly asked: 'Can we not have before again?' Its narrator, Scullery, was seen as a Jimmy Porter for the eighties, and Cartwright's gift for vivid similes is summed up in Louise's final speech: 'Why is life so tough? It's like walking through meat in high heels.' In the following decade, Cartwright's unique voice was joined by other, similarly intense writers.

The nasty nineties

In the nineties, a host of plays by young writers used explicit and directly confrontational material to explore the way we live and feel. Never before had so many plays been so blatant, aggressive or emotionally dark. The decade witnessed more and more new writers (as well as some older hands) being drawn to the extremes of experience. Ideas were kidnapped and taken to the limit. If drama dealt with masculinity, it showed rape; if it got to grips with sex, it showed fellatio or anal intercourse; when nudity was involved, so was humiliation; if violence was wanted, torture was staged; when drugs were the issue, addiction was shown. While men behaved badly, so did women. And often the language was gross, the jokes sick, the images indelible. Theatre broke all taboos, chipping away at the binary oppositions that structure our sense of reality. Although drama has always represented human cruelty, never before had it seemed so common. For these reasons, the label 'in-yer-face' – often used in reviews – describes nineties drama more accurately than other coinages, such as 'new brutalism' or 'theatre of urban ennui', neither of which achieved much currency.

The line between offensive and acceptable words had certainly shifted. A survey by the Broadcasting Standards Commission found that 'cunt', 'motherfucker' and 'fuck' were the strongest, while 'God', 'bloody' and 'damn' were the weakest. And just as religious insults were less offensive than sexual and Oedipal ones, so racial slurs took the place of seaside bawdy: 'nigger', 'Paki' and 'Jew' were judged much stronger than 'tart'. Taboos had shifted from sexual to racial terms. You can't imagine a critic today referring, as Tynan did in 1952, to Orson Welles's Othello as

'Citizen Coon'. But what offends some audiences leaves others unfazed. 'Cunt' is used only once in Shelagh Stephenson's *An Experiment with an Air Pump*, but when the play was put on in Manchester in 1998, it attracted several letters of complaint. After the piece transferred to London's Hampstead theatre a few months later, no one protested.

By the nineties, nudity was no longer a symbol of liberation, but had become more problematic, often associated with vulnerability, with being victimized. To be noticed, you had to use nudity in ever more provocative ways. When Ursula Martinez staged *A Family Outing* in 1998, she advertised it with a poster that showed not only herself nude but her parents as well. And it was the older bodies that drew the eye. Similarly, in DV8 dance company's 1998 show, *Bound to Please*, there was a scene in which Diana Payne-Myers, an elderly woman, appeared naked and kissed a much younger man. This dramatic reversal of the stereotypical idea of an old man falling for a younger woman created a palpable sense of shock in the auditorium. People felt it 'wasn't right'. But as the programme note said, 'Who decides what is socially acceptable behaviour?'

Occasionally, even the boundary between the real and the representation came down. For example, critic Michael Coveney remembers that during *Sabotage: The Body Show*, put on at the Glasgow Mayfest in 1993, there was a peepshow where a couple performed 'stilted pornographic poses and then made gentle love'. For the first time in his theatregoing experience he saw 'hard and indisputable evidence of onstage sexual arousal: you never saw a chap standing to attention in *Oh! Calcutta!*, *Carte Blanche*, *Let My People Come* and other such limp festivities'. Not that it was easy to pander to the fashion for overt theatre. When Michael White, who'd produced *Oh! Calcutta!*, tried to repeat its success in 1996, with *Voyeurz*, a story featuring lipstick lesbians and sado-masochistic gear, people stayed away in droves.

As always, violence onstage raised questions about how realistic drama can be. In Simon Moore's version of the Stephen King horror story, *Misery* (Criterion, 1992), some people felt queasy enough to walk out when the hero, a kidnapped novelist, has his leg amputated by his female captor. So although it lacked the camera angles and clever cutting of the Rob Reiner film version, *Misery* onstage was equally tense because of its delight in sadistic detail and its overall air of claustrophobia.

One of the decade's most notorious acts of violence – at the opening of David Mamet's *Oleanna*, directed by Harold Pinter at the Royal Court in June 1993 – brought into question the division between performers and audience. When the play's professor, who has been accused of sexual harassment, finally snaps and attacks his accuser, a female student, some men in the audience cheered. In New York, there had been shouts of 'Hit the bitch!' In both cases, the violence onstage was nowhere near as disturbing as the violence in the stalls. Masculinity in crisis? Perhaps. What is certain is that, instead of being observers willing to grapple with the issues raised by the play, these spectators had become part of the problem.

Sometimes a play became controversial because of media emphasis on one aspect of performance. Clare Dowie's 1998 *Easy Access (for the Boys)* was a unsettlingly ambiguous study of child abuse, but because Dowie had used her young daughter for the play's prerecorded video sequences, which had a 'paedophile' voice-over, the *Guardian* newspaper highlighted this at the expense of the rest of the show. And while Kay Trainor's 1992 study of incest, *Bad Girl*, was not the first play to examine the subject, it outraged some people because of its programme, which showed a schoolgirl's legs, one in a sensible shoe, the other in fishnets and high heels. Not for the first time, fuss about publicity distracted attention from a play's content. It was, after all, the decade when even the Royal Shakespeare Company jumped on the Quentin Tarantino bandwagon by using a poster of a blood-soaked Toby Stephens to advertise its *Coriolanus* (1994–5). In a letter to the *Independent*, marketing manager Andrew Canham said the play was 'sold in a visual style which mimics the current trend for violent thrillers', and pointed out that the number of students buying standby tickets had 'increased by a staggering 1,140 per cent'.

The gradual shift in sensibility that resulted in the majority of young writers starting to use a new theatrical vocabulary, which included both highly explicit stage pictures and innovations in structure, also affected older writers. Pinter and Churchill led the way. Both continued to innovate, both developed the short play form, both explored uncomfortable emotions.

Pinter's work became more explicitly political and hard-hitting. At the start of the decade, his most uncompromising play was *Party Time* (Almeida, 1991), which ends with the powerful image of a political prisoner talking about his suffering: 'I sit sucking the dark. It's what I have. The dark is in my mouth and I suck it. It's the only thing I have.' Then *Moonlight* (Almeida, 1993) uncovered bitter emotional truths about parents and children in a prolonged deathbed scene, and *Ashes to Ashes* (Royal Court, 1996) reminded audiences that Europe today is not immune to genocide. Many critics mocked Pinter's work, seeing his vision of murderous oppression as exaggerated. 'It couldn't happen here,' they said.

Churchill's work in the nineties (*Mad Forest*, *The Skriker*, *Thyestes* and *Blue Heart*) expressed a delight in language and a freedom in the use of form that was theatrically exciting. Her adaptation of Seneca's *Thyestes* (Royal Court, 1994) was marketed as the ancestor not just of *Hamlet* but of *Reservoir Dogs*. Directed by James Macdonald, it featured video sequences, which gave a sense of surveillance, and focused attention on the clash between explicit horror – Thyestes eating his own children – and our voyeuristic fascination with violence. Her *Blue Heart* (Royal Court, 1997) was made up of two miniatures: *Heart's Desire*, which stopped and started manically, and *Blue Kettle*, which was gradually taken over by the words 'blue' and 'kettle' dropped randomly into the dialogue. In the first part, parents wait for the return of their daughter from Australia, and the stops and starts and rewinds of the dialogue convey the frustrations of family life. What you remember about *Heart's Desire* is not only the wild staging – with the kitchen visited by an SS officer, an emu and a gang of children – but also the married couple's mutual hatred, the sister-in-law's fear of death, and the husband's amazing dream of self-cannibalism. Even sadder was *Blue Kettle*, where a man preyed on old women – chosen because they'd given up their babies for adoption – by cruelly pretending to each one that he was her long-lost son. Churchill has lost none of her power to delight and disturb.

Other authors also became more daring. For example, Martin Crimp's *The Treatment* (Royal Court, 1993) dealt savagely with the rat-eat-rat world of showbiz in New York. Although the play showed fellatio onstage, most reviewers mentioned only the scene in which a man's eyes are gouged out with a fork. In March 1997, his Court follow-up, *Attempts on Her Life*, was a postmodern extravaganza that could be read as a series of provocative suggestions for creating a new kind of theatre. The recipe was: subvert the idea of a coherent character; turn scenes into flexible scenarios; substitute brief messages or poetic clusters for text; mix clever dialogue with brutal images; stage the show as an art installation. The playtext doesn't specify who says which lines, but Tim Albery's production brought out the acuity and humour of Crimp's writing, with its characteristic irony, and its pointed comments on the pointlessness of searching for a point.

Jim Cartwright also caught the mood of the nineties. In 1992, the National Theatre's production of his *The Rise and Fall of Little Voice* starred Alison Steadman as the boozy, blowsy and foul-mouthed Mari. Although this was a comedy, Cartwright's view of the North's older generation of working-class men and women felt characteristically bleak. If the play's portrait of LV, the sad, shy daughter who finally finds her own voice, seemed sentimental, this was balanced by its feisty women's emotional pain. Seeing Steadman end up in the gutter felt like a kick in the groin. Even more ferocious was Cartwright's *I Licked a Slag's Deodorant* (Royal Court, 1996), a blatant account of the awkward intimacy between a fetishistic Man and a crack-addled Slag. While its poetic prose is studded with lurid similes – 'I'm lonely like a dying spunk up a cunt' – what is disturbing is the play's vision of two types of chronic desperation, one chillingly quiet, the other unbearably frantic.

Other writers, such as Bond, Brenton, Berkoff and Barker – whose legacy continued to inspire the young playwrights of the nineties – produced work in that decade that was neither original nor thrilling. Bond practically disappeared from the theatrical scene, and Brenton's satirical work with Tariq Ali – *Moscow Gold* and *Ugly Rumours* – was entertaining but banal. His *Berlin Bertie* (Royal Court, 1992), a response to the recent changes in eastern Europe, lacked the epic sweep of his best work. Similarly, Barker's recent plays, such as *Und* (Wrestling School, 1999), were not as arresting as his earlier visions. And although the twenty-fifth anniversary production of Berkoff's *East* (Churchill theatre, Bromley, 1999) advertised the play as having 'set the ground rules for hard-hitting urban drama' two decades 'before *Trainspotting* and *Mojo*', Berkoff's nineties plays – *Kvetch*, *Brighton Beach Scumbags*, *Acapulco* – were predictable in form and content. In the West End, his one-man show, *Dog* (originally called *Pitbull*), was provocative enough to be heckled, but much of his work came dangerously close to self-parody.

Finally, John Osborne, the so-called Angry Young Man of the fifties, who had once done so much to rewrite theatrical sensibility, made an unexpected comeback in the nineties. Aptly enough, Osborne's only new play in this decade, *Déjà Vu* (Comedy, 1991) revisited *Look Back in Anger*, with familiar characters such as J.P. and Cliff, Alison and Helena. Was that an ironing board onstage? Yes, it was. Oh, very postmodern. Watching the play from the circle, the pleasure of listening to the familiar tone of Osborne's ranting Jimmy Porter soon palled as his reactionary opinions and pontificating blasts of verbiage filled the air. Osborne's distinctive theatrical voice seemed compromised by the noisy prejudices of his dotage. Suddenly it felt as if the old sensibility was past its sell-by date and that the times were crying out for something new.

2 Come to the shock-fest

> We're all as bad as each other. All hungry little cannibals at our own
> cannibal party. So fuck the milk of human kindness and welcome to
> the abattoir!
>
> (Cougar in Philip Ridley's *The Fastest Clock in the Universe*)

Because they dramatize the messy jumble of events, metaphors make
good history, and most accounts of theatre are full of them: writers
explode onto the scene; revolutions break out in theatres; new waves
build up and sweep all before them. The most famous 'revolution' in
British postwar theatre was the press night of John Osborne's *Look Back
in Anger*. Because of the cultural importance of this event, theatre histo-
rians might be tempted to date the start of the new wave of nineties
drama with the opening of Sarah Kane's *Blasted* on 18 January 1995. This
would be a mistake. Although the controversy it excited made Kane's
play a significant cultural moment, it was not the first play of its kind.
Long before *Blasted*, other provocative plays had explored the outer
edges of sensibility. Not so much postcards from the edge as urgent,
noisy invitations, they seemed to call out: come to the shock-fest.

If it was the more shocking writers that caused the most sensation
and did most to put British theatre back into sync with youth culture,
why did this happen in the nineties? The short answer is that the decade
was characterized by a new sense of possibility that was translated into
unprecedented theatrical freedom. The fall of the Berlin Wall and the
exit of Margaret Thatcher showed those under twenty-five that, despite
the evidence of political ossification, change was possible; the end of
Cold War ideological partisanship freed young imaginations. Youth
could be critical of capitalism without writing state-of-the-nation plays;
it could be sceptical of male power without being dogmatically feminist;
it could express outrage without being politically correct. Picking
among the tattered remains of modernism, and encouraged by postmodernism's notion that 'anything goes', theatre shook off the style
police and began to explore a new-found freedom.

At the very beginning of the nineties, however, the image of new
drama was dire. Newspaper articles spoke of theatre's 'crisis of new

writing'. In May 1991, the *Guardian*'s critic Michael Billington pointed out that 'new drama no longer occupies the central position it has in British theatre over the past 35 years'. The best plays at the Royal Court were often American or Irish imports, such as John Guare's *Six Degrees of Separation* or Brian Friel's *Faith Healer* (both 1992). As playwright Nick Ward argues, 'Never had the theatre been so out of touch with youth.'

But things were about to change. A handful of artistic directors emerged who were willing to give young writers permission to travel to hell and report on what they found. They were supported, says Jonathan Meth of Writernet, by 'enlightened individuals who had a determination to support new writing'. This included heads of funding bodies, such as the Arts Council and London Arts Board, as well as business sponsors. But if the Royal Court was eventually to lead the new trend for provocative plays, it didn't start it. Because it entered the decade with an embattled mentality, as artistic director Max Stafford-Clark fought off threats to its subsidy, the initiative passed to west London. At the hundred-seat Bush theatre, situated above a pub in Shepherd's Bush, a new artistic director, Dominic Dromgoole, arrived in 1990. He thought 'the situation of new writing was so desperate that the only thing to do was to celebrate diversity'. With an average of ten new plays a year, the Bush developed its eclectic policy of reviving new writing.

Dromgoole, who stayed at the Bush until 1996, agrees that the nineties were a time of unprecedented opportunity. 'In the eighties, most theatres wanted well-meaning, well-reasoned, victim-based plays,' he says. 'But in the nineties, some theatres gave young writers complete freedom. There were no ideologies, no rules, no "taste" – writers were free to follow their imaginations.' Some 'went to extremes', creating the trend for 'a new Jacobeanism'; others explored more lyrical moods. He thinks that showing 'explicit sex onstage is naff; if you want to show cruelty, you need to be more subtle'. For him, some of the cruellest moments of the decade occur in otherwise tender-hearted plays, such as Billy Roche's Wexford trilogy (Bush, 1992), with shock being 'less about blood and violence, and more about feelings of desperation'.

Although some new writers were reacting against past models of theatrical practice, most were responding directly to the new cultural climate of the nineties. Wanting to criticize the world, they soon found the language, in the widest sense, to do it. After all, compared to television or film, you could say or do almost anything onstage.

One play that seemed to capture the prevailing mood was Jonathan Harvey's *Beautiful Thing*, which opened at the Bush in 1993. With its story of working-class boys discovering their gay sexuality, it touched on the theme of masculinity in crisis, and gave audiences permission to laugh about sexual and emotional confusion. Its foul-mouthed and funny one-liners made the audience roar. Original if not confrontational, the feelings it explored were very idealized, very 'feelgood'. Even so, when it transferred to the West End in 1994, it sparked a media panic, with papers screaming about a 'plague of pink plays'. However nonsensical, the controversy made theatre seem relevant and exciting.

If Dromgoole at the Bush was quick on the uptake, his theatre was too small to revive new writing by itself. For that to happen, the Royal Court, with its two stages and its heritage of 1956, had to join in. A new artistic director, Stephen Daldry (who began work in 1992), gave the theatre its opportunity. At first, Daldry brought in American work and gave space to companies such as DV8 dance theatre. But he gradually realized that the way to create a writing renaissance was to produce as much new work by younger writers as quickly as possible. 'From autumn 1994, the Court doubled the amount of new productions in the [sixty-seat] Theatre Upstairs and focused on young writers,' says Daldry. 'The huge success of this season showed that there was a growing urgency in young people to express themselves through writing for theatre and that the only crisis in new writing was one of opportunity.' Established ideas about what could or could not be done were questioned, with the result that runs were shortened, more first-time writers were put on and some even premiered on the main stage. Daldry transformed the Court's Theatre Upstairs into a launching pad for young unknowns. He also programmed seasons with hip titles such as 'Coming On Strong' and 'Storming'. A case of shrewd marketing, it was also a way of integrating formerly separate aspects of the Court's work.

The result was a rash of funky plays by young authors that brought an excitement to new drama. During his short tenure, Daldry put on between twelve and nineteen productions a year and introduced about forty first-time writers. A natural impresario, he not only enjoyed shocking people, but was skilled at getting funding for new projects. As he said in 1994: 'While the financial odds against producing new plays have worsened, there is an energy emerging from a new generation of writers unshackled by the bitterness of the past decade.' Adept at playing the media, he not only programmed provocative plays, but defended them vigorously in public.

So while the nineties were an era of cuts in arts subsidies, what mattered more was the cultural climate. As Ian Rickson, Daldry's successor at the Court since 1998, says: 'The writers who grew up under Thatcher experienced two things: they were disempowered and simultaneously empowered. On the one hand, the state was strengthened at the expense of the individual; on the other, the only way of achieving anything was to do it yourself.' Young writers seized the chances offered by this DIY culture. 'Thatcherism provided both a climate of anger and the motivation to do something about it.' Whereas many seventies and eighties plays came from a left-wing point of view, nineties plays were based in a more 'privatized dissent'. For Graham Whybrow, literary manager at the Court since 1994, new writing, 'if it is to be exciting, will often have an oppositional spirit', which can be expressed both in form and content. 'Part of this is its tendency to surprise, provoke and shock.'

While the Court under Daldry helped new writers, the National Studio (part of the National Theatre) also played a vital role, developing plays through collaborative workshops and rehearsals, as did organizations such as the Soho Theatre Company, Paines Plough and the London New Play Festival. In the regions, local reps, courses and self-help groups were just as important in nurturing new talent.

If things were beginning to stir in London, they were equally canny in Edinburgh and Glasgow. In July 1992, after twenty-five years in Edinburgh's Grassmarket, the Traverse moved to a new building in Cambridge Street. Under artistic director Ian Brown, it produced provocative new work, such as local actor Simon Donald's *The Life of Stuff* – an urban fairy tale fuelled by drugs and violence – and Canadian-born Brad Fraser's spooky *Unidentified Human Remains and the True Nature of Love* (both 1992). Many confrontational plays that arrived in London were first seen in Scotland. Older Scottish writers – such as Chris Hannan – became better known south of the border. Brown, who was at the Traverse from 1988 to 1996, says that his policy was based on two strands: developing Scottish work with Scottish actors and finding the best international new writers. 'I was a risk-taker; I had a taste for doing plays that are a bit between-the-eyes: most London theatres didn't dare put on Brad Fraser because of the explicit sex,' he says. 'But you can't reduce new writing to confrontational plays: other Scottish writers such as David Greig and David Harrower were writing quieter plays.' In 1993, he was accused of 'running a gay ghetto', but 'that was simply because there was a lot of gay work around that year'. The growth of Glasgow's Mayfest also signalled a revival of Scottish drama, which culminated in the production of *Trainspotting*, one of the quintessential plays of the decade.

But Britain was also having an extended cultural conversation with North America. One theory is that the in-yer-face sensibility owed much to American models. 'Okay, we'd lost the knack of hitting the zeitgeist where it hurt. But it was cruel indeed to find that as we dropped the baton, the Yanks had picked it up,' says playwright David Edgar. According to him, the two texts that turned things around were Tony Kushner's *Angels in America* (National Theatre, 1992) and David Mamet's *Oleanna* (Royal Court, 1993) – they reminded writers of the sorts of play the British used to do so well.

In 1993, there were plenty of other American models on offer. From April to July, the Court ran an 'American Season' (which included *Oleanna* and Howard Korder's *Search and Destroy*, as well as Martin Crimp's *The Treatment*), while the Hampstead theatre hosted Canadian plays by Brad Fraser and Judith Thompson. Thompson's *Lion in the Streets* had two unforgettable scenes: in front of appalled neighbours, a young wife strips to attract her bored husband; then a man forces his fiancée to say that the time she was raped 'was the only fuck' she 'ever respected'. *The Times*'s Benedict Nightingale describes work such as this as 'quirkily episodic pieces' which saw urban rootlessness as 'a spiritual madhouse whose inmates were linked by loveless sex, offhand despair, serial killers and telephone answering machines'. From the United States came Wendy McLeod's kooky *The House of Yes* (Gate, 1993), about incest and gun culture, and Scott McPherson's taboo-breaking *Marvin's Room* (Hampstead, 1993), about terminal illness. But important as such work was, there were also home-grown examples of provocative writing.

Philip Ridley's *Ghost from a Perfect Place*

In 1991, Philip Ridley kicked off the decade with *The Pitchfork Disney*. Put on at the Bush, its sexy young men caused gasps of astonishment by eating cockroaches and breaking fingers: one character comes onstage and immediately vomits. More startling still were the play's vivid and excruciating verbal images: of sudden ageing, of a boy stabbed through the neck, of a snake being fried alive, of a penis scraping along the tarmac, of excrement 'like brown worms'. Ridley is fascinated by the simultaneous attraction and repulsion of the gross and the grotesque: his character Cosmo talks about 'Man's need for the shivers. Afraid of blood, wanting blood', and concludes that the reason the fairground ghost train is so popular is that there are no ghosts. Imaginary fears run deep.

According to Mike Bradwell – Dromgoole's successor at the Bush – *The Pitchfork Disney* was one of three plays that showed that Dromgoole had 'hit his stride'; the others were Chris Hannan's *The Evil Doers* (1990) and Roy MacGregor's *Our Own Kind* (1991). Hannan's play – which he describes as 'a running dog-fight' around Glasgow – reversed the usual traffic from Edinburgh to London by opening at the Bush and then going north; MacGregor's play was an award-winning debut that showed the repercussions of a racist murder. The origins of *The Pitchfork Disney* lie in Ridley's experience of sitting in an East End pub, sadly drunk on Southern Comfort whiskey. Then he sees a nineteen-year-old man in a sequinned jacket come onstage and start to eat slugs and worms and beetles. As the audience groans in disgust, Ridley feels his depression lift.

Ridley's second play, *The Fastest Clock in the Universe*, put on in May 1992 at London's Hampstead theatre, was also strong meat. *The Times* saw Ridley's story about a man who is totally neurotic about ageing as a 'grotesque comedy' influenced by Pinter, Orton and Howard Barker. On a set decorated with stuffed birds, tension rises as Ridley's language sizzles with images of sex and violence, but the most awful moment is when a young woman is beaten and loses her unborn baby. In the audience, I could feel the revulsion. But you never know exactly what will cause offence. 'In *The Fastest Clock in the Universe*,' says Ridley, 'I had Cougar Glass, a thirtysomething man, trying to seduce a schoolboy onstage – blatant paedophilia.' A boy was 'about to be raped, but no one batted an eyelid, even though the papers were full of stories of boys being abused'. What audiences complained about most was neither the abuse nor the miscarriage, but the description of a mink being skinned alive. 'All that really bothered them was cruelty to animals.'

In April 1994, even more controversy greeted the Hampstead theatre's production of Ridley's *Ghost from a Perfect Place*. Veteran critic Michael Billington used his weekly *Guardian* column to open the attack. He began by taking issue with *Observer* critic Michael Coveney's statement (made in his book, *The Aisle Is Full of Noises*) that: 'I am all for violence in the theatre and in the cinema. Up there, beyond us, to gawp at, is where it belongs.' Perturbed by the 'blank cheque that Coveney gives to theatrical violence', Billington went on to attack Ridley's play as 'profoundly anti-feminist' and 'degrading and quasi-pornographic in its use of violence'. Had he not been reviewing, he said, he would have walked out at the point when a young woman onstage threatens an older man with a pair of scissors. Arguing that the play was 'primarily concerned to titillate', he said it was different in kind from Shakespeare's *King Lear*, Bond's *Saved* or Mamet's *Oleanna*, and ended with a call to discriminate between 'art and titillatory violence'.

Three days later, Jenny Topper, Hampstead's artistic director, and Matthew Lloyd, who had directed all of Ridley's plays, hit back. Lloyd was 'amazed' that Billington missed the 'cathartic, tragic structure of the play' and pointed out that if 'he was titillated I'm afraid that reveals more about him than about the play'. He also said that 'the secret of effective stage violence is that the audience must be persuaded above all by the acting'. What 'gives the scene its already notorious power is that the emotional drives of the characters are so truthfully rendered'. Because Ridley – like Bond – tells us where the violence comes from, he earns the right to show it. Topper agreed, pointing out that she was in a better position than Billington to judge whether Ridley's 'complex and brave play' was antifeminist or not. Having 'rejected countless plays that I have thought exploitative of women', Topper said she 'always thought carefully about acts of violence and sex being depicted on stage', and concluded that Ridley's play was 'based in truth'. 'The violence in the play was in no way spurious,' says Topper. 'It was grounded in character and plot.' She adds that older members of her audience are less shocked by violent acts than by bad language.

One explanation for the originality of Ridley's imagination is that, as far as theatre goes, he is an outsider. Born in Bethnal Green in London's East End in 1964, he has always been fascinated by powerful images: his autobiographical introduction to his published plays is full of childhood shocks and adolescent freak-outs. By the age of ten he wanted to be a painter, and eventually studied fine art at St Martin's School of Art, where he also acted in an experimental theatre group and began making films. It was the time when the 'Brit pack' of young artists such as Damien Hirst were starting out. 'I've always been involved in the visual arts and started out by illustrating my own stories,' Ridley says. 'I was part of the London art scene at a very exciting time; I knew most of the people that went on to be in the controversial *Sensation* show at the Royal Academy in 1997.' Like them, he developed a language of strong images; unlike them, he chose theatre:

All my plays have that *Sensation* sensibility; their images and set pieces are garish and brash. For me, the visual side of drama has always been vital. I've always seen images as engines of emotion. I've always sought that one icon-like image that will convey a wordless meaning, an image-aria, if you like.

Ridley's prolific career includes screenplays, such as *The Krays* and *The Reflecting Skin* (both 1990), several novels, radio plays, as well as many children's novels and plays for young people.

Advertised as 'a scorchingly nasty blend of comedy, spectacle and terror where a monster from the past meets the monsters of the present', *Ghost from a Perfect Place* begins with the return of a sixties gangster, Travis Flood, to his old stomping ground in Bethnal Green, ostensibly to publicize his autobiography. He pays a call on Rio, a tart he has met in a graveyard, but finds only Torchie, her Gran, at home. Both of them conjure up the past ('the perfect place' of the title), but while the gangster's vision is nostalgic, Torchie's is full of pain: her daughter was raped at the age of fourteen, and died in childbirth. Rio arrives, but Travis is no longer in the mood for sex. When he tries to leave without paying, Rio clubs him to the ground. As Act II opens, he is tied up, and Rio leads a girl gang – Miss Sulphur, aged eighteen, and Miss Kerosene, twelve – singing and dancing in front of him. When he mocks them, they torture him by grinding burning cigars into his chest and face. To stop the pain, he confesses the worst thing he ever did, which was to rape Rio's mother. Realizing that he is her father, Rio dissolves the gang and releases Travis, who admits that his book is full of lies.

Watching *Ghost from a Perfect Place* at the Hampstead theatre was both an exciting and excruciating experience, with energetic, noisy acting and a stark contrast between Travis, the dapper, old-style villain with his buttonhole lily (the play's motif), and the aggressive girl gang, all pony tails and gold lamé miniskirts. Choosing John Wood, a great classical actor, to play Travis suggested links with Shakespeare and Greek tragedy; while Trevyn McDowell's Rio looked like a Madonna clone, very different from her previous role as Rosamund in the BBC's *Middlemarch*. When the characters acted out their life stories, the theatrical panache of doing so was heightened by Ridley's verbal clarity. At the same time, disturbing emotional material about subjects such as the loss of a child, teenage rape, secret birth and guilt snaked under the play's glitzy surface. During the long torture scene, thoughts about pain mingled with curiosity about how the 'burning' make-up was done.

As well as visual stage pictures, the play had powerful verbal images: people burnt in their beds, kicked in the balls, having their faces savagely scratched, being threatened, raped. Words conjured up blood-soaked mattresses, dead baby rats. Such eldritch lyricism was not to everyone's taste. The *Mail on Sunday* reported that it was 'too much for a couple of middle-aged women, who voted with their feet, muttering "Isn't it *awful*" as they went' and the *Financial Times* said that 'one woman in the audience fled during the cigar-burn treatment'.

Lauded as a 'knuckle-duster in words', 'a masterpiece of killer-bimbo menace', with its 'in-yer-face castrating trio' of 'Furies', Ridley's writing was praised even when the brutality of his imagination was deplored. Charles Spencer of the *Telegraph* found Ridley's play 'compelling, original and about as nasty as you can get'. Its effect was that 'one moment you are laughing wildly, the next staring fixedly at the floor and praying that you won't part company with your supper'. He found the torture scene 'repulsive' and the play's ending 'sentimental'. Neil Smith in *What's On*, a London listings magazine, argued that Ridley trivializes the women's case by 'sapping their strength with internal divisions and lesbian rivalry', making the play 'more a sex fantasy for kinky males than a portrait of female emancipation'. Such criticisms, says director Matthew Lloyd, are misguided. The play is 'the tragedy of a cruel man learning the human cost of his cruelty'. Travis, after all, 'goads his assailants into hurting him because he realizes his own need for retribution' – a point missed by most reviewers. Since 'the person in control of this scene is the victim in the chair, not his torturers', the issue is a morally complex one.

Ridley, as the *Daily Mail* pointed out, had 'rekindled the flames of interest in the Krays with his award-winning screenplay', and now returned to the problem of violence. In *Ghost from a Perfect Place*, brutality is not only used as a way of showing Travis's almost religious sense of guilt, but also as a criticism of nostalgia. Here the target is working-class sentimentality. One of the myths about the Krays is that they were honourable villains, philanthropists who harmed only 'their own kind'. Yesterday's hard men did a public service, dressed smartly and were celebrities; today's criminals are thrill-seeking deviants – nobodies. Travis complains that he hardly recognizes the East End, now a 'wasteland' disfigured by dirt and graffiti. By showing how violence breeds more violence, how horrible its consequences are and how it is justified by telling untrue stories about it, Ridley makes a political point. The optimistic ending of the first production, which some reviewers criticized, implies that change is possible.

Ridley prefers to think of the play's ending not as optimistic but as neutral. 'Rio has woken up and she can now make a choice.' At the end, two people are left onstage: Rio and her Gran. One knows the truth, the other doesn't. 'Who's better off?' asks Ridley. In fact, the rapid departure of Travis at the end defuses the play's most emotionally fraught moment: the mutual recognition of father and daughter. A faint odour of incest hangs in the air. Says Ridley: 'I may turn up the colours a bit, but what I write is true. I'm also trying to find something mythic in that underclass that's living on the edge. A lot of critics have said that my plays have more in common with Greek tragedy than with contemporary drama, and I think that's true. For example, *The Pitchfork Disney* is set in real time, in one location and is full of long monologues.'

Other influences are Sam Shepard and Tennessee Williams. 'Something about both the Deep South of America and London's East End produce dynamic, strong women and sexually confused males,' says Ridley. With its Victorian plot about a daughter discovering her long-lost father, *Ghost from a Perfect Place* owes much to Dickens, 'but it uses elements of melodrama in a postmodernist way'. Its starting point was the film script of *The Krays*. 'I was talking to these gangsters to see if I could get any good bits of dialogue, and they were saying how it used to be a godfather society, and one let slip that what now scared him most was the girl gangs.' So the idea of 'a matriarchal society taking revenge on the patriarchs grew into the play'. But the 'key is that the three main characters have all been deluded or lied to themselves about the past'.

Ridley was working through ideas about memory and about 'the sins of the fathers catching up on their kids', and when he got to Act II he 'thought that, as in Greek tragedy, the only thing that can shatter this stalemate is an act of violence', and the 'only thing that can make the various parts of these histories fall into place is a symbolic cleansing, a sacrifice'. He was upset when critics called the violence gratuitous, because 'if you look at the narrative threads of the play, it is the inevitable outcome of the story.' Why were critics so hostile? 'I think some of them saw the violence as a symbolic act by a new generation against John Wood and everything he represented. Someone told me: "You wouldn't have had that reaction if you were burning Berkoff."'

The intensity of the response to the torture in Act II 'made people forget that Act I is a really cosy, funny scene about two old codgers chatting about the past'. Ridley didn't play the violence for laughs, 'nor as a postmodernist joke – which is the only palatable way of doing violence these days, although making something palatable has never been high on my agenda'. Gender politics also came into play: 'Seeing men being violent onstage is fine, but vicious girls are another matter.' 'It touched a raw spot,' agrees Topper, 'because it showed that young women could be as violent as young men, which no one else was saying at the time.'

In the published playtext, Ridley prophetically quotes poet Andrew Motion: 'The fire is out at the heart of the world:/ All tame creatures have grown up wild.' During the same month that *Ghost from a Perfect Place* opened, the *Daily Mail* reported that two thirteen-year-old schoolgirls in Shoreham-by-Sea, West Sussex, were 'tied up, beaten and burned in a horrific attack by two older girls' who called themselves the 'Kray Sisters'. They'd apparently been influenced by Ridley's film. But Ridley points out that getting heated up about the issue of violence distracts from the heart of his play, which is more about loss than aggression.

What makes *Ghost from a Perfect Place* Ridley's best work is the tension between its vivid gothic images and its emotional subtext of love, loss and sacrifice. While some parts of the play – for example, the Ten Commandments of Saint Donna, Rio's sanctified mother – could easily be dismissed as lurid, juvenile fantasy, the ending brings out the underlying feelings in an imaginative and forceful way. The most riveting moment is not the torture but the conversation in which Travis tells Rio about his rape of her mother, and how the daughter gave herself to him to save her parents from being beaten. As Rio suddenly makes an imaginative leap and tells her mother's side of the story, the idea of self-sacrifice becomes powerfully moving. The idea of a child protecting her parents is complicated because the figure onstage, Rio, is playing the role of her long-dead mother, and acting out the trauma of her own conception. Psychologically, it is not only an adolescent fantasy but also a reminder of the strength of youthful feelings and idealism.

At the same time, Ridley's concern with storytelling has all the force of a cautionary tale. *Ghost from a Perfect Place* shows what happens when people are so obsessed about fabricating their own stories that they forget to listen to other people's. One day, the play implies, the story that is being told may actually be about you. Travis realizes this; Torchie doesn't. Rio experiences it as a revelation that will change her life. Despite its clamour, the play's best moments have a still sadness, a quiet realization of pain and loss, and of the need for courage to bear them, which is both touching and a tribute to human resilience.

At the start of the decade, Ridley was almost alone in exploring ideas no one else dared to touch, but soon some of his trademarks – violent stage images, blatant language, pop culture references – became staples of the new drama. Because of his background in visual art, Ridley was ahead of his time, using shock tactics before the Royal Court made confrontation fashionable. 'My plays tend to be garish and amoral,' he says. 'One American critic described them as the Marquis de Sade meets Liberace. I don't think he meant it as a compliment, but I've always taken it as one.' Never politically correct, all of Ridley's plays used shock, but always with a reason. 'The violence towards animals, for example, is just a device, often used in fine art, to question mortality in a godless world.' By 1999, with *The Pitchfork Disney* and *The Fastest Clock in the Universe* getting New York premieres, and *Ghost from a Perfect Place* enjoying a London fringe revival, Ridley had a chance to enjoy the climate for provocative writing he himself had helped create.

Phyllis Nagy's *Butterfly Kiss*

At the same time as Ridley played out his singular vision of London's East End, Phyllis Nagy was widening the scope of theatrical possibility. In 1992, her *Weldon Rising* (Royal Court/Liverpool Playhouse) explored the effect of a random murder on a group of New York lesbians and gays, using a mix of formal innovation, emotional honesty and an ironic worldview. If what provoked some critics was the lesbian love scene – which *The Times* called 'fairly robust' – the hardest thing to bear in *Weldon Rising* is Natty's regret at being too afraid to intervene and save his lover from being stabbed by a homophobe. The most moving thing about the play is the way that fear is shown as crippling and isolating. *Weldon Rising* was the first play programmed by Stephen Daldry in his role as new artistic director of the Royal Court, and it sent a signal, influencing other young writers.

Weldon Rising was sharply written and controversial. The British gay press attacked Nagy for creating 'unsympathetic' characters and appealing to 'male voyeuristic fantasies' by showing two lesbians having sex. This was ironic, because Nagy is as intensely 'gay-sympathetic' as any other 'gay writer'. What she insists on is the portrayal of fully rounded human beings. 'People's foibles are what persuades audiences to your

47

point of view,' she says. It is 'unhealthy' to deny that people have divided characters and that everyone is capable of lying, cheating and doing wrong. Both straight and gay audiences, however, often find it easier 'to accept lesbian and gay characters who fret about their gayness' than to watch gays who behave just like everyone else. Besides, the final ten minutes of *Weldon Rising*, with its vivid image of naked women embracing, were celebratory. Individual identity was being affirmed in the face of calamity.

If *Weldon Rising* announced the arrival of a new talent, Nagy's next play – staged in the same month as Ridley's *Ghost from a Perfect Place* – confirmed her promise. With its story about a daughter who kills her mother, *Butterfly Kiss* scandalized many people, who were as confused by its innovative structure as they were troubled by its emotional content. Once again, the shockable were dismayed by a lesbian kiss, although the really disturbing thing about the play was its underlying sense of unease.

Set in a jail cell, *Butterfly Kiss* is a memory play in which twenty-five-year-old Lily Ross, having been arrested and charged with her mother's murder, remembers the events that led to her imprisonment. Intercut with her past is the story of how her lover, Martha, searches in vain for a reason for the murder. With a beguiling mix of irony and intensity, the play moves through a number of disquieting scenes from Lily's life. Living with her mother, Jenny, and grandmother – after her father, Sloan, left home to live with his mistress – Lily is a young woman with great ambition but few achievements. When she meets Martha in a gay bar, happiness seems to be within her grasp. Then her lover goes away on a business trip, and Lily shoots her mother in the head.

Masterly in its balanced tone and perfectly controlled in its complex structure, *Butterfly Kiss* moves between past and present, fantasy and reality, pain and amused detachment. At north London's trendy Almeida theatre, the simultaneous scenes took place on a curving white set that was both prison cell and family kitchen. I have a vivid image of this white expanse splashed with blood, but this is an invented memory because, although Lily's grandmother scrubs the stains of the crime obsessively, no blood was spilt during the production. On the back wall was a pristine cabinet with rows of pinned butterflies in the shape of the Stars and the Stripes, a constant reminder that the play was a comment on the American Dream. Because actress Elizabeth Berridge played Lily's older self and younger self in the same way, without behaving like a teenager, you had a strong sense of her being in the present, remembering rather than acting out her past. Director Steven Pimlott's lightness of touch brought out the intimacy of the final scene, as Lily stroked her mother's hair with the barrel of the gun. The play is as seductive and elusive as its title, which means 'a caress given by winking one eye so that the lashes brush against the face of the receiver'.

Butterfly Kiss irritated some critics. The *Telegraph* complained that the play, which had a set that looked like a 'modish installation' from the Saatchi Gallery, was just an 'artily attenuated drama in which the sequence of events is jumbled up', while *What's On* asked whether our fascination with serial killers came from 'our passion to figure out what makes them tick' or whether 'our jaded mindsets require ever more visceral horrors to stimulate them?'. By contrast, praise came from the *Sunday Times*'s John Peter ('a hauntingly and brilliantly inconclusive play'), the *Daily Express*'s Maureen Paton ('a brilliant new drama of paradox'), and the *Observer*'s Michael Coveney ('a hard-edged, often dazzlingly well-written fable').

Born in 1962, Nagy is a New Yorker who never intended to become a playwright. She studied Music Theory and Composition at New York University, attended a creative writing course at Hollins College, Virginia, and 'drifted into the dramatic writing programme at New York University', during which she wrote, in 1983, an early version of *Butterfly Kiss*. She then worked in real estate and on the *New York Times*, painstakingly developing her interest in writing plays during her spare time. A further draft of *Butterfly Kiss* was written in 1989. Two years later, she quit work and took part in an exchange scheme between New Dramatists, in New York, and the Royal Court: while Martin Crimp went to New York, she visited London, and moved there permanently in 1992. *Weldon Rising* was put on later that year.

'My inspirations are always musical,' says Nagy. The structure of her plays is related to a musical model, so that the 'build of a scene or the build of a moral revelation is achieved through the accumulation of detail, which stops and is picked up, and is then recapitulated in a similar way to music'. She also uses popular songs to 'push the right emotional buttons': Donna Summer's gay anthem 'Could It Be Magic?' in *Weldon Rising* and 'My Melancholy Baby' and 'Shine On Harvest Moon' in *Butterfly Kiss*. But her biggest influences are Chekhov, Beckett, and modernist novels. The Americans that inspired her most are contemporary writers such as John Guare – especially his *Landscape of the Body* –

and Albert Innaurato, with *The Transfiguration of Benno Blimpie*, in which a sixteen-year-old fat boy eats so much that he dies.

Murder makes a big splash in Nagy's work. 'I'm fascinated by the nature of violence and what makes those who commit violent acts different from those who can't,' she says. While in *Weldon Rising* murder is a random act, in *Butterfly Kiss* it's personal. Nagy is interested in violence when it raises questions about individual responsibility. In *Weldon Rising*, this involved making uncomfortable suggestions about human selfishness; in *Butterfly Kiss*, it dared audiences to consider the possibility of murder being a loving act. But Nagy uses shock sparingly; she is not interested in staging atrocity. What she does is to carefully balance the visceral emotions of pain and hatred with a sense of intellectual control. Her plays are also wickedly funny. 'If you can make people laugh, they will listen to almost anything you have to say.'

So what is *Butterfly Kiss* trying to say? On the broadest level, the play is a provocation. Show me the average American family, says Nagy, and I'll show you an emotional nightmare. Here, the family is the fundamental unit of social pressure: Lily's mother and grandmother keep hassling her about who she should marry and what she should be. In *Butterfly Kiss*, both the 'average family' and the American Dream are mercilessly satirized.

The play is not a whodunit but a whydunit. Its meaning comes from Lily's act of matricide, which is never completely explained. Nagy says, 'The play implicitly gives you the information to come to a conclusion.' All 'the behaviour that leads up to Lily's final action is contained in the play – there is always an answer, but you have to be willing to engage with the play and come up with an answer yourself.' If 'what you want is a passive experience, then theatre is not the right medium'. But, she argues, while classic plays that don't easily yield up their secrets are often praised, 'new plays that don't give direct answers are always attacked'.

Butterfly Kiss certainly contains plenty of material for psychological speculation. The blatant elements of Lily's past include scenes in which her father offers his fourteen-year-old daughter to his buddy, an ex-marine; Jenny desperately tries to dance with her; her grandmother forces Lily to spy on her parents' lovemaking; her father leaves his wife and parades his mistress. An early joke about the 'booze gene' suggests a history of unhappiness. Eating disorders are briefly mentioned. The absence of 'pain cells' is joked about. Lily complains that nobody notices her, that her family never thanks her. In her father's wallet, she finds a photo of his mistress obscuring her own. A later sneer about her having turned out to be a 'big nothing' signals the pressure she is under. Eventually, her father gives her a gun.

But despite the profusion of psychological clues – topped by Oedipal hints that culminate in Lily telling her mother that she is moving in with Martha: 'She reminds me of Daddy's girlfriend' – none of this adds up to a traditional explanation. Each of these incidents signals a family in trouble, but none of them is a reason for murder. What they create is a strong sense of quiet desperation. Lily can't bear the lack of love in her family, nor the constant pressure to achieve, nor her own frustrated expectations. In the end, she solves the problem by shooting her way out of trouble: she'll never be a composer, but murder makes her famous, an achiever. And she also concocts a reason for herself, saying to Martha at the end of Act I: 'My mother asked me to kill her.'

The last scene – the murder – is more violent the more gently it is played. Lily brushes her mother's hair, like she has done a million times before. This time she uses a gun; she sings to her mother. Then shoots her. Jenny can no longer distinguish between what her daughter is and what she wants her to be. Is she mad, or just dreaming? At one point, she realizes what will happen to her and accepts it. Mother and daughter both know the road they're going down; death is a gift. A mercy killing? 'No,' says Nagy, 'A sick dog is not being put down, but an active decision is being made. The murder is the only thing Lily could have done.'

The matricide is both an insane act by a sane woman and a sane act by an insane woman. What is subverted is any idea that a simple explanation is possible. Lily's murder of her mother is meant to be inexplicable because that way it stays disturbing, praying on the mind. Whether you take a psychological slant on it, or just see it in the great literary tradition of existential murders, it remains a puzzle, forcefully reminding you that there are many actions that make perfect sense to the person doing them but are incomprehensible to everyone else. As Martha says, it is 'painful' to read the speculations of 'strangers'. In the end, no one knows what makes Lily tick. 'When a play doesn't tell you what to think, it's bound to be agitating,' says Nagy. 'I don't like forcing people to feel one way or the other.'

Butterfly Kiss is also troubling because it is about a matricide. 'Mother–daughter matricide is the only taboo,' argues Nagy. 'When a son kills his mother, it can be seen as understandable and even heroic. A man can break with his mother symbolically and it's a rite of passage.' But 'when a daughter does it, it's seen as fundamentally unnatural, a violation of the sacred bond between mother and daughter'. In literature, 'the relationship between mother and daughter can be explored, but the bond is always reaffirmed. Literature tells me that women are seen as emotionally unable to make the break with their mothers.' In *Butterfly Kiss*, the matricide smashes this view of the family. In doing so, it reminds us that ugly feelings are normal too.

What is shocking about Nagy's play is not the lesbian kiss, nor the final gunshot, but the picture – which we glimpse through the fractures of a highly elliptical style – of neediness and cowardice. The play's emotional core is about needing to be taken care of and to take care of others. The paradox is that the only way Lily can take care of her mother is to kill her. Her act of decision is also an act of defiance. Nagy examines states of emotional intelligence by using a sophisticated structure, with shifting timescales, fantasy reruns of past events and simultaneous scenes. However abstract on paper, the reason this works onstage is that everything happens in the theatrical present. In performance, everything appears to be real, yet in the playtext Nagy mentions that some scenes are set in the 'imagined past'. Lily's memory of her seduction of her father's best friend, for example, feels very adult: it could be her fantasy, or it could be an actual traumatic moment. When she tells her lawyer that her father seduced his buddy for her, it is clear that what really happened is less important than her sense of alienation from her father.

With *Butterfly Kiss*, Nagy's career took off. One year later, her *Disappeared* (Leicester Haymarket, 1995) examined personal loneliness and urban anonymity by telling the story of a woman who walks out of a New York bar and vanishes. Then came *The Strip* (Royal Court, 1995), a postmodern odyssey that showed Nagy's imagination in full flight. Structurally innovative and highly influential, it confirmed her mastery of theatrical form, despite its lack of a compelling emotional core. In *Never Land* (Royal Court, 1998), an outstanding example of imaginative writing and emotional understanding, Nagy explored the geography of family emotions, the desire for a home from home, and the nature of prejudice. Dipping and diving between the crevices of the said and unsaid, frequently interrupting social chatter or family bickering with blasts of emotion or fragments of dream, *Never Land* is a haunting, intimate and poetic play.

Nagy's theatre is difficult, an acquired taste. More than any other writer, with the exception of Martin Crimp, her work can be read in terms of postmodern ideas about indeterminacy and avoidance of closure. But her intellectual edge and ironic tone are never cold or unemotional. At the same time, it is much easier to recall the story of a Nagy play than to explain what it is really all about. As she says, 'We do need to ponder over the meaning of good plays beyond the moment in which we watch them. This is the essence of resonance.' Whether shocking, irritating or unsettling, Nagy's theatre subverts audience expectations. 'Provocation, because it stimulates thought, offers us a way forward.' In her work, meaning percolates slowly to the surface, seeping into consciousness long after the curtain has come down. A unique voice in nineties theatre, Nagy doesn't provide a comfortable theatrical experience, but you do feel that she embraces life wholly, in its warmth as well as its terrors.

Tracy Letts's *Killer Joe*

While Nagy was experimenting with the language of theatre, another American writer was reminding British audiences that they didn't have to go to the movies to see a detective thriller. *Killer Joe*, written by a male actor named Tracy Letts, came from Chicago to the Edinburgh Traverse, a successful example of director Ian Brown's policy of finding new international voices. The play won a Fringe First award in August 1994, then transferred to the Bush in January 1995 and to the West End soon after. It is the kind of play, said Steve Grant in the London listings magazine *Time Out*, that sends its audiences 'blinking their way into the night with looks of gleeful incredulity'.

Opening the Bush's 'A Walk on the Wild Side' season, *Killer Joe* was followed by Nick Ward's *The Present* and Harry Gibson's *Trainspotting*. Letts's play, says Dominic Dromgoole, was one of three 'by young men who look at the back end of the modern world in funny and unpleasant ways. They look at people who are very confused, and explore the wastage. It's dirty writing, the flip side of the New Age thing: the big spiritual smile that characterized new writing in the early nineties.'

He was also responding to the growing strength of the Royal Court, where Stephen Daldry's first season included Sarah Kane's *Blasted*. 'Putting three very different plays together in a season is always a marketing ploy,' says Dromgoole, 'a way of staying hot.'

Set in a trailer home on the outskirts of Dallas, Texas, *Killer Joe* is peopled with the poor white trash of America. While the playtext has an evocative epigraph from William Faulkner's *As I Lay Dying* – 'How often have I lain beneath rain on a strange roof, thinking of home?' – the set is full of 'seedy and cheap' decorations, and 'other detritus of the poor'. The action starts with Chris arriving in the middle of the night. His step-mother, Sharla, wearing 'only a man's sweat-stained tee-shirt that falls above her ass', lets him in. When Ansel, his redneck father, appears, Chris complains that Sharla 'answered the door with her beaver puckered out like it was tryin' to shake my hand'.

After this opening, *Killer Joe* quickly turns into a thriller. Chris is in debt and, to save his life, wants to hire a crooked cop, 'Killer Joe' Cooper, to murder his mother, so that the whole family can enjoy her life insurance. But unable to pay Joe in advance, Chris and Ansel agree to let him have a 'retainer': Chris's sister, Dottie, a twenty-year-old virgin who walks in her sleep. At a candlelit dinner, Joe makes her strip and model a 'sexy black evening dress'. By Act II, he has moved in with Dottie, despite Chris's misgivings. Before long, 'mom' is killed and Joe has to be paid. Then come the plot twists: the insurance policy has been made out to Rex, mom's lover; Dottie falls in love with Joe; Rex is manipulated by Sharla, his secret lover. After a vicious scene during which Joe forces Sharla to mimic fellatio on a chicken leg, there follows a parody of a family meal during which Joe announces his impending marriage to Dottie. Chris objects, there is a violent struggle and Dottie shoots Chris and Ansel. The final image is of Dottie pointing the gun at Joe's head, saying, 'I'm gonna have a baby.'

Critics loved *Killer Joe*. As well as praising the superb timing of Chicago's Hired Gun company – directed with immaculate precision by Wilson Milam – they admired the writing, which Michael Billington called 'eldritch Southern Gothic' with echoes of Faulkner, Sam Shepard and Tennessee Williams. The play, raved *Today* newspaper, was 'raw as a fresh knife wound and just as bloody'; a 'claustrophobic remix of *Blood Simple* and *True Romance*', said *Time Out*. A key moment was high-lighted by the *Independent*'s Paul Taylor. After Joe hints that he'll accept Dottie as a 'retainer', Ansel shouts 'GODDAMN IT!' – not because his daughter is being bartered but because the television is malfunctioning. As Irving Wardle wrote in the *Independent on Sunday*, the family is morally blind: they 'piously attend their victim's funeral, hold hands for grace at dinner' but have a 'stunted response' to 'shock events'. In the *Guardian*, Tom Morris pointed out that the play's 'enduring impact' is not its violence, but 'the ease with which violent thoughts are accommodated'. Responding to the media panic about representations of violence, Morris said that *Killer Joe* is a 'moral play', arguing that 'if we believe something is moral, we will stomach any amount of shock'.

How did critics respond to the most disturbing scene, when Joe makes Dottie strip and handle his erection? For *The Times*'s Jeremy Kingston this was a 'gracious courtship', for the *Daily Express*'s Maureen Paton 'cold-blooded yet sexually mesmerising', and for the *Financial Times*'s Sarah Hemming it was 'like watching a spider move in on a fly, yet it is also astonishingly beautiful'. Billington saw Joe 'shyly and gracefully' courting Dottie and 'only when he forces her to strip are you reminded this man is something more than a gentleman caller'. No London critic, male or female, protested. No one seemed outraged by the abuse of power involved, when a much older man forces a naive young woman into having sex.

In the close confines of the Bush theatre, *Killer Joe* was heavy with naturalistic detail, from the trailer's greasy dirt to the television's ranting evangelist, but what was electrifying was the uncompromising acting of Hired Gun. Each of the characters was as vivid as a cartoon. When fat Ansel lazily rubbed his crotch and slumped in front of the television, it perfectly summed up the hopeless impoverishment of his world. Equally memorable was the savage impact of the violence and the tension that grew in the audience when Joe told Dottie to strip. At that point, the scene seemed too intimate to watch. A brutal bargain had been made, and everyone was too stunned to stop it. With the audience jammed tight, there was a strong feeling of complicity.

Killer Joe is full of dialogue that shows what happens when language becomes meaningless. At one point, Dottie asks: 'Are you gonna kill my momma?' To which Joe replies: 'I'm not sure. Why?' 'Just curious,' says Dottie politely. When language is emptied of meaning, there are no values, just habitual phrases. In the play, moral language is constantly used to describe immoral acts. When Chris says Joe will 'do this right', he has murder in mind. Violence feeds off the inarticulateness bred by a diet of junk food, junk television and junk drugs. Lashing out is a form of self-expression. Social deprivation results in desperation and desperation leads to miscalculation: the strength of *Killer Joe* lies in its relentless logic.

Born in 1965 in Oklahoma, Letts worked as an actor for Chicago's Steppenwolf Company before becoming a founder member of Hired Gun, which produced *Killer Joe*, his first play. Letts tells several stories about the play's origins. In one version it is based 'on a combination of true stories I pulled from newspaper articles', in another on one 'newspaper clipping about a Florida family'. Either way, 'it's risky material but it's about what's happening here and now. It's scary but these people really exist. Domestic violence is a popular issue since O. J. Simpson put it on the agenda.' Letts is the first to admit that he talks 'shit' about his own work, but what seems to be genuine is his dislike of the 'easy comparisons' some critics made with other writers. 'I hate the references to Sam Shepard. My real inspirations were Jim Thompson, the fifties pulp-fiction writer, Faulkner, even Sam Peckinpah.'

A key line in the play is Chris's description of his mom: 'Look at it this way. Is she doin' anybody any good?' 'What people find unsettling about Killer Joe,' says Letts, 'is that they don't know who to align themselves with. Some people want Joe killed; others say he's the only one with any real integrity.' Chris 'has a vague understanding that there's something moral out there, but he doesn't know what it is: he's trying to figure it out'.

The play, says Letts, 'is a return to the old Chicago school of rock 'n' roll, kick-ass theatre.' Chicago theatre is 'more dark, hard-edged and gritty than New York. The consensus here is that most New York actors are pansies.' At first, many American theatres rejected the play on grounds of taste and decency. 'They were scared of the unknown; they wanted to tidy it up; they wanted to put underwear on Sharla.' One theatre that rejected it 'called the seduction episode "the scene where the psychotic cop rapes the retarded girl"', says Letts. 'Actually, it's a pretty sad, pretty erotic scene. Here are two damaged people who find some solace in each other.' But Letts couldn't duck accusations of misogyny. 'I got accosted at parties, and not only by women,' he says. 'But I consider myself a feminist or a womanist. At the end of the play, the question is really about how you take control of your life – it's about empowerment.' The play's ending could be read as symbolizing a biblical (eye for an eye) morality.

Letts has no problem with stage violence. 'When I go and see plays, violence – for better or worse – keeps me interested. It's confrontation brought to its physical conclusion; it's drama.' But if Letts's play was everywhere applauded, was it because its structure – that of a tense, naturalistic thriller – made it a less demanding viewing experience than, say, Butterfly Kiss or Blasted? The popularity of Killer Joe had little to do with its morality and everything to do with its resemblance to a cult film. Like a movie, it offered the thrill of overt sex and violence; like a Jacobean drama, it excused the excess by thoroughly punishing the villain. Its morality acted as an alibi, licensing the audience's enjoyment. At the same time, it sent a clear signal that theatre could give audiences a forceful sense of life on the edge, a vision of human hopelessness all the more powerful for being so cinematic and so humorous.

Harry Gibson's *Trainspotting*

Irvine Welsh's 1993 book, *Trainspotting*, was a cult best seller that lent its name to a generation. When it reached number ten in the Top Hundred Books of the Century, promoted by Waterstone's bookshop chain, commentators suggested that this may be the only grown-up fiction young clubbers read. By gradually colonizing global culture with T-shirts, a film version, soundtrack CDs and a special website, *Trainspotting* did for drug-taking what *Pulp Fiction* did for violence. But before it became a multimillion-pound film, directed by Danny Boyle in 1995, the book was made into a sellout stage version that brought new audiences into the theatre. Judging by its amazing success, you'd imagine that *Trainspotting* had been written by a couple of twentysomething street kids. You'd be wrong. As Harry Gibson, who turned Welsh's 'great dirty book' into a play, says: 'The novel was written by a thirty-five-year-old, adapted by a forty-five-year-old and produced by a fiftysomething-year-old: we all drew on experiences we'd had long before in-yer-face was fashionable.' All three were well-educated university graduates, and their success is another reminder that provocative theatre was not solely an English metropolitan phenomenon.

In *Trainspotting*, Welsh tells the stories of a group of Scottish junkies, with a wacky humour and dark, stylized language. It is a book mainly about boys, and one that shows drug culture as both a fantasy playground and a descent into hell. Typically, these are young men without work and without family. Parents are there just to bail them out. Politically, *Trainspotting* is a smack in the mouth to liberal sensibilities because it shows working-class Edinburgh druggies not as victims but as pleasure-seekers. Little wonder that *The Face* magazine dubbed Welsh 'the poet laureate of the chemical generation'. Of course, *Trainspotting* is less interested in social realism than in insolence and shock: in one scene, a man sticks a syringe into his penis. According to the playtext's blurb, other 'raw tales' include 'two dossers' 'called up to interview for the same shite job neither wants; a gallus lassie, goaded by four failed-Oxbridge twats from the Uni, takes bloody revenge; a skag boy tries to kick it one last time.' The 'bloody revenge' refers to the scene in which a waitress describes how she took her revenge on abusive, sexist customers by dipping a used tampon in their soup and mixing excrement in their food. Neither this scene – nor the one in which two women mock the men who wolf-whistle at them – were included in the sanitized film version. In-yer-face feminism remains unmarketable.

The play begins with the exclamation 'Fuck!', as Mark tells a hilariously gross tale about waking up in a strange bed after a binge, only to find he has 'pished', 'puked up' and 'shat masel'. From then on, the play takes off, with a cast of four playing all the parts: Mark (Renton), Tommy, Franco (Begbie) and Alison, plus other junkies such as Sick Boy, Mother Superior, and sundry other characters. With its direct address to the audience, spoken narratives and imaginative use of simple props, *Trainspotting* demonstrates the power of rough theatre. Unlike the film, the play ditches the novel's heist plot and emphasizes its stories.

These include Laura asking Tommy to 'Fuck me in the erse' and then putting Vick's Vapour Rub on his penis instead of Vaseline; Mark and Tommy's master class in how to 'fuck up' a job interview; the cot death of Alison's baby; Mark losing his opium suppositories in a blocked toilet and delving deep to retrieve them; Begbie digging a hole in the turf and rubbing his 'knob' in it while schoolgirls race by; Tommy buying a ticket to an Iggy Pop gig instead of a birthday present for his girlfriend; 'loved-up' friends arguing over a squirrel; Mark having sex with his dead brother's pregnant girlfriend during the wake; Tommy getting AIDS after boasting he could handle 'skag'; and the final scene in old Leith Central Station when Mark and Begbie meet a drunk, who turns out to be Begbie's father. With grim irony, he asks the lads if they're 'trainspottin' in a derelict station.

Trainspotting without trains is the image of desolation that hangs over the play, in stark contrast to the image of escape that ends the novel. 'Ending the book with Renton's escape to Amsterdam is arguably less powerful than the idea of people being left behind,' says Gibson. But *Trainspotting* also suggests other metaphors: for example, the 'tracks' or needle marks on an addict's arm. And in its cyclical structure, it implies that addiction has no narrative: the last line of the play is a repeat of the first. Was Gibson describing youths going around in circles? 'Every production has its own biology: you have to let it end in the way that particular production wants to end. I leave it to the actors: "You are the band; this is your show."' Since the first version, there have been four or five different endings.

Both humorous and sinister, *Trainspotting* is set in Leith, Edinburgh's old dockland, and its demotic is inescapably funny and lurid, whether borrowing from rhyming slang – 'Ah'm happy steying oan the rock 'n' roll [dole]' – or playfully vulgar – 'You'd shag the crack ay dawn if it had hairs oan it!' – or cruelly revealing of its characters' hopelessness – junkie Alison prefers heroin to sex, saying 'That [drug injection] beats any meat injection. That beats any fuckin cock in the world'. *Trainspotting* is loaded with metaphors as addictive as its subject matter. Less an adaptation of the book than a staging of some of its narratives, the play's sick jokes and schoolboy humour remind you of William Burroughs's *The Naked Lunch* and other drug-culture classics.

In his introduction to the playtext, scornfully titled 'Drugs and the Theatre, Darlings', Welsh says that the success of *Trainspotting* took him by surprise, especially when it became 'a classic text without which no home is complete, blah, blah. Certainly, I had next to nothing to do with its adaptation for the stage.' That was Gibson's idea. At the time, he was play reader for the Glasgow Citizens theatre.

> Most of the plays were shite so I thought I'd better do something myself. I wandered into John Smith's bookshop in Hillhead and asked the manageress for the latest hot read, and she said: 'We've just got one left.' She brought the last dogeared copy of *Trainspotting* from the staff lavatory. 'Everybody's reading it and everybody's stealing it.'

Born in 1950, Gibson is the son of an Aberdeen shipwright who migrated to Oxford to work at the Cowley car plant. After reading English at Oxford University, Gibson 'eventually worked in theatre because it's the only thing I enjoyed'. Having been a stage manager, actor, director and writer, he is proudest of mounting 'the first revival of *East* outside London, in 1978'. Berkoff's play was 'the biggest influence' on *Trainspotting*. A Joy Division fan, Gibson's other inspirations include experiences at the Everyman in Liverpool, where a workshop production was attended by 'lots of housewives, and a woman in the audience said: "The trouble with most theatre is that the actors don't speak to us."' For Gibson, 'a genuine communal theatre is one where actors speak directly to the audience instead of imagining a blank fourth wall.'

Directed by Ian Brown, *Trainspotting* was one of the hits of the 1994 Glasgow Mayfest. Emphasizing the play's 'enormous wit and humour', the *Independent* praised the performances, calling Ewen Bremner's Mark 'an angular, fidgety youth, nervous and loud by turns'. The *Guardian* commented on how the 'bleak tragedy of a no-hope needle-sharing generation' was conveyed by 'a breathlessly dynamic production full of dangerous, deranged performances that articulate the fearful nihilism of the dispossessed'. And while the *Scotsman* pointed out the irony of bringing Leith junkies to the Gorbals, none of the reviewers foresaw just how big the play would become. First, it transferred to the Traverse. A year later it was revived at the Citizens, then transferred to London, then a new version was put on during the Edinburgh Festival. It moved back to London and was put on twice in the West End. There have been two national tours and countless revivals since 1996.

When I saw *Trainspotting* at the Bush in April 1995, the press officer told me that middle-aged theatre critics wouldn't understand it. For once, she was mistaken. Most of the critics rated the show highly, pointing out how Gibson's adaptation gave shape to an episodic novel by using the technique of one narrator commenting on another, one snippet of dialogue being taken up by another. For example, after Mark draws us in by explaining: 'Smack's an honest drug', Alison soon tells us to wise up: "Smack's an honest drug." Shite. Pure shite.' Not every word of the heavily accented dialogue was clear, but the repetition of key phrases had an almost incantatory feel – as did the rituals of 'cooking up' and 'shooting up'.

The set of *Trainspotting* made the Bush's claustrophobic space seedy, with its stained mattress, crusty toilet bowl and flickering candlelight. Dark and shadow-flecked in atmosphere, the play felt gleeful in its trawl through degradation, explicit in its nightmarish vision of the hell that addiction inflicts on the body, and occasionally unexpectedly tender: as when three friends go to a funfair or two men embrace. Actors Ewen Bremner, Susan Vidler, James Cunningham and Malcolm Shields played to the audience superbly. Above all, what struck you was the play's masterly theatricality. In Scene 6, Mark describes a heroin party, saying: 'Alison wis thair.' He looks over to her; she doesn't move. 'Ye wir thair,' he insists, and sulkily she joins in as Mark carries on: 'Alison wis cookin.' Of course, when Tommy injects heroin into his penis, people became uneasy, but no one walked out. Welsh says that 'members of the audience have been know to faint' during the injection scenes, which shows just how powerful intimate theatre can be.

One of the paradoxes of *Trainspotting* is that it is the kind of play that sends you out into the night so elated by the experience of watching it that you forget just how degraded its characters are. Both the book and the play were advertised by a picture of youths wearing skull masks. You can see why the *Guardian*'s Lyn Gardner wrote: 'You are constantly reminded of "the skull beneath the skin". But in this instance, the skull is grinning.' Yes, but not always. When Alison's baby dies, Mark observes that 'her thin white face is like a skull wrapped in milky clingfilm'.

What the stage version omitted, as the *Sunday Times* pointed out, was the novel's politics. Welsh's Renton 'blames Westminster for the death of his brother on army duty in Ulster, but he is also vitriolic about the IRA's claims to be freedom fighters. The second point is omitted by Gibson; so is Mark's bitter dismissal of Scottish patriotism'. 'Mark hates decency and sees patriotism as representing decency,' says Gibson. 'I kept that point, but decided to cut much of Irvine's abuse of Scotland because I wanted *Trainspotting* to be common to all housing schemes the world over, not just a parochial phenomenon.' By 1999, the play had been translated into ten languages and produced around the world, from Rio to Zagreb.

As *Trainspotting* was revived and revived again, questions arose about its message. When it transferred to the West End, the *Independent* accused it of 'moral tourism', saying that 'hell's a popular place, so long as you have a two-way ticket'. The *Sunday Telegraph* said it peddled 'a smart tough-guy complacency'. For Michael Billington, the play 'never gets to grips with the key question: why the characters succumbed to drugs in the first place' – he compared it unfavourably to 'American plays about narcotics such as *A Hatful of Rain* and *The Connection*'. Gibson is well aware that *Trainspotting* can be seen as glamorizing dirt. 'Compared to New York, we're much more open to the wild and the raw. At first, critics said it was fab; then they started asking: "What is it saying?" And that question has bothered me too. And I do wonder how close it really is to sensationalizing pain.'

A key moment is Mark's 'Life's boring and futile' speech, which is repeated with irony by Alison. Gibson says, 'This struck me as having a terrible ring of truth about it. It's like Beckett's "Keep going, going on, call that going, call that on". That seems to be the rock-bottom fact that really does face so many people.' Moments like this resonated with young audiences. The *Glasgow Herald*'s Carole Woddis commented: 'They loved the incipient anarchy of it, they groaned with the desperate degradation of it, and they thrilled to the dramatic urgency of it.' But if the *Sunday Express*'s Clive Hirschhorn was moved by a Scottish spectator 'with pierced nostrils' who cried when Tommy got AIDS, Billington disliked the 'young, nattily clad' audience's 'easy, self-gratifying laughter'. 'We've had rowdy kids in the audience,' says Gibson, 'though they tend to get a bit bored and keep going out for booze. We were told by lots of regional theatres that they'd never been so full for years.' When I saw the

West End revival of *Trainspotting*, its young spectators behaved as if they were at a rock concert. This was one of the few plays ever reviewed by the *New Musical Express*.

By the time *Trainspotting* was made into a film, it had become a cultural symbol that attracted both love and outrage. Its fans praised it for being youthful, funny and true to life, and supported Welsh's argument that people use drugs as 'life enhancers' and to get away from 'the horror and dullness of straight, mainstream life'. In the eighties, young people moved from taking the 'state-sponsored poisons of alcohol and tobacco' to 'private sector' drugs such as heroin, cocaine and Ecstasy. End of story. The *Times Literary Supplement* pointed out that *Trainspotting* 'carries a simple, right-on message of abstinence' while itself 'abstaining from authorial condemnation of addicts'.

But the backlash against *Trainspotting* was not long delayed. When Welsh's novel *Filth* was published in 1998, journalist Bryan Appleyard pointed out that while in the sixties drugs were a symbol of liberation, by the nineties they caused only decay and devastation. As the Verve sang, 'The drugs don't work.' For playwright David Greig, who defines political drama as one that 'posits the possibility of change', the character of Renton was a 'lifestyle icon' (a short haircut was named after him), whose addiction symbolizes political somnolence. He deplored the play's ending, with its despairing message: 'Things remain the same.' In general, the case against *Trainspotting* is that 'dirty' plays enabled 'an educated, reasonably affluent middle class' to 'vicariously enjoy' the 'empty lives of the junkies'. In reply, Ian Brown points out that, when Welsh wrote the book, 'he felt nobody was talking about needle-sharing and people were dying of ignorance', and that his anger made *Trainspotting* 'a very moral, profoundly anti-drugs piece'.

'It's preposterous to think *Trainspotting* glamorizes drug abuse,' argues Gibson.

> I can see how this might apply to the film, because it's so sumptuously colourful and euphoric. I've spoken to young people who came out of the play and said how dark and terrible it was, and much harder-hitting and [more] moving than the film. In Perth, a couple of Australian lads, who ate popcorn throughout the show, complained that it was 'a real downer'.

For the New York production, Gibson

restructured the play to make it clearer that people turn to drugs as an anaesthetic. The play is about the culture of poverty, boredom and violence, and there's always some drug around that's cheaper than food – and you curl up with your drugs and one-bar electric fire because, in social terms, you're surplus DNA.

When Renton says 'how amazing heroin is, the other characters always point out that it's pure shite'.

But *Trainspotting* is not just about drugs, it is also about friendship, loyalty and betrayal: heroin is a metaphor for not being able to talk about your emotions. None of the junkies can connect with their feelings. Taking drugs is a way of avoiding pain. The *New Statesman*'s Boyd Tonkin saw heroin as symbolizing a 'deeper craving – for intimacy, for solidarity, for companionship'. Gibson says, 'I knew that for a two-hour show I needed to have one relationship which ran through it, so I created the character of Tommy out of various bits of Irvine's characters and I made the friendship between Mark and Tommy central.' The play is 'ultimately about a betrayal of love. Mark is a desperately lonely person.' One production played up 'the sexual quality of the moment when they embrace, with heroin bonding them together in the same way as a sex act – then Alison says, "Och, why don't they just fuck each other?", and they spring apart.'

Gibson also defused suggestions about Welsh's misogyny by including two explicitly feminist scenes. *Trainspotting* shows women as both victims and victors. 'In Scotland, sexism and homophobia are really acute,' says Gibson. 'Women don't have much of a place in that sort of rough, backstreet society. They tend to have to look after the men and quietly suffer.' In the play, they have 'two big speeches which express women's anger, shame, insight and amazing grace'.

Trainspotting was a wake-up call. Like the film *Shallow Grave*, it showed that genteel Edinburgh could be as much an edge city as rough Glasgow. Like other drug culture classics, it seemed to advocate transgression just for the hell of it. Like Tarantino, Welsh inspired many imitators. A potent symbol of a generation's attitude, *Trainspotting* crossed easily from one cultural medium to another. It certainly gave theatre a shot in the arm.

The success of writers such as Philip Ridley and Phyllis Nagy, and of plays such as *Killer Joe* and *Trainspotting*, publicized the arrival of a new sensibility. As Dominic Dromgoole says, the Bush was looking for new writing that was 'juicier, more energetic and textured, with more exciting language'. By 1995, many more theatres were rushing to promote explicit plays by young writers and the trickle became a flood. In November 1995, the *Financial Times*'s Sarah Hemming was asking who, following the death of John Osborne, would take on the mantle of anger:

> We are looking for plays that burn with rage, that dislodge complacency, that disturb their audiences, and for young writers who have taken the batons handed on by more recent angry men – Brenton, Barker, Bond and Berkoff – and run with them, proving that theatre can still be a radical, shocking medium.

By 1996, the critics had become even more upbeat. Billington, who had been reviewing since 1971, wrote: 'I cannot recall a time when there were so many exciting dramatists in the twentysomething age-group: what is more, they are speaking to audiences of their own generation.' In *The Times*, Benedict Nightingale pointed out that *Look Back in Anger* had once 'caused such a stir that the theatre was clearly "the place to be at"', and said that 'there is a similar buzz in the air now'.

But as well as the Bush, the Traverse and the Court, other London spaces such as the Finborough, Hampstead, Old Red Lion, Theatre Royal Stratford East and the Tricycle made a powerful contribution to new writing. And regional work was vital too: Birmingham and Bolton, Leeds and Manchester, Salisbury and Sheffield. Most importantly, theatres everywhere attracted younger audiences, who discovered plays that explored a world they recognized as their own.

3 Anthony Neilson

It's a simple question;
Do we bear monsters?
Or do we create them?

(Wehner in *Normal*)

In February 1998, the *Daily Mail* ran a story that both flattered the national pride of its readers and stoked their prejudices. Headlined 'Britain saved this boy from Hitler, now he wants to save us from our own vulgarity', it told the tale of Peter Wolff, a Berlin-born Jew who'd fled the Hitler regime in 1937 and, after settling in Britain, built up a clothing business that became a major supplier of ladies' wear to Marks & Spencer. Having made millions, he sold his company and set up a trust to combat 'the growing trend of "filth and violence" on the West End stage'. Claiming that 'so many people I know are becoming reluctant to go to the theatre because there is too much filth and violence', Wolff said he wanted 'to help a group of playwrights to write good theatre without needing to put twenty f[uck]s in it'. His idols were David Hare, Tom Stoppard and Arthur Miller. His pet hate was Anthony Neilson, whose *The Censor* particularly incensed him. 'It was so vulgar,' he said. 'How many penises do you need to see in a play?' This was one of those rhetorical questions that illustrates the hysterical backlash provoked by confrontational theatre: there were no penises onstage in *The Censor* – nor in any of Neilson's plays.

Born in March 1967, Neilson grew up in Edinburgh. His mother, Beth Robens, was an actress; his father, Sandy Neilson, a director. 'I was a rehearsal-room baby,' says Neilson. His first acting experience was as a 'little kid in a British Rail advert', and he absorbed much theatre 'naturally' from his parents. 'It was an exciting time: my parents were involved in Scottish theatre in the seventies, when 7:84 and Wildcat were taking off, and I've always wanted to recapture the energy and urgency of that time.' But the plays that had the 'most impact on me as a kid were those by Donald Campbell.' Campbell's play, *The Jesuit*, 'caused a fuss at the time because of the language', but it was his *The Widows of Clyth* that really hit Neilson in the gut.

I was eleven when I saw it at the Traverse. There's a moment
when the women find out that their husbands have died at sea,
and my mother let out this horrendous scream. I was absolutely
chilled. Because she was my mother, the emotional force was
doubled.

Since then, 'I've always struggled with the idea that theatre should be like
that, that it really has to have that very direct, very basic force.' Neilson
believes that theatre 'should be an emotional experience – you should
come out feeling something. You are there; you are with people. It
should be like going to see a good live band.' What annoys him is that
most theatre 'seems to be purely cerebral'. To Neilson, provocative theatre is 'equivalent to punk rock'. Every 'fifteen years or so, a kick up the
arse is good for theatre. It needs it. A certain amount of shock is necessary – in-yer-face theatre reinvigorates the mainstream.'

After a troubled schooling, Neilson studied drama in Edinburgh for
a year before going to the Welsh College of Music and Drama in Cardiff.
He acted in Peter Weiss's *The Marat/Sade* and Dennis Potter's *Son of
Man*, but was 'thrown out' after a year, in 1987. He says he is 'one of those
people that institutions feel they have to break'. The 'alternative' lifestyle
of his parents 'instilled a questioning attitude' in his character, but what
he remembers most about growing up is a sense of instability. 'For the
first three years of my life we lived in one room in Aberdeen.' Then, in
Edinburgh, 'I remember bailiffs and the constant threat of eviction' and
'my mother having nervous breakdowns'. 'The odd thing about me was
that I was culturally middle class, but, at the same time, we sometimes
lived near the poverty line.' Although not a overtly political writer, Neilson remains acutely sensitive to questions of social justice.

After Cardiff, Neilson went back to Edinburgh, and entered a BBC
young playwright's competition. 'I had no particular interest in writing,'
he says, but he remembers having 'a weird clear feeling' that if he did
write a play, it would be put on. *The Colours of the King's Rose* – which
Neilson describes as 'something cinematic for the ears' – was broadcast
by BBC radio in 1988, and he then wrote *Welfare My Lovely* for the Traverse theatre in 1990. Other radio and stage plays followed. In between,
he moved to London.

One of the problems Neilson had at Cardiff was that he 'was never
happy being an actor'. He wasn't happy being told what to do; he always
wanted to think of the bigger picture. For this reason, he has often

directed his own work. He also has a vision of a small-venue experiential theatre – where the audience participate by living the emotions shown onstage and doesn't just sit back and contemplate the play intellectually. The development of such experiential drama was an essential part of the new confrontational aesthetic of the nineties.

Neilson gradually developed his own approach to writing and rehearsal. 'I would have less and less of the script finished by the time we went into rehearsal,' he says. 'And it got to the point when I was making it up as we went along.' He would 'take bits in and try them with the actors and see whether they worked.' Then he would rewrite, quickly and intensively. 'They were always getting the last part of the script very close to opening.' What effect did that have? 'Well, actors normally temper their playing because they have a view of how the whole play will develop, and the audience can guess where the play is heading by the way the actors behave at the start.' With his method, however, the 'audience has less to go on'. While rehearsal sessions normally last all day, 'mine were three or four hours at most'. This enabled actors to 'discover the play as it unfolds' and allowed Neilson 'to tailor the play to an actor's strengths'. Often it meant that his plays were 'a lot more ragged on the first night than on the last'. It sounds ramshackle, but it does have its advantages: 'The actors get the chance to make a journey during the run; they haven't rehearsed the play to death; they still take risks; they still have an edge.' The result is a type of theatre that is experiential for both performers and audiences.

Writers such as Neilson don't always fit snugly into the British theatre system. 'I don't like submitting my work to committees; there always comes a point where you've rewritten a play to oblivion. You lose its energy.' When he writes, 'it's for the moment, to have an impact, not to produce a work of literature'. In a piece published in *Time Out* magazine, Neilson satirized the theatre establishment. Among his ideas for scaring ordinary people away is to give theatres names such as 'Royal', 'Duke's' and 'Ambassadors'. 'None the less,' he writes, theatre had better stage 'something controversial now and then or people will get suspicious. So what new writing venues there are cause little *frissons* with "yoof" plays featuring guns and techno music, or – even better – drugs, which are good because, despite being illegal, they and their incapacitated users pose no threat . . .' He goes on to advise, tongue firmly in cheek, that theatres should 'try and keep off politics and sex'.

In pursuit of a 'more extreme kind of theatre', and before he moved to London, Neilson wrote *Normal: The Düsseldorf Ripper* for the Edinburgh Festival, to which he used to go every year. 'I knew the Edinburgh Festival very well and I knew that you needed a certain angle' so that 'people skimming through the brochure would be drawn by your show'. To sensation-hungry fringe audiences, he dangled the bait of a play about a serial killer.

Normal

Long before Sarah Kane and Mark Ravenhill hit the headlines in the mid-nineties, Neilson was exploring the darker side of the human psyche. His first major play, *Normal: The Düsseldorf Ripper*, opened at Edinburgh's Pleasance theatre in August 1991, became a contentious fringe success and then transferred to London's Finborough, an Earl's Court pub theatre that was a small but crucial laboratory for new writing. In *Normal*, Neilson uses a battery of theatrical devices to tell the story of Peter Kurten, the 'Düsseldorf Ripper', a serial killer who terrorized Germany between February 1929 and May 1930, and who inspired *M*, Fritz Lang's 1931 Expressionist film. Written with a flair for vivid images, *Normal* – the play's subtitle was dropped from the published text – raises questions about sexual violence and its social origins. Like other serial-killer shockers, it at first seems to debate the notion that, in the clichéd phrase, there is a murderer inside us all. But more importantly, it also suggests that theatre is a place where the representation of horror can cross the boundary between actors and audience.

Normal has three characters: Peter Kurten (the Ripper), Frau Kurten, his wife, and Justus Wehner, his defence lawyer. Beginning with a scene set in a life-size version of a penny-arcade model, in which the Ripper, armed with a pair of 'ludicrously oversized scissors' cuts the neck of a large model swan, the play explores Kurten's world. Divided into thirty-one scenes, it follows conversations between Kurten and his young defence lawyer, who wants to prove that his client is insane. What emerges is not just the story of a brutal killer but a picture of a dreadful childhood. The Kurten family lived in one room; there was no privacy; the father beat his children and tried to rape one of his daughters. 'Did you ever see your mother's cunt?' taunts Kurten, who denies being insane. While still a boy, he was initiated by the local dog-catcher into the joys of killing strays. He made the 'astonishing discovery' that blood gave him sexual pleasure, and started 'fucking dogs and sheep and pigs whilst

68

sticking them with knives'. At first appalled, Wehner gradually gets drawn into Kurten's imagination. He meets Kurten's wife and seduces her – only to be told that she was just doing her husband's bidding. In the end, despite Wehner's reasoned defence, Kurten is found guilty, pronounced 'normal' and executed. Years later, Wehner describes the model of Kurten in the penny arcade, explaining how 'once/ having found no victim in the Hofgarten/ he had/ he had cut/ the head/ from a sleeping swan/ and drunk its gushing blood.' In a short epilogue, Wehner comments that, under the Nazi regime, 'I/ and a great many "normal" men/ were to do things we had never thought ourselves capable of.'

Onstage, *Normal*'s argument was emphasized, as Jeremy Kingston pointed out in *The Times*, by Kurten and Wehner being 'dressed identically in grey suits and sombre ties'. If his abnormal upbringing helps explain Kurten's sense of his own 'normality', Neilson also suggests that his character's fevered imagination and lust for blood can infect those from cosy middle-class homes. What kind of a society, he asks, is it that allows a man so obviously insane to be judged normal and executed? In an act of grim absurdity, Kurten was condemned to death by guillotine nine times over.

Put on in a hot, tiny space, *Normal* had an angular Expressionist set that recalled Lang's film and suggested a scaffold. The play also used a whole toolbox of theatrical devices: direct address to the audience, directional lighting, a mannequin, letters home; one scene was played entirely in the dark, another split the murder's narrative between Kurten and Wehner. At one moment, the style was that of a slapstick silent movie, at another it was described as a 'scream of rage' or a 'daydream'. When Kurten is executed, it is Frau Kurten who drops her head. Even the shape of the swan was reminiscent of the German imperial eagle. Some scenes were particularly suggestive. 'When Kurten rants from the top of the stairs,' wrote Kingston, 'the panel in front of him suddenly looks like a podium and his arms, stabbing at the air, are Hitler's.' Under the name Psychopathia Sexualis, Neilson directed three actors he knew from college (Jon Sotherton, Juliet Prew, Craig Edwards) and 'got away with a lot: mainly due to the actors barrelling their way through certain unsayable sections of the play'. As played by Sotherton, who looked like a cross between Nazi propaganda minister Goebbels and a matinee idol, Kurten represented less the banality of evil than its magnetism.

One scene had a greater impact than all the others. Called 'The Art of Murder', it came just before the verdict that pronounced Kurten 'normal'. Played under an eerie red light, it was a long fantasy in which Kurten directed Wehner to murder Frau Kurten. At first, Wehner hit her with an oversize hammer. She fell, got up, tried to escape. Then Wehner caught her. The stage directions give the gruesome details:

> He strikes her again. **Kurten** indicates that **Wehner** should strangle her. He does this and she falls limp. **Wehner** backs away and she suddenly sits up, coughing and spluttering. **Wehner** strangles her again. She collapses. He backs off. She starts to crawl away. **Wehner** grabs her and **Kurten** directs him to break her legs, which he does ...

After more attacks, she finally dies. The sequence lasted about six minutes, but felt much longer. The directions specify that the action should be 'quite relentless'. 'We deliberately did it as long as you could bear it – and then some,' says Neilson. In performance, the most unsettling moment was when Frau Kurten jumps off the stage and rushes into the audience, suddenly putting the public into a quandary: do we help her or stay put? Wehner follows, catches her and drags her back onstage. Then the killing continues.

Although a couple of critics had reservations about the play's production values, most praised its taut and energetic writing. The *Scotsman* appreciated Neilson's 'deep research', while the *Guardian* said that 'a lot of white face make-up and Grand Guignol style' gave *Normal* 'an air of modish nihilism'. But while some accused Wehner of being a 'caricature' liberal, 'prudish, naive, and sexually repressed', Kurten was praised as a terrible embodiment of a man who 'murders for pleasure'. In *What's On* magazine, the murder scene was described as 'brutal, shocking and distressing in its prolonged fumbling'. By contrast, critic Ian Shuttleworth thought that Neilson's argument, which linked the Ripper's depravity with his deprivation, was 'highly questionable' because of the 'pornographically violent murder'. Did the play's aggression really compromise its ideas?

'If you're going to do something about a serial killer,' says Neilson, 'it's important to show what they do.' The murder sequence was largely inspired by Hitchcock's 1966 film, *Torn Curtain*, which has a long scene in which a man is butchered. Like the film, Neilson's version shows how hard it is to kill someone. Reactions to it were predictable, but came from an unexpected quarter. 'I was accused of misogyny by men, not by women. Because it was a guy killing a woman, it tended to shock middle-

aged, middle-class men.' Some went into fits of 'overprotectiveness'.
But what was the point of the scene? Neilson says:

> A lot of people found it distressing and wriggled about, but my
> point is: 'You came to see a play about a serial killer – what is your
> problem?' It was done in quite a caricatured way, but its power
> came from the fact that it went on and on. And although the
> hammer we used was an exaggerated size, totally unrealistic, the
> actress was screaming as if it was a real one. It was an intense,
> horrible experience.

It was further intensified by the fact that the sequence was in sharp contrast to the play's other scenes and because the lawyer moved in a dream-
like way. 'When Frau Kurten ran into the audience, and he dragged her
back, people were craning their necks to see what was happening,' says
Neilson. 'They'd paid to see it, so they were interested. This fascination
with violence is a natural human reaction. Let's not pretend to be
"absolutely disgusted".'

The standard theory is that people are fascinated by serial killers
because of the suspicion that there may be a seed of the desire to kill in
all of us, and fiction provides a safe place in which to indulge this
notion. Neilson disagrees: 'If you're not a person that can do appalling
things, you're fascinated by how another human being can.' For him, it is
otherness that fascinates. With extreme human behaviour, 'you always
find yourself asking: "What are they lacking?" or "What am I lacking?"'
Difference is what interests him. Just asking 'What does this tell me
about who I am?' is a narrow way of looking at the problem. For Neilson, there is a wider issue about what we see as the boundaries of being
human. 'People go around with lots of crazy fantasies in their heads', but
'your fantasy life is not necessarily a comment on how you live – it's just
how your imagination works'.

What were Neilson's inspirations for *Normal*? 'My conscious influences were cinematic: *M*, *The Cabinet of Dr Caligari*, *Nosferatu*, Hitchcock's films. As a writer, everything you see comes into play, but you mash
it up until you're not aware of the separate elements.' Other influences
include Edinburgh's Museum of Childhood, with its penny-arcade slot
machines and 'creepy dolls', and Howard Brenton's *Christie in Love*.

The question of influences reminds Neilson of his background. He
says: 'I am liberal, quite left-wing. But I also think: what have I done to
question my upbringing? Have I asked myself the really tough questions?

Am I a liberal just because my parents were?' In the play, he uses the device of Wehner's letters home to show how his character's liberalism is all about pleasing his parents. When Wehner meets Kurten, 'for the first time he sees a life completely different to his own, unimaginably different'. A world of poverty, 'a world were everything is inverted. Maybe everyone should sit down and look at what they absolutely despise and see if there is anything of that in them.'

Normal also introduced a more intimate theme. 'What fascinated me about the Düsseldorf Ripper was not so much that he was a killer,' says Neilson, 'but how his character was predetermined in childhood.' The play is less about murder than about how our upbringing shapes our definition of normality. Kurten is a grim example of how, 'if you bring people up in a completely brutal environment, they will take that as the norm'. We learn 'how to love from the relationships we see around us – if you are taught that love is beating the shit out of someone, then beating the shit out of someone may well become your expression of love'. Watching Fred and Rosemary West's children on television, Neilson got a glimpse of 'that terrible haunted expression in their eyes'. But all the horror in *Normal* came from archival records of Kurten's life. 'You name the perversion and he embraced it. When he's declared sane, you're meant to think: "What do you have to do to be judged insane?"'

Does the play explain how childhood predisposes people to violence? 'Look, it's not my duty as a writer to explain Kurten,' says Neilson. 'All I want to say is that he had a strange kind of courage to follow his own morality.' To thine own self be true? 'That's right. Here's my morality – fuck yours.' Like Kurten, Wehner is also a creation of his background. The collision between the two, both created by their upbringing, is the play's dramatic core. Both systems of values are anatomized, and both are found wanting. Since neither lives up to the ideal of society, this ideal is shown to be an illusion.

The main question that *Normal* raises is: how do you live in the knowledge that some people have moral views that are completely opposed to yours? But surely Kurten is an extreme example. 'OK,' says Neilson, 'he is uncommon – he gets an orgasm from blood – but he knows his morality is at odds with the rest of society's. He's a kind of rebel.' And there is 'a moral continuity between what he did and what the Nazis did'. *Normal* was 'not really meant to be an accurate picture of a murderer – for that, you need to look at a film such as *Henry: Portrait of Serial Killer* – but it used the idea of a serial killer as a symbolic device'.

Although Kurten was executed, his spirit leaked into the German nation. Under Nazism, abnormality became normal. In a sense, the play is about how atrocity can be rationalized.

Despite *Normal*'s ending, Neilson claims he has 'never been consciously political' in anything he has written: his energy goes into writing a story. 'Once you've anchored yourself in a good narrative, the work will tell you something about yourself.' As he says in the preface to his published work:

> Tell a story, and the themes will take care of themselves. The story is the route by which your subconscious finds expression in the real world. Preoccupying yourself with the mechanics of a narrative frees you from your ego and allows something more truthful to come through.

The most polished and poetic of Neilson's plays, *Normal* is full of detail and rich in theatrical inventiveness. The dialogues are razor-sharp and psychologically alive, the writing intelligent and aphoristic: 'Fear is really the dullest side of horror's coin.' Its lyrical style makes *Normal* a pleasure to read, even if it sometimes feels as if it has been crammed full of ideas.

Normal explores the psychological geography of Weimar Germany, a place that appeals to our culture – think of the success of *Cabaret* – because it symbolizes decadence and life on the edge of disaster. Yet Neilson is never nostalgic about decadence, nor does he shirk from drawing parallels with the present. The most disquieting thing in the play is that Wehner – the decent liberal rationalist – really knows so little about feeling, passion and love, while Kurten – the deranged maniac – has drunk deep of real emotion, however perverse. At one point, he compares his discovery of killing with finding 'a diamond/ washed up on the beach'. He is also alive to paradox, as when he says, 'Brutality belongs to love.' Kurten is finally a larger-than-life character, a gothic machiavel who is always ready with a clever answer, a man whose very existence calls into question all of Wehner's deepest convictions. Liberal values are tested by the extremes of experience and found to be shallow. If at times Neilson's satire on liberal sensibilities is a touch heavy-handed, what attracts and disturbs about *Normal* is his relish in the detail of horror, of the emotion that, says Kurten, 'causes your head to tighten and your scrotum to contract'. Out of an elaborate historical drama creeps a vision of how a human being can be both radically different and essentially the same.

The play's timing was fortuitous. When Neilson wrote it, he was interested in the psychology of serial killers and their potential as drama. Then, in summer 1991, the release of Jonathan Demme's film version of *The Silence of the Lambs* sparked off what he calls a 'serial-killer mania', which helped whip up interest in *Normal*. If in this instance Neilson proved that he had his finger on the pulse, his next play showed that he could go for the jugular.

Penetrator

Unlike television or cinema, theatre is virtually uncensored: it is a cultural outpost, a refuge from the world of 'family viewing'. Few plays illustrate the sheer danger of live performance as dramatically as Neilson's *Penetrator*. Commissioned by the BBC, but judged to be 'too extreme' for television, it was first put on at the Traverse in August 1993, then moved down to the Finborough before finally being put on at the Royal Court Theatre Upstairs in January 1994. In the printed playtext, Neilson describes it as a 'very personal project'. Not only was it 'loosely based on a real-life event', but it was also 'written for, and performed by, me and two long-standing friends. As a result, we were able to ad-lib freely and weave many of our own in-jokes into the play.' Audiences didn't have to wait long before finding out just how near the knuckle it was.

Penetrator begins with a soldier hitching a lift. A guttural voice-over intones: 'She hitched up her tiny skirt to reveal her gash, spreading the lips of her fuck-hole like some filthy tart, a flood of thick cunt-juice cascading down her long legs . . .' Cut to a fleapit flat where Max is masturbating over a porn mag. After he has finished, his flatmate Alan arrives. They take drugs, play cards, and banter. If Alan loses, Max will make his 'teddies fuck'. Then Tadge, Max's childhood friend, arrives. He is a soldier who has gone AWOL, and he is acting strangely, claiming that Norman Schwarzkopf is his father, and telling a story about being locked in a dark room and tortured by a gang of Penetrators. They were about to rape him with a wooden pole when he escaped. Tadge mimes the violence of his escape using Alan as a foil. Producing a huge knife, he accuses Alan of being a Penetrator, and disembowels one of the teddies. Then he threatens Alan. Max tries to calm him down. Tadge claims it was 'better before' they met Alan and forces Max to talk about the time they were children, lost in the woods, and Tadge pulled Max's trousers down. While Alan wants to get rid of Tadge, Max reveals that he knows

Alan has betrayed him by sleeping with his ex-girlfriend, Laura. In the end, Alan leaves, and Max and Tadge sit quietly. Tadge's last line recalls their childhood: 'I used to like coming to your house.'

I saw *Penetrator* at the Court's tiny Theatre Upstairs, located in the building's gloomy attic. Despite the comparative safety of the second row, its ninety minutes with no break were relentlessly frightening because of the acute sense of imminent danger and the real possibility of actors injuring themselves or one of the spectators. During Tadge's attack on Alan, with the vicious knife flashing through the air, the audience seemed to be collectively willing that nothing would go wrong. As the note to playtext says: 'The scene is designed to be played at the highest pitch of intensity.' And as Neilson comments, 'It's far and away the most draining scene I've ever seen played onstage but – if it's done right – uniquely shattering.' For once, such hype was justified. After the show, I staggered out like a survivor, glad to be alive.

Right from the start, *Penetrator* was ready to wrongfoot its audience. The opening porn fantasy woke people up simply because it is the kind of thing that men normally read in private – hearing it read in public broke a powerful taboo. Once in the flat, the tacky carpet, empty beer cans, cigarette butts and crisp packets was reminiscent of harmless student life. But Tadge soon changed that, telling a gross story about a guy who took some

> raw liver and he fucked it into his thermos and shagged that and
> he was in the bunk by me and every night he was like that with his
> flask and he didn't change the liver for three months, man, and it
> gave him some fucking, like, disease that made his cock drip pus.

Just when you thought that the play couldn't get any worse, it did. Tadge brought Alan to the ground; he ripped the teddy apart, covering the stage with stuffing. From the audience came a gasp of disbelief. Then the knife sequence began in earnest.

Most critics applauded *Penetrator* for its heightened emotions if not for its 'curiously flat' ending. The *Observer* saw it as 'an extremely well-written narrative in which robotic violence is gradually displaced by moral ambiguity and tenderness', while *The Times* called it 'heavy stuff' by 'an author who combines toughmindedness with a sense of humour of the more sardonic kind'. The cast – led by Neilson, who played 'cynical, misogynistic' Max, with James Cunningham as 'terrifyingly still, menacing Tadge' and Alan Francis as 'droll, peaceable' Alan – were justly praised.

Michael Coveney called the play a 'truly extraordinary piece of relentless realism' and Louise Doughty found that 'the explosion of violence towards the end is one of the most nail-biting scenes I have ever watched in a theatre'. In *Time Out*, Clare Bayley claimed that the 'debate around sexual politics is blasted open by work of this kind. Men: who'd be one?'

But it was the play's suggestion of ambiguous homoeroticism that gave critics the most problems. The *Guardian*'s Claire Armitstead thought the idea that 'homosexuality is a monster waiting to devour men whose defences are destroyed' was 'dangerous', while the *Evening Standard*'s Nicholas de Jongh said the play gave homophobia a bad name, treating it 'in sensational terms and as [an] inevitable fact of life, instead of exploring what drives some men to such states'.

Another dissenting voice was that of *Theatre Record* editor Ian Herbert, who wrote that the content of the play 'is so extreme, its horrors so relentlessly described that I actually found myself wondering whether it should have been put on at all'. Listing its 'sickening' horrors – especially Tadge's final speech with its furious 'shouting *ad infinitum* of two four-letter words' – he concluded: 'I'm no fan of censorship, but here is a case for self-censorship.' A year before Sarah Kane's *Blasted* – also put on at the Court – caused a media storm, it was already clear that confrontational theatre was stirring controversy. 'At the time we were preparing *Penetrator* for the Court,' says Neilson, '*Blasted* had its first read-through.' Kane saw Neilson's work and James Cunningham later appeared in her third play, *Cleansed*.

Penetrator has its origins in personal pain. When he wrote it, Neilson was 'splitting up with a long-term girlfriend so I was aware of the dark and tormenting aspects of sex, and jealousy. That whole murky world of confusion.' *Penetrator* is firstly about 'how sexuality can be transformed into a hugely destructive force'. It is also a play about male company. 'There's nothing like the ending of a long-term relationship with a woman to make you appreciate men; one tends to retreat to the cocoon of male companionship.'

The play begins with a deliberate provocation. Neilson was onstage every night during the opening monologue, and, he says, 'Waiting for the lights to come up, I'd be listening to this voice-over, and thinking: "Oh my God, what have I done?"' He writes about explicit sex, but he is not without inhibitions. And although he used the language of the 'soft end of the pornographic market, hearing it spoken out loud still has a huge impact. It's deeply uncomfortable.' If dragging shameful private fantasies into the public gaze was more 'in-yer-ear rather than in-yer-face', what about the end of the porn fantasy, which goes: 'I want you to/ I want you to shoot/ I want you to shoot me'? That, says Neilson, 'encapsulates the turning from sex towards something much darker.'

Some critics called Max a misogynist. 'He's not really misogynistic,' says Neilson; 'he's just recently had a bad experience with Laura. But Max is not bland about his opinions.' Critics 'tend to be hypersensitive to misogyny in a way that ordinary people are not'. When Max and Alan are by themselves at the start of the play, Max tells Alan about an argument he has had with a woman the night before. She argued that because 'I use the word cunt, I'm a potential rapist'. 'She was offended,' points out Alan. Max replies that she 'didn't seem to mind using the word *dickhead*' or 'bastard'. 'Yes,' says Alan, 'but nobody uses that literally.' 'The same with cunt,' says Max. 'If I wanted to insult someone, why would I compare them to a vagina? It happens to be a part of the anatomy that I'm quite *fond* of . . .' Just when you're tempted to agree, Max continues: 'She was just one of these fanny-bashers that Mikey collects so he can feel all right on.' Alan's response is an eloquent frown.

Alan leans towards political correctness. 'I knew people who were very PC about things,' says Neilson. 'And had a lot of female friends, but didn't get further involved. Any amount of admiration and respect for women is great and fine, but ultimately it is not much use to the woman unless the man's prepared to fuck them as well.' Is Alan a homemaker and a nag? 'Definitely,' says Neilson. 'In any domestic routine, even when it's just men together, someone always takes the traditionally feminine part.' But despite the fact that he plays the female role, Alan is the most heterosexual of the three men. Unlike Max and Tadge, he is untouched by homoeroticism. At the end, the revelation of Alan's betrayal of Max turns the play upside-down. It amounts to a satire on men: 'It takes this horrendous situation at knife-point to get Max to admit he's had even a vaguely homosexual experience. Then this is completely cancelled by his knowledge of Alan and Laura's infidelity.' Neilson sees this as 'true of men's priorities'. Sexual betrayal ranks high in the male psyche.

Tadge is based on a real person, whose experiences give a clue to the character's psychopathic tendencies. 'His father was in the police force,' says Neilson, 'so he was brought up in a very macho environment.' He had 'homosexual leanings but, because this was repellent to everything he was brought up to believe, he went into the army to prove himself as a man'. And 'the pull between those two things, and also perhaps the more ambiguous things that happen in an all-male environment, just set him off. Tore him apart.' The army doesn't drive Tadge mad, but his own unreconciled impulses do. *Penetrator* shows how sexual repression can turn into violence.

But while Tadge can only express his feelings through pornographic fantasies and violent imaginings about Penetrators, it is clear that what he wants is much more than a homoerotic experience. The most important line in the whole play is the last one: 'I used to like coming to your house.' Tadge 'hopes that if he was to involve himself in a purely masculine relationship, it might somehow be less complicated: he could understand how the other person worked,' says Neilson. 'But he also feels a revulsion at what he might be.' Does he dream of a uncomplicated childhood? 'Yeah, all the characters are yearning to go back to a world where sexuality, and all the complexity that it brings, did not dominate their lives.'

So the scene in which Max is forced to remember having his pants taken down by Tadge is not really about homosexual desire? 'No, it's not,' says Neilson. 'It's too simple to say that Max is "revealed" to be a homosexual. It's much more confused and ambiguous.' The point of the memory is that it demonstrates the emotional closeness of the boys in childhood. With that lost, Tadge is jealous of Alan's friendship with Max. 'When Max went to college, Tadge lost touch. A gulf opened up between them. Now he's groping back to childhood. It's a penetration through the depths of memory to the moment when he was truest.' And when the men finally sit down and share a packet of chocolate Rolos, they rediscover the emotional truth of friendship. The violence is what the audience have to go through to get to this tender, even sentimental, moment.

The main problem with *Penetrator* is that its soft centre tends to be forgotten because of its violence. But the softer emotions are what hold the play together. Tadge's feelings are grounded in a nostalgia for childhood, when emotions were intense and simple. He remembers looking after the weaker Max, sharing sweets with him, even his smell. 'Childhood can be seen as a world where you didn't have to deal with sexuality,' says Neilson. In the play, the men experience sexual relations as a burden, as inherently problematic. Whatever happened to Tadge in the army has driven him back to his childhood friend. And, because Alan has had sex with Laura, Max chooses the psychotic Tadge over his prissy flatmate. In this way, the simple loyalties of blokedom are reasserted.

Another of the play's arguments is that men can be as political correct as they want 'but they can't deny that there are fundamental differences between men and women. You cannot have a sexual relationship that is completely unsexist. It would be boring – brown rice sex.' But what about pornography? 'With pornography, you can get into it and enjoy it for what it is, but when things go bad in your relationships, you realize you've been fuelling your imagination with horrors.' Men in general 'take sexual betrayal very badly. They know their own minds. They hate to think of another man's pleasure coming out of their misery.'

Onstage, *Penetrator* works because it exploits what is particular to theatre. With film and television, says Neilson, 'The audience is just watching, but by going to the theatre people are putting themselves into a situation which is halfway between watching and participating.' With *Penetrator*, 'They saw something that couldn't exist in any other medium. It came from the gut: that's theatre's strength.' If some of the play's language was at the boundaries of taste, it was the knife scene that really raised the temperature. It got 'more and more frantic as the run went on. By the time it got to the Court it was cooking.' It 'played to the advantages of theatre, with real people onstage who are improvising: even we didn't know how violent it would be on any particular night.' There were times, says Neilson,

> When I was worried that Jim and Alan would get a bit carried away – once an ashtray narrowly missed my head. At the time, there was nothing in theatre that put you through so much danger. Alan got cut a few times, so he was worried; Jim was worried; I was worried. But the collective feeling was worth it. It was special.

It gave audiences a 'cathartic experience. Some people even said that they wanted to get up out of their seats and stop it.' To get to that point takes a lot of energy. 'Once you've been pulled through the scene, you feel like you're really there, which ultimately makes that moment of tenderness at the end much more powerful.'

But even the knife scene wouldn't have been so effective if it hadn't been for the astonishing moment when Tadge disembowels Alan's teddy. 'It's surprising how shocking that is,' says Neilson. 'Everybody was hit by that.' But why? 'Well, once the teddy had been cut to pieces, it signalled that anything was possible. After all, this was a literal symbol of the destruction of childhood. People are terribly protective of soft toys.' Audiences can invest as much emotion in inanimate objects as they do in living actors.

79

As theatre, *Penetrator* could only offer intensity of experience, 'really shaking its audiences, really putting them through something', by restricting the size of the venue. 'You can only do *Penetrator* in a small, sweaty theatre. But this reduces your audience.' The essence of *Penetrator* is that it is experiential. 'That's the only way of getting a feeling of excitement. If you just read it, it's dead; it's just a memory of energy.'

Even so, on the page, *Penetrator* has a brisk efficiency and a sense of momentum that engages your interest even if you haven't seen it onstage. Never inert, the dialogue is compelling and its central image, Tadge's paranoid fantasy of being violated, seems to sum up some of the worse fears of the decade. While it is not about a specific military scandal, nor about a precise political situation, it does suggest how the shadow of torture lurks at the edges of society. It also shows Neilson's willingness to peer into humanity's common darkness. Significantly, Tadge's paranoid fantasies occur in the 'black room'. His idea of his tormentors is reminiscent of Pinter's vision of torture: 'They can make you disappear. Like a black hole. A black hole where a person was.' The play also articulates a postfeminist male confusion (anticipating the New Laddism of television shows such as the BBC's *Men Behaving Badly*) and delves into emotionally truthful, if extreme, psychological recesses, showing both the ugly and the sentimental sides of men's feelings.

Penetrator stays in the mind because of its intensity, not because it has a neat message. 'The problem with plays that have a message is that they can't convince anyone,' says Neilson. 'I mean, have you ever seen something that makes you believe what you don't want to believe? Theatre does have an effect, but it's usually indirect.' He sees his role as 'providing intelligent entertainment, controversial plays that create an argument. Half the value of anything I write is in the bar afterwards.' By this criterion, his next major success, *The Censor*, was great bar food.

The Censor

In the nineties, British culture was one of the most highly censored in Europe. As theatre veteran Sheridan Morley pointed out in the *Spectator*, 'We are one of the last nations on earth still to employ film censors as government-funded guardians of our increasingly shaky public morality.' Indeed, Prime Minister John Major's 'back to basics' campaign of moral rearmament was no sooner announced than members of his government were exposed as mired in 'sleaze'. But while calls for more censorship seemed to be a simplistic solution to a variety of intractable social problems, theatre remained an island of freedom where plays such as Neilson's *The Censor* – winner of the best fringe play awards from the Writers Guild and *Time Out* – could discuss 'adult' subjects such as sex and censorship without any inhibitions.

The play opens with the Censor, who works in the 'shithole', an office that deals with pornographic materials that have no chance of getting a licence. Miss Fontaine, a filmmaker, tries to persuade him not to ban her film, which she claims is not just a 'skin flick', but a love story. Using a mix of brash seductiveness and articulate argument, she tries to make him see beyond the explicit images and understand the characters and subtext of her story. Miss Fontaine persuades this 'repressed anally fixated apparatchik' that the first scene of her movie – when 'the man's penis hardens and softens repeatedly throughout the scene' – means that the lovers are still 'in the early part of the relationship. They're still learning about each other.' Partly convinced, and more than a little enamoured, the Censor agrees to help her. Intercut with these scenes are brief glimpses into the Censor's home life. He is impotent and his wife seeks satisfaction elsewhere. Finally, Miss Fontaine cures the Censor's impotence by enacting his most intimate fantasy, which, she discovers, is watching women defecate. They make love. Soon after, he hears that she has been brutally murdered in New York. As he weeps, his wife mistakenly thinks that she has finally made emotional contact with him.

The Censor began life as a small-scale fringe play, the highlight of the Red Room's season at the Finborough in April 1997. 'Even after doing television,' says Neilson, 'in my heart, I remain on the fringe. My plays work best in a small space.' The play then transferred to the Royal Court, which at the time had taken up residence at the Duke of York's theatre in the West End. When performances of *The Wake*, a new play by Tom Murphy due to open in June, were cancelled, director Stephen Daldry had to find something to fill the gap. By placing both audience and actors on the stage, and leaving the rest of the Victorian theatre empty, he converted the 600-seat theatre into a sixty-seater, and put on a short season called 'Behind the Safety Curtain'. As well as *The Censor*, it included a new short play by Caryl Churchill, *This Is a Chair*. In September, Neilson's play transferred to the Court's other West End base, the Ambassadors theatre.

At the Duke of York's, *The Censor* was an intimate production, and its jet-black programme emphasized the darkness of the piece. It opened with orgasmic moans on the soundtrack, which both recalled the shock of *Penetrator*'s beginning and were a graphic comment on the repetitive nature of the Censor's job. Equally memorable was the gloom of the basement office, where the dark was broken by great shafts of light, forming patterns as they fell through huge ventilation fans from an immensely high ceiling – a dungeon in the cathedral of desire. Behind a gauze screen and red-neon frame, the eighty-minute performance saw the frigid Censor gradually warm to the seductive charm of Miss Fontaine, while his wife sat at the side of the stage, as distant as a memory, as nagging as a bad conscience. At the climax, the Censor's coprophiliac fantasy unfolds to the music of cello and birdsong. After the play finished, the audience left the theatre to the sound of Barbara Cook singing 'Till There Was You'.

While *The Censor* was on the fringe, the critics rated the play highly. Lyn Gardner in the *Guardian* called it 'considerably less loaded than [David Mamet's] *Oleanna* and as topical as [Ben Elton's] *Popcorn*. It is more unsettling than both, but in its own weird, urgent way almost beautiful.' When it came to the Court, several critics pointed out how timely the move was: it seemed like an intervention in the censorship debate that had been whipped up when Cronenberg's film *Crash* came before the British Board of Film Classification. Thus the *Daily Mail* called the play 'a healing, and finally tragic, love story', while *The Times* saw Neilson as 'one of that group of Royal Court writers who combine the desire to work on taboo subjects with a feeling for the theatrical effect of suspense, surprise and verbal precision'.

When *The Censor* was revived, however, reviews became more critical. The *Guardian*'s Michael Billington compared the play with Ariel Dorfmann's *The Reader*, saying that it 'comforts rather than challenges our liberal preconceptions'. Erroneously assuming that Neilson approved of Miss Fontaine's dream of a world where 'anything can be shown anywhere', Billington pointed out that 'you need only apply her arguments to violence – snuff movies for all? – to see how absurd they are'. In the *Financial Times*, David Benedict compared Miss Fontaine to 'the rabid, rabbit-boiling Alex in another three-way drama, [the film] *Fatal Attraction*', before concluding that 'this is a play which flatters you into thinking that you have thought long and hard about a given subject'. By contrast, the *Telegraph*'s Charles Spencer recommended *The Censor*, saying that 'Neilson confronts a taboo [on defecation] with an openness and honesty that I would describe as Lawrentian if I didn't believe D. H. Lawrence to be a grotesquely overblown writer'. In response, Benedict Nightingale of *The Times* reminded readers that, while the *Telegraph* 'a century ago denounced Ibsen's *Ghosts* as a "wretched, deplorable, loathsome history"', the same paper 'managed to find *The Censor* "poignant, funny, brilliantly controlled and profound"'. Nightingale thought that Neilson's play was improbable and concluded that it had 'a little too much of the sexual soapbox in its dramatic make-up'. After such mixed responses, it's hard to avoid thinking that the designer of the published playtext – which used crosses to deface the names of the critics whose puffs appear on the back cover – was also entering the fray.

Neilson has always been interested in censorship. 'Even when I was ten years old,' he says, 'I would write to the British Board of Censors and ask them why a film had been given a certain certificate – and they would write back.' Eventually, they even sent him an inch-thick dossier about how the Board operated. *The Censor* was an intervention in the debate about censorship, but 'ultimately, the subject interested me not on a political level but on a personal one. I was fascinated by the idea of self-censorship.' The figure of the Censor is a good metaphor for 'all the things we hold down and cut out of our minds'. In the play, Neilson put together 'the rather clichéd idea of the Censor being a fucked-up individual' with 'the notion of making the repellent look as if it could be beautiful'. Usually a play or a film chooses to be either a love story or a sex story; here Neilson was deliberately mixing the two genres. So *The Censor* is 'a kind of *Brief Encounter* with the sordid bits unedited'.

The Censor was Neilson's first attempt to put on 'an anti-shock play: I wanted people to come out of theatre *not* talking about the fact that they'd seen a woman take a shit onstage'. For many, this worked: the play was disturbing but not shocking. To Neilson's surprise, the right-wing press liked it 'better than anyone else'. His play, he says, exemplified 'the Trojan Horse ideal: you don't preach to the converted; you seek to change the minds of people who don't normally see this stuff'. The play is all about looking deeper than the surface, the moral being that 'if you can understand somebody, they're no longer alien'. Censorship is a symptom of 'not wanting to understand people', an example of alienation. 'The tabloids,' says Neilson, 'like to deal in simplified black and white issues, which is often totally unhelpful, irresponsible even'. Morality comes in shades of grey. So, in the play, the Censor has a point when he says, 'Without censorship there'd be no allegory, no metaphor, no restraint. I mean – *Brief Encounter* is a story about two lovers, but you don't have to see Trevor Howard's penis thrusting in and out of Celia Johnson.'

The play examines the way in which prejudices are rooted in personal pain. 'If you're trapped in a sad, sexless marriage,' says Neilson, 'you're bound to react badly, resentfully, to any mention of sex.' Like other individuals, censors tend to 'react very strongly when it's something that touches their own weak spots'. People 'tend to shut out things that make them feel uncomfortable – this is natural, but it can have social consequences.' It's a question of power.

But the play is above all a love story, one man's sentimental education. 'What interested me,' says Neilson, 'was the emotional side of the story.' But if the Censor blooms in this strange relationship, is Miss Fontaine's part underwritten? 'No, we made a conscious decision not to go into who she was, or where she was from,' says Neilson. 'You could even imagine her being a figment of his imagination – I wouldn't close off that interpretation.' One critic saw Miss Fontaine as Mary Poppins, dropping in, doing good, and then leaving. To vary the metaphor, 'She's a sexual Joan of Arc; she's on a mission.' She's a fanatic who thinks her film is important 'to the world', because soon 'sex will be completely divorced from reproduction' and it will be free to evolve into 'a completely universal non-verbal language'. No more repression; no more witch-hunts. Today's deviants are tomorrow's visionaries. In the end, she is a victim of her own desire for adventure. By killing her off, Neilson distances himself from the extremism of her philosophy.

Since *The Censor* is about ways of seeing, many critics quoted Miss Fontaine's idea of looking beyond the surface of the porn image: 'Could you tell, for instance, that the man's previous girlfriend was Asian? That the woman had been brought up in care?' When the Censor tries to show he has understood her work, Miss Fontaine is unimpressed: 'Where's the character, the subtext, the detail?' she asks. Of course, her ideas are well over the top. 'By the end,' says Neilson, 'the Censor is not really concerned with her philosophy; he's fallen in love. And that's why he doesn't pull her up on some of the more crazy things she comes out with.' Miss Fontaine is a missionary, so her ideas are distortions. But much of what she says also alludes to herself. By asking people to look closely at her film, she is inviting them to look more closely at herself. The play is a metaphor for looking closer. 'Anyone who really tries to understand someone they don't know is a bit of a saint because most of us just can't be bothered.'

'Miss Fontaine is the least important character,' says Neilson. 'By deliberately not explaining her, the play fixes the audience's attention on the Censor.' Here, the audience is asked to identify with male confusion and anger. But the play's most important moment is at the end, when the Censor watches the movie again and his smile shows that 'a small change has happened; sex has been restored to him as something more luminous and less dark'. The play affirms that 'we can make changes in ourselves through the sexual experiences we have with different people'. This makes the figure of the wife 'terribly important because she's his main relationship, and ultimately he's constantly returning to her'. At the end, 'she puts her arm around him'. Even though his wife misunderstands the reason for his tears, there is a connection between them; you feel they can talk to each other again. Ultimately, the play is 'like *Brief Encounter* – somebody has a fling, then goes back to their relationship'. Having accepted something in themselves, they go back to their main relationship feeling stronger.

But Neilson's play doesn't answer all the questions it raises. After all, while both the Censor and his wife are unhappy in their relationship, the effects of their infidelities are completely different: while the woman's affairs have led to communication breakdown, the man's affair strengthens the couple's relationship. It also ultimately reduces Miss Fontaine to an angel of mercy who cures the Censor's hang-ups, restores the sanctity of the couple, and then conveniently vanishes. 'My feeling with theatre is to produce an emotional reaction, not simply an intellectual one,' says Neilson. He agrees his play is not an argument for total freedom. 'If you remove censorship, if you completely free people, you have to be prepared for uncontrollable consequences. There are good reason for things being suppressed.' Yes, 'certain things need to be repressed in society, certain urges and instincts need to be repressed in ourselves'. But the paradox is that 'in repressing them, a lot of healthy things can be repressed as well'.

The Censor questions the assumption that sexuality is simply about the sex act. Key lines in the play are: 'Love is an emotion, sex a means of expression' and 'Sex is a language'. Neilson says that 'sex has many faces, and expresses many different emotions'. The play asks whether pornography could ultimately mean more than it usually does, and whether humans could communicate less in a verbal and more in an intuitive manner. Stephen Daldry once said, '*The Censor* is about trying to find a new morality.' 'That might be overstating things,' says Neilson, 'but it's a real question. It's very dysfunctional to make people feel criminal about wanting to have sex.'

Like *Normal* and *Penetrator*, the play is also about childhood. 'What we find erotic as adults is dictated to a certain extent by what happened to us accidentally as children,' says Neilson. 'This can be a shoe, spanking or some shit. In which case, this totally subverts our notion of sex being purely an adult behaviour.' While as rational adults, we like to think that we are in full control of our lives, Neilson reminds us that sexual desire is an emotional terrain where irrational fantasy and irrepressible urges run circles around reason and logic. His Censor finally reaches a temporary reconciliation with his past and his present. What is disturbing about the play is that, despite its rather stereotypical view of sexual healing, it nudges us gently to look closer at our own darker imaginings.

Written with wit and economy, *The Censor* is an amusing, if rather traditional, love story, which plays intriguing games with prejudices and fantasies. Yet, because it speaks frankly about sex and longing, it also has the power to annoy. As an example of experiential drama, it doesn't aim to develop arguments so much as trigger ideas and thoughts, mimicking the effect of real-life experiences.

One of the first writers of the decade to create an experiential theatre of extreme sensations, Neilson illustrates the importance of Scotland's contribution to new writing. Not only was his work first put on there, but his ambition to use the stage to 'make a difference' is based on vivid memories of the Scottish theatre of the seventies. Aptly enough for a writer who is concerned with childhood, he has drawn on his own early experiences. Although often underrated, Neilson's significance lies less in his skill as a writer than in his pioneering of a form of confrontational theatre that became central to the new aesthetic of British drama in the nineties. A great original, his plays have no direct models; at their best, they are bold trips into undiscovered territory, both psychologically and theatrically.

But Neilson's imagination is as narrow as it is powerful. For while it is true that he has written in different voices for radio, television and film, as well as theatre, his work is haunted by recurring images of sex and violence. As well as *Normal*, he directed Alan Francis and Mike Hayley's serial-killer comedy, *Jeffrey Dahmer Is Unwell* (Edinburgh Fringe, 1995). Even his minor plays, such as *The Year of the Family* (Finborough, 1994), feature sexual disturbance. In *Dirty Laundry*, a short written for the Finborough's 1995 'I'll Show You Mine' season (which also included Mark Ravenhill), two people are having sex and use infidelity as material for their fantasies. Nor has Neilson confined his interest in the extreme to the theatre. Commissioned to work on episodes of independent television's crime dramas *Prime Suspect* and *Cracker*, he was greeted with the words: 'So, you're the expert in serial killers.' As it turned out, his ideas were too transgressive, and the episodes were never made. Then, for Channel Four, he completed *The Debt-Collector*, a brutal 1998 film about an Edinburgh hard man.

To be fair, Neilson has tried to broaden his emotional repertoire. In *Heredity* (Royal Court, 1995), a touching and intimate play that takes place around a dying woman's bedside, he used strange, poetic monologues that were intended to 'convey a feeling of what life is like. These were meant to be felt, not analysed.' *Heredity* is a good example of what can go wrong if a writer steps out of line. 'After *Penetrator*, I tried to branch out in new directions,' Neilson says. 'My writing was better, but I suddenly no longer fitted in with the "boys with toys" stuff that was in vogue.' Theatres wanted another *Penetrator*, 'something with contentious material in it'. *Heredity* was put on for four nights in April 1995, but the Court felt that the poetic elements were irrelevant. So while Neilson was trying to move beyond narrative by introducing material that referred to 'that other life we have, of rumination and of fantasy, the Court just dropped it'. The message was: you're only as good as your shock value.

As a writer, Neilson is experienced enough to be ironic about his craft. 'Writing is like some nasty skin condition,' he says. He calls it 'a whore's game', in which too often 'the venue matters more than the writer'. Nor is the mass media any better, with its ratings chasing: 'Agents and TV producers hover over the fringe like vultures. They pick up writers, reshape them, put them through the mill, kick the shit out of them, drag them backwards through the hedge and then drop them – that's how the system works.' He argues that, in television especially, the individual voice has gradually been erased.

Neilson explains the amount of sex in his work by arguing that 'sexuality is the base rock of humanity', a paradoxical area between the urge to reproduce and the desire for pleasure. After all, he points out, 'The clitoris exists purely for pleasure.' He also believes that 'if you don't look at the sexuality of your characters, they tend to be bloodless.' Why? 'Because sex is still the single most unguarded aspect of our lives. Which is why such material appears in virtually everything I've done.' Just occasionally, he takes a more militant tone. 'There's a ridiculous level of shame about confronting our repressions, but it's important that we do.' For Neilson, sexuality is 'a truer world than our everyday one, one where we can just be ourselves'. After the sex is over, normality slips back. 'You might be in a café with your partner, talking away, but last night your tongue was just a inch away, to put it crudely, from their arsehole.' Because sexuality contains 'clues to who a person really is' we have built 'a taboo around it: it reveals too much about ourselves, and it is uncontrollable'.

What about violence? Neilson uses violence not to entertain, but to 'make a moral point'. His plays don't give you a gratuitous thrill, or empower you. 'You're meant to feel appalled,' he says. 'I think it's offensive when you're not appalled by violence.' In a small space where 'it is impossible to walk out', his theatre puts the audience through a simulated experience of violence, reclaiming brutality from the stylized glamour of cinema. The reality is that 'violence takes place in the same place as real life'. 'The fact that I'm not a violent person makes me write about violence because I don't really understand it, I want to get to grips with it.' He also makes a political point: 'Violence is usually perpetrated on the weak. It's not a brave act, but a cowardly one.'

Neilson says that his 'main purpose has been to move away from the notion that sex and violence have to be seen as extreme'. Although the content of his plays is explicit – 'I don't want to pussyfoot around' – they always have a softer core. Unconsciously echoing Tracy Letts, he says, 'In essence, all drama is about being extreme: that's why people go to the theatre.' But 'it may just be a generational thing: young people don't find this stuff as extreme as older audiences do.' Neilson says that he 'gets just as offended and embarrassed as anyone else by explicit material', but he tries not 'to shut it out'. 'I try to ask myself why I'm offended and to explore that. My hope is that I'll come to know myself better and thereby everyone else.' Behind the overt sex and violence, his work is a plea for compassion.

Neilson exemplifies a common paradox of cutting-edge writing: he is both tough and sentimental. For him, theatre 'has to give a voice to the poor, the deviant and the fucked up'. All his plays seek to redefine morality, all are partly about love. In print, they have a deceptive simplicity, a clarity that seems to lack shading and depth; onstage they feel full of energy, furious and daring. One of the first to exploit the new freedoms of nineties drama, Neilson created a theatre that often makes you feel that you've thought about an issue in depth. He has a seductive ability to suggest ideas rather than expound them. But although Neilson's aggressive naturalism makes him a powerful writer, his plays still seem like tasters for a major work he hasn't yet written, a play that would embrace life as wholeheartedly as his previous work has examined its more extreme manifestations.

4 Sarah Kane

And when I don't feel it, it's pointless.

(Grace/Graham in *Cleansed*)

Sarah Kane committed suicide on 20 February 1999. When I heard the news, I was just putting the finishing touches to the first draft of this chapter. Just as her plays had been among the most controversial of the decade, so her death had an extraordinary impact. Obituaries called her 'the most daunting, disturbing voice of her generation', 'a moralist of sometimes rebarbative rigour and mordant wit' and 'fiercely coura-geous'. In the *Independent*, Mark Ravenhill called her a 'contemporary writer with a classical sensibility who created a theatre of great moments of beauty and cruelty', work whose 'austere beauty' was 'a shock to the system'. Even in death she remained controversial: in the *Guardian*, Anthony Neilson contested the idea that her depression was the product of an 'existential despair', ascribing it instead to a chemical imbalance in the brain. In September 1999, her brother, Simon Kane, had to issue a press release pointing out that although her last play, *4:48 Psychosis*, deals with suicidal despair, it was not 'a thinly veiled suicide note'. Most critics, who originally hated her work, have since her death been more sympathetic. In the words of James Macdonald, who directed the first versions of *Blasted* and *Cleansed*, 'the clever ones have backtracked a long way since the days of *Blasted*, as the best critics once did [when] faced with the work of Osborne, Pinter, Bond'. The central problem with Kane's work is that, while she was alive, the power of her stage images tended to detract from the depth of her writing; now that she's dead, the fact that she killed herself threatens once more to obscure her achieve-ment. Examining her plays for clues to her mental state tends to limit the interpretation of her work, as does the tendency to sanctify a writer who has died young. I'd rather not glamorize Kane, nor read her work from the perspective of her death. For these reasons, I have decided to leave this chapter very much as it was first written, as a conversation with a living writer.

When Sarah Kane's *Blasted*, a first play by an unknown twenty-three-year-old, opened in January 1995, it not only became the focus of some of the most aggressive reviews of the decade, but also the centre of the biggest scandal to hit theatre since Mrs Whitehouse tried to close Howard Brenton's *The Romans in Britain* in 1981. As with Brenton's play, critics concentrated on the horrors of Kane's work at the expense of its essential optimism. Often seen as a 'depressing' or 'shocking' playwright, Kane doesn't recognize herself in such labels.

> I don't find my plays depressing or lacking in hope. But then I am someone whose favourite band is Joy Division because I find their songs uplifting. To create something beautiful about despair, or out of a feeling of despair, is for me the most hopeful, life-affirming thing a person can do.

Born in 1971, Kane grew up in Kelvedon Hatch, near Brentwood, Essex. Her mother was a teacher, her father a *Daily Mirror* journalist. They were Christians, and Kane became Evangelical while she was a teenager. She went to Shenfield Comprehensive school, and wrote short stories and poems. 'It never really occurred to me to write a play at that stage, probably because it's quite hard to sustain any piece of writing when you're that young.' Although Kane 'hated school until the sixth form', she also acknowledges that 'my English and drama teachers were excellent – I was encouraged to read and write and act, which were the things I wanted to do.' After school, Kane 'chose to do drama at Bristol [University] because it was the only course I could find any genuine enthusiasm for. Until I got there, when suddenly I found far more interesting things to do.'

At university, she took a confrontational attitude to some of her tutors. When one accused her of writing a 'pornographic essay', she threw porn mags at him at the next tutorial. Such provocations make good stories, but the truth is always more complex: her behaviour resulted in much inconvenience for herself. 'I got into a lot of trouble with the university authorities,' she says. 'It all took ages to sort out.'

Kane 'spent the first two years at Bristol avoiding the department as much as I could. I acted and directed and wrote – which was much more important and interesting than anything I was actually supposed to be doing.' In her first term, 'I played Bradshaw in Howard Barker's *Victory*, which was an unusually brilliant experience. His control of language is just extraordinary and I think I loved him all the more because none of the teaching staff seemed to share my enthusiasm.' After that, Kane stopped acting.

'I decided that acting is a powerless profession and I didn't want to be at the mercy of directors I didn't like. So I started directing. And then I wrote three twenty-minute monologues – *Comic Monologue*, *Starved* and *What She Said* – which was the sum total of my playwriting until I wrote *Blasted*.'

Kane left Bristol in 1992, with a First Class Honours Degree, and during the summer saw Jeremy Weller's *Mad* in Edinburgh. 'It was a project that brought together professional and non-professional actors who all had some experience of mental illness,' she says. 'It was a very unusual piece of theatre because it was totally experiential. As an audience member, I was taken to a place of extreme mental discomfort and distress – and then popped out the other end.' Instead of sitting, detached and mildly interested, and 'considering mental illness as an intellectual conceit', Kane was confronted by a full-on experience. '*Mad* took me to hell,' she says, 'and the night I saw it I made a decision about the kind of theatre I wanted to make – experiential.' She'd discovered the provocative aesthetic that was to change the face of British theatre in the nineties. *Mad* also had an effect on Kane's life. 'It was a bit like being given a vaccine. I was mildly ill for a few days afterwards but that jab of sickness protected me from a far more serious illness.'

In 1992, Kane started an MA in playwriting at Birmingham University. It 'seemed like the best way to get funding for another year before signing on. I needed to find out if I could write a full-length play with more than one person in it – to get a grant for doing that was ideal.' But Kane wasn't attracted by academic life. 'It's the same problem I had at Bristol – it was an academic course and I didn't want to be an academic.' She felt like an outsider.

'Inevitably what you're studying is what's already been discovered. As a writer, I wanted to do things that hadn't been done, to invent new forms, find new modes of representation. So sitting in seminars discussing the three-act structure switched me off completely.'

Also, 'the writers I was interested in talking to – Pinter, Bond, Barker – weren't the ones who were coming to talk to us. It was simultaneously academic and anecdotal – and I can't see the usefulness in that.'

Despite this, Birmingham was a crucial period in Kane's career. 'I wrote the first forty-five minutes of *Blasted* (up to the entrance of the soldier) while I was there, and it was given a workshop performance at the end of the course.' Then she moved to London and started working at the Bush theatre as a literary assistant while she finished the play. In all, *Blasted* went through about fifteen drafts. 'The Court decided to do a reading in January 1994, which James Macdonald directed, and I did one final draft after that, which was produced a year later.'

Talking about *Mad*, Kane says, 'It changed my life because it changed me, the way I think, the way I behave. If theatre can change lives, then it can change society.' She also argues that 'theatre is not an external force acting on society, but a part of it. It's a reflection of the way people within that society view the world.' In *Blasted*, Kane took the temperature of the times, and inadvertently brought down a plague on herself.

Blasted

Within days of opening at the Royal Court's Theatre Upstairs, Kane's *Blasted* became the most talked about play for years, the hottest show in town. Pretty soon, it became clear that it would be the most notorious play of the decade. But the 'oxygen of publicity' it generated made many people lose their heads: scribblers fell over each other to sneer at the 'naughtiest girl in class', titillating their readers with exaggerated accounts of sex and violence onstage. On television, newsreaders spread the panic, while cultural commentators sunk their claws into the scandal. Letters were written to the national papers; comparisons were made with the fuss caused by Edward Bond's *Saved* thirty years earlier. If moral panics are usually engendered by media fantasies, what was the fantasy that lay behind the *Blasted* scandal?

When the play was first put on, its title seemed to refer to a tabloid headline rather than to an explosive event. The programme, illustrated with a photograph of a grinning British Tommy of Second World War vintage, suggested a nostalgic glance at the past rather than an excoriating vision of the present. Only one detail spelt provocation: the soldier is giving a V-sign. By the time you'd climbed the endless stairs to the Theatre Upstairs – which seated only about sixty-five people – you would have seen a notice warning patrons that some scenes in the play were disturbing. For once, this routine warning was justified.

Stripped down to its bare essentials, the play's plot is this: located, according to the stage directions, in 'a very expensive hotel room in Leeds – the kind that is so expensive it could be anywhere', it begins with the arrival of Ian, a middle-aged hack, and Cate, a naive young woman. Ian's first words are: 'I've shat in better places than this.' He takes a bath, coughs like a man with lung cancer and rifles the minibar. With his shoulder holster, he appears to be more than just a journalist. Cate sucks her thumb, stutters when agitated and is prone to epileptic fits. Ian wants to have sex with her – after one of her faints, he rubs himself against her. Later, he tells her about the paranoia of being an undercover agent, and she fellates him – then bites his penis. She tells him that she used to love him, but that now he's 'a nightmare'. Suddenly the situation intensifies. A nameless soldier arrives, and Cate escapes. The soldier urinates on the bed, then the hotel is blasted apart by a bomb. In the ruins, the soldier tells Ian about the horrors of war. Ian comments: 'This isn't a story anyone wants to hear.' The soldier then rapes him, sucks out his eyes, eats them, and shoots himself. Cate returns. 'You're a nightmare,' she repeats, holding a baby. It dies and she buries it under the floorboards, then leaves to get some food. Helplessly blind, Ian masturbates, defecates and eats the baby. By now he's under the floorboards, with only his head poking out. He dies. Cate returns with provisions.

'The Court didn't really know what to do about *Blasted*,' says Kane. 'They were a bit embarrassed about it, so they programmed it just after Christmas when no one was going to the theatre and they hoped no one would notice.' At such a small venue, the premiere is usually spread over two press nights. For *Blasted*, however, most of the critics were free only on 18 January so that night most of the audience had notepads on their laps. And although only one person – the *Glasgow Herald*'s Carole Woddis – walked out, the smallness of the venue intensified the play's impact. Kane remembers the opening night: 'I looked around and realized that the director was near the front and almost everyone else was a critic. I think there were about three women in the audience.' Kane also says that:

> I wasn't at all aware that *Blasted* would scandalize anyone. At the
> time I wrote it, I didn't even expect it to be produced. Personally,
> I think it is a shocking play, but only in the sense that falling
> down the stairs is shocking – it's painful and it makes you aware
> of your own fragility, but one doesn't tend to be morally outraged
> about falling down stairs.

True enough, but the trouble with this analogy is that, whereas falls are accidents, plays are deliberate.

So are media outcries. After the show, one hurried phone call set off a feeding frenzy. Dashing into a call box outside the theatre, the *Daily Mail*'s Jack Tinker phoned in a review in which he complained of being 'driven into the arms of Disgusted of Tunbridge Wells', and calling the play 'utterly without dramatic merit'. Headlined 'This Disgusting Feast of Filth', his review set the agenda by questioning why the Court 'saw fit to stage it' and hinting that it was a waste of taxpayers' money. Convinced that this made it a news story, Tinker also alerted his paper's news desk. But if one man set off what the Court's director Stephen Daldry called 'a witch-hunt', other critics were right on his heels. The *Telegraph*'s Charles Spencer also phoned his news desk. A press photographer arrived at the Court within a hour. The next morning, Anne Mayer, the Court's press officer, got her first phone call at 7.30 a.m. She was still at home. After that, the calls never stopped. Extra staff were assigned to answering questions from journalists. The theatre was besieged by smuthounds looking for Kane. One day, Mayer found one under her desk. He left quietly.

In the media, lurid adjectives kept piling up. The most popular ones were 'disgusting', 'disturbing', 'degrading' and 'depressing'. Kane's 'atrocity play' attracted labels such as 'prurient psycho-fantasies', 'unadulterated brutalism' and 'degradation in the raw'. Purple passages likened it to 'having your face rammed into an overflowing ashtray' or said it left 'a sour taste in the mind'. The *Independent on Sunday*'s Irving Wardle couldn't recall 'an uglier play'; Sheridan Morley thought the Court should 'close for the winter' rather than put it on. Many questioned Daldry's wisdom in selecting *Blasted*. In *Time Out*, Jane Edwardes concluded: 'Kane has proved she can flex her muscles alongside the toughest of the men, now perhaps she will learn that repeatedly firing a gun at the audience can only lead to diminishing returns.'

The curious thing about the critics was that their cries of disgust were both ritualized and often frivolous. How seriously can you take a review that comments, 'Ah, those old familiar faeces'? That was the *Guardian*'s Michael Billington. Charles Spencer – recycling a phrase he'd used about Philip Ridley's *Ghost from a Perfect Place* – said that 'hardened theatre critics looked in danger of parting with their suppers', while Jonathan Miller coyly pointed out that, in the absence of a lavatory, 'poor Ian' had to 'do his poo on stage'. The critics, dubbed 'a group of men in comfortable shoes' by the Court's Carl Miller, were clearly enjoying themselves.

At the time, it felt as if the shrill chorus of condemnation was unanimous. In fact, the reviews were more balanced. Many mentioned Kane's youth and recognized her potential. Most explained their dislike of *Blasted* in reasonable, if literal, terms: the world of the play is incoherent and its message is lost in unrealistic plotting. What confused most critics was Kane's anti-naturalism. 'The reason the play falls apart,' argued Billington, 'is that there is no sense of external reality – who exactly is meant to be fighting whom out on the streets?' If the critics thought that *Blasted* wasn't realistic, or fairly balanced in its argument, they were right. But it says a lot about criticism that years after writers such as Caryl Churchill, Sarah Daniels or Phyllis Nagy had loosened the strait-jacket of naturalism, so many reviewers still expected plays to be realis-tic. As Kane says: 'I suspect that if *Blasted* had been a piece of social realism it wouldn't have been so harshly received.' You can see her point: Tracy Letts's *Killer Joe*, which opened in the same month, was widely praised, mainly because it made no demands on its spectators.

Even so, the critics were divided – but not by gender or politics. Kate Kellaway of the *Observer* attacked *Blasted*, while Louise Doughty of the *Mail on Sunday* defended it. When it came to cries for self-censorship, the liberal broadsheets went hand-in-hand with the tabloids. James Macdonald argues that the liberal broadsheets 'banged the (self-) cen-sorship drum loudest'. In fact, the *Observer*'s Michael Coveney praised *Blasted*, although his piece appeared after the show had closed. But the sturdiest defence of the play came from John Peter of the *Sunday Times*. Pointing out that violent plays 'make you question values' and that Kane's work was 'born of an unleavened, almost puritanical moral out-rage', Peter described her 'vision of a self-destroying society' as 'aimless, brutish, barren, cannibalistic, prurient, diseased and terror-stricken'. He concluded, however, 'We need these moral ordeals. Theatre is only alive if it is kicking.' But who was kicking whom?

Rarely has a young writer's debut grabbed so many headlines. On 19 January, for example, the London *Evening Standard* reported that 'so far, eight people have walked out of performances'. Hounded by reporters, Kane was protected by her agent, Mel Kenyon. Daldry, on a fund-raising trip to New York, was called back to appear on *Newsnight* and *The World at One*. Cartoons about Kane appeared in the newspapers. But the media frenzy also had its humorous side: at the *Mirror*, her father, who was proud of his daughter's play, was amused to see his colleagues, unaware that he was her father, doing everything to find her, except asking him.

Of course, controversy is good for theatre. It is 'what the Royal Court is for', wrote playwright Snoo Wilson. He claimed that the Court had tried to publicize *Blasted* in advance, but the truth is that they hadn't: Mayer says the hysteria was 'the biggest surprise' of her life. In the face of negative publicity, playwrights such as Bond and Pinter offered support.

Bond noted *Blasted*'s 'strange, almost hallucinatory quality', and Pinter said that its author was 'facing something actual and true and ugly and painful'. And Kane, pointing out that her play got more coverage than the actual rape and murder of an adolescent girl, said: 'The thing that shocks me most is that the media seem to have been more upset by the representation of violence than by violence itself.'

Because of the uproar, Macdonald and Daldry defended both *Blasted* and their decision to put it on. In the *Observer*, Macdonald argued that because theatre is a forum for debate, it should be used to address the issue of violence and our fascination with it. Praising the 'assurance, wit and economy' of *Blasted*'s writing, he called it 'a moral and compassionate piece of work'. With 'great heart and dramatic skill', it talks 'honestly about violence, but in order to do so it has to shock'. He believed the critics completely missed 'the strand of wry humour' in the play and lacked 'any sense of sympathy for the characters'. They didn't understand Kane's 'bold but assured treatment of theatrical time and place' and saw only a 'catalogue of unmentionable acts'. On BBC2's *Newsnight*, Daldry read out reviews of the original productions of *Look Back in Anger* and *Saved* – and predicted that one day *Blasted* would be hailed as a classic. In reply, Tinker used his favourable review of Tracy Letts's *Killer Joe* to return to the attack: *Blasted* was 'a bucket of bilge dumped over the audiences at the Royal Court', and Daldry's decision to put it on betrayed the ideals of subsidized theatre. As a result of the controversy, Daldry felt justified in his commitment to risky new writing: Kane had unwittingly given the Court a new mission.

One of the spin-offs of media attention was that members of the audience were asked what they thought about the play. As Kane says, 'It's important not to confuse press with audience. There was media outrage, but it was never a public outcry.' On 20 January, for example, the *Guardian* asked James, a Parisian, why he'd walked out of the show. 'It was not the most shocking thing I have ever seen,' he said. 'It was just gratuitous vulgarity.' By contrast, Andrew Lukas, a twenty-five-year-old student, said: 'It was more educational for me than therapeutic. It showed an aspect of moral degradation and there was something that everyone could learn from it.' When Jonathan Miller went, he found tabloid journalists trying to squeeze 'shock-horror' quotes from Middle-Englanders. Eavesdropping on one interview, he heard a 'lecturer from a college of further education' explaining 'how he thought the play a metaphor for our indifference to Bosnia'.

Audiences certainly felt passionately about *Blasted*. The Theatre Upstairs was so small that walking out was a strong statement. But one of the ironies about *Blasted* is that the media reaction seemed to prove exactly what the play argued: that journalists are sexist, irresponsible and hysterical. For example, the *Express* ran a story headlined 'RAPE PLAY GIRL GOES INTO HIDING', which told its readers that Kane had fled, when in fact she attended all performances.

So why were reactions to *Blasted* so violent? Kane gives two explanations. In the first, she says it was because critics were white, middle-class, middle-aged males:

> There's no doubt that there was a lot of pseudo-moral outrage in the press and it appeared to focus mainly on the play's content. There's been a failure of the critical establishment in this country to develop an adequate language with which to discuss drama. A list of a play's contents is not a review. So inevitably, a list of what happens in *Blasted* – middle-aged male journo rapes his girlfriend and gets buggered by a soldier who sucks his eyes out – isn't going to enamour me to your average middle-aged male theatre critic.

This explanation is unconvincing simply because theatre critics don't usually identify themselves with hard-bitten hacks such as Ian. And even if they did, would that really explain their reaction? A deeper explanation, which suggests that middle-aged men might have been disturbed by seeing a middle-aged man abusing a young woman – with the knowledge that the writer was a young woman – is more convincing psychologically, but doesn't explain why some female critics disliked the play.

Kane's second explanation carries more weight. 'Personally,' she says, 'I think the press outrage was due to the play being experiential rather than speculative. The title refers not only to the content but also to the impact it seems to have had on audiences. What makes the play experiential is its form.' *Blasted* is not a classic issue play that weighs up pros and cons. 'In *Blasted*, the form and content attempt to be one. The form is the meaning.' In its second half, the play collapses, 'putting the audience through the experience they have previously only witnessed'. Like Pinter, Kane rejects the complacent view that Britain is immune from civil war. 'There was a widespread attitude in this country that what was happening in central Europe could never happen here. In *Blasted*, it happened here.'

Blasted may have been too hot for Tinker and Spencer, but the critics enjoyed their moment in the limelight. Suddenly, their opinions were sought by the wider media; they were part of a scandal. Like their film colleagues, who denounced screen violence, theatre critics discovered a moral role. As self-appointed guardians, they claimed that taxpayers' money was safe with them. But whether genuinely appalled or opportunistically self-righteous, the critics blundered. What is every critic's nightmare? That an exceptional new writer emerges and goes unrecognized. In January 1995, it happened. None of us realized the depth of Kane's talent.

Why did the media frenzy get out of control? Perhaps the play tapped into serious anxieties about the problem of violence. Perhaps the combination of abuse and war touched a nerve. Or perhaps the *Daily Mail* was itching for a chance to attack a subsidized theatre for wasting public money – an idea that got readers into more of a lather than the play itself. Certainly, the intensity of media interest owed much to chance: *Blasted* opened during the 'silly season' after Christmas, when serious news stories were thin on the ground. On the other hand, if ever there was a play that deserved controversy, it was *Blasted*. Not only did it contain disturbing emotional material, but it adopted a deliberately unusual and provocative form. That such a play had been written by a young woman seemed to transgress the mainstream media's fantasy that sex and violence are the preserve of men.

With no interval, *Blasted* was a gruelling one hour and fifty minutes. When I saw it, its power to shock was obvious. It clearly made the tiny audience uneasy: two people walked out, others hid their eyes, some giggled. But the responses were mixed: some people were irritated by what they saw as puerile exhibitionism; others were moved by the starkness of the horror or by the psychological accuracy of the relationships. Here was a sensibility to make you clench your fists. One of the notes I made in the dark was: 'Men are animals.' After it was over, the audience sat stunned for a few moments. In the cramped bar after the show people were discussing it furiously. On the train home, I wrote: 'Kane's play makes you feel but it doesn't make you think.' This turned out to be wrong: it does make you think, but only after you've got over the shock of seeing it.

Blasted worked well onstage because of the vividness of its images – Ian's head poking out of the floor recalled Beckett as much as Bosnia – and the commitment of its actors: Pip Donaghy as Ian; Kate Ashfield as Cate and Dermot Kerrigan as the soldier. The contrast between Donaghy and Ashfield rammed home the play's point. Donaghy's seedy and reckless look summed up the balding, hard-drinking, chain-smoking journo. But when he stripped off, his paunch and bemused desperation occasionally made him a figure of pity as well as of lumbering brutality. Ashfield was sulky, earnest, naive and winsome. Her thumb-sucking and stammering soon indicated that something was wrong – her vulnerability laid her open to abuse. But by the end, while Ian's predatory masculinity shrinks into childish dependency, his victim grows into a survivor.

However powerful, the first production was not unproblematic. The playtext specifies that Ian dies before Cate's return at the very end of the play, which means that the last few minutes are played in hell, limbo or wherever. The idea is that the worst has happened, Ian's died, but then it gets even worse – rain falls on him. An example of Kane's dark humour, the scene remains a challenge to both directors and audiences. Similarly, in the playtext, Kane – like Beckett in *What Where* – divides the play into Spring, Summer, Autumn and Winter, indicating a symbolic cycle of violence. In the original production, this didn't come across.

With *Blasted*, it's easier to list the play's contents – anal rape, mastur-bation, micturition, defecation, fellatio, frottage, cannibalism and eye-gouging – than to appreciate the disciplined savagery of its language. For example, Ian says to Cate: 'You don't have to fuck me 'cause I'm dying, but don't push your cunt in my face then take it away 'cause I stick my tongue out.' He calls her brother, who has 'learning difficulties', a 'spaz', 'retard', 'a Joey'; blacks are 'coons', 'conkers', 'wogs', 'niggers', 'Pakis'; les-bians are 'lesbos' who 'suck gash'. In *Blasted*, what happens onstage looks pretty bad, but what's described is even worse. During its second half, accounts of atrocity in war pile up like corpses. The soldier says, 'Saw a child most of his face blown off, young girl I fucked hand up inside her trying to claw my liquid out.' In comparison, Ian's tabloid stories about kinky car dealers are positively humorous.

But apart from its horror, what was *Blasted* about? One way of answer-ing this question is to look at how it was written. 'Originally,' Kane says, 'I was writing a play about two people in a hotel room, in which there was a complete power imbalance, which resulted in the older man raping the younger woman.' Then something unexpected happened:

> At some point during the first couple of weeks of writing [in March 1993] I switched on the television. Srebrenica was under siege. An old woman was looking into the camera, crying. She said, 'Please, please, somebody help us. Somebody do something.' I knew

nobody was going to do a thing. Suddenly, I was completely uninterested in the play I was writing. What I wanted to write about was what I'd just seen on television. So my dilemma was: do I abandon my play (even though I'd written one scene I thought was really good) in order to move on to a subject I thought was more pressing? Slowly, it occurred to me that the play I was writing was about this. It was about violence, about rape, and it was about these things happening between people who know each other and ostensibly love each other.

Writing the play was a long process.

The first draft of *Blasted* was dreadful, full of huge dense monologues about the characters' backgrounds, every feeling stated, every thought spoken. A friend read it, and didn't say very much, but he gave me a copy of *Saved*. I'd read this years before, but I read it again in 1993. And that really was where I learned to write dialogue. At first, I thought Bond's approach would be of no use to me – I wanted my characters to be articulate and precise.

But Kane discovered that she didn't need long speeches. 'If each character can only say nine or ten words at a time, they become incredibly articulate and precise.' When 'I didn't let Ian elaborate on his racism, he just started to spill invective – it was a level of racism and violence that terrified me.' And although 'only three or four lines in the first draft made it to the final one', none of the work was wasted. The first draft meant 'I knew just about everything about these characters. Having brought it all to the surface, the job of later drafts was to bury it again, make it felt rather than spoken.' The emotional force of *Blasted* comes from the way Kane wrote it.

Kane then struggled with the connection between the two parts of the play.

I asked myself: 'What could possibly be the connection between a common rape in a Leeds hotel room and what's happening in Bosnia?' And then suddenly this penny dropped and I thought: 'Of course, it's obvious. One is the seed and the other is the tree.' And I do think that the seeds of full-scale war can always be found in peacetime civilization and I think the wall between so-called civilization and what happened in central Europe is very, very thin and it can get torn down at any time.

Next, Kane read other plays to see if anyone had done something similar before. 'If there's a precedent, I don't want to do it.' She couldn't find a precedent, but she still 'needed an event'. In early drafts, Ian merely hallucinated the soldier. 'And then I thought: "What this needs is what happens in war – suddenly, violently, without any warning, people's lives are completely ripped to pieces."' So Kane 'picked a moment in the play. I thought: "I'll plant a bomb, just blow the whole fucking thing up." And I loved the idea of that as well. Just blowing up the set.'

If what really annoyed audiences about the first production of *Blasted* was the way the naturalistic first half suddenly changed into a nightmarish and symbolic second half, Kane's experiment in form was not a coolly premeditated idea. It was forced on her by the need to turn two different plays into one. Her later rationalization is that 'war is confused and illogical, therefore it is wrong to use a form that is predictable'. She also argues that 'the element that most outrages those who seek to impose censorship is form. Beckett, Barker, Pinter, Bond – they have all been criticized not so much for the content of their work, but because they use non-naturalistic forms that elude simplistic interpretation.' Kane's play deliberately aimed to provoke: 'I more or less abandoned the audience to craft their own response to the imagery by denying them the safety of familiar form.' For Kane, the 'form is the meaning of the play, which is that people's lives are thrown into complete chaos with absolutely no warning whatsoever'.

If *Blasted*'s form was 'difficult', there was no problem with its stage imagery. Kane claims she was 'not particularly conscious of Beckett's influence', but also says: 'I was steeped in Beckett so it's not surprising that *Blasted* ends with an image of a man with his head poking out of the floor with the rain pouring through the ceiling onto his head.' In retrospect, 'I think the first third was influenced by Ibsen and Pinter, the middle section by Brecht and the final section by Beckett.' There were also other influences:

> There was a point at which I realized there was a connection with
> *King Lear*. And I thought: 'I'm writing about fatherhood. There's
> this scene where he goes mad; and there's this Dover scene with
> Cate when she unloads the gun – is she going to give him the gun
> or is she not?' And the only thing I didn't have is blindness. At the
> time, I was reading Bill Buford's *Among the Thugs*, about football
> violence. There was an undercover policeman who was pretending

to be a Manchester United supporter and he was found out. A guy attacked him, then sucked out one of his eyes, bit if off, spat it out on the floor and left him there. And I just couldn't fucking believe what I'd read; I couldn't believe that a human being could do this to another person. I put it in the play and everyone was shocked.

Blasted is pretty savage, but its violence was drawn from life. 'The only reason it's any more devastating than reading a newspaper,' says Kane, 'is that all the boring bits have been cut out.'

Kane is ambivalent about her characters. 'I really like Ian. I think he's funny. I can see that other people think he's a bastard. And I knew that they would. But I think he's extremely funny.' His character is based on 'a terrible moral dilemma' that arose 'when a man I knew who was dying of lung cancer was terribly ill, and started telling me the most appalling racist jokes I've ever heard'. Kane was

> completely torn: a) because they were very funny, and very good jokes; b) because I wanted to tell him I thought he was awful and I was glad he was dying of lung cancer; and c) because he was dying of lung cancer, I thought: 'This poor man is going to be dead and he probably wouldn't be saying this if he wasn't.'

Out of this 'turmoil' came Ian. 'Yes, of course I think he's a monster; I also think he's great.' But having created Ian, 'I wanted the soldier to be worse. And I knew it was going to be a real problem having someone come through that door who made Ian look like a pussycat.' So writing that part was 'probably the most difficult thing I've ever done'.

Is Cate simple-minded? 'No, absolutely not,' says Kane. 'That's a complete misinterpretation. She's naive. And yes, very fucking stupid: I mean, what's she doing in a hotel room in the first place? Of course, she's going to get raped.' But then 'isn't it utterly tragic that this happens to her?' Kane had 'nights during rehearsals when I would go home and cry and say to myself: "How could I create that beautiful woman in order for her to be so abused?" And I really did feel a bit sick and depraved.' A part of that feeling came from the sense 'that in the end Cate doesn't come out on top. If she had, I'm sure I would have felt completely exonerated.' But in real life, 'people like her never win'.

Blasted is a typically nineties play: it doesn't state a case but imposes its point of view. Kane doesn't have a message, she makes connections. Her vision of masculinity is not ideological but concrete: Ian abuses

Cate because she's in his power. He bullies her into submission. Aggressive, manipulative and predatory, Ian's actions illustrate the mindset of the middle-aged male. After all, Cate trusts him: he's a family friend; she was even once his girlfriend. Playwright Peter Whelan feels that the play makes more sense if you see Cate as Ian's daughter. However you view their relationship, Kane makes connections between the male urge to self-destruct and tabloid rhetoric, sexual fantasy, nationalist aspirations, football tribalism, homophobic feelings, racist hatred and open warfare. One typical contrast is between Ian's meat-eating and Cate's vegetarianism. This is then echoed in the play's imagery: talking about surgery on his lung, Ian says: 'When I came round, surgeon brought in this lump of rotting pork, stank. My lung.' But is Kane's account of male psychology believable? 'At Birmingham, there was a middle-aged bloke on the course,' she says, 'and he defended me when other students said my vision was too extreme. He admitted that many middle-aged men thought like Ian does.' An example of her insight is the way Ian manages to control Cate by making her feel guilty.

Blasted also raises questions without providing answers: what is the connection between maleness and violence? How does violence in the home become violence on the streets? When does the tabloid attitude to violence anaesthetize us to the real thing? Are most men really potential rapists? You could conclude that the play argues not only that all men are animals, but also that, while men abuse vulnerable women, they treat other men even worse. If masculinity is in crisis, then the effects of this are shown as a violent fallout of abuse. So is *Blasted* about the crisis of masculinity? 'Draw your own conclusions and I'll draw mine,' says Kane, rejecting any narrow interpretation.

Kane sums up her play's argument: 'The logical conclusion of the attitude that produces an isolated rape in England is the rape camps in Bosnia, and the logical conclusion to the way society expects men to behave is war.' You can recognize the truth of Kane's portrait of male psychology, without going the whole way with her. It's easier to agree with this 'logical conclusion' emotionally than to accept its intellectual implications. After all, not all men are rapists. Nor are they all self-destructive.

Kane shrugs off the idea that she's a moral writer. 'I find discussion about the morality of the play as inappropriate as the accusations of immorality. I've never felt that *Blasted* was moral. It doesn't sloganize.' Further, 'I really don't have any answers to any of the questions about violence, masculinity, morality, sexuality. What conclusions people draw are not my responsibility – I'm not in control of other people's minds and I don't want to be.' As she points out in her afterword to the *Frontline Intelligence* edition of *Blasted*, Kane deliberately avoids explaining herself to audiences because 'it relieves them of the effort of working things out for themselves'.

To prove that the media's moral panic says more about Britain than about *Blasted*, you only have to compare its reception in other countries. In Romania, for example, 'The idea of a soldier bursting into a room and raping the inhabitant isn't particularly difficult,' says Kane. 'What shocked them was the language, as they've only recently got rid of theatre censorship. They are used to doing things through strong images but not to saying "fuck" onstage.' In Germany, 'it was received very well, but I hated the first German production in Hamburg. It completely glamorized the violence. The director thought it was a stage version of Tarantino. It's not.' *Blasted* is about 'hope and love'; Tarantino films are not.

Some European productions were 'vastly different' to Kane's original intentions. One in Belgium was put on just after the child-abuse ring in Brussels had been exposed 'and the whole play became about the baby and there were people crying in the audience when the baby was buried. It bore very little relation to my play, but I accepted it as a genuine reinterpretation.' The same cannot be said about other versions. In one, after Cate has been raped, 'the lights came up and she's lying there completely naked with her legs apart, covered in blood, mouthing off at Ian. And I just wanted to die in despair.' Kane said to the director, 'Do you think it's either believable, interesting, feasible, or theatrically valid, that she's lying there completely naked in front of the man who's raped her? Do you not think that she might cover herself up?' And this 'has nothing to do with my feelings about nudity onstage. I've been naked onstage myself and I've no problems with that. It's simply about the truth of any given theatrical moment.'

The paradox of scandalous publicity is that while it enables more people to participate in an event than attend it, it also blinds those that see it. Because of the media attention, Kane soon found that 'no one could see the play any more'. At the Court, 'there was one night when the front row was filled with a group of lads determined to prove how funny they found it'. For reasons of scheduling, the play had a very short run, so only about 1,100 people saw it. This makes *Blasted* one of the most talked about but least seen British plays of the nineties.

Kane was also blinded by the glare of publicity:

> Any opinions I have about *Blasted* have been put together with
> hindsight. Writing my first play really was a process of groping
> about in the dark, making connections that I understood on an
> instinctive level but couldn't (and didn't want to) necessarily
> articulate.

When pressed, Kane falls back on the most general interpretation:

> For me, the play was about a crisis of living. How do we continue
> to live when life becomes so painful, so unbearable? *Blasted* really
> is a hopeful play because the characters do continue to scrape a
> life out of the ruins. There's a famous photograph of a woman in
> Bosnia hanging by her neck from a tree. That's lack of hope.
> That's shocking. My play is only a shadowy representation of a
> reality that's far harder to stomach. It's easier to get upset about
> that representation than about the reality because it's easier to do
> something about a play – ban it, censor it, take away the theatre's
> subsidy. But what can you do about that woman in the woods?
> Take away her funding?

Kane is conscious of the negative effects of her play's success. Two weeks
after it was on, she was given a script to read by the Court 'which was
about three people in a basement roasting a body and then eating it. And
I thought: "I wonder if this person has seen *Blasted*?"' There were 'some
extraordinary similarities' and since then 'there has been a glut of *Blasted*
copies'.

Despite seeing several different productions, Kane still claims that
her vision has not been fully realized:

> Directors frequently think the second half of *Blasted* is a
> metaphor, dream, nightmare (that's the word Cate uses), and that
> it's somehow more abstract than the first half. In a production that
> works well, I think the first half should seem incredibly real and
> the second half even more real. Probably, by the end, we should be
> wondering if the first half was a dream.

Blasted is Kane's best work. Harsh, humane and grimly humorous, it's
not an easy play, but it's written with passionate intensity. Rereading the
exchanges between Ian and Cate, you always have the sense of two people who've known each other for years and who share a whole life. You

never feel their interaction is wrong. Not only is the play written with a sense of compressed rage, its stage pictures also create powerful metaphors: Ian's blinding, for example, is both a personal disaster and a symbol of the media's moral blindness. And however disconcerting, the play's shift into a war zone in the second half is a perfect link between form and content.

Its meaning is also ambiguous. While writing *Blasted*, Kane 'had a conversation with David Greig about Aristotle's unities – time, place and action.' And 'I thought: "OK, what I have to do is keep the same place but alter the time and action." Or you can look at it another way: that the time and the action stay the same, but the place changes.' *Blasted* is not the first play to have a violent dislocation at its centre – Churchill and Brenton have done this before – but it is unique in that the dislocation can be read in two ways. On the one hand, the play stays in Leeds, and warns against complacency in Britain; on the other, it shifts to Bosnia, and confronts us with the reality of war, breaking down the distance imposed by geography and indifference. In the most compassionate way, it reminds us that war is both unendurable and must be endured, and argues that life is also both unendurable and must be endured. Like Beckett, Kane refuses to give in to despair: 'Once you have perceived that life is very cruel, the only response is to live with as much humanity, humour and freedom as you can.'

Phaedra's Love

Some writers choose to adapt a classic as a way of taking a rest from their own inner demons. Not so Kane. Her version of the Phaedra story begins with Hippolytus watching television in a darkened palace room, blowing his nose on one discarded sock, masturbating into another *'without a flicker of pleasure'*. 'He's depressed,' says a doctor. As the tale of his stepmother, Phaedra, and her passion for him, unfolds, an ancient tragedy transforms itself into a modern soap opera: 'Why shouldn't I call you mother, Mother? I thought that's what was required. One big happy family. The only popular royals ever.' But *Phaedra's Love* isn't just a barbed comment on Britain's dysfunctional royal family; it's also a study in extreme emotion. When Phaedra performs fellatio on Hippolytus, he feels nothing, and her passion for him ends in her suicide. She leaves a note blaming Hippolytus for raping her, and nemesis arrives in the shape of a mob that castrates him, grilling his genitals on a barbecue. '*A child pulls them out of the fire and throws them at another child, who screams and runs away.* His last line, as vultures gather, is: 'If there could have been more moments like this.'

After *Blasted*, the press tagged Kane as an 'angry young woman', and reviews of *Phaedra's Love* mixed praise and put-downs. For example, Michael Billington said, 'Viscerally, her play has undeniable power: intellectually, it's hard to see what point it is making.' Charles Spencer claimed to be 'seriously concerned about Sarah Kane's mental health', ending his review: 'It's not a theatre critic that's required here, it's a psychiatrist.' Younger, female critics were more appreciative: *What's On*'s Samantha Marlowe argued that Kane 'challenges theatrical conventions in a witty, intelligent and mischievous fashion', while the *Evening Standard*'s Kate Stratton said the play 'blows a range of dramatic raspberries at an unmistakable British society captured in galloping decay'. In *The Times*, Kate Bassett summed up:

> Speech is terse, truncated. Violence does not reach us by word of mouth. It is in our faces, almost literally as the cast thwack between clumps of seats. The trouble is that lashings of stage violence are not really shocking, just hard to believe.

Put on at the Gate theatre in west London in May 1996, *Phaedra's Love* was directed by Kane herself and lasted seventy minutes without a break. The set, designed by Vian Curtis, occupied the whole of this tiny theatre, leaving the audience perched on benches in the middle and on the edges of the room. The atmosphere was hot, claustrophobic. With the action happening all around, the feeling was one of eavesdropping on a problem family. While Hippolytus wallowed at one end of the set, messing about with a remote-controlled car, Phaedra brushed past audience members as she approached him. When she talked with her daughter Strophe, it was like listening to the 'Camillagate' tapes. But most dramatic of all was the play's ending, when a savage crowd rose up from among the audience and attacked Hippolytus. Being in the middle of the action made you feel complicit in the horror, even if the castration scene proved risible – as Hippolytus's genitals were flung the length of the theatre, several people laughed. More 'in-yer-lap', wrote critic David Nathan, than 'in-yer-face'.

The staging, says Kane, meant that 'the play could be at one moment intimate and personal, at the next epic and public'. One scene was glimpsed from across the theatre, another happened under your nose.

'And since it is a play that becomes more and more public, that's an entirely appropriate experience to have.'

Why did Kane adapt a classical tragedy? 'The Gate asked me to write a play based on a European classic,' she says. Her original choice was Georg Büchner's *Woyzeck*: 'I've wanted to direct it since I was 17. In the end, Woyzeck's only way of expressing himself is violence.' But the theatre was already planning a season of Büchner's plays 'so *Woyzeck* was out'. (As it happened, Kane did direct *Woyzeck*, on an open set, for the 1997 season.) But in 1995, her second choice was Bertolt Brecht's *Baal*, although the theatre anticipated problems with his estate. One scene in *Phaedra's Love*, that between Hippolytus and the priest, was originally written for *Baal*.

Finally, the Gate suggested a classical play. At first, Kane wasn't keen: 'I've always hated those plays – everything happens offstage.' But she chose Seneca 'because Caryl Churchill had done a version of one of his plays, *Thyestes*, which I liked very much'. (This was James Macdonald's 1994 production at the Court.) Kane read Seneca's *Phaedra* only once, and didn't look at either Euripides's version or Racine's until after she'd finished her play. She says, 'I wanted to keep the classical concerns of Greek theatre – love, hate, death, revenge, suicide – but use a completely contemporary urban poetry.' Instead of the violence happening offstage, Kane puts it centre stage. A similar inversion of the original, in the opposite direction, concerns Phaedra's suicide – for once, this is not shown.

'When I read Seneca's *Phaedra* I was struck by two things,' says Kane. 'Firstly, it's a play about a sexually corrupt royal family – which makes it highly contemporary – and secondly, Hippolytus is deeply unattractive. He's chaste, a puritan, a hater of mankind.' Rather than adapt the story, Kane rethought its psychology. 'Instead of pursuing what used to be seen as purity, my Hippolytus pursues honesty – even when that means he has to destroy himself and everyone else. The purity of his self-hatred makes him much more attractive than the virginal original.' But the play is also about the ability of language to describe unattractive emotions.

'What Hippolytus does to Phaedra is not rape – but the English language doesn't have words to describe the emotional decimation he inflicts. "Rape" is the best word Phaedra can find for it, the most violent and potent, so that's the word she uses.'

By making Hippolytus a grungy slob, who denies love by treating sex like junk food, Kane radically rewrote the story. *Phaedra's Love* is about love and faith, but it's also about depression. Hippolytus isn't just lazy, he's in despair. 'Through being very, very low comes an ability to live in the moment because there isn't anything else,' says Kane. 'Many people feel depression is about emptiness, but actually it's about being so full that everything cancels itself out. You can't have faith without doubt, nor love without hate.' You can see why Kane cites Albert Camus's *The Outsider* as one of her influences.

While she was writing *Phaedra's Love*, Kane herself 'was very depressed'. One of the things that obsessed her was honesty in relationships. At one point, a friend said to her: 'You've got your values wrong. You take honesty as an absolute. And it isn't. Life is an absolute. And within that you accept that there is dishonesty.' Kane couldn't accept this; nor can her Hippolytus – 'that's what kills him'. His tragedy is that everything comes together only at the moment of his death. For Kane, what makes depression bearable is humour; her play is a black comedy.

Writing was therapeutic: 'I'm simultaneously Hippolytus and Phaedra,' says Kane, 'both lethally cynical and obsessionally in love with someone who's completely unlovable. So every time I wrote a scene I was writing myself into two opposite states. I was connecting two extremes in my head. Which was both depressing and liberating.' For his creator, Hippolytus's truthfulness and directness are appealing. Like him, she's always wanted to be completely understood. And she can 'forgive him for being a shit' because he has a sense of humour. Phaedra, on the other hand, is 'not actually very in touch with herself', but she does pursue what she thinks she wants even unto death. Kane sees this nihilism as 'the most extreme form of romanticism'.

But the play is about faith as well as love. Its discussion of God centres on the 'insurance theory' of belief: 'If you're not sure God exists you can cover your arse,' says Kane, 'living your life carefully just in case, as the priest does in my play, or you can live your life as you want to live it. If there is a God who can't accept the honesty of that, then tough.' In the play, Hippolytus uses the same expression: 'I have no intention of covering my arse. I killed a woman and I will be punished . . .' Like Kane, he is fascinated by the idea of doing wrong deliberately. For him, moral choices are expressions of personal freedom.

As always, Kane's political points (about the hypocrisy of having a God-sanctioned monarchy) arise during the examination of extremes of feeling. If the violence of Phaedra's emotions shows the irrationality of desire – 'Can't switch this off. Can't crush it. Can't. Wake up with it, burning me. I think I'll crack open I want him so much . . .' –

Hippolytus's truth-seeking is an essay in confrontation. In the end, both choose self-destruction. Phaedra hangs herself; Hippolytus breaks from his police escort and '*hurls himself into the crowd*'. Bitterly disillusioned with love (he's angriest when Phaedra mentions his former girlfriend), Hippolytus consoles himself by attacking hypocrisy. Phaedra's suicide and her accusation of rape galvanize him into life – he's suddenly in touch with his emotions. To maintain this feeling, he seeks damnation with reckless impiety. A play that rings with loud emotions stars a man who's searching for something to feel, a reminder that Kane is less interested in atrocity than in the psychology of desperation.

Kane justifies the horror in her work by saying that

> sometimes we have to descend into hell imaginatively in order to avoid going there in reality. For me, it's crucial to commit to memory events we haven't experienced – in order to avoid them happening. I'd rather risk overdose in the theatre than in life.

Yet she rejects the comforting idea that violence is perpetuated only by men. 'My main source of thinking about how violence happens is myself, and in some ways all of my characters are me.' Kane emphasizes that her themes 'are the problems we have as human beings'. 'I am not writing about sexual politics. Class, race or gender divisions are a symptom of societies based on violence or the threat of violence, not the cause.'

Kane's work also has moments of accidental clairvoyance. The scene in which Strophe asks Hippolytus whether he's had sex with Phaedra was written in 1995, but its evasiveness sounds like President Bill Clinton being questioned about his affair with Monica Lewinsky: 'Did you have sex with her?'/ 'I don't think so.'/ 'Was there any sexual contact between you?'/ 'Sexual contact?'/ 'You know exactly what I mean.' Later, the brief comment about the most popular member of the royal family dying has, after the death of Diana, Princess of Wales, also acquired extra meaning.

Phaedra's Love is not Kane's most successful play. Despite the intensity of its vision of depression, incest and uncontrollable desire, it is difficult to take some of it seriously. The dialogue veers from exchanges that are genuinely disturbing (Theseus's grief) to boneheaded declarations such as: 'Fuck God; fuck the monarchy.' Some scenes – such as those between the Doctor and Phaedra and between Hipploytus and the Priest – are less convincing than others. Kane's great strength is her ability to delve into the nastier recesses of the human spirit and come up with emotionally fraught dialogue; her weakness in *Phaedra's Love* is a lack of discrimination between what works onstage and what is maddeningly banal. Compared to *Blasted*, *Phaedra's Love* never really takes the audience on an emotional journey, and only fitfully connects to the feelings that inspired it. Both the fragility of the characters and their tenderness are drowned out by the confusion of untamed emotions. It is a powerful play, but an imperfect one.

Cleansed

Kane's reputation has stuck to her like a sickness she can't shake off. When her third play, *Cleansed*, opened at the Court in May 1998, the memory of *Blasted* still dominated its reviews. Many critics couldn't resist reminding their readers about the outcry that greeted her debut: the *Daily Express*'s Robert Gore-Langton called it 'the most vicious play of the decade', while Michael Billington summed up judiciously: 'Everyone, including me, so over-reacted to her first play, *Blasted*, that it becomes difficult to judge her work with cool clarity.'

'In an institution designed to rid society of its undesirables,' says the blurb of *Cleansed*'s playtext, 'a group of inmates try to save themselves through love.' Set in what the stage directions ironically call 'a university', the play is a highly symbolic story which has four interweaving storylines that defy easy summary. The main one is about Grace's search for Graham, her brother, an addict who's been murdered by Tinker, a sadistic guard or doctor at the institution. Grace wears Graham's clothes, dances with his spirit, makes love to him, and finally – after receiving a penis transplant – becomes him. Juxtaposed with this story of incest and sibling bonding is the romance of two men, Carl and Rod, who discuss love and betrayal. Carl, who promises eternal love, betrays his lover; Rod, who lives for the moment, dies for love. In a subplot, Robin, a disturbed nineteen-year-old, falls for Grace when she tries to teach him to read. After learning to use an abacus, he realizes how long his sentence is and hangs himself. The last story is Tinker's: he visits a peepshow and imposes Grace's identity onto that of the erotic dancer. He seduces her, then turns nasty. At the end, Tinker has his own 'Grace', Grace looks identical to Graham, Carl is dressed in Grace's clothes. But despite the punctuation of Grace's final speech by the word 'pointless', the play ends in a blaze of sunlight.

As usual, most reviews began by listing the play's atrocities: Graham's eye is injected with heroin, Carl's tongue is sliced off, a broomstick is shoved up his rectum, amputations are followed by rats nibbling at limbs, people are beaten up and executed, a penis is transplanted and breasts are sliced off. And, yes, there's nudity, sex and masturbation. Sheridan Morley called Kane 'a naughty schoolgirl desperately trying to shock an increasingly bored and languid audience'. But other reviewers took Kane's influences seriously, from 'the Bard's ultra-nasty *Titus Andronicus*' to Pinter, Bond and Barker. The *Times*'s Benedict Nightingale suggested that readers 'think of the sadistic tortures of Kafka's *Penal Colony* and the bureaucratic cruelties of Pinter's *Hothouse*; [and] stir in the surreal violence of Bond's *Early Morning*'.

A few critics – perhaps provoked by the fact that the play's sadist is named after the *Daily Mail* critic who'd led the charge against *Blasted* – objected to Kane's work being staged. Charles Spencer saw it as a 'cynical attempt' by Ian Rickson, the new artistic director of the Court, 'to retain its reputation for cutting edge theatre'. Even those who liked *Cleansed*, such as David Benedict of the *Independent*, had doubts. He said that, after leaving the theatre, the play 'clings to you like a shroud', but despite a thrilling production, it showed 'clear weaknesses in the writing'. What was never in doubt, however, was the sheer force of Kane's vision, which inspired adjectives such as 'unforgiving', 'feverish', 'compelling', 'hermetic' and 'dazzling' – 'her handling of image and metaphor sets her apart from almost every other playwright of her generation'. As Rickson says, 'Kane is a true poet of the theatre. She has the bravery to take us to the deepest, darkest places with striking theatrical language.' However ambiguous its meaning, there is little doubt about the play's theatrical impact.

In the first production, on the main stage of the cavernous Duke of York's theatre in the West End, *Cleansed*'s twenty scenes lasted ninety minutes with no interval. What impressed me most was the series of vivid images. The quiet snowfall as Tinker cooks up heroin for Graham; Carl and Rod sitting on a green and exchanging rings; Grace putting on Graham's old clothes in the sanatorium; Carl being loudly beaten by unseen assailants in a sports hall; Grace and Graham miming a dance together; a sunflower bursting out of the floor after they make love; Tinker watching an erotic dancer in a gloomy gallery; Grace teaching Robin to write; Carl being dismembered in a muddy field; a ferociously loud execution followed by a burst of daffodils; the hot blaze of light and electricity while Grace is tortured; Carl and Rod listening to the Lennon/McCartney song 'Things We Said Today'; the bonfire of books;

the relentlessness of the numbers counted out by Robin on the abacus; Grace wearing a transplanted penis.

The audience, many of whom were gay, was very small but appreciative. People loved the play's gender confusions, laughing at Robin's clumsiness as he and Grace swap clothes, and were also gripped by the raw emotion onstage; only one person walked out. Despite the tortures, the play's view of the world felt idealistic, wild, strange, occasionally annoying – provocative theatre at its cruel best. The play's themes came at you with their pants down, defying criticism by being over-the-top.

Designed by Jeremy Herbert (who'd worked on Churchill's *Thyestes*), the staging featured hip leathers and urbanwear, rats represented by twitching bags with tails, blood by ribbons, fire by an orange-lit cloth. Directed by James Macdonald, some scenes were shown as if from above, in others the stage tilted; mutilation was deliberately unrealistic. But was the production a triumph of style over content?

A parable about love in a time of madness, *Cleansed* is full of metaphors of addiction, need, loss and suffering. As its title, and Grace's name, suggest, the play flirts with quasi-religious notions of purification and redemption. But while the central theme is the ability of love to survive fascistic, institutional cruelty (with clear overtones of ethnic cleansing), the precise meaning of Kane's play is deliberately elusive. Here Kane is grappling with a theatrical language capable of generating a multiplicity of meanings. 'Almost every line in *Cleansed* has more than one meaning,' she says.

In a play about love, each of the four main relationships is different, each symbolic. Grace and Graham represent the fantasy of incestuous, identity-sharing twins; Carl and Rod are the classic couple, one member of which is idealistic, the other realistic; Tinker and the dancer represent domination and alienated love; Grace and Robin experience a teacher and pupil, mother and child rapport. In each case, the relationship is difficult and makes suggestive assumptions about gender and identity: Grace becomes Graham without ceasing to be female; Carl and Rod are the same sex but have opposite sensibilities; Tinker has the power to abuse the dancer, but she's complicit in her victimization; Robin is needy and falls in love with care and knowledge, which kill him. Less sensationally, and more sentimentally, identity is affirmed through love. *Cleansed*'s idealism lies in its conviction that love is the one basis of hope in an evil world. It presents a vision of a tough love that can survive not only physical torture but also the need to tell the truth about ourselves.

At one viewing, it's hard to take in all the meanings of Kane's most ambitious and intellectual play. As a text, *Cleansed* is written sparely, but packs in a lot of emotions. While it does convey a sense of redemption through love, it also has a sado-masochistic feel. People are cleansed by pain and terror; Grace is burnt clean by torture. To make up for the loss of her brother, she gives up her own identity. Then she takes up her dead brother's identity as a way of loving him, as a way of finding herself and as a way of changing. Armed with incest love, she survives the worst tortures imaginable. Like Hippolytus, she ends up saying that, if you can't feel, life is 'pointless'. Carl and Rod differ because, while Carl dreams of everlasting love, Rod is only certain of the moment and makes no promises. He's right, of course. Carl betrays him. But despite hideous torture, Carl also survives. Robin tries to love Grace and buys her chocolates, but is disturbed by the dancer's sexuality and his own emptiness. Tinker's confusion with the dancer suggest a crisis of masculinity: Eros colonized by the language of pornography. *Cleansed* is about the dangerous emotions of losing yourself, trusting the other, facing death. Here Kane's voice is uniquely shrill, bleakly humorous and pared down.

Cleansed's original production gave a glimpse of what theatre might be like in the future, the product of an ongoing conversation with live art. It was strongly influenced by the theatrical freedom suggested by performance art or installations. Kane's explanation – 'As soon as I've used one theatrical form, it becomes redundant. So each time I've tried to do something different' – sounds like a tribute to Churchill. *Cleansed*'s origins lie in 'a particular fit I was having about all this naturalistic rubbish that was being produced'. She decided to write a play that 'could never be turned into a film, that could never be shot for television, that could never be turned into a novel'. *Cleansed*, she claims, can only be staged. 'I knew some of the stage directions were impossible, but I also genuinely believe you can do anything onstage. There's absolutely nothing you can't represent one way or another.'

In the last four performances, Suzan Sylvester (the actress playing Grace) pulled out because of a back injury, and Kane took her part. What did she gain from performing in it? 'The play suddenly became extremely clear to me.' The characters 'are all emanating great love and going after what they need. The obstacles in the way are extremely unpleasant, but that's not what the play is about. What drives people is need.'

Cleansed is the second of an informal trilogy that examines hope, faith and love during a time of war (the third play was never finished).

'It has violent things in it,' says Kane, 'but is essentially a love story. I started it before *Blasted* was produced and it took three-and-half years to write – I had to keep taking breaks because the material was so difficult. For me, there's an enormous amount of despair in the play because I felt an enormous amount of despair when I was writing it. But there are beautiful things in it too.' One of her starting points was Roland Barthes's *A Lover's Discourse*. At one point, he compares the situation of a rejected lover with that of a prisoner in Dachau.

'When I first read that I was appalled he could make the connection, but I couldn't stop thinking about it. And gradually I realized that Barthes is right: it is all about loss of self. When you love obsessively, you lose your sense of self. And if you lose the object of your love, you have no resources to fall back on. It can completely destroy you.'

Because 'the concentration camps are about dehumanizing people before they are killed', Kane's daring link between incarceration and infatuation allows her 'to raise some questions about these two extreme and apparently different situations'.

Cleansed's structure is certainly innovative, and was inspired by an unexpected source. 'It's based on *Woyzeck*,' she says. And influenced by Orwell's *Nineteen Eighty-Four* and Strindberg's *The Ghost Sonata*. But 'I wanted to strip everything down; I wanted it to be as minimal and poetic as possible; and I didn't want to waste any words.' At the same time, the play's pace is deliberately relentless: 'I didn't want to give anyone in the audience time to calm down.'

Although Kane firmly rejects any easy correspondence between her life and her writing, there are parallels between her Evangelical experiences and the quasi-religious images in *Cleansed*. For example, at one point Rod says: 'You'd have watched them crucify me.' 'I was a Christian until I was about 17,' says Kane. 'It was spirit-filled born-again lunacy. So the reading I did in my formative years was the Bible, which is incredibly violent.' However tongue-in-cheek, such statements are suggestive. Kane is certainly drawn to extremes. 'If you want to write about extreme love you can only write about it in an extreme way,' she says. 'Both *Blasted* and *Cleansed* are about distressing things which we'd like to think we would survive. If people can still love after that, then love *is* the most powerful thing.' *Cleansed* discusses identity and sexuality, but in a highly metaphorical way. As designer Jeremy Herbert says: 'Cutting a hand off is not about what physically happens to you – in this case, it's about no longer being able to express your love with your hands.' And

James Macdonald adds: 'The experience of love may be a kind of hell, but feeling it you're more alive than not feeling it.' When Grace gets a sex-change, all she says is: 'I felt it.' As in *Phaedra's Love*, the search for feeling is what makes Kane's work so emotionally fraught.

The play's horrors are based on true accounts. 'Robin is based on a young black man who was on Robben Island with Nelson Mandela,' says Kane.

> He was eighteen years old; he was put in Robben Island and told he would be there for forty-five years. Didn't mean anything to him, he was illiterate. Some of the other prisoners taught him to read and write. He learnt to count, realized what forty-five years was and hung himself.

The impaling scene comes from reports about Bosnia: 'It's a form of crucifixion which Serbian soldiers used against Muslims. And I tend to think that anything that has been imagined, there's someone somewhere who's done it.'

In *Cleansed*, the characters lose themselves, find their bearings again, survive or go under. In a stark but idealistic way, it suggests that love is strong and that lovers endure. Using provocative theatrical language, it also conjures up a world of pain. Without a trace of naturalism, it works more by suggestion than by explanation. 'When I was writing *Cleansed*,' says Kane, 'I reread Kafka's *The Trial* – it's one of those books where nothing is specified, but somehow you get it.' The same feeling of metaphoric truth permeates the play.

'*Cleansed*,' says Kane, was 'written by someone who believed utterly in the power of love. My next play, *Crave*, was written at a time when I thought the world was a pretty grim place.' Now, every time 'I let my cat out I think some vivisectionist is going to put washing powder in its eyes. That indicates a general depression about the world, don't you think?'

Crave

To shake off her 'bad girl' reputation, Kane presented a rehearsed reading of her fourth play, *Crave*, under the pseudonym Marie Kelvedon. As the playtext points out: 'Anonymity liberated Sarah to write for – and see her work played in front of – an audience unswayed by the influence of the *Blasted* phenomenon.' She also used the pseudonym because the play was unfinished, and Kane is fanatical about her work. The published playtext of *Crave* had an erratum slip that corrected 'I feel I' to 'I feel'. It's the kind of attention to detail characteristic of Pinter. The playtext also has a fictional biography of Kelvedon: 'Since leaving Holloway, she has worked as a mini-cab driver, a roadie with the Manic Street Preachers and as a continuity announcer for BBC World Service. She now lives in Cambridgeshire with her cat, Grotowski.'

Crave was directed by Vicky Featherstone and opened at the Traverse, Edinburgh, in August 1998. Her most difficult work, it was produced by Paines Plough, a company that cultivates new writers. In the play's poetic monologues, her use of language is richer, more allusive and more sensuous than before. As the introduction to the playtext says, having 'pioneered a new theatre where brutality and action express an emotional narrative, here she deploys language like music'. In performance, the effect was intoxicating. It was proof that Kane never rests, never stands still. The minute you categorize her, she moves on to explore different feelings, a different style, another extreme.

Crave has four characters, A, B, C and M, who, in its first production, sat on a row of chairs reminiscent of a chat show. As its title implies, the play is about aching need and suggests that what we most crave may be the same thing that cripples us emotionally. The play can be read in several different ways: as an account of two couples, as one mind's mental collapse or even as the overlapping feelings of four people who've never met. What's certain is that the emotions explored are not only edgy and desolate but also surreal and humorous ('As a child I liked to piss on the carpet. The carpet rotted and I blamed it on the dog').

If you read *Crave* carefully, it slowly becomes clear that most lines can have more than one meaning, depending on which character you imagine is being addressed. *Crave* is one of the more complex plays of the nineties, needing four different reading strategies to fully uncover its meanings:

First, the rationalist approach can attempt to work it out as a coherent play. For example, an older man, the abuser, is infatuated with a young black girl who cannot reciprocate because she is haunted by an abused past that she can neither remember nor forget. At the same time, an older woman tries to seduce a young man in the hope that he will father the child she is desperate for. In this case, A stands for abuser, B for boy, C for child and M for mother. The trouble with this approach is that it tends to limit interpretations of a deliberately open-ended text.

Second, an Eng Lit approach can examine the play's echoes of the

Bible, Shakespeare and T. S. Eliot. At one point, Kane considered providing footnotes in the same way as Eliot had done with *The Waste Land*, but decided against this because the notes would have been longer than the play and would have attracted more attention than the text.

Third, *Crave* feels like Kane's most personal work. Private allusions, from the 'mark of Cain' to the number 199714424 mean that it is an ideal candidate for biographical criticism. *Crave* has references to *Blasted* and *Cleansed* as well as to Kane's breakdowns and hospitalizations. The play can always be read, in the words of its publicity, as 'the disintegration of *a* human mind under the pressures of love, loss and desire'.

Fourth, *Crave* can be experienced as a performance. Watching it, you don't have time to work it out; your mind is simply dazzled by its images and the way its phrases collide, clash and mix. The more you try to analyse these impressions, the more the magic evaporates. But the problem remains that *Crave* is more of a poem than a play: however well you describe the stage picture of the first production – four characters on four swivel chairs – it seems trivial compared to the words.

As a poem, *Crave* is more suggestive than transparent. With its constant assertions of hope – and good intentions – followed by despair – and backsliding – it is a paradoxical work. In it, there is a constant struggle between loss of control and a desperate need to retain control. The longest speech is a reiterative poem in praise of the little, everyday things of love. But even here there is a note of subversive irony. Although the text doesn't specify, the speech can be read as the words of an abuser to his victim. But as in *Blasted*, the moral complexity of the work comes from the sense of complicity that the scenario implies.

Like Martin Crimp's *Attempts on Her Life*, *Crave* is an ambitious attempt to recast theatrical form. In its mixture of truth-telling and humour, it is reminiscent of Forced Entertainment's *Speak Bitterness*. It is also a reminder of how much Kane owes to Churchill in her ability and willingness to present her unique voice in a different structure with each new play. Like Pinter, Kane uses language strictly and severely; like Bond, she examines violence in its personal and social meanings; like Barker, she's capable of great flights of imagination. *Crave*'s intensity tends to provoke visual images: damaged lives, feelings of love and loss, permeate the piece like stains on a Polaroid photograph. As disturbing as an overheard confession, *Crave* also resembles a sinister tour around a city at night, where people's faces are suddenly lit up in the headlights of passing cars, then consumed by the dark.

Kane feels that the main emotions behind her work have not been understood.

> *Blasted* is a hopeful play. It's a lot more fucking hopeful than *Crave*, which oddly, other people have characterized as uplifting. I was a lot more hopeful at twenty-two than I am now, but strangely enough the one work of mine which I think fails to negate my own personal despair (*Crave*) other people find uplifting. The plays that I consider to be about hope (*Blasted*), faith (*Phaedra's Love*) and love (*Crave*) seem to have depressed everyone else.

Kane was not the first writer in the nineties to break the rules, but her notoriety meant that, more than any other, she publicized both the idea of transgression and the notion that a new sensibility had arrived. 'Writers such as Kane,' says James Macdonald, 'are reacting to a new complacency and to a lack of risk-taking in theatre.' Not only have her plays been innovative in form, they have also abounded in striking theatrical images. Although her obsession with atrocity tends to blind spectators to the tenderness and affection in her work, Kane is a purist who's always trying to make form and content one, and constantly seeks new dramatic voices to represent her vision of the truth. Not only is her best work experiential, it also puts into question the ruling conventions of naturalism. Her use of shock tactics – premeditated as they often are – should not detract from the fact that she's a highly thoughtful playwright, both fascinated by emotional extremes and well aware of theatrical tradition. Even when unsuccessful, she's courageous and passionately serious. And although her work is not explicitly political – Bosnia is never mentioned – it does implicitly criticize a society built on violence and denial.

If Kane's concern with violence says much about contemporary society, her relations with the media also typify the times. Her short 1997 film, *Skin* – an explicit portrait of a racist thug who falls for a black woman – excited controversy because Channel Four decided to change its transmission time from 9.30 to 11.30 p.m. on account of its scenes of racist violence and body carving. But despite being hounded and labelled, Kane is not averse to using the media herself. During the 1998 Edinburgh Festival, she wrote pieces for the *Guardian* about the 'performance' of Manchester United football team, as well as stories about herself vomiting in the toilet after drinking a bottle of gin. At other times, her suspicions about the media seem justified. 'I'd quite like to review plays,' she says. 'In fact, I was asked to review Pinter's *Ashes to Ashes* for the *Observer*. I was really keen to do it, and then they phoned me up and said: "If you don't like it, that would be great", and I thought: "This is a set-up, so I didn't do it."'

Kane is the quintessential in-yer-face writer of the decade. At a time when many felt 'impotent rage' with conventional politics, *Blasted*, in Anthony Neilson's words, 'spoke for a generation which has a dulled, numb feeling – not apathy, but a feeling that nothing you do will make any difference.' The play 'expressed the feeling that horror coming into your living room is the only way you can feel something and get yourself motivated.' Director Tom Morris sums up the parallels between *Penetrator* and *Blasted*:

> Like *Blasted*, *Penetrator*'s subject was the distorted and violent landscape of the sexual imagination; like *Blasted*, its argument was a crude parallel between the male sexual psyche and the mentality of war; like *Blasted*, it was calculated to make its point unmissably by putting horrifying violence into a tiny studio theatre where the audience was only feet away from the action.

As Kane says, 'What I can do is put people through an intense experience. Maybe in a small way from that you can change things.'

Kane guards her privacy sternly and has no time for questions about gender or sexuality in regard to her work. 'When people talk about me as a writer, that's what I am, and that's how I want my work to be judged – on its quality, not on the basis of my age, gender, class, sexuality or race. I am what I am – not what other people want me to be.' As a writer, 'I don't believe I have a responsibility to the audience. My responsibility is to the truth, however difficult that truth happens to be.'

5 Mark Ravenhill

I think we all need stories, we make up stories so that we can get by.

(Robbie in *Shopping and Fucking*)

If Sarah Kane's *Blasted* publicized the effrontery of the new wave, Mark Ravenhill's *Shopping and Fucking* proved that a new sensibility had well and truly arrived. When this controversial shockfest opened at the Royal Court on 1 October 1996, the theatre had moved from its historic premises in Sloane Square – closed for lottery-funded rebuilding – and had taken up residence in the middle of London's West End. Well aware of the publicity value of moving into a staid part of town – for tourists, 'Theatreland' is synonymous with musicals and light entertainment – the Court proudly announced: 'There goes the neighbourhood.' Two Victorian theatres, the Duke of York's and the Ambassadors, were rented and their interiors given a makeover. Out went all the traditional glitter, in came the dark and distressed look. Boring old theatres suddenly became cool spaces. The smaller building, the Ambassadors, was converted into two theatres and it was here that Ravenhill's first full-length play had its debut.

Born in June 1966 and brought up in 'bland' Haywards Heath, West Sussex, Ravenhill discovered theatre early. 'From the ages of ten to sixteen,' he says, 'I used to go to after-school drama classes. When I was about thirteen, I read a biography of Louis Braille and wrote a little play so that me and a friend could do lots of acting blind. It was all very weepy.' After school, Ravenhill took A-levels at a sixth-form college in Chichester and then read Drama and English at Bristol University between 1984 and 1987. 'I originally wanted to act,' he says, 'but I quickly realized that other people were better at it than me.' Instead, he directed student productions and in his final year wrote *Blood Brood*, which was put on at the Edinburgh Festival. 'It was the story of the Kray twins in blank verse, inspired by Steven Berkoff's *East*.'

Ravenhill's first job was administrative assistant at the Soho Poly, a new writing theatre. 'Apart from licking stamps and cleaning loos,' he says, 'I was in contact with directors, actors and writers, so I learnt all about how a new play gets put on.' After leaving the company, he became a freelance director, taught drama and worked at the Finborough theatre, run by Phil

Willmott's Steam Industry. In 1993, Carl Miller directed his *Close to You*, a comedy about 'outing' a gay MP, for the London New Play Festival. Although it played during the day and wasn't reviewed, it still proved controversial. 'Half the committee,' says festival director Phil Setren, 'found the play absolutely abhorrent and thought we would get a bad name for doing it, and the other half said that this is someone who writes clever dialogue and thought we had to do it.' Even without press coverage, 'we've never had a bigger seller: parade a group of ravers onstage carrying a "Queer as fuck" banner and the public will come in droves'.

Then, for Christmas 1994, Ravenhill directed *Hansel and Gretel*, a show written by Sheila Goff for the Midlands Arts Centre in Birmingham. 'We did a week of previews in a theatre full of screaming kids,' he says, 'and I thought: "Oh God, when I get back to London I just want to do something really adult."' He contacted Louise Mulvey (who later became the Finborough's literary manager) and said: 'Let's get something together very quickly – and let's make it really, really rude.' Put on as a fund-raiser for Red Admiral, an Aids counselling project, 'I'll Show You Mine' was a season of short erotic pieces. With contributions from Anthony Neilson and Robert Young, it was 'a kind of *Oh! Calcutta!*'. Ravenhill wrote *Fist*, which had two men talking about sex for ten minutes. During the week-long season, Ravenhill invited director Max Stafford-Clark. 'Afterwards, he asked me: "Have you got a full-length play?" and I lied and said: "Yes." Then I had to write one.'

Ravenhill finished the first draft in Spring 1995. He began with 'a group of young people living in a flat and got the story to tell itself'. His starting point was imagining 'characters whose whole vocabulary had been defined by the market, who had been brought up in a decade when all that mattered was buying and selling'. The play's theme was simple: 'These were extreme characters pushed to extreme situations. The market had filtered into every aspect of their lives. Sex, which should have been private, had become a public transaction.' At first, its title was *Fucking Diana*.

> I was a few scenes into it when Sheila Goff told me she'd run into an old schoolfriend, someone she hadn't seen for twenty years. She didn't like this woman so when asked what she was doing, Sheila just said: 'Oh, I'm writing a shopping and fucking novel.' She just wanted to shock her.

But the idea of shopping and fucking – with its ironic reference to novelists such as Jackie Collins – seemed just right.

In May 1996, Ravenhill returned to the Finborough to direct David Eldridge's second play, *A Week with Tony*. A month later, Stafford-Clark directed *Shopping and Fucking* in a two-week workshop at the National Studio and rehearsals followed in August. The collaborative process threw up new ideas. 'Antony Ryding, who played Gary, asked questions about how his character, after leaving home at fourteen and coming to London, was getting by financially – and came up with the idea of being a rent boy,' says Ravenhill. 'He did some research and the character changed quite a lot.' Workshopping also increased the cast's involvement in the play. 'You get a particular quality of acting when actors are really engaged in making a play.' *Shopping and Fucking* went through about seven or eight drafts, with changes being made up to the last minute. 'In the final week of rehearsals, I improved the scene where Lulu disconnects the phones.'

What were Ravenhill's inspirations? 'Mainly American novels of the late eighties, early nineties: Douglas Coupland's *Generation X*, Bret Easton Ellis's *Less Than Zero*, Tama Janowitz's *Slaves of New York* and Jay McInerney's *Bright Lights, Big City*.' He thought that 'they managed to capture the essence of what a generation had experienced, a sense of materialism and a kind of moral vacuum', and they 'reflected my sense of the world better than any British fiction or drama'. For him, 'the starting point for a young contemporary dramatist is something that is quite sardonic, quite ironic, quite cynical, because that's the predominant sensibility of the generation that's under thirty'.

The only things he'd seen onstage that had the same effect were Martin Crimp's work, such as *Dealing with Clair*, and Brad Fraser's *Unidentified Human Remains and the True Nature of Love* and *Poor Super Man* (Traverse, 1994). Other influences? 'On the level of dialogue, David Mamet; on the level of theatrical possibility, Caryl Churchill.' Her *Top Girls* is 'the best play of the past twenty years. I still reread it at least once a year.' Nearer home, 'Anthony Neilson's sense of stagecraft was important to me.'

But Ravenhill didn't feel part of a movement. 'When I was writing *Shopping and Fucking*, I hadn't seen *Blasted*. I'd been put off by the reviews, which suggested it was a mess.' Then while supervising some student dissertations, he found 'one which was about representations of violence, including *Blasted*, so I read the play'. Within five pages, he realized that it was one of the best-written contemporary plays. Impressed by its 'brilliant, almost classical structure', he thought it 'achieved a perfect balance between word and image'. At this point, he hadn't read *Trainspotting*, nor seen the play, nor any Tarantino films. But, during the week he began *Shopping and Fucking*, he saw Phyllida Lloyd's version of *The Threepenny Opera* at the Donmar Warehouse, with Tom Hollander as Macheath. 'Its savage, sardonic wit seemed to release a great howl of anger and despair.'

More important than direct influences were the years of practical experience. 'I'd thought a lot about how to tell a story dramatically, and I'd learnt as much from film as from theatre.' Structure was particularly important. 'Actually, *Shopping and Fucking* has a dramatic climax in the traditional place – in terms of structure, it's quite an old-fashioned play', an ironic echo of John Osborne's description of *Look Back in Anger* as 'a formal, rather old-fashioned play'.

Shopping and Fucking

Those looking for scandal didn't have to go further than the title of Ravenhill's play. When it was accepted for production by Max Stafford-Clark's Out of Joint company, Sonia Friedman, the producer, was given legal advice that the title could not appear on posters or in adverts. Under a Victorian law – the Indecent Advertisements Act 1889, amended by the Indecent Displays (Control) Act 1981 – the word 'fuck' is banned from public display. Originally drafted to stamp out the explicit adverts that prostitutes once put in shop windows, a law designed to curb a real-life activity was used to ban adverts for a play that represented, among other things, that activity. To solve the problem, the first posters for *Shopping and Fucking* used the image of a splintered fork to obscure the offending word. The next solution involved asterisks, so the title became *Shopping and F***ing*, and promotional postcards advertised the play's West End transfer with a quote from the *Evening Standard*: 'Entert***ing, Sh*cking & St*mulating.'

Friedman said: 'We can use the F-word on stage', but 'in anything unsolicited – posters, leaflets, direct-mail letters – we cannot print it without risking prosecution'. A passionate polemic on the subject by Carl Miller appeared on the Court's website. He pointed out how little had changed since Tynan first said 'fuck' on television in 1965:

> Over 30 years later, we still can't tell people the name of one of the plays in the autumn season. If you see posters, leaflets and

advertisements for Mark Ravenhill's new play in the Theatre Upstairs, they will coyly censor the title [. . .] If you ring up to ask what the title is, the box office staff still cannot tell you. Thanks to the Indecent Advertisements Act of 1889, they lay the theatre open to prosecution if it is called anything more explicit than *Shopping and Effing* [. . .] only once you have committed to buy a ticket, can the full horror of the title be revealed.

When the play went on its national tour, the posters with the splintered fork were acceptable in seven towns, but in another three the local authority rejected even the asterisk version. So in Bracknell, Warwick and Newbury, good citizens were encouraged to see a play advertised as *Shopping and*. While metropolitan audiences were 'virtually unshockable', says Stafford-Clark, spectators in smaller cities were less blasé. In Swansea, in what Ravenhill calls the 'Welsh bible belt', a dozen Christians made a block booking and ten minutes into the show stood up and began singing hymns. Police had to be called.

While such incidents helped make *Shopping and Fucking* notorious, and advertised the play far more effectively than any advert, they were rare. More common were heavy-handed jokes about alternative titles: *Shopping and Shagging* or *Shopping and Bonking*. In polite society, it was coyly called *Shopping and Flower Arranging*. Legends sprang up about punters asking the box office if they could 'watch the fucking and miss the shopping'. In a way, the brouhaha merely emphasized the gap between what youth considered normal – 'Me and my friends never gave the play's title a second thought,' says Ravenhill – and what the wider society felt was rude. The play's title is also a good example of the Court's tradition of mischief-making: neither Stephen Daldry nor Stafford-Clark is immune to the temptation of being a bit naughty.

Shopping and Fucking begins with Lulu and Robbie trying to get their flatmate Mark to eat from a carton of takeaway food. In a series of rapid scenes, their attempts at self-improvement come under threat. Mark books into a clinic to cure his drug addiction, has sex with another addict and is thrown out. On the streets, he finds Gary, a teenage rent boy who falls for him. Meanwhile, Lulu's attempt to get a job involves stripping off for middle-aged Brian, who tests her by giving her 300 Ecstasy tablets to sell. In a fit of stoned idealism, Robbie gives away the drugs and Brian threatens the couple with torture. To raise the money they owe him, they sell telephone sex. The climax of the story comes when Mark brings Gary to meet Lulu and Robbie. They play a truth and dare game, which includes a gross story about having sex with Diana and Fergie in a gents toilet, and which culminates in Gary's offer to pay off their debts if they penetrate him with a knife and give him a 'a good hurt'. Later, Brian arrives and expounds his philosophy that 'Money is civilization'; he settles his accounts with Robbie and Lulu. The play ends with harmony restored as the three flatmates share a meal.

The original Out of Joint production of *Shopping and Fucking* opened with the music shrieking 'Life's a bitch!' and ended with the song 'Love is the sweetest thing . . .' In between, Stafford-Clark created a coherent world crammed with memorable theatrical images for the play's themes: the takeaway dinners, the video sequences, the bag of coins won in an arcade. With its pumping music and flashing neon messages – 'home', 'E', 'meat', 'sweet' – the piece was slick, exciting, its bright surface glowing with colour, its characters as vivid as cartoons. Brian was chillingly detached, while Robbie, Mark and Lulu mixed the artificiality of Ken and Barbie dolls with the desperation of youth. Only the boyish pathos of Antony Ryding's Gary was genuinely touching. Although its snappy scenes gave the play a sporadic feel, and the sight of Mark rising with his mouth bloody after rimming Gary provoked groans, the action really took off during the truth and dare games of the second half. Ravenhill was careful to make the gang-rape of Gary consensual: he twice asks to be abused. In a small theatre, the effect was experiential: Ravenhill says he wrote the play for 'a close-up audience of 65 people'. At the end, as the *Guardian*'s Michael Billington noted, 'the chief sensory impression' is the 'smell of the cheap microwave-cooked food', 'a symbol of society's conspicuous waste'.

On the night I saw *Shopping and Fucking*, the sense of occasion was heightened by the play's late start. Harold Pinter's *Ashes to Ashes*, which was on in the adjacent theatre space, had to finish before *Shopping and Fucking* could begin because the only thing that divided the two spaces was a curtain. So Ravenhill's play began at about 9.15 p.m. By chance, I sat just behind a black homeless man who, making the most of the 10p standing tickets, was sheltering from the cold October night. During the play, the tramp's constant bemused glances at the mainly white, middle-class audience were perfectly eloquent: what are these nice people doing watching these horrors?

He might have been even more surprised by the critical reaction to the play, which was generally favourable. The *Daily Mail*'s irrepressible

Jack Tinker reminded his readers that 'whereas I led the chorus of disapproval' against *Blasted*, 'I can only applaud' the Court's 'courage in staging this dangerous and, no doubt to some, offensive work'. This time, no critics took the bait. Although several mentioned the scenes of rape and rimming – in what Billington called a 'deeply uneven, in-your-face play' – most realized its achievement in putting onstage a world where sex is a commercial transaction and consumption sexually arousing. Most also noted the play's balance between raw dialogue and bigger themes. Only John Gross in the *Sunday Telegraph* made a sustained case against the play, arguing that it encourages 'complacent self-pity (it is always somebody else's fault) and glib pessimism (taking the worst for the most representative)': it 'wallows in the conditions it describes'.

Other critics noted the values inherent in the play: for example, *Time Out*'s Jane Edwardes said: 'When Lulu is invited to take her top off at an interview, she is more worried about the stolen M&S frozen meals [falling out of her jacket] than revealing her tits.' The *Sunday Express*'s James Christopher – in a review that was reprinted in the programme of the play's West End transfer – said that scandal was what made the Court 'chic'. In general, the critical reaction surprised Ravenhill, who thought his play – like *Blasted* – would get 'mauled'. He now thinks that *Blasted* 'softened up the critics', so that when they saw *Shopping and Fucking*, they were 'more prepared to take it on board'. In less than two years, the climate for provocative drama had changed.

Shopping and Fucking was put on twice at the Ambassadors, toured Britain, and became, with help from the British Council, a cultural ambassador to Sweden, Ireland, Italy, Australia and Israel. In June 1997, it came back to the West End – and was revived yet again six months later. By now, most critics had become blasé, the older ones nodding ruefully that 'the shocks of 50 years ago are no longer the shocks of today'. Only its title continued, in critic Sheridan Morley's words, to give 'typesetters and broadcasters headaches'. When it opened at the Gielgud theatre in Shaftesbury Avenue, many pointed out that the necessary coyness about the title contrasted with the explicit sexuality on display just around the corner in Soho, London's 'red light' district: in *Time Out*, Steve Grant noticed the 'nicely ironic twist' of the title's asterisks in a location 'outside which people not only shout "Fuck" but are often looking for one'.

Seeing *Shopping and Fucking* for the second time here, it was clear that the distance imposed by putting the play behind a proscenium arch not only lessened its impact but also released more of its humour. It had also built up a cult following, the audience boasting a strong gay presence: the play had been advertised in the window of Clone Zone, a Soho shop specializing in gay gear, as well as in the gay press. Apparently, ticket sales shot up after it was reviewed in *Attitude*, a gay style magazine. This young, hip, metropolitan crowd was difficult to shock and completely sympathetic to the black humour of the piece. On television, Emma Freud claimed that its 'graphic depiction of rent boys and drug-dealing pulled an enthusiastic young audience into the theatre', while Sonia Friedman pointed out that not only were most of the audience in their mid-twenties, but also they refused to book, simply turning up and buying tickets as if for the cinema. But not everyone was impressed. Simon Nye – writer of the BBC's *Men Behaving Badly* – walked out of the play, calling it 'miserable', and Ravenhill also points out in dismay that some young people reacted as if the whole play was meant to be 'ironic, cool, unfeeling'.

Is *Shopping and Fucking* any more than a play that, in Stafford-Clark's words, 'titillates the middle-classes', part of the 'long tradition' in which liberals enjoy being publicly 'spanked'? Certainly, the theatricality of the play's original staging, the wit of the dialogue and the glitz of the set tended to obscure the darkness of the piece. The scenes of overt sex or explicit violence were not as disturbing as the feeling that the characters were lost, somewhat clueless, prone to psychological collapse, vulnerable to exploitation. Stafford-Clark's staging was clean, cool and restrained, but rather unemotional. Worst of all, some scenes did feel as if they were celebrating rather than criticizing the values of the throwaway culture.

While much of Ravenhill's writing in *Shopping and Fucking* is laid-back, almost casual, what is impressive is the thematic unity of the play. Full of powerful metaphors of consumption and sexuality, the piece displays a set of distorted mirror images. Mark's initial telling of the shopping story – a fantasy in which he buys Lulu and Robbie from a 'fat man' in the supermarket – is reprised at the end when he retells a mutated version of it; Mark is throw out of the clinic because he has 'lick and go' sex in a toilet, which is reflected in the gross toilet cubicle story about Diana and Fergie; Lulu's problem with sharing individual ready meals is mirrored by Gary's offer of pot noodles to Mark; Robbie gets sacked from his McJob after being attacked by a customer wielding a plastic fork, while Lulu witnesses an attack on a shop assistant with a real knife; Mark wants sex to be a simple transaction, but Gary wants it to hurt; the

Rule Number One of drug dealing ('He who sells shall not use') is mirrored by Brian's 'We need something [. . .] a set of rules'; Robbie's 'Fuck money' is challenged by Brian's 'Money is civilization'. In a telling irony, Mark offers Gary a choice between being loved and being bought: Gary prefers to be bought, another echo of the play's shopping story. *Shopping and Fucking* may lack a naturalistic plot and well-rounded characters, but its strength is density of metaphor and theatrical flair.

If the play's main theme is that each character becomes involved in some kind of 'transaction', this is set in the context of a nineties boys' story. The play's gender confusions are about definitions of maleness: Gary, the abuse victim who wants to die; Mark, the emotional dependent who is also a junkie; Robbie, the bisexual. In scene after scene, the boys foul up and it is Lulu, the woman, who holds things together. When Robbie gets sacked, Lulu gets work. When drug dealing needs to be done, she knows the 'first rule'. When Robbie gives away the Ecstasy, it is Lulu who begs Brian for time to repay the money. She is also the one who shoplifts food for them all. At one point, she says, 'Boys grow up you know and stop playing with each other's willies.' Except that here they don't. And when boys won't grow up, the only woman in the cast is forced to play mummy. 'People picked up on the crisis of masculinity quite quickly,' says Ravenhill, though he claims he wasn't aware of the theme while writing.

'The people in the play are just trying to make sense of a world without religion or ideology,' says Ravenhill. 'They're kids without parental guidance – they're out there on their own having to discover a morality and a way to live as they go along.' But it would be wrong to see them as victims. 'They are quite tough and optimistic, they keep trying out new schemes, they don't moan.' In a way, 'that's the provocation: they don't call on the government to sort out their lives; they don't say they should get more unemployment benefit; they don't have a political vocabulary.' More practically, 'if they moaned, it wouldn't be engaging for an audience'. Ravenhill's aim is to keep the audience on its toes by juggling with conflicting feelings of empathy and criticism.

One thing that no 'middle-aged critic picked up' was Ravenhill's playful attitude to his characters, who are named after members of the pop group Take That. 'I never remember the names of characters, so I thought it's not worth spending time agonizing over them,' he says. He took the names from a CD that was lying on his desk. The choice of names meant that young people not only 'fell about laughing' when they read the play, but also 'felt an ownership of it, felt it was written for them and was about them'. Lulu's name was not only a reference to the single she recorded with Take That, but also an in-joke: in 1994, Ravenhill had written a BBC World Service radio adaptation of Wedekind's 'Lulu' plays.

The most problematic aspect of *Shopping and Fucking* is Ravenhill's unrealistic idea of character. For example, Andrew Davies, who adapted *Pride and Prejudice* for the BBC, says the characters 'don't have a life to sustain them for more than ninety minutes'. Ravenhill replies that 'although we are still reassured by a nineteenth-century notion of character, there are plenty of good plays that don't use that idea of character'. What about *Shopping and Fucking*? 'No, they're not the product of accumulated detail, but are quite pared down and spare; they're the sum of their actions.' His theory is that this 'allows the actor to add to them and the audience to project onto them. My characters are more open. The weakness is that people think I'm dismissive of human beings.'

What audiences did feel was that Gary was central to the play, a symbol of neglect, abuse, urban drift. But why did Ravenhill defuse the horror of the climax by making Gary's rape consensual? 'I wanted the power situation at that moment to be dialectical,' he says. Gary 'seems to be the victim, but actually it's the others who have become victims because he's led them to a point where he expects them to do something which horrifies them – and they've got to do it'. In most power relations 'there's something more complex going on than just a simple oppressor and oppressed. It's more ambiguous.' Although much of the bleakness of the play comes from the fact that fourteen-year-old Gary is a no-hoper, his death in the original production was never signalled explicitly enough to be really moving. His fate was left hanging in the air.

No such uncertainty affected the play's marketing. The programme of *Shopping and Fucking* used the arguments of big names – from John Webster to Laurence Olivier and Edward Bond – in favour of showing violence onstage. It quoted Sarah Kane (saying that if you don't represent something, you risk 'denying its existence') and Kenneth Tynan, who in 1965 wrote: 'Unless we can use the theatre as a platform on which to demonstrate the serious problems of today, particularly violence, we feel that we are not serving a useful purpose in society.' James Christopher spoke of the play's 'unnerving knack of opening our eyes to the horrors of our daily lives'. Like other controversial plays before it, *Shopping and Fucking* was justified on utilitarian grounds. For its defenders, its message was: we have made an ugly world – what can we do about it?

But did the play really need such a justification?

Shopping and Fucking was certainly discussed in a wide-ranging way, not only in the press but on public platforms. On one panel, Stafford-Clark drew attention to the 'qualified optimism' of the play's ending. After Thatcherism, he said, there was no longer any consensus about liberalism, and in theatre there were 'no happy endings'. New audiences were more embarrassed by the word 'socialism' than by the word 'cunt'. Ravenhill agreed. His play, he said, was a implicit critique of Thatcher's dictum that 'There is no such thing as society'; if her vision was true, this is what you got, a 'cynical and hardened' attitude, angry that a 'sense of society has disappeared'. *Shopping and Fucking* captured the 'low-level anger of the twenty to thirty generation'. On the same panel, Stephen Daldry argued that young audiences no longer wanted the old-fashioned thesis play, but preferred 'a personalized internal search without necessarily a clear answer'. Ravenhill said that the main characteristic of new audiences is that they 'don't believe' what the media tell them: 'We are very cynical, sceptical, distrusting.' His play shows a world in which the liberal imagination has lost its youthful disciples.

Shopping and Fucking offers a snapshot of Generation X. As Stafford-Clark says, 'It's a play about urban dysfunctionals, not surviving, almost drowning.' Here is a nation where the grown-ups, represented by Brian, have a vestige of old values (the video of his son playing the cello) but also advocate the most excessive spirit of capitalism, whose moral lesson is: 'Get the money first.' When Gary complains about being abused, his social worker, another grown-up, offers him a leaflet. Young people have been abandoned. However funky and uninhibited, they are dazed, confused and boiling over. With all adults corrupt, there is little to relieve the pain and the tedium except shopping and fucking. And these are not the children of the sink estate. 'People still imagine that a stage character who takes heroin or swears is from an underclass,' says Ravenhill; 'the image is that heroin addiction just happens on Glasgow housing estates.' But no, these young characters are the children of middle-class, middle Britain, and their crisis is part of a country's redefinition of its self-image.

The sensibility of *Shopping and Fucking* is not only youthful but also postmodern. A very knowing play, it makes frequent use of discourses, creating the effect of a collage. When Robbie says that 'a long time ago there were big stories' but now 'we're all making up our own stories', he recalls theories about the end of grand narratives; when Mark says, 'I have a tendency to define myself purely in terms of my relationship to others', he parodies therapy-speak. Other discourses include Lulu's quotation from Chekhov, her parody of postcolonial ideas while serving ready-made food ('You've got a fucking empire under cellophane'), Brian's paean in praise of money, the Diana story and, above all, the mutating shopping story. Here everything is about stories and surfaces. On one level, the play is a very postmodern mix of savage critique and playful entertainment; on another, the evident longing of its characters for something more than postmodern irony, for narratives that make sense of the world, links the play with an older tradition of committed drama. Ravenhill denies knowing much about postmodern theory, but the content of his play argues that he is better read than he admits.

The reason for including about seventeen stories in the play is due not only to postmodern stylishness but also to theatrical technique. 'I thought it would be quite effective dramatically for the characters to tell each other stories,' says Ravenhill. Some of these were more provocative than others. The blatant one about sex with the royals had to be changed on tour after Diana, Princess of Wales, died on 31 August 1997. 'On the day after, we were afraid the audience would be too shocked if the Diana story came first. It would have killed the laughter.' So Ravenhill 'just swapped the order of the stories, having Fergie first and Diana second'. People laughed at Fergie and 'then they suddenly thought: "Oh no, it's going to be Diana next", and there was a kind of uncomfortable laughter.'

By 1999, it was becoming difficult to keep track of overseas productions of *Shopping and Fucking*, with more than twenty versions and translations into most major languages. The first German production at the Baracke in Berlin, directed by Thomas Ostermeier, showed how theatre traditions differ. 'A German audience is used to having no points of empathy with the characters,' says Ravenhill. 'In the text, it's the fact that Gary says he wants to be anally stabbed that's upsetting, but a character can say that on a German stage and it's completely unmoving.' So what they did was 'anal stabbing with the knife, lasting about seven minutes, and lots of blood – that moment had to be played explicitly and in real time.' In German theatre, naturalism is frowned on as intellectually unjustifiable, so the play's set – a room with a sofa – was itself scandalous. For Ravenhill, the most disturbing aspect of the play is 'what the characters want and feel, not the rimming or the anal sex. It's their lack of understanding of the world and their isolation from each other which is shocking.'

Half of the play shows the cynicism of the *Trainspotting* generation and the other half challenges it – in Mark's sudden love for Gary; in Robbie's message: 'You're not alone'; in Lulu's plea for the boys to 'grow up', there is hope, however muted. So while Ravenhill creates a supermarket society where everyone's for sale and anything can be packaged, he shows his compassion by suggesting, with quiet optimism, that love, mutual caring and the search for new values are possible. 'There is a little bit of optimism at the end,' he says. 'I just wanted to suggest that they might be able to sort things out. Earlier, Lulu has been quite obsessed with the fact that they can't share their food, but now they do.'

Whatever its legendary shock value, the tone of *Shopping and Fucking* is predominantly ironic, tongue in cheek. Its brutal scenes are finally less surprising than its tender-hearted idealism: at the end, Brian abandons drug dealing and gives Lulu and Robbie their money back. Similarly sentimental and ironic is the fact that his ideals are inspired by Walt Disney's *The Lion King*. Tucked inside a knowing, unnaturalistic, episodic play is some cosy wishful thinking. Ravenhill shows how the brief cultural moment that was hyped as Cool Britannia is a place of small consolations and large contradictions, but while he calls *Shopping and Fucking* a 'piece of Britpop', his next play was darker, more cerebral, 'like Kraftwerk'.

Faust Is Dead, *Sleeping Around* and *Handbag*

After making a thrilling debut that introduced an original voice to British theatre, Ravenhill wrote three plays that, in various ways, proved problematic. The first of these, a free adaptation of the Faust story, featured Alain, a French postmodernist philosopher who is on the American chatshow circuit to publicize his book on the Death of Man and the End of History. He quits his university post after upsetting the institution's sponsors, and hooks up with Pete, the wayward son of a computer software magnate. Together, they journey into the Californian desert, having sex and taking drugs. On the Internet, they meet Donny, a disturbed boy who cuts himself. Challenged to prove his authenticity, Donny kills himself. Alain is then hospitalized and Pete returns to his father.

Commissioned by Nick Philippou of the Actors Touring Company, which specializes in radically updating classics, Ravenhill agreed to do a contemporary version of *Faust*. Director Philippou had already worked with Stewart Laing on a project called *Brainy*, which looked at Foucault's time in California in parallel with the Faust story. *Brainy* was put on in Glasgow in 1995 and, although Ravenhill never saw it, ideas from the project seeped into his *Faust*. 'When Foucault was in the States,' says Ravenhill, 'he drove to Death Valley with a student and they took LSD and had sex.' This idea of shaking off academic life and setting out on an adventure became one of the play's motifs.

Unwilling to simply update the notion of a pact with the Devil, by substituting a drug dealer or company executive for Mephistopheles, Ravenhill abandoned the idea of a pact, but was stuck with the name *Faust* because ATC had already advertised the play. Ravenhill knew the Marlowe and Goethe versions of the story, and Philippou introduced him to Lenau, a German Romantic poet who wrote his *Faust* in 1836. Instead of starting in Faust's study, says Ravenhill, 'Lenau begins with Faust dissecting a body. He realizes the limits of knowledge when he's looked at every organ but still can't understand how people work.' The image of cutting the body recurs in Ravenhill's play. Another striking scene is quoted in the programme for the ATC version. 'At the end, Faust doesn't believe he's real any more. He sees this knife and thinks it's a dream, then stabs himself and realizes, too late, that it is real – quite a postmodern idea.'

As well as reading about Faust, Ravenhill studied Foucault and Baudrillard. 'I read a lot, starting with the *Baudrillard for Beginners* book.' Ravenhill felt that such theorists were 'being quite chic, having these dangerous thoughts about violence and sexuality, but they lacked any responsibility'. In the play, he uses examples of Baudrillard's riddles about a cannibal who eats a woman, and about a woman who rips her eyes out and sends them to her lover, to examine cruelty and the nature of seduction. 'They're little teasers he used to give his students. He was playing a smart intellectual game, but his nihilistic philosophy seems like an easy option.' He sees postmodern theory as 'an act of revenge' for the failure of the 1968 student movement in Paris. For Ravenhill, philosophy's retreat from social responsibility is deeply reactionary. His play dramatizes the 'meeting of somebody with a very chic notion of violence with people for whom violence is real'.

When Alain – played by Canadian video-maker Alain Pelletier (who looks like Foucault) – meets Pete, he discovers that both have lost their sense of reality. Compared to the academic, Pete has more experience of life, but his world is filtered through the Internet and video cameras. Because Pete comes from a good family, he can handle Alain. Having stolen some secret software, he is confident of his power. But Donny isn't. 'Donny's the person at the end of food chain,' says Ravenhill, 'the poor bastard for whom academia should be doing something to improve the quality of life rather than disappearing into intellectual conundrums.' Alain is Faustian in that he has had enough of studying and wants to live a little. With his paradoxical puzzles, he seems to be the seducer, but, when Pete shows him the Internet, he becomes the seduced. Ravenhill's Alain keeps changing places, one moment being Faust, the next Mephistopheles, which not only underlines the idea that good and evil coexist, but also dramatizes postmodern ideas about the volatility of character and the indeterminacy of the subject.

After a week's workshop in October 1996, followed by a further rehearsal period, the eighty-minute *Faust* began a tour of Britain in Hemel Hempstead the following February, although most reviewers saw it soon after at the Lyric Studio, Hammersmith. On a claustrophobic set, which had screens for the brash motel interiors and an atmosphere so dark that critics could barely take notes, Ravenhill's allusions to junk culture and hyper-reality mixed freely with a wry scepticism as funny as it was bleak: on a video screen, one impoverished rioter defends his theft of a video machine by saying that having food is pointless if you have nothing to watch while eating. With its contemporary references (to Bill Gates and Kurt Cobain, Saddam Hussein and Boris Yeltsin, CNN and MTV, Prozac and the Internet, chaos theory and the millennium), understated acting and repetition of key lines, *Faust* appealed more to the intellect than to the emotions. The scene in which Alain and Pete get stoned and have sex in Death Valley expressed both their desire for freedom and their alienation: when Alain fellates him, Pete doesn't feel a thing. The play is dark, not only because good and evil blend into one but also because the system remains all powerful. Capitalism rules; humanity has gone down the plughole.

When the video sequences were on, audiences sat back and enjoyed them, unaware that they were Ravenhill's biggest problem. 'Because Donny only appears on video, you don't really connect with him, so audiences missed the fact that he's the real victim,' says Ravenhill. 'By the end of the play's London run, I thought that Donny was the most important character.' But if Donny remained a virtual presence (there was only enough money for two actors), Pelletier's video images of the chorus, which break up the narrative with humorous if sad stories of life in Los Angeles, exemplified the production's multimedia approach. During workshops, the chorus members made their contribution. 'We used American students living in London,' says Ravenhill. 'I met them and talked about this sense of disconnection from reality, and one of them said: "Oh yeah, I know what you mean, I'm the kind of a person who could stand in the middle of an earthquake and just be like 'Woah, neat earthquake!'" Ravenhill used the line in his play.

One critic's response to *Faust* had an unexpected side effect. 'John Peter's review in the *Sunday Times*,' says Ravenhill, 'said that this brilliantly self-denying piece of mythology suggests that the Faust myth may be dead.' So Ravenhill thought that a 'more honest' title would be *Faust Is Dead*. As a compromise, the published playtext was called *Faust (Faust Is Dead)*, and subsequent productions use the new name. Another critic identified Francis Fukuyama as a source for Alain because the latter's announcement of the End of History echoes the title of Fukuyama's controversial book, *The End of History and the Last Man*.

A second production in April 1998 at the Tuesday Laboratory in Los Angeles gave Ravenhill the chance to bring Donny alive. Scene 14 was rewritten to put Donny onstage so that audiences could see him cutting himself. Alain intellectualizes self-mutilation as 'an initiation rite' and 'a moment of control', but Pete's response is sardonic: 'Either that or he's a loser who cuts himself.' The scene is partly a critique of mutilation chic. 'There's a lot of rather trendy performance art in which people cut themselves,' says Ravenhill, 'but I find it repulsive.' He is sceptical about 'academic writing about the body and the fascination with piercing', and criticizes the attitude that people cutting themselves are somehow 'interesting': usually 'it just means there's something deeply wrong'. In LA, 'they told me that cutting has almost taken over from anorexia. People who are powerless find the only thing they can control is their bodies, however perversely.'

The other main change in *Faust Is Dead* was the ending. 'Alain has a completely nihilist philosophy, so I wanted an upbeat ending which questioned that.' In the rewritten version, Donny is prepared to look after Alain, but he is not prepared to stay with Pete. Ravenhill's feeling was that 'the international capitalist is irredeemable, but the academic, if he connects with reality,' can find redemption. The LA production also used live actors rather than video images for the chorus. 'Each member of the chorus,' says Ravenhill, 'was from a different ethnic group, which is what choruses are all about: the voice of the city'. How did they come across? 'Bleak, but also very funny.' Before this, Ravenhill had never been to LA, so his ideas about the place came from books, such as Dennis Cooper's *Closer*, *Try* and *Frisk*, or movies, such as Greg Araki's *Living*

End, Totally Fucked Up and *Nowhere*. 'My chorus has a similar voice to these', queer rather than gay, morbid rather than wholesome, edgy rather than mainstream.

Although only 'a small hard core' thought *Faust* was better than *Shopping and Fucking*, it was still controversial. At the Lyric, one man, sporting a bow tie, scrunched up his programme and walked out, saying: 'That's like no *Faust* I've ever seen.' A woman in Hemel Hempstead declared: 'It's not *quite* as I remember the play.' When ATC conducted an audience survey, it found that the average age was twenty-three, with many just eighteen. 'Young audiences didn't seem bothered by the intellectual content,' says Ravenhill. 'They liked the video, and accepted the emptiness of the piece.' Using his characteristic mix of postmodern ideas and traditional morality, Ravenhill's *Faust Is Dead* is a good example of the decade's freedom in turning old myths into new sources of meaning.

Ravenhill's next two plays, *Sleeping Around* and *Handbag*, share a common problem: in both, so much of his energy went into the form of the plays that other qualities, such as character development or emotional empathy, are lacking. *Sleeping Around* was a collaborative project, conceived in 1997, when Ravenhill was literary director of Paines Plough. The idea was to use several writers to create a new version of Schnitzler's *La Ronde*. At first, says Ravenhill, 'We played with the possibility of having twelve writers write a scene each, but that was unmanageable, so we decided on four.' Being a national touring company, Paines Plough chose writers from Scotland, Wales and Ireland, and Ravenhill developed the play with Stephen Greenhorn, Abi Morgan and Hilary Fannin at the National Studio. First they researched contemporary notions of class, interviewing people who work in marketing, advertising and academia. Then they dispersed to write, spent another week at the studio, followed by another bout of writing. At this point, 'we realized we'd created an absolutely horrendous Frankenstein monster. It didn't work at all.' With only a week before rehearsals, the play was frantically cut and reshaped, so that 'only one line of the earlier draft survived'.

First put on at the Salisbury Playhouse in March 1998, *Sleeping Around* was performed by John Lloyd Fillingham and Sophie Stanton, who played all the roles. Despite their enthusiasm and precision, the play was an experiment in form that didn't quite work. It sagged in places and the variety of different voices never quite gelled. But if the total effect was incoherent, the play still offered rueful images of the sex wars of the nineties. What appeals is its sensibility, which contrasts sharply with more mainstream adaptations of the same play.

In 1998, two new versions of *La Ronde* were put on at the Donmar Warehouse, a coincidence that offered a chance to compare two different worldviews. In October, David Hare's mainstream version, called *The Blue Room*, was literary and sophisticated, yet also chilly and bloodless. It got acres of publicity, mainly because it starred the Hollywood actress Nicole Kidman opposite Iain Glen. Media interest was aroused when she took her clothes off, and led to distasteful discussions about whether or not she had cellulite. When I saw *The Blue Room*, the audience was not offended by the partial nudity, but by the play's representation of class arrogance: when the rich student, after having sex with the foreign au pair, tells her angrily to 'do your job', there was a gasp of outrage. For a brief moment, in Blair's Britain, blatant class power was offensive.

By contrast, *Sleeping Around*'s style was much sexier, raunchier, cruder, yet also oddly poetic. In the opening scene, a woman masturbated a man at the launch of a scheme to project a corporate logo onto the surface of the moon. Despite the play's humour, it was the emotional bleakness of the relationships that hit you. In the saddest scene, a woman begs her AIDS-stricken lover to have sex with her. As in Terry Johnson's *Dead Funny*, the most shocking aspect of the play was its painful picture of couples who stay together but don't have sex. A kaleidoscope of lovelessness, emotional frustration and deep need, *Sleeping Around* made for compelling viewing. In its casual assertion that Britain was a place where people still believe in 'the potential of a moment's true connection with another human being', the play also offered a touch of optimism.

Whereas *The Blue Room* was hailed as 'pure theatrical Viagra' by middle-aged critics, *Sleeping Around* won most praise from a much younger audience. At the Salisbury Playhouse, says Ravenhill, 'There was this usher, a student, who said: "I love this play: it's the only thing that's been on here that's about people like me."' Other young people said: 'Hey, this is about real life.' After all, the sex in the play, however frank, was less important than its raw feelings and sense of confusion. It was also a celebration of acting. 'At the curtain call you could feel a real warmth from the audience,' says Ravenhill. *Sleeping Around* had mixed reviews but, despite its uneven texture, it did give a revealing glimpse into sexuality on the eve of the millennium. As Michael Billington pointed out, 'Women are seen as the initiators of sex but also the ones less likely to be fulfilled.' He also commented that 'the irony is that, while dramatists attack the notion of sex as just another consumer appetite, it is also being used as a marketing ploy to attract young audiences'.

Like *Sleeping Around*, *Handbag* was an ambitious project that didn't quite work. Telling two stories simultaneously – one about contemporary parenting and one about Oscar Wilde's *The Importance of Being Earnest* – it was developed, like *Faust*, by ACT. The play, says director Nick Philippou, attracted 'a mixed audience, half fifty-year-olds and half teenagers'. In discussions after the show, which toured during 1998, the older generation was attracted mainly by the idea of playing games with Wilde's text, while younger people were more open to its ideas about alternative parenting. Ravenhill had assumed that everybody knew Wilde's play, so he was 'surprised when a lot of young people said they'd never heard of Lady Bracknell'.

Why deconstruct Oscar Wilde? 'I'd directed a production at university,' says Ravenhill, 'and I'd always thought that the moment when Miss Prism swaps the baby with the book was strange, funny, quite frightening.' Ravenhill also wanted to put Wilde's play into a broader historical context. Whereas Alan Bennett's *Forty Years On* and Tom Stoppard's *Travesties* see *The Importance of Being Earnest* as 'a bubbly, almost Absurdist piece of theatre, I was more attracted to the emotional darkness that underlies the laughter'. His version also articulates the gay unconscious of the original.

On paper, *Handbag*'s plot is quite complex. In the nineties strand, a pair of middle-class lesbian and gay couples (Mauretta and Suzanne; David and Tom) decide to make a baby by artificial insemination. By the time it is born, however, David is picking up Phil, a homeless junkie, and Suzanne is trying to seduce Lorraine, a young vulnerable woman. Both couples are too stressed to cope with the baby. The women employ Lorraine as a childminder, but she meets Phil, neglects the baby, gets the sack, kidnaps the baby and sets up home with Phil. When the baby develops breathing problems, Phil tries to revive it by burning it with a cigarette. The plot's Victorian strand is a prequel to *The Importance of Being Earnest*, set twenty-eight years before Wilde's play begins. Augusta, the future Lady Bracknell, arrives from Ireland to stay with her pregnant sister, Constance. Soon after its birth, Constance's baby is handed to Miss Prism, a nanny whose main interest is novel-writing. Meanwhile, Cardew, a philanthropist with a penchant for young boys, is searching for Eustace, one of his escaped charges. When a hostile crowd burns down his house, he flees to Worthing. As he leaves, Prism gives him the baby. It grows up to become the Jack Worthing of Wilde's play.

Ravenhill's title refers, of course, to one of the most famous exclamations in British drama. In Wilde's play, the formidable Lady Bracknell exclaims 'A handbag?' when Jack tells her that his parentage is obscure because he was found on Victoria Station in a handbag. In Ravenhill's version, baby Jack is given to Cardew deliberately and not lost accidentally. Equally deliberate is the first production's subtitle: 'The Importance of Being Someone'; here, identity is no accident, but rather a quest and a construct. But while some critics, notably the *Financial Times*'s Alastair Macaulay, saw *Handbag* as one of a 'post-mod genre of clever plays' that refer to Bennett and Stoppard, the play's other references eluded older spectators. Of the critics, only Samantha Marlowe in *What's On* noticed that Handbag is a form of house music and that the Teletubby Tinky Winky (a cult figure for clubbers, who was denounced as gay by American preacher Jerry Falwell in 1999) also carries a red handbag. Apart from the last track by Suede, the play's music was indeed wall-to-wall Handbag. In such ways, *Handbag* appealed uneasily to both young and old.

Onstage, the complicated plot is never confusing, and both plot lines are spattered with images of desire and desperation. In one sequence, there is anal sex, in another masturbation, in a third, heroin injection. Phil at one point wets himself, at another shoots up. While the baby cries, Phil and Lorraine have sex. In the words of the *Evening Standard*, *Handbag* is 'another of Ravenhill's withering celebrations of good-time nihilism built around chaotic acts of sexual excess'. The sex, says Ravenhill, 'is a useful way of getting characters into close contact with each other. It's revealing and funny.' Most critics quoted Ravenhill's line of cod-Wilde – 'Labour? Isn't that something that happens in Manchester?' – and pointed out that Miss Prism's final judgement – 'To him who needs the child, the child shall be given. That's what justice means' – echoed Bertolt Brecht's *The Caucasian Chalk Circle*. You can also detect touches of Feydeau, Coward and Wilde. So is Ravenhill the Stoppard of the Chemical Generation?

'Critics liked the Brecht reference,' says Ravenhill, 'because they recognized it. But I put it in quite late just as a joke.' Nowadays, he argues, *The Caucasian Chalk Circle* 'looks simplistic: here's the good mother, here's the bad mother – as neat as if it's come out of a Christmas cracker.' Ravenhill's version of Brecht is more of a sick joke: after all, Prism is giving the baby to a paedophile. 'It's more morally ambivalent than Brecht.' When a pram is wheeled onstage, it's hard to avoid an echo of Bond's

Saved, but the play's main inspiration was Caryl Churchill. Early during the writing, Ravenhill went to see Peter Hall's revival of *Cloud Nine* at the Old Vic (March 1997). 'I was amazed by how well it worked and how it didn't seem dated at all. I found it really funny, really moving, and very theatrical.'

Although *Handbag*, with its complex structure, recalls *Cloud Nine*, Ravenhill never manages to achieve Churchill's emotional empathy. And while the dialogue is written with his usual flair for explicit expressions of desire and conflict, the modern scenes work much better than the Victorian ones. But even here, the image of the rent boy cutting himself, having anal sex and injecting heroin seems overfamiliar, almost mannered. Despite the play's humour, the main problem is that most of the characters are frankly unsympathetic. Onstage, the doubling of the roles, with each actor playing both a modern and a Victorian character, encouraged the audience to make comparisons between the past and the present. 'The doubling came from *Cloud Nine*,' says Ravenhill. 'Seeing how quickly the actors could do the costume changes was fun.' It also had a political point: with Lorraine and Prism both played by Faith Flint, 'you can't help asking: how much have we moved on since the 1890s? After all, Lorraine is a hired servant – just like Prism.'

Handbag voices contemporary anxieties about parenting in an age of sexual diversity. 'When I wrote it,' says Ravenhill, 'stories about destructive nannies, baby-stealing and artificial insemination were very much in the air, and then a rash of baby plays appeared': Edward Albee's *The Play About the Baby* (Almeida), David Lewis's *Sperm Wars* (Orange Tree) and Liz Lochhead's *Perfect Days* (Traverse). Billington described this litter as a 'theatrical baby-boom'. *Handbag* is clearly an intervention in the long-standing debate about parenting: what is natural and what is learnt? By giving the baby to two non-heterosexual couples, Ravenhill argues that the realm of what society considers 'natural' has no monopoly on bringing up children, but, by making the whole experiment a disaster, he also plays into the hands of those who believe that only married couples should have children.

The failure of the two modern couples in the play comes from Ravenhill's polemical view of his characters. They are 'all infantilized,' he says. 'They live in a greedy society in which the emphasis is on each individual's needs. They've become completely self-centred.' The middle-class ghetto is as alienating as any council estate. 'Walled up with these huge mortgages, they're selfish people trying to do something selfless, having a child.' The central meaning of the play is 'that it is impossible to have children as a selfless act in a society that is basically selfish, that can create the Lorraines and Phils'. The comedy and tragedy of the play is that 'if you have hoards of excluded people, you can never be a happy middle-class person because you're always looking over your shoulder'. Isn't this too negative? 'Not really – it's a social problem and therefore it can be solved. It's not existentially bleak.'

There is also a danger that lost boys such as Phil, however moving as characters, have become a Ravenhill trademark. 'Yeah, it's tricky. I had Phil in early drafts, but he was shadowy,' he says. Then, one day, 'I was waiting in the rain, under some awnings in Camden, next to this junkie guy who was talking to a friend.' Listening to him, Ravenhill found the character of Phil. Being a junkie, Phil is a liar, 'so you can't really trust what he says'. He is also the 'most constructive parent in the play – but under pressure he has no resources at all to cope'. Ravenhill once worked with addicts in a rehab unit, so

> a lot of the drug culture is based on real life. One ex-junkie told me that he'd lived in this big block in Glasgow and human life was so cheap that, if somebody died, they'd just put them in a bin-bag and throw them out of the window. There were human bodies in bin-bags at the base of the flats. The image of putting a baby in a bin-bag stayed with me and appears at the end of *Handbag*.

Much of *Handbag*'s intellectual flair comes from Ravenhill's ideas about our relationship with the Victorians. 'More than any other period in history, the Victorian era provides us with images that are the reverse of what we are now,' he says. When its starched and crinolined characters come onstage, audiences tend to see them as 'completely different from us, sexually repressed and class-bound'. But Ravenhill wanted to goad audiences into questioning the idea of progress: if modern parenting is as alienating as Victorian parenting, how different are we? If today's middle classes also rely on servants, are we the new Victorians? 'Today, there's a huge gulf between rich and poor, and men and women lead segregated lives, particularly in gay milieus – so much for progress.'

Equally provocative is Ravenhill's sympathetic portrait of Cardew. If some audiences saw him as a child abuser, Ravenhill feels that although he has 'a very strong attachment to young boys, and his huge energy probably comes from his libido, it never reaches the point of physical abuse'. *Handbag* implicitly argues that projecting today's sensibility about sex onto the past can result in distorted views of ways of feeling that are now lost to us.

The play's most theatrical moment is the time warp in Scene 9 when Phil injects heroin and time-travels in and out of the Victorian era. Although it is never explained, in performance it works as a device linking the past and present. One of the reasons for its success is that it comes late in the play, at a point when audiences are wondering what the link between the two strands will be. Ravenhill says that, when Phil time-travelled, he could 'sense this feeling of relief' as audiences realized the play would make sense.

As with all of Ravenhill's work, collaboration during workshops was crucial. Originally, the play had a different beginning. 'When we discussed it,' says Ravenhill, 'everybody wanted to open with a scene about conceiving the baby, so I wrote one in rehearsals.' He phoned a student at Goldsmiths College, London, who was in a gay couple and who wanted to have a baby, 'and he told me details like the cup and the porn mag'. At the time, there was a debate about political correctness, with some people feeling it would be 'inappropriate to masturbate with porn when you're trying for a child. On the other hand, some people find it impossible to masturbate without porn . . .' Like much of Ravenhill's other work, *Handbag* is both a journey into the heart of postmodern culture and a quizzical account of *fin de siècle* morality.

Some Explicit Polaroids

Ravenhill's *Some Explicit Polaroids* – a ninety-minute play produced by Max Stafford-Clark's Out of Joint company in September 1999 – was widely seen as the follow-up to *Shopping and Fucking*, with some commentators unaware that Ravenhill had written three plays in the interim. But if, thematically, *Some Explicit Polaroids* has much in common with his debut, taking once again a sceptical look at contemporary consumer society, its origins lie in theatre history. Based on Ernst Toller's 1927 play, *Hoppla, wirleben!* (*Hurrah, We Live!*) – which tells the story of a revolutionary who returns home after eight years in an asylum to find that his old comrades have become corrupt conformists – Ravenhill's version combines a seventies state-of-the-nation play with a acerbic critique of both nineties youth culture and traditional leftist militancy.

In it, Nick, a left-wing radical, is released from prison after serving fifteen years for a savage attack in 1984 on Jonathan, a capitalist entrepreneur. He calls on Helen, his former partner, and finds that she has turned into a New Labour councillor with ambitions to become an MP. She doesn't want him to stay, so Nick drifts around the city, meeting Nadia, a lapdancer who spouts self-help clichés, and lives with Tim, an HIV-posi-tive man whose boyfriend is Victor, a 'Russian doll' addicted to trash. But while these youngsters just want to party, Nick struggles to adjust to a world whose values he doesn't understand. When Nadia is beaten up by her boyfriend, he wants her to react with the same anger he feels, but she responds by 'thinking positive'. Meanwhile, Helen, who is being black-mailed about her radical past by Jonathan, persuades Nick to meet him. As old leftie and new entrepreneur come face to face, it seems that both miss the struggle. As Jonathan says: 'Nostalgia's a tricky bitch, isn't she?' In the end, however, Nick turns down Jonathan's offer of work in Eastern Europe and goes back to Helen, who this time allows him to stay.

Directed by Max Stafford-Clark, *Some Explicit Polaroids* was seen on the main stage at the New Ambassadors, by then vacated by the Royal Court and restored to its former shape as a proscenium theatre. Within this traditional setting, Ravenhill's parable sported the junk phrases and gadgets of contemporary life: Nadia speaks in psychobabble; Victor wears a spiky, sado-masochistic-chic collar; Tim says he 'downloaded' Victor after seeing Polaroids of his 'fucking crazy body' on his Internet homepage; one telephone answering machine message begins: 'Me returning your call returning my call returning . . .'; a bleeper tells Tim when it's time to take his pills. In this production, the mix of pounding techno music and flashing images on a wide video screen gave a sense of the frenzy of city life, as well as recalling the multimedia effects of Toller's original play. The idea of the Polaroid camera, with its instantly gratifying but short-lived images, worked as a powerful metaphor for nineties pop culture.

By 1999, critical responses to a play that included explicit sex no longer dwelt on outrageous stage images but focused more on the piece's ideas. However, while *Some Explicit Polaroids* was praised as an account of contemporary social rootlessness – with the *Daily Express* calling its author 'the poet for the off-message, off-your-face Britain' – its politics were less well received. *The Times* said that it was 'a nostalgic lament for the end of class struggle', while the *Independent* saw Nick as 'a hollow Rip Van Winkle-figure'. Just as the *Sunday Telegraph* mocked the 'nonsense' of having a 'Hard Left tough' representing a 'vanished idealis-tic past, and the best hope for the future', so even the *Guardian* felt that the play 'sometimes falls prey to the soundbite values it condemns'.

Although *Some Explicit Polaroids* is about ideas, it is emotionally fuelled by its theme of anger. Almost every scene has some allusion to anger. In an ending lit by a muted ray of hope, Helen says to Nick 'I want you to be angry', hoping to reignite the excitement of their shared past. Nick's anger echoes both the Angry Young Men of the fifties and the Angry Brigade urban terrorists of the early seventies. Yet, significantly, he kidnapped and tortured Jonathan in 1984, a year that recalls both George Orwell's dystopia and the last Miners' Strike. It was, says Ravenhill, 'the last great moment of class struggle before the Tory government defeated the unions, which meant that many on the left had to rethink their ideas quite radically'. At university in the mid-eighties, he was attracted to the Socialist Workers Party for 'about three months', and Nick embodies the militancy of Trotskyist activists. In Scene 3, his anger at social injustice ('You've gotta fight back') is juxtaposed with Nadia's incredulous laughter: she just finds his fury funny. But the anger in *Some Explicit Polaroids* is not merely political: Tim is angry because of his terminal illness; Nadia tries desperately to justify her lover's anger against her by calling him 'frightened' and 'a child inside'; Jonathan is angry for the pain he has suffered and the scars he still bears; and Helen is 'so fucking weary of always being angry'. Even Nick's anger comes as much from frustration and emotional hunger as from political conviction. For Helen, it is what both attracts and repels her about him. As Ravenhill says, 'Anger is a necessary part of being human.'

More clearly than in any of his previous plays, Ravenhill's characters interact in a dialectical way, changing with every new confrontation. Nick goes from initial incomprehension, to anger, to trying to shake some sense of reality into Nadia, to giving up and drifting into a 'totally fucking meaningless' life, to longing to return to prison (a clear echo of Toller's play), to a final uneasy truce with the new reality. At the same time, Nadia, Tim and Victor begin by totally embracing the trash aesthetics of contemporary culture and end up by making their own discoveries. Nadia finds out through Jonathan that her self-delusions are lies; Tim decides that death is preferable to endless uncertainty; and Victor discovers the pain of his love for Tim. In the end, while Nadia is left with a perishable Polaroid photo of Victor (with a fading shadow on it that looks like Tim's ghost), Helen chooses Nick as her living memory. Even though their relationship will not be easy, the audience knows that both Nick and Helen have reconnected themselves to their past.

The play's characters exemplify Ravenhill's use of dramatic irony and contradiction: although the twentysomethings are free of ideology, which, he says, 'allows you to be open to new ideas and new experiences', they are also 'lost and confused'. By contrast, Nick and Helen are firmly grounded in ideological beliefs, but Helen is seen as 'dull' and Nick cannot join in with youth's frantic partying. Ravenhill's contrast between the lifestyles of today's bright young things and those who were once angry, antagonistic and politically active reflects badly on both. The militant leftist certainties, the 'bigger picture' that Nick once believed in, seem simplistic when juxtaposed with Helen's concern with trying to make life more bearable for the poor; the hectic fantasy of Tim, Nadia and Victor's 'happy world' seems fatuous when confronted with the realities of HIV infection, domestic violence and loveless sex. By bringing Nick into conflict with Helen, Tim, Nadia and Victor, Ravenhill forces all of his characters to look again at what they feel, believe and want to do. Conflict is what enables each of them to break out, however briefly, of the prison of loneliness.

Some Explicit Polaroids is the first Ravenhill play that really connects to a deep and painfully emotional core. Scenes 7 and 9, both set in a hospital, focus on Tim. In the first, he refuses to take his medicine because the endless postponement of death seems worse than a predictable, if terminal, illness. By not taking his pills, Tim tries to regain control over his life – 'I want to know where I am' – even though it kills him. The only way Nadia and Victor can persuade him to take his pills is by starting to have sex with each other. Suddenly excluded, he gives in. But two scenes later, he is dead, and Victor rages against his corpse, hitting the dead body. When Tim, now a ghost, talks to him, he sulks. Then he asks Tim to tell him he loves him even if it is untrue. When Tim asks Victor to masturbate him, the grim humour of this 'one final request' wrestles with the sense of loss. 'Why,' asks Victor, 'do you only say "I love you" when you feel orgasm coming on?' Masturbating a corpse is a powerful image of futility, and Tim's realization, too late, that he does love Victor makes the scene a gut-wrenching one. 'It's hard to write about illness without being sentimental,' says Ravenhill, who here successfully avoids 'conventional ways of representing dying'. In both scenes, Tim's rage against disease and death is both emotionally truthful and symbolic, suggesting a image of gay life that is sad without being mawkish, humane without being 'feelgood'.

But while such moments do connect with strongly felt emotions,

Some Explicit Polaroids is by no means perfect. Although Ravenhill is well aware of what is wrong with the superficial interactions of the clubbing generation or the banalities of self-help therapy, his play is an uneasy mix of character and ideas. The word 'explicit' in the play's title refers both to sex (such as Victor's proud boast, 'I've got a fantastic cock') and to the way the characters openly proclaim their worldview. Tempting Nick with Ecstasy, the twentysomethings revel in their hedonism, refusing to put a moral value on anything. Just as Helen has learnt to forget the 'bigger picture', so Nadia attacks Nick's attempts at generalization: when he tells her not to let men 'walk all over' her, she says her assailant was not a 'man' but an individual. This theme is echoed by Tim's 'Nothing's a pattern unless you make it a pattern' and Victor's 'Nothing is fixed any more'. Most explicit is the contrast between Nick's rage against injustice and youth's sense of personal responsibility. Just as Victor sums up the failure of socialist regimes (in a speech about their ugliness that ends with 'big fucking lie') so Tim clearly states the new generation's focus on the particular: 'We're all responsible for our own actions okay? We don't blame other people. That's very nineteen eighty-four.'

But are Ravenhill's characters just walking points of view? 'It's like an optical illusion,' says Ravenhill. 'Some people see completely rounded three-dimensional characters; others see only cardboard cut-outs.' Each of the characters is 'meant to have attractive and unattractive characteristics' and 'the aim is for you to feel torn between liking and disliking the characters'. But none of his characters is easy to sympathize with. Nick and Helen are not an attractive couple, and Nick is not Ravenhill's mouthpiece. Nick's disparaging phrase about Helen's work in reforming bus timetables ('just rearranging the same old shit backwards and forward') is both a scornful attack on reformism and an unpleasant put-down by a 'holier than thou' revolutionary. Ravenhill is less successful at showing the loss of political idealism than at conveying the need for memory and of keeping faith with the past.

While it is always clear that Ravenhill's sympathies lie with a leftist point of view, and he is occasionally as didactic here as he was in *Shopping and Fucking*, as a writer he takes care to be scrupulously fair to the opposition. Ironically enough, Jonathan tends to be a more attractive figure than either Nick or Helen. He is dynamic and clever, and refuses to wallow in his injuries. His vision of capitalism is deliberately seductive and his language is strongly reminiscent of Brian's from *Shopping and Fucking*. Jonathan is a powerful character, whose charm comes from the fact that he was based on Maurice Saatchi, the advertising tycoon, whom Ravenhill met while researching the play. He was 'very charming, very intelligent, yet with a worldview which is completely at odds with mine'.

Although Ravenhill's play does articulate a powerful sense of despair, you do long to hear something more conclusive, more compelling than his characteristically ironic tone. He disagrees: 'Audiences get resentful if they are hectored from the stage. Just as in life, people who argue and don't listen are boring and unbearable.' If there is no easy solution to a problem, he says, 'it's pointless offering an easy answer. I sympathize with Brecht, when in the epilogue to *The Good Person of Szechwan*, he says that he can't solve the problem and asks the audience what the answer is.' As director Max Stafford-Clark says, '*Some Explicit Polaroids* is a political play; it looks at the values people had twenty years ago and the absence of them now, and asks whether this is a loss or an improvement.' The answer, unsurprisingly, is both yes and no. But isn't this a cop-out? 'I don't think so,' says Ravenhill. 'One of the major shifts in audience attitudes is that now people don't expect someone to give them a neat answer after two hours in the theatre.' If anything, 'they feel rather insulted if you do. The thing is to more urgently and more cogently ask the right questions. I want to shake up the audience.'

However Brechtian, *Some Explicit Polaroids* is both fun to watch and proof that the obits for political theatre have been just a touch premature. For however incomplete the arguments, however unsympathetic the characters, the play is richly written and, more than Ravenhill's previous work, repays deeper study. Because he has cast his state-of-the-nation play in a defiantly nineties mode, it never preaches or takes sides in a simplistic way. Ravenhill offers food for thought rather than a ready-made meal.

While the play was on tour, Ravenhill was reported as having ruffled feathers by arguing that the original Angry Young Men – such as John Osborne, Arnold Wesker and John Arden – were 'straight boys' whose historic mission was to clear theatre of the 'feyness and falseness' of gay writers such as Noël Coward and Terence Rattigan. Although the heady days of 1956, when *Look Back in Anger* opened, are usually seen in terms of class, with gritty kitchen-sink realists driving out 'snobbish, dilettante and pampered' effeminates, what most commentators missed was the question of sexual orientation. This reinterpretation of the fifties was apt because *Some Explicit Polaroids* is a good illustration of playwright David Edgar's idea that 'without Osborne we certainly wouldn't have had Ravenhill'. In particular, there are passages in the play that hint at the anger that Ravenhill undoubtedly feels about the alienation of contemporary life and how this affects both twentysomethings and the older generation of radicals. The main problem, however, is that Ravenhill is so concerned not to bore his audience that he cuts short the political discussions and truncates any speech before it can rise to the level of a Jimmy Porter tirade. Alert as always to contemporary currents of feeling, one of Ravenhill's major strengths may turn out to be his biggest weakness: his unparalleled feeling for the Zeitgeist could one day make him seem old-fashioned.

Controversy has followed Ravenhill around like a hungry dog. After the storyline he wrote for third series of the BBC's cult soap opera, *This Life*, was dropped, and the series abandoned, there was wild media speculation that he'd killed off the main characters and introduced too many gay ones. All untrue. Then, in March 1998, Education Secretary David Blunkett denounced *Shopping and Fucking* as full of foul language and a waste of public money. Had he seen or read it? Apparently not. As Stafford-Clark commented, 'It is shameful that there are puritans and philistines in the Labour Party who are just as damaging as those in the Conservative Party.' On one occasion, when Ravenhill appeared on a panel with David Hare to discuss new writing (London New Play Festival, May 1998), some journalists wanted to turn a perfectly amicable occasion into a battle between the old generation and the new. On another occasion, Ravenhill was attacked for refusing an invitation to a Buckingham Palace reception.

Ravenhill does have a flair for publicity. His Rule Number One is 'Don't be boring'. In April 1997, at the Eighth Birmingham Theatre Conference, he appeared in an orange 'Girl Power' T-shirt. In one newspaper article, he spoke of sharing a house in Brixton with actress Emily Watson when both were unemployed, hanging around 'all day in baggy jumpers' and living on lentils while he started writing. In another article, he explored his childhood obsession with the BBC science-fiction series *Dr Who*. 'My characters in *Shopping and Fucking* make up an alternative family – just like *Dr Who*. Rather than being lost in time, they are lost in the city.' And 'just like in *Dr Who*, there are monsters in the *Shopping and Fucking* world. When my characters leave the flat it is never very long before something awful happens.' These troubled urbanites live in 'homes with microwaves but no kettle'.

Is Ravenhill a gay playwright? 'Not at all,' he says. 'For a long time, gay playwrights were expected to be witty, warm-hearted and feelgood', so he found it 'quite liberating' that he started writing 'at a point when audiences didn't expect a coming-out speech or AIDS-related plot'. *Shopping and Fucking* was one of the first plays where the sexual orientation of the characters was rarely mentioned in reviews. 'A couple of years earlier, it would have been perceived much more as a gay play, simply because it put gay sex onstage.' So while Jonathan Harvey's *Beautiful Thing* was seen in 1994 as part of a 'plague of pink plays', Ravenhill's work caused no such hysteria. But Ravenhill is 'not keen on being a "gay man"' because, he argues, the label has been appropriated by consumer culture. He has been more attracted to 'being queer, a sexual outlaw' than 'being gay, in the sense of assimilationist'. The 'agenda of much gay drama tries to prove that gay people are just like straight people, but with better soft furnishings', but 'the notion of queer is much more about being a radically different person'. If you compare *Beautiful Thing* with *Shopping and Fucking*, in Harvey's play 'gay relationships are as romantic as straight teens'. Puppy love? 'Yeah. But the sexual agenda of *Shopping and Fucking* is completely different, with the energy coming from the queer side of the divide.' If being queer is an assertion of difference, it can also be a form of radical chic, which is why Ravenhill prefers a jokey label such as 'post-gay'.

One of the first to recognize that the 'blank fictions' of American culture – with their emphasis on the extreme, the marginal and the violent – applied equally to today's Britain, Ravenhill has blended the bleakness of 'apocalypse culture' with more traditional humanistic concerns. Despite its mediation through irony, there is a lot of anger in his work, which is full of potent theatrical metaphors critical of mainstream culture, whether of commercial capitalism or of gender identity. The most lacerating images of his plays challenge standard platitudes about the market economy and sexuality; instead, they remind us of a much darker reality, peopled by the homeless, the addicted, the lost.

Ravenhill is not an angry young man, but a more paradoxical figure: his plays may explore contemporary life, using gadgets, pop culture icons and poststructuralist ideas, but his values are traditional. His motive is always moral, his politics leftist. Not for him the relativism of postmodern philosophy; he much prefers traditionally humanistic values. If his best work has a mixture of postmodern playfulness and traditional left-wing morality that is sharply critical of contemporary society, do his plays lack heart? 'Heart is in the eye of the beholder,' he says. 'Some people find my plays cold and don't really connect with them, but other people find them really compassionate and feel for the characters.' Aren't shock tactics incompatible with compassion? 'Newspapers like plays to be shocking, but I don't think people are easily shocked.' English audiences are more open-minded than the media give them credit for.

With their social observation, witty dialogue and touches of sentimentality, Ravenhill's plays have an unmistakable tone of voice, ironic, amused, slightly detached. But judged purely as a writer, Ravenhill is less impressive than many of his contemporaries. Compared to such painstaking stylists as Phyllis Nagy or Sarah Kane, he lacks finish and his plays rely on collaboration and workshopping: he is more a collective theatre-maker than a solitary writer. He is also much more than just a play-maker: acting as a publicist and advocate of new writing, he has also had an important role in championing younger writers such as Linda McLean, whose *Riddance* was staged by Paines Plough in 1999. More than most of his contemporaries, he has worked hard to establish a new range of sensibilities. And all the signs are that he will continue to grow. If his chosen territory, which lies uneasily between postmodern irony and engaged criticism, remains problematic, Ravenhill's commitment to exploring it puts him in the avant-garde of today's drama.

6 Boys together

He's one of my best mates isn't he? But he's a cunt.

(Potts in Jez Butterworth's *Mojo*)

The nineties was the decade of the boys. Wherever you looked, blokes were thrusting their way into the limelight: on the telly men behaved badly and in the cinema they did the full monty. They played fantasy football and acted dumb and dumber. On every sofa you could find two blokes, boasting about sex and setting fire to their farts, while the beer cans and fag ends piled up around them. Men got off their faces but rarely off their butts. They watched topless darts and went to war. You can see why some wags call masculinity the 'fun identity'. And for the *Loaded* Generation, there was not only beer, footie and totty – there was also thoughtful, middle-aged and middle-class angst in books such as Nick Hornby's *Fever Pitch* and *High Fidelity*. Everywhere, masculinities multiplied like suspect rashes; men were invited to see themselves as in crisis or to contact the wild man within by thumping drums in a wood at night. For andropausal men, therapy was recommended. Academic books about gender started to take men seriously; personal stories about fathers began to appear. New Men hung on, but New Lads pushed past them. Despite (some said because of) thirty years of feminism, even women were drawn into aping the blokes, becoming ladettes, babes or MAWs (Model, Actress or Whatever). 'Yoof TV' welcomed lads male and female, men's work declined and offices became 'feminized'; the family became a no-man's land of missing fathers.

While in the eighties it was plays by women that headed new writing, and often made cutting-edge experiments in form, by the nineties the fad was for boys' plays. When *The Times*'s Benedict Nightingale drew up his list of top ten writers in 1996, eight were men, most of whom had written testosterone-heavy work. A year later, the *Sunday Times* national student drama festival was dominated by lads' plays. As playwright Timberlake Wertenbaker says, the advent of boys' plays was partly a reaction – by both media and theatre managements – to the women's plays of the eighties: 'Suddenly, they were hungry for a different kind of play: male violence and homo-erotica.' But although boys' plays were fashionable, they weren't new: think of David Mamet's *Glengarry Glen Ross*. Still, they wouldn't have had such a impact if they didn't reflect changes in society. As Ian Rickson, Stephen Daldry's successor at the Court, says: 'One of the most important issues of the late twentieth century has been the crisis in masculinity – in the workplace and the family – and that's why there's been a lot of boys' plays.'

By the middle of the decade, boys' plays were everywhere and dealt with every kind of male discomfort. In the West End, the huge success of Yasmina Reza's *Art* (Wyndham's, 1996), a play about male friendship under strain, testifies to the subject's popularity. It also shows, not for the first time, that women could write about men as well as men themselves. Even laddish writers benefited from female help. As Jonathan Lewis, whose *Our Boys* (Cockpit, 1993; Derby Playhouse, 1995) took apart notions of maleness in a military hospital, says: 'Miranda Foster helped me finish the play – she rewrote it with me, editing out the superfluous funny lines, shaping it, pushing the action forward, rounding out the characters.'

Since war games are classic male territory, several plays marched to a military theme. In *Killers* (Royal Court, 1992), Adam Pernak contrasted legal and illegal murder by comparing two brothers, one a war hero, the other a psychopath. Sometimes such stage dramas turned into real-life crises. Jeremy Weller's Grassmarket Project production of *Soldiers* (1998) collapsed when one performer – a Bosnian militiaman – fled after he was recognized onstage and accused of war crimes. Elsewhere, theatre continued its tradition of questioning the costs of military life. Who can forget the flag-draped coffin in *Trainspotting*?

Male violence was also typified by the gangster play. Bad boys enjoyed aping gangsters in work such as Jez Butterworth's *Mojo* and Louis Mellis and David Scinto's *Gangster No 1* (Almeida, 1995). Even older writers, such as Mick Mahoney, the so-called 'hooligan playwright', followed suit with the politically incorrect *Swaggers* (Old Red Lion, 1996). With its bragging youths, plays such as Parv Bancil's *Crazyhorse* (Paines Plough, 1997), opened up a world of petty crime, while Nick Grosso's *Real Classy Affair* (Royal Court, 1998) attracted large young audiences to the Court, proving that gangsters and crims were hip again.

Of course, sport was a field where men could bond at the same time as competing with each other. Football became fashionable once more and soccer manager Bill Shankley's quip, 'Football is not a matter of life and death – it's more important than that', was quoted again and again. Some plays, such as Paul Hodson's adaptation of Nick Hornby's *Fever Pitch* (1994) or David Farr's *Elton John's Glasses* (Palace, Watford, 1997), were relatively harmless accounts of men at play. Much more disturbing was Hodson's adaptation of John King's cult book, *The Football Factory* (Gardner Arts Centre, Brighton, 1998), which confronted audiences with the image of the ultra-vicious hooligan – as subtle as a cosh. Here the solution to impotence was to run with the tribe and 'beat the shit' out of everyone else. But, claimed the *Guardian*, the play attracted audiences made up of 'likely lads' with only the 'odd middle-class mincer'. Equally typical were plays about indoor games, especially those set around card tables – as exemplified by Patrick Marber's *Dealer's Choice* (National, 1995) or William Gaminara's *According to Hoyle* (Hampstead, 1995), which artistic director Jenny Topper calls 'the feminine version of men alone at the gambler's table'. Even the classic men's plays of the past were viewed differently. After Mark Ravenhill saw the Court's 1996 revival of David Storey's *The Changing Room*, set during a rugby match, he suggested with typical irony that, while audiences went to see the first 1971 production because it spoke to them about working-class life, now 'we went to check out the dicks'.

Irish writers also contributed their share of boys' plays. Mark O'Rowe's award-winning *Howie the Rookie* (Bush, 1999) was a flamboyantly written tale of a wild feud, with a provocative stress on aggression and changing loyalties that revealed the shifting sands on which male friendship is built; Jimmy Murphy's *Brothers of the Brush* (Soho Theatre Company, 1993) was both about work and male friendship; Daragh Carville's *Language Roulette* (Tinderbox, 1996), about a reunion of old friends, had a violent climax which centred on sexual betrayal; and Alex Johnston's *Deep Space* (Bedrock, 1998) featured a pair of male students, one of whom used rape to prove his masculinity. Even Gary Mitchell's *Trust* (Royal Court, 1999) was less concerned with the wider politics of the hardline Loyalist community in which it was set than with the family politics of a local fixer who is unable to make a man out of his teenage son.

Often, male competitiveness was shown in excruciating detail. For example, in Mark O'Rowe's *From Both Hips* (Fishamble, 1997), an innocent man, Paul, has been shot by mistake by Willy, a policeman. When they meet again, Paul boasts that, despite being shot, he didn't cry. 'I took what happened like a man. I didn't lose control of my bladder like a woman.' Willy, on the other hand, was so shocked by what he'd done that he fell on his knees, 'whingeing like a three-year-old, going wee-wee like a baby'. His humiliation can only be expunged by violence.

From Mamet's harassed professor in *Oleanna* to Roy Williams's strutting teenagers in *Lift Off* (Royal Court, 1999), the anxieties of men were rarely hidden from view. The same situations – loyalty, betrayal and self-destruction – were played out time and again. Not all boy's plays were equally confrontational, but most focused on the questioning of masculinity. Even so, there is a danger in being too reductive. If *Trainspotting* and *Shopping and Fucking* are seen as, according to playwright David Edgar, examples of the 'girl-in-a-boys'-gang play', this is a polemical oversimplification that reduces interpretation to one theme. If both plays feature a single woman who holds a male milieu together, which says much about our notion of men's capabilities, they also treat wider issues such as addiction and consumerism.

When nineties plays explored the problems of blokedom, they usually did so in a highly explicit way. The male urge to self-destruction was often represented by extreme images, such as eye-gouging or anal rape. Murder was common, abuse frequent. While bad language marked off the new confrontational sensibility from the milder offerings of mainstream theatre, it was the pain of the emotions explored that made watching them a troubling experience. As Rod Dungate wrote in the programme for his rent-boy drama, *Playing by the Rules* (Birmingham Rep, 1992): 'If we watch documentaries or read reports in the newspapers it is easy for us to cut ourselves off from the truth.' Much harder to do so while watching a live performance. In nineties drama, boys will always be boys: when they get together, they usually end up tearing each other apart.

Naomi Wallace's *The War Boys*

One of the best boys' plays of the decade was written by a woman. Naomi Wallace's debut, *The War Boys*, was a seventy-five-minute one-act play directed by Kate Valentine and put on at the Finborough theatre in February 1993. Praised as an 'unflinching study of racism and sexism', it at first caused controversy not because of its subject matter but because of its author's gender. Most reviewers were surprised that a woman could describe the male psyche in such convincing detail. It won her, in the words of *Time Out* magazine, 'exceptional acclaim for the daring way she stormed traditional male preserves by writing about a wholly male experience'. People were, says Wallace, 'surprised not just by the fact that a woman could stand on her legs, and write too, but by the complexity of the writing'.

The controversy over a woman writing a man's play shows the residue of literalism in British culture. After all, why shouldn't women write convincingly about men? As *The Times* noted, the 'sneer commonly levelled against plays by women' is that while 'men can write about women tremendously well, women write best about their own sex'. Wallace says, 'Women did not write about war because for a long time we were not supposed to write about male experience.' For her, the idea that 'universal' experience has to be 'white, male and straight' is absurd, and she points out that all writing involves creating something outside your own experience: 'Some of the greatest novels on war were by men who hadn't even been to war.'

Born in Kentucky in 1960, Wallace's nationality is a reminder that the Anglo-American connection has had a crucial input into British theatre. Being raised in the second poorest state in the USA was also significant: 'I'm interested in war and violence because, in Kentucky, a state of violence and war is inflicted daily on the majority of people through poverty and the class system,' she says. Wallace is one of six children, her parents being a former *Time–Life* journalist father and a left-wing Dutch mother. 'My mother's family were active against fascism during the last European war, running safe houses for Jews, and she wanted her children to grow up with an indignation against injustice.'

Although Wallace has received 'rough rides' from critics in Britain, she appreciates the fact that 'there's an open tradition of political theatre in Britain'. She started out as a poet but became interested in theatre because 'writing poetry is such a private enterprise and I felt that I wanted to collaborate – theatre is a more public forum'. Although Wallace has strong leftwing views, she has never seen her work 'as something to give people answers. To disturb, yes, that's what I'd like my work to do, but to disturb people in a way that they would come back for more.' Questioning is 'what really moves us forward'.

The War Boys is about the white vigilantes who patrol the Tex–Mex border and hunt down the 'wetbacks' or 'beaners' crossing it illegally. As a note in the playtext points out, it is based on the Light Up the Border Brigade, composed mostly of young men, who 'work as a paramilitary force' in an area that has become 'a militarized zone'. Where did Wallace's subject come from? 'I read a small article about the situation in *The Nation*,' she says, 'and I wanted to show a group of people who were racist, but without dehumanizing them.' She has 'always been interested in how mainstream culture affects us in very intimate ways. We underestimate how much culture influences how we see ourselves and how we see others.' Culture's representation of both men and women 'deforms or perverts our sexuality. Men must behave in one way – straight and macho – and women must behave in another.' Coming to terms with 'an exploitative culture takes some time. Some damage has already been done to all of us who grow up in a capitalist, sexist and racist culture. I wanted to show that.' And specifically, 'I wanted to show what happens when one of the vigilante gang is not white.'

One important influence on Wallace's theatrical imagination has been playwright Tony Kushner, who taught her at Iowa University. Another has been Edward Bond. She says,

> I was rereading his essay, 'On Violence', and what I really appreci-
> ate about it is how he sees culture as a very active and brutalizing
> force. We tend to see violence only in terms of war and crime.
> The daily violence that's inflicted on the majority of people is
> almost invisible.

At the same time, Wallace was also reading Caryl Churchill and Bertolt Brecht.

> I don't like violence onstage that's divorced from history or from
> society. Purely sensational violence doesn't interest me because
> it's not complex – to show violence in a void is both sentimental
> and conservative. I'm interested in questions about how individu-
> als are made violent.

The War Boys opens with David, Greg and George, all in their early twen-ties, scanning the border. Their laddish banter immediately reveals their attitudes and their backgrounds: David is college-educated, Greg is half-Mexican working class, and George a country 'home-boy'. In critic Irving Wardle's words, David 'is a young lawyer who exercises a cynically sadis-tic hold over his working-class cronies'. To pass the time, they play a game where each puts on a one-man show, telling a story about their lives and how they ended up watching the border: Greg recalls how his father for-bade him to marry Evalina, a Mexican-American girl he'd got pregnant; David tells how he was bullied to stick radishes in his sister's vagina to prove he wasn't a 'pussy'; and George remembers a hunting trip during which he upset his dad by scaring away a buck – and then grew a camel's hump. The radishes and the camel are surreal touches to stories that show the various ways in which masculinity can be constructed – and the way men carry a legacy of shame. But it is uncertain whether these tales are true or just an act: Wallace uses them to challenge the tradition of employing monologues as revelations of a character's inner life. In the end, the men's rivalries get out of hand and Greg snaps, unable to reconcile the 'Mejican' and 'WASP' halves of his character. He takes David's gun, threatens the others, and then crosses into Mexico. The punch line is that the gun has MADE IN THE USA stamped on it, so Greg gives it back in disgust.

Near its start, the play is deliberately provocative in its attack on one of the icons of American society: the Pledge of Allegiance. David issues Greg with a challenge: 'I would like to bet you five dollars you can't, excuse my coarseness, jerk off while I'm saying the Pledge of Allegiance.' Greg loses, but, at the end of the play, he get his own back as he forces David to say the pledge. A more disturbing aspect of the men's macho banter is their casual reference to the rape of female captives before they're handed over for a ten-dollar bounty. But the play's most white-knuckle moment is when Greg wrestles David to the ground and threatens to bring his boot down on the other's abdomen. What gives this a double impact is that Greg has just been telling a story about how his patriarchal father stamped on Evalina's abdomen to abort Greg's child. So the gesture is both a replay of a horrific event and an expression of Greg and David's rivalry. It is also a theatrical shock because the first time that Greg tells the story he doesn't mention the attack. 'The incident shows how acts of violence are passed on from father to son,' says Wallace.

In *The War Boys*, Wallace indicates how male identity is a construct. The reason for this is political: 'Change is only possible if something is constructed in the first place.' In the play, 'culture represses sexuality – every time David tries to kiss his first girlfriend he hears the jingles of American consumer culture'. Consumerism is a metaphorical substitute for desire, and the result of this repression of human feeling is violence. George and Greg 'strike out against others because they lack power. All of them act in a racist manner because it makes them feel good, feel strong, if only for a moment.' They feel they're 'on the right side – in this way, basic human needs are perverted by culture.'

Critical reactions to *The War Boys* acknowledged its politics. As the *Guardian*'s Claire Armitstead said, 'In language, rhythm and imagination, Naomi Wallace is trespassing on traditional male preserves, where women exist only as anecdotes', but she also explores 'the rocky psychological terrain of US cultural politics. Sex and race are revealed as cornerstones of the same ugly colonial urge.' The men fall 'into a frenzy of self-loathing from which only the bi-cultural Greg can escape'. The *Evening Standard*'s Michael Arditti found the play 'redolent of the locker room': while 'the dialogue oozes testosterone', the plot suggests that racism is 'rooted in male insecurities'. In *The War Boys*, male insecurity and self-doubt are projected onto the 'beaners', while the men's emotional inertia is expressed by the repetitiveness of their banter. What works theatrically is that the monologues invite sympathy and complicity at the same time as showing us the disturbing effects of the dysfunctional family on rich and poor alike. 'I'm interested in making a link between the dysfunctional family and the dysfunctional society,' says Wallace. 'There's this idea that if the family goes wrong, it sends messed-up people into society and then they mess up society. I think it's the other way round.'

To British audiences, *The War Boys* seemed to be a metaphor of America as a macho culture and evil imperium, a country paranoid about defending its borders from a demonized other, yet at the same time corrupt enough to profit from the trade in labour. The racial mix is fraught with contradictions and conflicts. But although it is set in a particular geographical and social situation, the play also has a general lesson. By taking an abstract theoretical idea – that maleness and sexuality are a social construct – and dramatizing it through the Brechtian device of storytelling, Wallace both gives the theory an individual form and shows how contradictions arise in real life. In *The War Boys*, gender identity is literally performed as if it were a role. Watching the play, you feel as though you can see the boys' personalities being formed before your eyes. In their surreal fantasies, Wallace uses an anti-naturalistic device which, however, never loses contact with the emotional subtext. And, as the Bush theatre's Dominic Dromgoole says: 'Wallace presents male violence and aggression without proselytizing about it.' With imaginative sympathy, she paints a clear picture of male emotional neediness and pain. The boys are old enough for war, but they still need a lot of healing.

In her subsequent plays, Wallace experimented with form, deepened her account of character and elaborated her vision of history. *In the Heart of America* (Bush, 1994) mixed tenderness with anger in its attack on the xenophobia engendered by the Gulf War. It broke taboos by creating a dramatic space for a Palestinian-American character and by making links between war and eroticism. Like Trevor Griffiths's underrated *The Gulf Between Us* (West Yorkshire Playhouse, 1992), Wallace's play was not an antiwar tract but an imaginative revisioning of what war means and how the human body suffers it. Her *One Flea Spare* (Bush, 1995) was set in London during the Great Plague of 1665 and looked at an elderly woman's sexuality. Even more theatrically ambitious, *Slaughter City* (Royal Shakespeare Company, 1996) examined labour history from the nineteenth century to the present. The set, hung with the dead meat of an abattoir, was blatantly symbolic, the writing marvellously expansive and humane. In March 1997, her adaptation of William Wharton's *Birdy* opened in the West End. It addressed the theme of male bonding and male fears with insight and humour, but was grounded by some clumsy staging. Despite such setbacks, Wallace's best work is never humourless or preachy, but combines moments of resonant poetry with emotional truth, and political engagement with a highly contemporary sensibility.

Jez Butterworth's *Mojo*

While Wallace drew political lessons from her account of boys trying to become men, other writers in the nineties celebrated the sheer excitement of being a lad. One of the results of the fashion for boy's plays was that some writers got chances they'd never have dreamed of a decade before. Among the first to benefit was Jez Butterworth, a twenty-six-year-old Cambridge graduate whose first play, *Mojo*, was produced not in a studio theatre but on the main stage of the Royal Court. A calculated risk by artistic director Stephen Daldry, it was hyped as the first time since *Look Back in Anger* in 1956 that a first play had jumped straight onto the main stage. Hailed at its premiere in July 1995 as the 'most dazzling' debut in years, *Mojo* went on to win numerous prizes, including an Olivier Award for Best New Comedy and the George Devine and *Evening Standard* awards for most promising new playwright. Versions of the play were produced as far afield as New York, Chicago, Johannesburg and Sydney, its popularity making it one of the most significant plays of the decade. In 1996, it was revived in the West End, and a film version was released two years later. Like other gangster plays, it dips in and out of violence, but, more significantly, its theme is men.

Mojo begins with thundering drums, pounding bass and screaming guitar chords. Loud. Silver Johnny, a seventeen-year-old rock 'n' roll protégé, hip-swivels across the stage. Next moment, he has gone and we're upstairs at Ezra's Atlantic club in Soho. It is July 1958, and the place is run by a gang of petty villains – Sweets, Potts, Skinny and Baby – who spend their time blitzed on amphetamines. While they bicker and lark about, a sinister gangster, Sam Ross, kills their boss, Ezra, and steals their hottest property, Silver Johnny. Terrified, the gang, now led by Mickey (Ezra's number two), barricade themselves in the club, and prepare for an attack. Although he is Ezra's son and heir, Baby realizes that Mickey is now in charge and suggests they run the club together. Mickey has other ideas, and throws the young man out. But when the lights go up for the final scene, everything has changed. Baby's back: he has killed Sam Ross and retrieved Silver Johnny. Now he unmasks Mickey as the man who betrayed Ezra to Ross. Panic breaks out, but when Skinny sides with Mickey, Baby shoots him and then beats up Mickey. From being a layabout, Baby has grown into a figure of psychotic grandeur. As dawn breaks, an uneasy calm returns.

The simple plot is spun out with a barrage of dazzling dialogue, which owes as much to casual obscenity as to pill-popping jokes, a typical refrain being: 'My piss is black'/ 'It's the white ones. Don't eat no more of the white ones.' *Mojo* is full of instantly memorable phrases. Discussing Silver Johnny's value as a star performer, Sweets says that a woman told him that 'when Silver Johnny sings my pussyhair stands up'; remembering what happened to his father, Baby says, 'There's nothing like someone cutting your dad in two for clearing the mind.' What makes Butterworth's writing exciting is its mix of quick-fire humour and baroque elaboration. Typically, he first sets up a situation in plain language, then repeats it using a colourful metaphor. For example, Silver Johnny is first described as a marketable commodity because he makes girls 'shit when he sings', and next because he 'makes polite young ladies come their cocoa in public'. Another device is the constant use of verbal tags (such as 'fish are jumping') and visual puns (when Sweets asks Baby if he can ask him a question, Baby points a gun at him and says: 'Fire away'). The virtuosity of Butterworth's language games is reminiscent of Mamet and Pinter, of Stoppard's *Rosencrantz and Guildenstern Are Dead* and Tarantino's *Reservoir Dogs*, of Absurd drama as well as film noir. Here, the incessant talk of these dim-witted, speed-soaked Kray wannabes is a way of fending off fear.

As well as using heightened language, *Mojo* employs visual images that are peculiarly vivid. Not only has Ezra been chopped in half, but his body has been dumped in two dustbins, which are dragged onstage in a grim parody of Beckett. At one point, Baby comes in, holding five toffee apples, his childish glee juxtaposed with the fact that he is about to be told that his father is dead; at another point, a big box is delivered to the club, sparking off a panic: is Johnny's head inside? No, all it contains is his suit. Other visual gags include the gang's newly acquired Derringer pistol, which turns out to be a tiny revolver ('It's a sign. It says: "We are the men with the small gun"'), a sharp contrast with Baby's vicious cut-lass. Much of the play's design – glitzy jackets, noir shadows and sequins – seems to echo Philip Ridley's work.

The first production of *Mojo* was instantly appealing, with the Court's stage giving off clouds of dust shot through with flashing lights. The image on the playtext's cover – Silver Johnny sporting a very nasty black eye – summed up the play's punch. From the first thunder of music, the motormouth, high-octane dialogue ripped and roared, leav-ing the audience to piece together the plot – a simple double-cross story – from the frenetic chatter of second-rate crims. Baby, a cool incarna-tion of evil from Tom Hollander, whose mockery was as light as it was ominous, contrasted with the more good-natured craziness of Andy Serkis as Potts and Matt Bardock as Sweets. But by the end of the evening, full of death 'n' drugs 'n' rock 'n' roll, the effect was more drain-ing than exhilarating.

Because it began on such a rapid high, *Mojo*'s energy had nowhere to go and finally became wearisome. However enjoyable, the play's crack-ling one-liners and visual gags barely concealed its sadistic side: hung up by the ankles in the last scene, Silver Johnny looked less like a star than a piece of meat. The casual brutality of the climax, which was played for laughs, was simply depressing. Shot in the head by the tiny pistol, Skinny complains that there is blood on his new trousers and that his teeth 'have gone wiggly'. Asking again and again, 'What if I die?', he finally collapses and dies. 'The audience is helpless with laughter,' wrote *Theatre Record*'s Ian Herbert. 'We have been dehumanised, and we're loving it.'

Other critics were sufficiently fired by *Mojo*'s verbal fireworks to write classic 'Good, but' reviews. Most hailed the brilliance of the writ-ing, the verbal panache, the influence of other playwrights and of pop culture, and even the homoerotic subtext – and almost everyone was excited by director Ian Rickson's staging of this gangland story. Also praised was the look of the play, its 'seedy glamour, with jukeboxes lean-ing against sweating black walls and cardboard boxes overflowing with records'. Good, but: most critics also felt that the flashiness of the dia-logue concealed a stalled plot and a lack of interest in fifties culture; they also pointed out the moral void at the heart of the work. Most ended their reviews by looking forward to Butterworth's follow-up.

Unusually for a new play, *Mojo* was rapidly revived by the Court in October 1996, with a new cast and a slightly rewritten text. But its inherent weaknesses were more evident than ever. The *Independent* pointed out that the play's 'slick and dubious elision of the Tarantino morality of the present day and the morality of the Fifties' lets the 'playwright off the hook of being faithful to either', while the *Sunday Times* saw its 'brutish humour' as 'one of the hallmarks of our cynically angry decade', and the *Telegraph* worried about the 'stylistic nihilism' of the Court's new writers. The *Financial Times* concluded that *Mojo* 'for all its brilliance, is a mere exercise in style'.

Born in 1969, Jeremy Butterworth grew up in St Albans. However spectacular his Royal Court debut, his talent didn't drop from the sky. He read English at Cambridge, where his contemporaries included writer David Farr, and he has been writing since the age of eighteen. For Edinburgh, he first co-wrote an adaptation of Katherine Whitehorn's *Cooking in a Bedsitter* and then, in 1993, *Huge*, about two failed comedy writers. *Mojo* – the title, he says, refers to the way the characters see Silver Johnny as a talisman, and 'a focus for all their sexual aggression and energy' – took a year to write, and was accepted by the Court within a week. Its writer in residence, David Lan, helped with rewrites. Like many young writers, Butterworth rejects any talk of theatrical influences, claiming to have seen very few plays. But, for all his disclaimers, he soon learnt that 'the real juice lies in the tension between what's onstage and what's off. It's what's left *off* which ignites what's *on*.' In *Mojo*, Ezra and Ross never appear onstage, but are a constant presence. What was Butterworth's inspiration while writing the play? 'I listened to a lot of Tom Waits.' More mundanely, he was helped by his elder brother, Tom. Together, they also wrote *Christmas*, a Channel Four film. Where did *Mojo*'s exuberantly artificial street slang come from? 'The idea was to create something that had a poetic edge. I did some research, but after a while I thought: I'm going to make it all up. It makes it seem less like archaeology.' For Butterworth, the 'heart of the story' is 'Mickey's guilt and Baby's pain'. Both states of mind are silent, solitary and male.

With its all-man cast, *Mojo* is clearly a study of blokedom. While much of the plot, which tiptoes around the power struggle between two gangsters, happens offstage, what you actually see is male relationships: Sweets and Potts, Baby and Skinny, Mickey and Skinny, and Baby and Mickey. Frantically pill-popping and muddle-jawing down the byways of youth subculture, Sweets and Potts are strays from a buddy movie.

Sadly, their maleness is all mouth and no trousers; when the going gets tough, they go to pieces.

With Baby and Skinny, we're back in the playground: Skinny has a crush on Baby and wears the same clothes as his hero. Baby resents this and torments Skinny, squeezing his 'nuts' or threatening to cut them off. He makes him kiss his 'pegs'. Before he gets shot, Skinny stands up to the bully: 'Shut your fucking mouth, Jew. You don't belong here. You've got no place here. None of us want you.' It's the language of schoolkids. Equally juvenile is Skinny's hero worship of his stepfather, Uncle Tommy, much to Sweets's and Potts's amusement. His regard for Mickey, another father figure, comes from the same place. And in a play about power, the final struggle between Ezra's right-hand man, Mickey, and his son, Baby, has shades of a Shakespearean history play. Mickey turns out to be a study in failed masculinity – never as cool and strong as he'd like to be. In gruesome Jacobean style, Baby becomes a symbol of maleness as psychopathology.

Starting off as a lazy couch potato – a Prince Hal with no Falstaff – Baby grows into his inheritance by becoming a vicious Renaissance avenger. He tells Mickey he has no feelings. Told of his dad's death, he is numb. Sweets explains why: 'There's dads and dads. You're thinking of a *dad*. Like in a book. Fucking figure of something.' But Baby's dad was different, a 'bloke' who 'waits for you [to] come home from school [and] stuffs his hands down your pants'. The key to Baby's character is a nineties cliché: once a victim of abuse, he has now become an abuser. In one of the play's longest speeches, Baby remembers his terror when Ezra took him for a drive in the country. He was nine and, noticing a 'bag of sharp knives' on the front seat, was convinced his father meant to kill him. This is emotional dynamite – in performance, you feel the fear coming off the stage. But Dad has other ideas. He kills a cow and cuts it up for sale. Baby remembers being 'covered in blood'. More an exercise in black humour than a psychological portrait, the story still underlines the play's main theme: boys will be bloody boys.

The trouble with *Mojo*'s scintillating language, blokeish atmosphere and modish hints of homoeroticism is that they tend to divert attention from its more serious theme, the father and son relationships. As Butterworth says, 'It's a story about men's fantasies and desires – sexual desires, desire to succeed, fatherly love.' But although the central relationship is that of a father and his son, with the son taking on his father's mantle, Ezra never appears onstage. This is dramatically effective, but it does mean that the audience only sees Baby's side of the relationship. In other words, it never sees the relationship but only its effects on Baby. Instead of Ezra, there is a parade of surrogate fathers led by Mickey, whose bossiness and maturity are finally revealed as empty, based on lies and betrayal. Similarly, Skinny's hero worship of Baby is a form of displaced father love from a boy whose real father has been replaced by an 'uncle' at home.

So *Mojo* starts as a gangster thriller and ends as a study of absent fathers. Its images of masculinity also shoulder a simple and powerful message: these boys have never grown up. And maybe never will. In common with many nineties films, the play also embodies one way of thinking about masculinity in crisis: the boys may be all fucked up but at least they're cool. Ian Rickson says that the play, 'with its femaleless world, has a critique of machismo culture': after all, aren't the men shown to be inadequate? It is 'a play about damage and healing in a father-led world'. But, surely, whenever Butterworth introduces deep emotions, he defuses their impact with cruel humour, encouraging audiences to laugh. 'But often laughter is to do with discomfort,' says Rickson. A safety valve? 'Yes.'

With its record-breaking swearword count and glaring anachronisms, *Mojo* is less about the fifties than about today. It is less *Absolute Beginners* than *Pulp Fiction*, less a critique of gangland involvement in the music biz than an example of idealized criminality, less an account of the corrosive effects of American consumer culture than a tale of male aggression. A good example of postmodern sensibility, *Mojo* assumes that its media-literate audience will pick up its cultural references, from the Coasters' 'Yakety Yak' to the Beckettian dustbins. More than most new writing, *Mojo* is self-consciously literary, a text in the theoretical sense of referring to other texts, songs and cultural symbols. With half the dialogue elaborate fantasy, the emotionally truthful exchanges tend to get drowned out. It is a very knowing tale about characters who are living in a movie world, detached from life, where style dominates substance and surface effects are more important than depth or compassion.

But *Mojo* also suggests that even as we laugh at stage violence, our liberal consciences are troubled by it. When a social problem is intractable, you can either take refuge in a nostalgic past or look for metaphors that help you understand the present. *Mojo* advocates a third way, turning the contemporary problem of fatherless men and violent crime into a fantasy world, tempting the audience to sit back and just enjoy the rock 'n' roll. But as the show goes on, its lack of heart and moral emptiness turns laughter brittle and makes you long for a life beyond playground machismo.

Simon Block's *Not a Game for Boys*

Whatever its deficiencies, *Mojo* sent a signal to theatres that rude boys and brat packs were fashionable. By August 1995, the *Financial Times*'s Sarah Hemming could write: 'Maybe it's something they are putting in the beer, but it seems men are self-destructing all over our stages.' After mentioning Patrick Marber's *Dealer's Choice*, with its all-male cast, and DV8 dance company's *Enter Achilles*, which satirized pub machismo, she went on to review one of the more sensitive of the new wave of plays about laddishness, *Not a Game for Boys*, Simon Block's Royal Court debut. This time, the game in question is not football but table tennis. And as usual with boys' plays, the match turns out to be a metaphor for life.

Set in what the playtext calls a 'cheesy, closed bar of a run-down table tennis club', *Not a Game for Boys* is about a cab-drivers' ping-pong team – Eric, Oscar and Tony – who play one evening a week. Tonight, they must win their games to stay in Division One. But while all three use the sport as an escape from their personal lives, middle-aged Oscar has doubts about its importance after witnessing fellow player Fat Derek collapse and die during a game, and young Tony is more concerned about his sex life than about the match. Only Eric, whose wife, Elaine, is nursing his senile and incontinent mother and whose grown-up kids are giving him grief, is desperate to avoid relegation. For him, the match is – in the words of the play's marketing – 'a matter of life and death'. At first, Tony is torn between playing with his mates and going home to talk to his lover, Lisa, who is threatening to leave him. Then it looks as if Oscar will deliberately lose his games in order to give up the sport. Eventually, Oscar changes his mind but Tony, afraid that he'll lose Lisa, walks out on the team. Eric's attempt to persuade him to stay ends in blows.

Not a Game for Boys offers a wide range of ideas about blokedom, from Eric's macho comment about the 'tit factor' when he is up against a female player (who wins) to Tony's abject description of Lisa: 'She's worth a hundred of me.' When Eric finally confronts Oscar about deliberately losing his games, he begins with the classic male phrase: 'I've known you longer than my own wife.' To which Oscar replies: 'Is this

167

some kind of advanced male-bonding, Eric?' But Eric remains fixated on the game: 'It's all I've got. You've no conception of the pressure I'm under at home.' 'Anxiety gives you a hard-on,' snarls Oscar. In an effort to persuade his mate to win the next game, Eric crosses one of the traditional male's great dividing lines: physical contact. He clutches Oscar's knee. Later, after declaring that he'd 'sooner fuck broken glass' than go home, Eric tells a story about driving a couple of lesbians home from a 'fertilization clinic': 'Big dyke turns to little dyke and says the only reason men lasted this long's 'cause women like something to laugh at.'

But loyalty is no laughing matter. When Lisa hangs up the phone on him, Tony is outraged: 'Shit, Ozzie, that's blackmail, isn't it? Once you give in to that kind of thing they've got you, haven't they?' Crucially, 'she's not interested in my team loyalty. *She's* my team.' When Oscar fails to cover for Tony's sexual escapades, the younger man is angry: 'Whatever happened to loyalty, Ozzie?' 'Boys together right or wrong?' mocks Oscar, 'that's fine when things are bubbling nicely', but he disapproves of Tony's promiscuity. 'Behave like a *man*,' he urges, 'and accept the consequence of your actions.' Later, Eric's insistence that loyalty is '*all* we've fucking got' and 'When all else fails there *is* loyalty between mates' is called into question when Oscar loses his games on purpose. Having witnessed Fat Derek's death, Oscar no longer sees the game as all-important.

When pushed, the men's attitudes to women are adversarial. After Tony tells Eric that he has 'been fucking this gorgeous fare in the back of my cab', Eric can't believe he wants to tell Lisa about it. 'I feel the *urge* to confess,' Tony says; 'honesty is the best policy.' 'Who the fuck told you that,' retorts Eric, 'a *woman*?' But manly as they'd like to be, these men are also desperate. At one point, Tony tells Oscar his philosophy of life, gleaned from men's magazines: 'We are men, so we behave like men, so forgive yourself or go fucking mad.' But when he says he wants to dump Lisa, Oscar brings him back to earth: 'Without Lisa you are *nothing*.' But Oscar is compromised because he lives alone and, symbolically enough, carries a gun that turns out not to be loaded.

Each man represents an unsuccessful way of life. Eric slaves all day in his cab to keep a family he has excluded himself from; Oscar is independent but lonely; Tony is a man-child who can't face commitment. While they don shorts to play their juvenile game, the women get on with the messy business of life. These men can't get away with traditional roles any more, but have still not been able to discover a new way of being grown-up. 'Is this masculinity in crisis?' asked *What's On*'s

Roger Foss. 'You end up with the familiar feeling that the women are left coping with the realities of living while the boys just play with their toys.' The point is that wives are no longer nice little women who keep quiet and look after their menfolk. Eric, Oscar and Tony are in a mess because their world has been challenged and they don't know how to evolve.

The first thing audiences noticed about the Court's production of *Not a Game for Boys* was the meticulously naturalistic set by Nettie Edwards, which turned the whole of the Theatre Upstairs space into a club bar. With its nylon carpet, curly beer mats, dusty sporting trophies, wall notices and Mortal Kombat video machine, the place looked and smelt authentic. Dressed in shorts and sports gear, the three men seemed more vulnerable than their cabbie personas would lead you to expect. Fiftysomething Eric's bullish language was in stark contrast with the sight of him playing a child's game.

While *Not a Game for Boys* can't resist using metaphors of games-manship – sexual infidelity is 'playing away' – Block also tackles subjects such as the onset of middle age, the futility of always having to compete and the results of emotional deprivation. He writes with a mix of sharp one-liners – 'It's a dog eat dogturd world' – and a joy in orotund formal-ity that draws on the Jewish cockney tradition: for example, 'moment of deceasement' is used instead of 'time of death'. Employing a single set-ting in real time, Block uses the device of the big match to solve one of the problems of writing for theatre, getting the characters on and off the stage. As each man goes to play his match, the other two stay and talk. A naturalistic writer who is equally at home with screenplays, although a plan to turn *Not a Game for Boys* into a series for Channel Four televi-sion came to nothing, Block exposes masculine inadequacies with humour and compassion.

The danger with a play that bounces jokes off every surface in sight is that the laughs can completely defuse the pain. In *Not a Game for Boys*, the balance between hilarity and discomfort works because even though the two women – Elaine and Lisa – never appear, they're always present. As the *Guardian*'s Lyn Gardner pointed out, the 'absent women' dominate the play. We only know about Elaine through hearing Eric's side of their phone calls; we only know Lisa through what Tony and Oscar say about her. In both cases, the disturbing emotional material, especially the descriptions of Eric's senile mother, is powerful because it is never shown.

Born in 1966, Block is a Londoner who first went to Southampton University to study Biochemistry, then changed to Psychology, and finally completed an MPhil in Criminology at Cambridge. His jobs have included:

> shovelling vast quantities of elephant droppings at London Zoo, interviewing George Best, selling double-glazing, taking bets for William Hill, teaching archery to small children, silver service waiting, bar-tending, running a life drawing class, bus driving for London transport and picking mangoes in the Middle East.

At Cambridge, he wrote a revue, and was then asked to write a sitcom series, *Every Silver Lining*, for BBC television in 1993. His ambition to write for theatre was realized when a friend, Paul Cahidi, needed a monologue for his end-of-year show at drama school in 1994. Block wrote *Last Director of the BBC* and it 'went down a storm', he says. 'This was my first experience of a hard-core audience: actors, agents, casting directors, and I thought, yes, I can do this.' Director Richard Georgeson asked him for a play and Block wrote *Not a Game for Boys*. It was developed at the National Studio and the Court picked it up from there.

What was Block's inspiration? Although he was influenced by Williams and Miller, Pinter and Mamet, as well as by Elvis Costello, Joseph Heller and Raymond Carver, the play was based on his experience of playing table tennis. His team mates would play 'five nights a week if they could; a lot were married. So I started to wonder: a) how they got away with it; and b) why did they want to play so much?' It was, he concluded, a combination of getting away from family pressure, a search for excitement and a desire for some kind of glory. In one team, there was a 'young man with a young family. He'd play table tennis, stay at the bar until it closed and then play snooker all night. Then to work. He'd do that two or three nights a week.' Despite being a soft sport, table tennis can be crucial to a man's sense of self: the way he plays is an expression of the way he is. It is 'a few minutes a week when he can just be himself, without any additional pressures, when he can put everything else behind them, let it all hang out'.

The drama of *Not a Game for Boys* is simple: Tony has to decide between two points of view. 'Should he stay with the boys, or go home and sort out the most important relationship in his life? He doesn't quite trust his own experience,' says Block. Although the play shows how machismo hides inadequacy, none of the characters is truly macho. Tony, for example, 'is having sex in the back of his cab, not because he's macho but because he can't face a commitment he can't admit he needs'.

Tony doesn't enjoy his sexual escapades because he knows he is risking his relationship with Lisa. There is 'no swagger behind what he's doing'.

As each man exits to play their offstage opponents, the remaining two show us a different aspect of male friendship. Eric and Oscar have been friends for thirty years; Oscar and Tony are mentor and pupil, while Eric and Tone often seem to be like father and son. 'Eric and Oscar have a genuine friendship,' says Block, 'based on an intimate knowledge of each other. Eric accepts that Oscar's a lonely old fart who loves large women and Oscar accepts that Eric bangs on and on about his life.' For Tony, 'Oscar's a kind of teacher – somebody to looks up to and respect. Part of the problem is that he respects him too much, which stops him looking to his own experience.' Tony tries too hard to emulate Oscar. 'Eric is the opposite extreme – a man in a messy married life.' Eric also tries 'to be the team captain not only in the game but in Tony's personal life as well'. He likes giving him 'the benefit of his experience, but all his advice is coloured by the fact that he simply wants Tony to play as well as he can'.

There is little in the play to suggest a political agenda, except for the discussion about men's magazines, which quoted and mocked their advice. 'At the time of writing,' says Block, 'male magazines were trying to sell more copies by pushing a particular line on how young men should behave: do what you like; other people are not your problem.' At the same time, 'women's magazines were "advising" women about what men were *really* thinking. So each sex was being "advised" on what the other wanted from relationships. Specious bollocks really.'

The account of men's magazines in the play suggests that powerful organizations can give permission to men to behave badly. Block shows that although men know the difference between right and wrong, they sometimes use the permission that lad culture gives them as an excuse to follow their worst instincts.

Block is aware of the perils of writing a boys' play. 'My play wasn't an attempt to be shocking – though some critics reacted as if it was and then attacked it for failing.' Perceptive reviews by Lyn Gardner and Sarah Hemming stressed the point that the relationship of the men with their women was what underpinned their lives and the world of the play. Although *Not a Game for Boys* is about male bonding, its emotional core is provided by its women. The characters' relationships with women are more important than their friendships with men. Oscar knows this, even if his own life is lonely; Eric knows it, but fights off the knowledge; and

Tony learns it during the course of the play. In the end, Block doesn't give an answer to Tony's problem about whether to stay single or to commit to Lisa. Although Tony runs out on the team, causing it to be relegated, we don't know whether Lisa is waiting at home or has already left him. For all its compassion, Block's play refuses to offer any consolations.

David Eldridge's *Serving It Up*

Block's comprehensive survey of masculinity in crisis revolves around betrayal, a theme that is also central to David Eldridge's *Serving It Up*. When he began writing the play, he thought, 'OK, these two fellas are best mates, what's the worst possible thing that could happen, that would break this friendship up?' His answer was: 'One of them shagging the other's mum.' That act of betrayal became 'the seed of the whole play'. Aged twenty-two when he made his debut, at the Bush in February 1996, Eldridge was hailed as a precocious talent, with the *Daily Mail's* Jack Tinker claiming he had 'all the verbal swagger, all the fine-tuned insight, all the confident theatricality of an established writer'.

Brought up in Romford, Essex, Eldridge worked on a shoe stall in the market while going to Brentwood, a nearby independent school. 'Growing up,' he says, 'I often felt I lived a double life.' When he was in the sixth form, his interest in theatre was kindled by his English and drama teachers and he remembers being moved by John Wood's King Lear. Eldridge studied English and Drama at Exeter university, where other students 'found it hard to believe that the bloke with the thick Essex accent was "public school"'. At first, he was 'gagging to be a director', but soon realized that 'there were things I wanted to say that I couldn't express by interpreting someone else's work'. He began to write and his first short play, *Cabbage for Tea, Tea, Tea*, was put on at Exeter.

At the end of his second year, 'while I was meant to be revising *The Faerie Queen*, I was amusing myself on my computer and started to write some dialogue,' says Eldridge. The exchanges between his characters, Nick and Sonny, 'were written at eleven o'clock at night to get me through the boredom of revising' and became the first scene of *Serving It Up*. Encouraged by Peter Thomson, his professor of drama, he completed the play and sent it to several London theatres in Autumn 1994. Soho Theatre Company invited him to a writers' workshop; Mark Ravenhill read his play at the Finborough and so did Dominic Dromgoole at the Bush. On his twenty-second birthday, the Bush accepted the play. At first, it had a clumsier title, *1995 (Let Them Eat Cake)*, but, on Dromgoole's advice, Eldridge changed it. The new version, *Serving It Up*, means 'drug dealing', but it also suggests 'serving it up to the girls', as well as alluding to the way Sonny's mother constantly serves cake to family and visitors.

Set in London's East End, *Serving It Up* starts with two lads, Sonny and his best mate Nick, sitting on a park bench, talking about which 'bird' is a good 'shag'. Sonny tells Nick that he should have put that 'bird down at the fish shop' in 'her place' by ejaculating 'all over her stomach'. Then he says: 'Got a right fit mum she has. Wouldn't mind fucking a mum, eh, Nicky-boy? Nice old piece of roughage to teach you a lesson or two.' It turns out that this is exactly what Nick is doing – with Sonny's mum, Val. Nor has he been the first. When Val and her husband Charlie quarrel, he accuses her of other affairs with Sonny's friends. Meanwhile, Sonny and Nick are also seen in relation to Wendy and Teresa, two hard-faced local girls. By the end of Act II, Sonny finds out about his mum's affair with Nick after a misunderstanding during which the truth slips out. Sonny then cuts Nick's face open with a knife.

The second play in the Bush's award-winning 'London Fragments' season, *Serving It Up* was directed by Jonathan Lloyd and showed a world that with its rather bleak staging, all concrete benches and rock-hard sofas, felt both unyielding and hopeless. Yet in the street-smart banter of its youths, it was also often hilarious. Both manly and boyish, Sonny and Nick are shown 'taking the piss', playing the fool and acting hard. At the same time, there was a real note of sadness about Nick's guilty secret, which undermines their friendship. Occasionally, the audience response was a touch cruel. In the published playtext, Eldridge says that 'for me this play is as much about disaffected middle age as youth and it always saddened me when audiences laughed at Charlie's fall at the end of Act I, and Val stuffing her face with cake at the end'. Sympathizing too closely with the boys can blind you to the other characters. 'But', he says, 'the laughter may have had more to do with embarrassment and nervousness than cruelty.'

Most of the critics were impressed by Eldridge's debut. The *Guardian* review began by noting that 'new writers are currently appearing at a faster rate in the British theatre than at any time since the post-Osborne fifties', and went on to say that Eldridge implies that 'fascists like Sonny' are created by 'a mixture of parental pampering and the England-first, look-after-number-one philosophy which has spread like a poison through society' and resulted in 'a new form of thuggery'. Also praised were the play's lifelike complexity and its 'portrait of female resistance to macho bombast'. On the other hand, *The Times* complained about its 'two hours of in-yer-face boorishness'.

Serving It Up, says Eldridge, was influenced by the usual suspects: 'sub-Pinter, post-Bond, Tarantino-generation'. But his real hero is Trevor Griffiths and he prefers Robert Holman to Tarantino. At university, he was inspired by Edward Bond's *Saved* and Arnold Wesker's trilogy, especially by Wesker's insistence that his characters were not caricatures and that his 'harsh' picture of East End life was not due to 'disgust' but to anger at the waste of life. Eldridge wanted to represent the 'siege mentality' of the white East End families left behind, because of either lack of money or ambition, when their neighbours migrated out of London, and also

> to show racism to be as ugly as it is. I can't forget one event: this fella, who'd done my brother a favour, came around. He was talking to my dad, and started going on and on about black people. It was really sickening – he said that blacks are animals, and if they want to live in this country we should give them a bag of nails and a couple of sheets of corrugated iron and they could build their own shanty towns.

The same comment appears in one of Sonny's speeches in Act II, Scene 2.

At university, Eldridge had been 'very angry that those living in East London's deprived council estates scarcely find their voices heard'. One of his intentions in the play was to argue against 'the Politically Correct aspects of student thought, which have no idea about the realities of life in the East End'. But the play is more than 'two fingers to this attitude: I was trying to say that, although we know Sonny's a cunt, in lots of respects he's still a human being – he's not an animal'. No right-on student 'would have any time for Sonny: he would have simply been dismissed as a racist thug'. Within a nineties boys' story lies a seventies state-of-the-nation play, although its politics are often expressed in casual asides, as in Sonny's ideas about the importance of money: 'If you got the spondooli anything's possible. Thirty quid and your train fare to King's Cross – you've got low-life with a dose. Thirty million and a yacht and Fergie will be sucking your cock.'

Nick and Sonny are best mates, but their friendship is based on deception. They are also moving apart in other ways. Nick wants to better himself and get a job, while Sonny is content to lie around, getting stoned, thieving and dealing. As in other boys' plays, there is also an element of sexual rivalry. Nick is more successful with girls such as Wendy and Teresa – and it is a misunderstanding over this that leads to the climactic revelation about him and Val. If Sonny's instinctive reaction to any situation is brutality, Nick is capable of moments of sensitivity and shame. Eldridge's portraits are unsentimental, but not simplistic. Nor does he reduce the young men's motivations to one factor, such as inarticulacy or poverty.

The characterization is also more subtle than it at first appears. 'Sonny does learn, albeit in small way,' Eldridge says. 'When Sonny brings flowers to say sorry to Wendy, part of the reason is that he's sorry for what's happened in the previous two scenes, when we've seen him quarrel with his best mate and Ryan, an old schoolfriend.' The contrast between the image we're given of Sonny as a young boy, with his dreams of playing cricket for Middlesex, and the reality of his life as a young man solicits sympathy. But is Sonny doomed to turn into his dad? 'For most of the play you do feel that, but when he attacks and cuts Nick, you don't really know where that's going to lead.' In a way, 'Sonny's brutal attack may perversely be an opportunity for him to change.'

When Sonny finds out about Nick and his mum, the play serves up some agonizing lines. One refers to the jumper Nick has bought for Val: 'Shit,' says Sonny, 'you still left the price tag on. Nine fucking ninety-nine – is that what she was worth?' Then: 'We're meant to be mates', followed by 'Shit, I would die for you, you cunt.' These cries of agony, and especially the fantasy of dying for a friend, are powerful assertions of male identity, and contrast with Nick and Sonny's earlier bravado about dying young.

Sonny's sexism is rooted in traditional attitudes. When he says that it is wrong to beat up women, you feel he really means it. 'He'd never hit a girl,' says Eldridge. Nick, by contrast, has a father who beats his wife, so coming around to Sonny's house is important because it represents a surrogate family. Part of his attraction to Val comes from the feeling of warmth and safety of a substitute family.

Serving It Up delivers a well-prepared climax so 'the audience always saw what was going to happen thirty seconds before it did,' says Eldridge. 'I always loved watching people recoil with hands covering their mouths as they realized one mate was going to tell the other mate he'd been shagging his mum.' Other audiences proved that you can't deny Sonny his humanity, even if his language was offensive. The Bush hosted a special matinee for Asian children from Hackney, and they recognized Sonny as a human being, with all his flaws, and not 'a hate figure'.

However unevenly written, *Serving It Up* offers a powerful picture of the self-destructive male. If Nick's fling with Val is more a sneaky piece of sexual opportunism than a premeditated betrayal of his friend, Sonny's vicious attack on him is a savage assertion of male power that takes the form of a will to destroy. This is both self-destructive – witness Sonny's fascination with an early death – and destructive of everything around him, from relationships to his mum's Royal Wedding mug. Instead of growing up, as his childhood friend Ryan does, Sonny merely intensifies his brutality. Commenting on his temper, Val says: 'It's like putting up with a bloody kid.' Yet despite the sheer randomness of his violence – he cuts a man's face at a bus stop because he won't give him a potato chip – there is an element of psychological panic in his behaviour that reveals his vulnerability. At the same time, Sonny is also a symbol of a social problem: bullet-headed, unemployed young men who are out of control. And while Nick is the play's glimmer of hope – he does try to get a job – Sonny remains a grim figure of testosterone-heavy masculinity.

Two of Eldridge's subsequent plays – *Summer Begins* (Donmar, 1997) and *Falling* (Hampstead, 1999) – have proved that he is a highly observant writer. But while he has cultivated compassion and humanity, the edginess of his early writing has become diluted, and his experiments in form – especially the device of having crucial scenes happen offstage – tend to distance the audience from the drama. Like other young writers of the nineties, Eldridge gets irritated when critics say he is indifferent to plot. 'An ABC plot is not necessarily the be-all and end-all of writing. I'm much more interested in character than in tub-thumping plots.' But despite its confidence, his latest work hasn't yet found a really satisfying match between emotional content and theatrical form.

With its frankness and sense of pace, however, *Serving It Up* is a roaring boys' story with a form that does successfully subvert audience expectations. While the plot seems to be driving towards a vicious climax, Sonny's attack on Nick is never shown. The last scene has two couples onstage – Wendy and Teresa discuss the attack, while Val and Charlie are barely able to talk. The young women call the boys 'monsters', then Wendy realizes: 'We're all monsters, Trese.' Charlie refuses Val's motherly offers of cake and she is left eating it herself, crying. Here the grievous bodily harm is less important than grievous emotional harm. As Michael Billington wrote, the final image of Val 'heedlessly feeding her face while all around disintegrates' was 'infinitely more disturbing than anything' in *Trainspotting*. There is more to a good boy's play than just testosterone.

Although words such as 'manliness' now seem hopelessly archaic, the boys' plays of the nineties remind us that men still aspire to be heroic, either as games players or gangsters. Whether they are American vigilantes or British criminals, table-tennis-playing cabbies or East End lads, they live for action, they need to bond, they boast of prowess, they jeer at weakness. However foul-mouthed or foul-tempered, these boys also gave the British stage a new sense of risk and excitement. With the advent of what the *Independent*'s David Benedict called 'testosterone theatre' – first plays written by young men, which hardly mentioned women – it sometimes seemed as if an antifeminist backlash had colonized theatre. But although lads' plays proliferated, the messages they sent were not always incompatible with feminism. Each play ended up with a balance sheet: men's strengths and weaknesses. Usually, men's vulnerability outweighed their power. Perhaps the most provocative aspect of boys' plays was not their tendency to flirt with homoeroticism, but their frank acknowledgement that men are needy.

What such diverse plays as *The War Boys*, *Mojo*, *Not a Game for Boys* and *Serving It Up* have in common are not only their ideas of loyalty and betrayal but also the picture they paint of the attraction of depravity for young men. With the power granted to them by the state, the boys in Wallace's play can behave towards women in a way that would be unthinkable in everyday life; left to themselves, Butterworth's gang wallow in drink, drugs and futile bragging; Block's Tony is sexually incontinent because he thinks that men's magazines have given him permission to misbehave; Eldridge's Sonny and Nick not only seek oblivion through excessive drinking and drug-taking, they also aspire to be sexual predators. In each case, depraved behaviour seems so much more attractive than mature ways of relating to men and women.

In the boys' plays of the nineties, most of which followed traditionally linear patterns of narrative, there were stacks of images of the wounded male, but what was missing was any real exploration of how a new masculinity – which might go beyond traditional macho posturing or 'new' self-conscious angst – could be created. Instead, the evidence of the plays seems to be that men not only can't grow up but don't even want to. As Philip Ridley said in 1990, 'Men never leave the playground.'

7 Sex wars

> I know who you are. I love your scar, I love everything about you
> that hurts.
>
> (Larry in Patrick Marber's *Closer*)

The nineties was the decade of peace processes, not least in the war of
the sexes. But if some of the truces seemed real, no arms were actually
decommissioned. If anything, the suspicions and tensions between
men and women seemed to have deepened. One best-selling self-help
book saw the gulf between them as so large that each seemed to come
from a different planet. At the same time, fashion emphasized bisexu-
ality and adverts showed androgynous youths. As divorce rates continued to rise, moralists and media pundits bemoaned the attrition of the
family. The famous couples of the nineties – from Charles and Diana
to Hugh Grant and Liz Hurley, and from Kenneth Branagh and Emma
Thompson to Paul and Sheryl Gascoigne – looked like emotional disaster areas. On television, soap operas flaunted their love-crossed
stars. For romance, the fantasy was four weddings for every funeral,
and it helped if you had a name such as Harry or Sally, or lived in Seat-
tle. Still, if all else failed, you could just be friends. Women could con-
sole themselves by complaining about male 'fuckwittage' and men
could always go back to their hobbies. Amid falling sperm counts and
'oestrogen storms', the advent of Viagra and the Birth Technologies
may have given people more control, but they did little to soothe troubled feelings. While thirty years of 'genderquake' seemed to have
changed relations between the sexes, there was a nagging feeling that
much remained the same. Although Girl Power, ladettes and postfem-
inism symbolized new roles for women, their relationships with men
were as problematic as ever.

You can see why the programme note to Murray Gold's *50 Revolutions* (Oxford Stage Company, 1999) says: 'No one knows exactly what
has happened to sex in the nineties'. While 'society's tolerance of sexual
behaviour, freedom, orientations and minorities has never been so high',
many people 'have simply accepted that sex has taken over the world, in
terms of imagery'. With 'the entirety of youth culture' advertising it, 'sex
is easy to have, which is not the same as saying that everyone is having it

easily'. Although Gold's play did not succeed in following up such insights, other plays did.

Instead of gently hedging around the theme of adultery in suburbia, the most provocative new plays saw sexuality as raw, aggressive and often very troubling. Sex acts onstage were usually explicit: masturbation, anal sex, rape or acts of fellatio and cunnilingus. Even when nothing was shown, there was no doubt about what was happening. For example, Julian Perkins's *Images of Tiffin* (Old Red Lion, 1993) opened with a very noisy act of offstage sex. Generally, guilt was less in evidence than outright aggression; sex and violence were intimately mixed. In Sarah Kane's *Blasted*, a middle-aged man abuses a naive young woman in a Leeds hotel. In Tracy Letts's *Killer Joe*, a middle-aged man abuses a naive young woman in a trailer park. Both put on in January 1995, the two plays used radically different forms, but both contained the same message. Another graphic example of this mix of sex and pain was the scene in Kevin Hood's *So Special* (Royal Exchange, Manchester, 1998) when Porsh and Sam bond by simultaneously piercing each other's nipples. Love hurts. In Irvine Welsh's *Headstate* (Boilerhouse, 1994) perverse feelings are glumly accepted: 'It's warped, it's twisted and it's perverted, but it's still there.' Occasionally, personal problems were equated with bigger scenarios: the metaphor of sex war in Richard Zajdlic's *Infidelities* (Tabard, 1990) discussed sexual betrayal in the context of two army couples whose men serve in Northern Ireland; in Wendy Hammond's *Jersey City* (London New Play Festival, 1993), a fifteen-year-old victim of child abuse finds much in common with a youth escaping the violence in El Salvador.

The sex act was often seen less as an exploration of liberating eroticism than of a desperate attempt to communicate. In Patrick Marber's *Closer*, for example, one character begs for a 'mercy fuck'. When, in Joe Penhall's *Pale Horse* (Royal Court, 1995), Charles and Lucy spend the night in a hotel, their views about what happened diverge significantly. He is in a 'jolly mood' until she says that what they did was 'just a fuck', 'a quick fuck to keep our spirits up': 'It doesn't mean anything.' In Simon Bennett's *Drummers* (Out of Joint, 1999), Ray's furious resentments culminate in his rape of his younger brother, Barry.

In many nineties plays, the key notion was that of psychological damage. In Mike Packer's foul-mouthed *Card Boys* (Bush, 1999), Plato and Kath conceive the idealistic idea of retiring from a life of prostitution to grow marijuana in the countryside and bring up Kath's baby, but she is so damaged that she can't stop working. Mark O'Rowe's *Howie the Rookie* (Bush, 1999) is shot through with a series of lusty encounters that are hilarious but also sad, desolate and unloving. So damaged are the characters in many nineties plays that you can see why Mark Ravenhill has suggested that it is heterosexuality that is in crisis rather than masculinity: 'The male and female parts of our psyches are pushing further and further apart and to bring them together onstage can only result in a huge conflict.'

As traditional definitions of sexuality were increasingly questioned, gender confusion and sexual ambiguity became typical nineties tropes. Who exactly is sleeping with whom in Mark Ravenhill's *Shopping and Fucking*? In his *Some Explicit Polaroids*, Helen says she has had a relationship with a woman 'for a few years', although 'there's been a few blokes as well'. In Samuel Adamson's debut, *Clocks and Whistles*, last in the Bush's 1996 'London Fragments' season, the ambiguous love triangle between Henry, Anne and bisexual Trevor reaches a cruel emotional climax that is partly defused by the play's subtle, ironic tone. Sex has little to do with love, but depends a lot on power.

Happy couples were often seen as being under siege. In *Chimps* (Hampstead, 1997), Simon Block shows what happens when a pair of salesmen exploit a young couple's conflicts in order to sell them a useless but expensive brick-treatment product. As every decision becomes a question of trust, the relationship between Mark the self-employed fantasist and Stevie the breadwinning realist starts to falter. It is the kind of play that has you shifting in your seat with anxiety. A similar scenario was played out in Joe Penhall's *Love and Understanding* (Bush, 1997), where Neal, a workaholic doctor, and his partner Rachel, an overworked nurse, are torn apart when the freewheeling Richie comes to stay. Ryan Craig's *Happy Savages* (Lyric, Hammersmith, 1998) – a witty study of two couples and their infidelities – sounded a equally grim note: 'Nothing changes. Everything just gets worse. And what's the point of that?'

Sexual conflict may have been relentless, but occasionally it was mitigated by conscience. In Conor McPherson's vampire story, *St Nicholas* (Bush, 1997), a theatre critic is obsessed by a young actress, talks his way into the house where she is staying, and, turned on by a porno mag he finds in the toilet, plans to rape her. But when he finds her asleep in bed, he changes his mind: 'Reason had crept into the room behind me and caressed my neck.'

While many plays in previous new waves had something urgent to say about the family, most in-yer-face plays rejected mums and dads, and ignored uncles, aunts, grandparents and siblings. Others abandoned normality and concentrated on dysfunctional and problematic relationships. Even soft-hearted plays – such as Michael Wynne's *The Knocky* (Royal Court, 1994) or Ayub Khan-Din's *East Is East* (Tamasha/Royal Court/Birmingham Rep, 1996) – had their cruel moments. In one, a Liverpudlian mother betrays her son to the police, in the other, a Pakistani father beats his Mancunian wife. In Helen Blakeman's *Caravan* (Bush, 1997), what starts off as a teen seduction, a light-hearted piece of sex play with ice cream, suddenly turns into a date rape, resulting in pregnancy. The stale marriage of Leo and Pauline Black in David Greig's *The Architect* (Traverse, 1996) peters out in a kind of exhausted confusion, while the love affairs of their children – Martin, who picks up Billy in a public lavatory, and Dorothy, who meets trucker Joe while hitchhiking – are emotional minefields. Occasionally, the tensions within the family break out in gobsmacking aggression, as when Martin accuses Dorothy, who is sunbathing, of showing too much leg: 'You don't think of your sister having a cunt, do you? Barbie-smooth, you imagine.' 'You've got a warped mind,' she replies.

Instead of showing families, many plays showed groups of ill-assorted people, often held together only by their problems. Originally titled *Damaged*, Simon Bent's *Goldhawk Road* (Bush, 1996) looked at people who, in director Paul Miller's words, are 'at odds with themselves, each other and the rest of the world'. Incestuous dysfunctionality is both staged and parodied in Bent's *Sugar Sugar* (Bush, 1998), in which Dennis says: 'So I want to kill my father and sleep with my mother? I'm angry with my dad for betraying me by sleeping with my mother? Yeah, right.' Even Conor McPherson's *This Lime Tree Bower* (Crypt Arts Centre, Dublin, 1995), a great yarn about a robbery, is spotted with teenage sexual fantasy, casual adult sex and rape. Guilt-ridden and surreal, arid and ridiculous, the effect is both wildly humorous and rather sad. In drama as in life, if all happy relationships seemed to be the same, each unhappy relationship was unhappy in its own particular way.

Nick Grosso's *Peaches* and *Sweetheart*

Nick Grosso's *Peaches* – which opened at the Royal Court in November 1994 – was immediately recognized as one of the most promising debuts of the decade. Here was a twenty-six-year-old whose 'really sparkling' play was praised as an 'evocation of the agonies of adolescence', and his writing admired for its 'delicious dialogue'. In the *Telegraph*, Charles Spencer said it was the 'kind of play' that 'made him glad to be middle-aged, married and *hors de combat* in the battle of the sexes'. In language as familiar as a pair of trainers, yet as hip as a trendy club, *Peaches* conjures up the urban lives and loves of Generation X.

Born in 1968, Grosso was brought up in St John's Wood and Kentish Town, London. His talent was spotted early. 'When I was at primary school,' he says, 'they wanted kids to go to Saturday workshops with famous writers, such as Ted Hughes, and I was picked. I used to hate it because I missed the football. My mum had to drag me by the ear.' Although, he says, 'English was always my best subject', by the time he went to Hampstead Comprehensive he had had enough of Saturday classes. Despite his precocity, Grosso claims he 'never really read books', and studied neither English literature nor drama.

Then, at twenty-one, Grosso 'discovered writing' and started working on stories. In 1993, he became a member of the Court's Young People's Theatre, joined the writers group led by playwright Andrew Alty, and had a monologue, *Mama Don't*, produced. 'I knew nothing about theatre,' he says. Such disclaimers sound like a smart pose, but Grosso points out that inexperience had practical advantages: 'It sets you free.' He 'soaked up' the writers group and then 'went off to Berlin and wrote *Peaches*. It took three weeks and I sent it to the Court.' He talked to Caryl Churchill after seeing her on a public platform at the National Theatre; she read his play and championed it. It 'was a question of being around at the right moment': Daldry was launching his first season of new writing.

When he wrote *Peaches*, Grosso gradually learnt that 'drama is only interesting if it has a subtext, but if you write something with a subtext in mind, it's no longer interesting. It has to be instinctive.' His characters are 'never really talking about what they seem to be talking about, which is what happens in real life'. *Peaches* follows Frank, who has just finished college, and watches him chat with blokes and 'peaches' (attractive girls). The Court's staging not only had a crack young cast deftly directed by James Macdonald, but also scenic backgrounds that showed filmed street scenes, countryside, and shots of motorway traffic for the episodes set in cars.

Reviews were favourable: the play 'simply says, with devastating honesty, that all most young guys ever think or talk about is women', and it was noted that 'New Man is banished' as 'a group of young lads saunters around the pubs of North West London, boosting their insecure egos, preserving their cool, and fantasising about women drooling over their bodies'. Most reviews mentioned the play's opening. Frank is at an end-of-term bash at a Leeds nightclub. Cherry tells him that she has 'got the biggest crush' on him. His reply is typically bemused: 'You're joking!' She is giggly, slightly drunk and says she has fancied him 'since the First Year'. She feels like a fool for telling him. 'Don't worry,' Frank says. 'It happens all the time.' That's Frank all over. When he leaves, Cherry tells her friends different versions of the encounter. That's Cherry all over. When, a couple of scenes later, Frank and Cherry are alone at her sister's place, Frank asks her where the bedroom is. 'Everyone thinks we're at it, we might as well do it,' he reasons. Cherry isn't impressed by this approach and turns him down. In the next scene, when Frank tells his mate what happened, he claims it was *he* who turned *her* down.

When Frank is alone with Cherry, says Grosso, 'he wants something closer, but there's a conflict between what he would rather do and what he feels he should do'. *Peaches* is about the thrill of the chase. But although he might have a 'quick shag' or a one-night stand, Frank will never be fulfilled. 'To feed his ego, he needs to know he could charm the pants off most women. Knowing he has this power is more important to him than any sex act.' The *Guardian*'s Michael Billington noted that, with women, Frank 'always seems to be putting on an act'; only with his mates 'does he seem totally relaxed'. Grosso adds: 'Perhaps he puts on an act with blokes as well; he never articulates his true feelings with anyone.' Is this an example of the crisis of masculinity? 'My male characters are at the age when they dream a lot – and some of them are loafers.' They love banter and bluster, speaking a language that uses 'shit' and 'you're joking' every few seconds. Some critics labelled this 'inarticulate', but, Grosso points out, 'There's a lot of smartness involved in appearing dumb.' Certainly, the subtext is about young people attempting to come to terms with what they really feel rather than what they think they ought to feel.

The women tend to be more sensitive, more feeling: when Pippa talks about her mum being lonely, she cries – and only then does Frank think he can talk to her properly. But when Frank tells Pippa his philosophy ('as far as I'm concerned, all women are up for it – it's as simple as that') she says that he talks 'more shit' than any of his mates. If Frank is a typical bloke, women know how to prick his confidence. In the last scene, Frank sums up his view of men and women: 'We're different shapes, I mean you musta noticed. Our minds are different, we talk about differ-

ent things – girls talk about castles in the sky, guys talk about sand castles – things that *exist*! Girls talk about books, guys talk about peaches
. . .!' The women, says Grosso, are 'more centred, less boastful – they're
feisty, sassy, quite street-smart, quite independent, strong-minded.'

As far as sex is concerned, says Grosso, '*Peaches* is about talking about
doing it rather than actually doing it.' All the relationships are casual, the
communication fractured, a society of slackers who can't tell exactly
what's going on. But if the youngsters of his first play were puzzled and
lost, those of his second were scarcely less troubled.

In *Sweetheart*, directed by Roxana Silbert and first put on at the
Court in February 1996, Grosso's vision of the Blank Generation has
widened: now most of the characters are in relationships, some have
'meeja' jobs and higher expectations. Instead of Frank, here comes
Charlie, who assumes all women are 'sweet' on him. In a series of smart
dialogues, Grosso shows how Charlie can be both attractive to women
and a turn-off. Like Frank, says Grosso, 'Charlie is a magpie. Whatever
piece of information he gets from one scene, he uses in the next.' Both
attach a lot of importance to being cool. 'Although women find both
Charlie and Frank attractive, Charlie is different – he struggles more,
society fails him more. He can't work things out.'

Charlie doesn't have a job, so people see him as a 'layabout'. And his
alienation from the mainstream is expressed by his habit of calling ordinary folk 'cunts'. Charlie doesn't want to be a 'cunt' – the worst fate is getting a job, just 'like all the other cunts'. With *Peaches*, says Grosso,

> There was only one 'cunt' in the text and, when it was said, there
> used to be a sharp intake of breath in the audience. But in *Sweet-
> heart* there were over fifty 'cunts'. One theatre on the national
> tour wrote a letter saying: 'We can't possibly put on a play which
> has more than fifty cunts in it.' They'd actually counted them. The
> regional press commented on what they saw as the excessive
> amount of strong language, making it into a controversy. But by
> the time I wrote *Real Classy Affair*, my third play, 'cunt' was no
> longer such a taboo. This reminds me of that Lenny Bruce sketch
> where he says 'nigger' so many times that it just loses its force.
> The minute you don't attach importance to a word it loses its
> power.

Sweetheart suggests that women are keen to have careers and that men
are helpless dreamers. 'The women are more grounded,' says Grosso,

'more rooted in reality: most of them work. Women are becoming much more employable than men.' And the generation whose younger sisters are into Girl Power can be as laddish as the blokes: for example, Emma sees Micky Bainbridge as 'a walking hard-on, a prick on legs. I swear he thought the whole world fancied him.' Such observations give the play its charm, but the sex war is fraught with non sequiturs. When Ruby says, 'You haven't got a very good vocabulary', Charlie replies, 'What's that?' And when he meets a new woman, his first question is: 'What shall we fight about?' because he thinks 'that's what men and women do'. Because communication is difficult, men and women skirmish, and the wounds take the form of embarrassment, misunderstanding, frustration.

To many reviewers, *Sweetheart*'s subtext was youth under pressure from the demands of adulthood; the play shows how the 'classless cama-raderie' of comprehensive schools changes when mates go their separate ways. Seen as 'an anatomy of emptiness', it also emphasized style and location. Grosso even specifies which records play in which scenes. As these flicked past, in the Court's pacy production, northwest London postcodes flashed up on the backdrop, underlining the sense of place.

For younger audiences, Grosso's plays were instantly familiar. They pulsed with youthful energy; they had attitude. Older spectators found his slacking boys and laddish girls more troubling. It is not just the casual bad language, nor the casual sex and casual drugs, but emptiness of spirit, gnawing insecurity and meaningless banalities. If, for these young hedonists, getting 'hammered' or 'off my nut' is more important than politics, it is also true, Grosso points out, 'that each character thinks they're left-wing, while also being non-political'. In fact, the politics of both plays can be summed up by the sense of disenchantment many of their characters feel. When, at the end of *Sweetheart*, Charlie's girlfriend – who works as a nurse – leaves him, he struggles to make sense of it, pointing out that nurses are more important but less valued that media folk: 'What good's a *fucking* newsreader . . .!? when you're dying of AIDS on your deathbed?'

Peaches and *Sweetheart* show the disaffection and disorientation of Thatcher's Children. Their relationships are fraught with insecurity and pain: half the time they don't know what they want or how to get it. Here the sex war is scary not because it is violent but because it is confusing – these hip youngsters only have good intentions and words, and the words often fail them. In both plays, there is a sex war but very little sex. Instead, there is a void that is filled not so much with damage as with hurt. Grosso's most typical characters talk and talk and talk, but the more confident they seem, the deeper their insecurities.

Grosso's dialogues are always sharply written, funny and acutely observed. His emphasis on character and subtext means that there is always a lot going on psychologically. But the most provocative aspect of his plays is their experiment with form. 'My tutor always claimed that nothing happens in my writing,' he says. 'There's no drama, just dialogue.' But just because 'nothing's happening on the plot level, doesn't mean that nothing's happening on the psychological and subtextual level'. The idea of a three-act drama with a climax strikes him as old-fashioned and uninteresting. Imagine 'a play about a couple of people standing at a bus stop: they take the same bus and every journey is the same, the same stops and the same people getting on and off.' Other writers 'would spice up this story by throwing in some bullshit, like a terrorist hijack. I prefer simply to write about an everyday journey. That alone is sufficiently fascinating to me.' It also 'amuses me that in the nineties people still expect revelations and explanations to be criteria for good drama. Personally, I'm not into explanations and revelations.'

If being confronted with such a deliberate anti-dramatic form can feel both frustrating and irritating, Grosso is unrepentant: 'It's quite simple: if you want a plot, don't come to my plays.' However pugnacious his attitude to form, not all audiences have a problem with it. During *Real Classy Affair*, a hit for the Court in October 1998, the *Independent* printed a vox pop of audience reactions: 'One man said that although he could guess how the play would end, the plot wasn't what mattered: "It was more about peeping into people's small lives."'

But the main problem with Grosso's determined indeterminacy is that it implies a scepticism about change. In the absence of a plot that delivers a punchy conclusion, Grosso's plays tend to wind down rather than end. The main difference between the first and second editions of *Sweetheart* is that the revised version omits the whole of the last scene without any loss of meaning. What such quiet endings, such undramatic dramas convey is a note of resignation, a lack of any hope of change. Grosso defends this on the grounds of psychological realism: 'I'm writing about people who are trapped. Some people want Charlie to change, they want him to see the light and become a well-adjusted human being, but that's just not going to happen.' However frustrating the absence of closure, Grosso's first two plays are minor comic masterpieces that perfectly capture a nineties sensibility.

Patrick Marber's *Closer*

While feelings of hurt in Grosso's work are a matter of subtext, other writers articulated a much more overt sense of sexual conflict. Patrick Marber's *Closer*, arguably the decade's key play about relationships, and certainly one of its most successful, opened at the National Theatre's intimate 300-seat Cottesloe theatre in May 1997, transferred first to the larger Lyttelton stage and then to the Lyric, Shaftesbury Avenue, where it ran for eight months. Versions were staged in New York, and in thirty countries from Australia to Argentina, Iceland to Israel. With rave reviews, *Closer* attracted both media attention and extreme audience reactions: some people broke down, sobbed openly, ran for the exit; others cuddled during the interval and one couple allegedly had sex in a theatre box.

The play starts in a hospital, where journalist Dan has brought Alice, a streetwise waif and sometime stripper, after she has been knocked down by a cab. They fall in love. Eighteen months later, Dan has written a novel based on Alice's life and is having his photograph taken by Anna. He falls for her, but she rejects him. Just as, for his book, he once imagined what it would be like to be Alice, Dan now pretends to be Anna on the Internet. In cyberspace, 'she' seduces Larry, a doctor, and arranges to meet him. When Larry meets the real Anna, he makes a fool of himself. But they get over the misunderstanding, fall in love and marry. Six months later, Dan and Anna are having an affair. When Dan tells Alice, she leaves; when Anna tells Larry, he demands to know the sexual details of her affair. Act II opens in a lapdance club, where Larry meets Alice. They begin an affair. Anna wants a divorce, but Larry begs her for a 'sympathy fuck'; when she tells Dan about it, he wants to know the details. He is jealous, but still dreams of Alice. Anna eventually goes back to Larry, who vindictively tells Dan of his affair with Alice. A month later, Dan and Alice are together again, but they quarrel when he asks her about the sexual details of her affair. Six months on, Anna and Larry have separated; and Alice has been killed by a car in New York.

Elegantly structured, the play has four characters, who are shown over four and a half years, their story told in twelve scenes, six either side of the interval. Although no two of the scenes happen in the same place, and the four characters never appear together onstage, the play has a formal balance that encourages the use of dance metaphors to describe it:

'quadrille', 'square dance', 'like a dance in which partners swap all the time'. Every pair of scenes seems to mirror the previous pair: in the first two, couples meet; in the next two, they deceive each other; in Scenes 5 and 6, betrayal reaches a climax. Over this formal 'musical' structure looms an architectural symbol. At the start, Alice tells Dan that she has been to London's Postman's Park, home to the Watts Memorial of Heroic Deeds, an open-air gallery created by the Victorian painter G. F. Watts and made up of plaques commemorating selfless acts of heroism by ordinary people. At the end of the play, Dan tells Anna that Alice's real name was Jane Jones. She 'made herself up', taking her name from one of the plaques: Alice Ayres, who died horrifically after saving three children from a fire in 1885. Likewise, the play's characters have symbolic professions: dermatologist and stripper (skin trade), obits journalist and photographer (distilled memory). Marber says that Anna, Dan and Larry are 'lookers', while Alice is 'looked at'. These symbols suggest we can manipulate surface reality, that we can be who we want to be. This fluidity of identity is also suggested by the Internet scene, by Anna's fascination with strangers and by Dan's desire to be a novelist instead of a journalist. But the play also argues that, however fluid our identities, we're still at the mercy of our emotions.

For many critics, *Closer* was a case of love at first sight. Reading the reviews, it was easy to guess that the play would scoop awards. For the *Daily Mail*'s Michael Coveney it was the 'the best-acted', 'sexiest' and 'most profoundly uplifting' play in town, and for the *Sunday Times*'s John Peter 'one of the best plays about sexual politics in the language'. Everyone defended the play's provocative boldness. The *Telegraph*'s Charles Spencer thought the 'f-words and the c-words' were 'entirely justified' by their 'poetic intensity', while the *Evening Standard*'s Nick Curtis pointed out that of the many four-letter words, '"love" is undoubtedly the most brutal'. The *Mail on Sunday*'s Georgina Brown said that Marber's mix of 'physical restraint with verbal savagery' was a 'far more potent shock tactic' than nudity, but 'as far as the battle of the sexes is concerned, Marber the playwright refuses to take sides'. Even *Melody Maker* joined the chorus of approval: 'Forget any notion you may have had about theatre being boring. *Closer* is sex and danger, delivered by emotional letterbomb.'

But when *Closer* transferred to the Lyttelton, the *Independent*'s Paul Taylor took a cooler view. He found it was 'the kind of "searing" male lowdown on the awfulness of men that wins rather more moral Brownie points for courageous self-exposure than it actually deserves'. While Marber 'makes dutiful efforts' to show women 'as far from beyond reproach', 'his heart is in exposing the men' and their sexual insecurity. 'Not so,' says Marber, 'I have no moral position vis-à-vis my characters.' Taylor concluded that he detected a 'faint odour of sanctimony': 'after all, a man who points out that men are shits is not in a morally high-risk position these days'. Perhaps not, but Marber also shows that if men can no longer feel superior to women in terms of virtue, they can attempt to be superior by boasting about their depravity or through the exaggeration of their protestations of guilt.

Onstage, as directed by Marber himself, *Closer* was a seductive show. Watching it, you could never be sure you wouldn't feel a flush of recognition, a sudden memory of some past deception, an odd suspicion of partners past or present. It was a play that seemed to peer into your heart. As the first production unfolded, the glazed Doulton tiles of the Postman's Park memorial, visible throughout on the back wall of the stage, became reminders less of heroism than of mortality. Underneath them, discarded props from previous scenes began to pile up, symbols of the silt of emotional memory. *Closer* could be uncomfortable: for example, when Anna talks about faking orgasms, the women in the audience seemed to be laughing louder than the men. At the end, a light shone on the Alice Ayres plaque: was this a touch of nostalgia for a golden age of altruism or a reminder of the importance of memory?

Closer certainly touched a chord, and the media tried to find out what ordinary members of the audience thought about it. Some people, such as Anthony Sadler, a retired teacher from Eastbourne, were baffled by its success. 'Who do you know,' he asked, 'who conducts their physical and emotional relationships in this way and using such basic language?' One woman thought 'it was trying to shock, but in such an old-fashioned sensationalist way'. She took her parents, and all three were embarrassed. Another woman found it 'raunchy and violent' but saw that 'beyond the shocking, in-your-face stuff, there are some moving human moments'. Thirty-seven-year-old writer Shane Watson blamed her boredom on the play's bias towards men, its 'emphasis on sex, on being macho'. In the *Sunday Times*, journalist Lesley Garner concluded that *Closer* offers 'lots of trauma but no catharsis'. In the London *Evening Standard*, journalists Louise Chunn and Neil Norman gave a man and a woman's view of the play. Chunn said that the experience was 'uncomfortable' because the men and women were so 'bloody typical', while Norman commented: 'It may be just a play, but this time it's personal.' During one exchange, he found his 'hands clasping themselves a tad tighter'. When journalist Ben Smith went, he made the 'huge mistake' of taking his girlfriend. Squirming in his seat, he felt as if someone had 'found my secret diary'. After the show, apparently, she asked him questions such as: 'So, do you really think about ex-girlfriends when you wank rather than about me?' Incidents such as these indicate that theatre could inflict collateral damage.

From the stage, the actors also noticed the show's effect. Liza Walker (Alice) found that couples either tended to get 'really huggy' after the show or 'move further away from each other'. During the lapdance scene, she could sense audiences tensing up, thinking she would strip completely. Similarly, Mark Strong (Dan) points out that audiences in the small Cottesloe theatre felt 'brutalized' and didn't laugh much; 'in the bigger Lyttelton they were more dispassionate and distanced', and laughed more. In New York, says Marber, the play was seen as a 'coarser beast' because audiences were less used to provocative dialogue.

Closer was hip enough to have its own website (www.closer.co.uk), sporting a design that reflected the play's structure of short exchanges, with apposite quotes from Noël Coward, Milan Kundera and Dorothy Parker. Best of all was the site's discussion section, where – amid the fan mail – appeared criticisms written by someone who signed himself, or herself, 'Dan'. Inspired by the play's Internet sequence, some people speculated fruitlessly that 'Dan' might be Marber in disguise. In fact, it wasn't, says Marber, who logged on at 8 p.m. on 25 June 1998 for a cyberchat. When asked about his influences, he said: 'Pinter, Mamet, Miller, Stoppard, etc., etc.' What about the play's title? 'I went through loads of titles before stealing this one from Joy Division. It's their second album.' When asked about the play's blatant language, he explained: 'I never intended to shock with the language. It is simply the case that I felt the people in the play would speak as they do.' But his most revealing comment was about the sex war. 'No,' he said, 'I don't hate men, but I don't think they are as nice as women in general.'

Marber sums up his life succinctly: 'Born in 1964, grew up in Wimbledon, middle-class, Jewish, went to Oxford, started doing comedy, started writing for television, radio, wrote a play, directed a couple of plays, wrote another play. No life plan.' First a television writer, Marber worked on satirical shows such as the BBC's *The Day Today* and *Knowing Me, Knowing You (with Alan Partridge)*. 'Great comedy,' he said in one interview, 'is sadistic.' Marber has always liked theatre: as a youth, he used to go to the National. Later, one of his inspirations was Theatre de Complicite's *A Minute Too Late*, especially its 'weird disjunction between the comic and the tragic, when for the first time it struck me that you could work within the comic form and still be incredibly beautiful and moving'.

Closer was Marber's second play. Like his first, *Dealer's Choice*, it was directed by Marber, developed at the National Studio and put on at the National Theatre. Describing *Dealer's Choice*, which examined male rivalry and father–son relationships in the context of a poker game, Marber once said, 'It's obviously true that most male relationships are structured on a fundamental bluff, which is that we are men and must not show our true feelings.' One of the decade's great boys' plays, *Dealer's Choice* also provided one starting point for *Closer*. While on tour in Atlanta, the cast took Marber to a lapdancing club, which was 'an extraordinary bacchanalian whirlpool of complex power relationships', he says. Another starting point for *Closer* was Marber's desire to write 'a play that was true to love as I and others felt it'. In his mind was Steven Soderbergh's 1989 film *sex, lies and videotape*. He also wanted to write something that expressed 'what is happening after feminist politics and the age of the New Man, when no one knows what's going on any more'.

Marber was aware of the risks of writing a follow-up to a successful first play. 'The second play is difficult – like the second album – because you write the first one with a joyful naivety; you don't really know what you're doing.' Much of *Closer*'s energy, freshness and ferocity may be due to its having been written in a week, although Marber constantly rewrote the play while he directed it. 'At least a third of *Closer* was rewritten in rehearsals, because of what the actors brought to it.' But while *Dealer's Choice* feels broadly comic and naturalistic, *Closer* is bleaker and more poetic. It is 'about love, sex and other crimes of the heart', says Marber. 'It was always part of the conception of the play that I would write about big ugly emotions contained within some formally beautiful structure: which makes it crueller.' The main 'problem with writing about sex is self-censorship.' He was scared about writing so frankly about sex 'because people might think it's about me. It *is* about me, but it's also about everyone I know, both male and female.' Its 'power comes from the fact that you don't usually see these private conversations onstage'.

Marber is inspired by 'well-made plays' and 'well-constructed novels'; he admires the novels of Martin Amis and Quentin Tarantino's films make him laugh. The plays he has chosen to direct are also significant. For BBC2, he directed *After Miss Julie*, his adaptation of Strindberg's *Miss Julie* (a play that is mentioned in Stoppard's *The Real Thing*, itself an influence on *Closer*). Marber has directed a stage version of Dennis Potter's *Blue Remembered Hills* (National), Craig Raine's '*1953*' (Almeida) and Mamet's *The Old Neighborhood* (Royal Court). Both Alice and Larry could have strayed from a Dennis Potter series, but Raine's influence is more specific. Influenced by his *Rich*, Marber noted how poetry's 'formal compression' opens up 'a multitude of meanings'. In *Closer*, Larry's 'Ever seen a human heart? It looks like a fist wrapped in blood' sounds like Raine. *Closer* also echoes Mamet's *Sexual Perversity in Chicago*; the flashback in Scene 8 is a distant reminder of Pinter's *Betrayal*; the two couples obliquely suggest Coward's *Private Lives*; and Larry's joke about how a nurse refused to sleep with him until he left private practice is a reminder that Marber originally wrote a much more political play.

If one of *Closer*'s pleasures is its sheer intelligence, in performance the play's cerebral delights make us drop our guard and become prone to its emotional punch. With its programme, which showed a Man Ray photographic x-ray of male and female fingers, *Closer* was marketed as an examination of the human heart. So what is the diagnosis?

Closer emphasizes the differences between the sexes. In almost every skirmish, men come off slightly worse than women. Take the oft-quoted dialogue between Anna and Dan in Scene 8:

ANNA: You don't *make* me come. I <u>come</u> . . . you're . . . 'in the
    area' . . . providing valiant assistance.

DAN: You make *me* come.

ANNA: You're a man, you'd come if the tooth fairy winked at you.

Then, in Scene 9, a key speech is Anna's account of the different attitudes men and women have to psychological baggage: 'We arrive with our . . . "baggage" and for a while they're brilliant, they're "Baggage Handlers". We say: "Where's *your* baggage?" They deny all knowledge of it . . . "*They're in love*" . . . they have none. *Then* . . . just as you're relaxing . . . a Great Big Juggernaut arrives . . . with *their* baggage. It Got Held Up.'

Two scenes earlier, Larry is explicit about male fantasies: 'If you women could see one minute of our Home Movies – the shit that slops through our minds every day – you'd string us up by our balls, you really would.'

If Marber does emphasize the differences between the sexes, he also tries to even up the score. His men can be manipulative, but then so can his women. In the end, if he seems to blame men more than women, he is also clear about the reason: 'For me, *Closer* is about people who tell the truth.' The most dramatic scenes in the play are those in which the men want to know the details of the women's infidelity: this passion for knowledge is seen as self-destructive. It is also a male thing. Neither of the women want to know the details of their partner's infidelity. This notion of truth as searing conflict also gives the play its emotional intensity. In the programme, there is an apt quotation from Adam Phillips's *Monogamy*: 'Infidelity is as much about the drama of truth-telling as it is about the drama of sexuality.'

During the Internet scene, the truth of sexual desire contrasts with the lie that Dan tells by pretending to be Anna. Sitting at separate desks in separate rooms, Dan and Larry type messages that appear on a huge screen behind them. Here the anonymity of cyberspace allows anybody to assume any identity. 'The scene only works,' says Marber, 'because Larry is a net virgin.' Revealing the 'uncensored male libido', it got fewer laughs in the play's previews; after the reviews hailed it as a comic masterpiece, 'audiences reacted differently'. Marber says he was updating Shakespeare's *Twelfth Night*, where a woman pretends to be a man. But the deception of pretending to be a woman on the Internet is mild when compared to Dan and Anna having a secret affair for a year.

One of the most theatrically successful scenes in *Closer* is the double splitting-up scene, where on one half of the stage Dan tells Alice that their relationship is over and Anna does the same on the other half. The scene brings Act I to a climax with Larry threatening Anna and demanding to know where, when and how she had sex with Dan. It is a shocking scene, not least because Larry manages to hurt himself more than Anna. But his drive to know the truth is mixed up with his desire to provoke Anna to go beyond the guilty politeness of her responses. It is also a way of possessing her even as he loses her. Knowing all there is to know is less about understanding than about winning. Later, when trying to crush Dan, Larry uses his knowledge as a form of heavy moral artillery.

Alice, a drifter who makes up her own identity, is the play's most symbolic character. The scar on her leg, which is explained in several different ways, suggests both the endless mutability of the stories we tell about ourselves and the emotional scars we always carry. Because Alice takes her name from the Postman's Park memorial, it is tempting to equate her attitude – a mix of wilfulness and moral absolutism – with heroism. Compared with Dan's cowardice and opportunism, the openness of her feelings and the frankness of their expression are appealing. But Marber's irony subverts such easy explanations. Alice's willpower manifesto – 'I didn't *fall* in love, I chose to' – is based on her idea that she fell for Dan because he cut the crusts off his sandwiches; he later points out that he only did this once because the bread 'broke in my hands'. However understanding, Marber's portrait of Alice, with its hints of a traumatized past, is finally only skin-deep. Certainly, her behaviour can't carry the moral authority of the Postman's Park symbolism, nor can Dan's for rescuing her. In fact, the play's central symbol is not meant to stand up to examination. For Marber, it is an image not of heroism but of memory: 'How do we remember love? What are old love affairs for?' A good question, but neither he, nor his play, gives an answer.

Chance in *Closer* is always balanced by necessity. In the programme, there is a quotation from Newton: 'To every action there is always opposed an equal reaction.' One of the play's props is a Newton's cradle, with metal balls that bounce off each other. But, of course, humans are less resilient than metal, and only three out of the play's four characters survive. Alice's death feels like a mix of chance and necessity. Is she a suicide rescued for a while by the hope of love? 'I don't feel that,' says Marber. 'She's not trying to kill herself; she was simply looking in the wrong direction while crossing the road.'

In the end, the key to *Closer* is its account of the irrationality of desire. Every time the characters swap partners, no reasons are given. There are no rationalizations for infidelity, no elaborate explanations. Sexual attraction is as much a mystery here as it is in Jacobean drama. Marber fills this silence with the tumult of wounded feelings and the rawness of betrayal. He never tells us why Dan falls for Anna, or why Anna accepts Larry, or why Dan and Anna betray Alice and Larry. Much of *Closer*'s power comes from the way it shows chaotic emotions without burdening itself with explanations. What disturbs is its reminder that, for all our reasonableness, we are at the mercy of unreasonable passions.

But does the play suffer from a lack of compassion? While the writing is vivid, punchy and often funny, it can also be irritatingly fidgety, compulsively comic. Marber says, 'I find writing comic lines much easier than constructing dramatic situations.' As critic Kate Kellaway points out, Marber 'speeds dialogue up. The pace is incredible and his characters can say anything they like (including the almost unsayable) with velocity and precision.' The comedian's sharpness makes *Closer* exciting, but the excitement sometimes defuses the pain. The headlong rush for the punch line feels like a lack of compassion. As Marber says, 'Some of my dialogue reveals the paranoia of the stand-up – if you're not quick and interesting, the audience will leave.' The speed of Marber's writing means that, while the play frequently touches intimacy, it never really lingers.

In *Closer* love is problematic. The closer you get, the more pain you suffer. Underneath its cool poise and aphoristic dialogue, its manipulative characters and their cowardly behaviour, there is stark neediness. 'Men want intimacy just as much as women do,' says Marber. In the play, he never lets us off the hook, forcing us to ask the same questions about each of his characters: why do we love? Why do we lie to the one we love? Why do we want to hurt the one we love? Answering such questions may lead you to agree with his conclusion: 'It is a pessimistic play.'

Che Walker's *Been So Long*

If Marber's account of emotional unreason is pessimistic, Che Walker's debut, *Been So Long*, offers a vision of sexual joy that is anything but. Aptly enough for someone who has always had 'a fascination with the dynamics of how men and women relate', the play is a love story that weaves in and out of a revenge fantasy. Set in a 'loser's pub' run by Barney the wise bartender, it opens with Gil, a young white man, looking for Raymond LeGendre, a black sex legend who apparently stole his girl some three years previously. Then two streetwise black women, Yvonne and Simone, come onto the scene. When provoked, Yvonne pulls a razor on Gil. After he leaves, Raymond appears and falls for Simone. A couple of scenes later, Gil finally catches up with Raymond, tries to kill him, fails, and is comforted by Yvonne. While Raymond and Simone struggle to overcome their past experiences and square up to the robust love their romance will need, Yvonne takes Gil for a walk.

Walker was born in 1968, and lives in Camden, north London, where the play is set. Theatre runs in the family: his mother, Ann Mitchell, played Dolly in *Widows*, an eighties ITV series about the wives of imprisoned criminals. 'My family is full of cockneys,' says Walker, 'so I know about strong women.' His father is director Rob Walker, who ran the Half Moon theatre during the early eighties. A rehearsal-room baby, Che left school at sixteen, and eventually began a drama course at Webber Douglas on his twenty-first birthday. Qualifying as an actor, he worked with Edward Bond and Dennis Potter. As acting jobs dried up, he started writing, especially during the long hours when he worked as a security guard. In 1995, he played Cal in *My Old Flame*, his own short film for Carlton TV. After putting on a short play, *Sticks and Stones*, at Camden's Interchange studio, where Walker studied and taught, he wrote a brief version of *Been So Long* in 1995. After many rewrites, it was produced by the Royal Court at the Ambassadors in April 1998.

What were Walker's inspirations? 'I was very affected by Philip Ridley's work; I was in his *The Pitchfork Disney* at the Glasgow Citizens in 1993' (one critic described his performance as 'pathos and menace personified'). He was also inspired by *Ragamuffin*, a piece by Amani Naphtali, who had been to the same secondary school. '*Ragamuffin*, which I saw four times in 1989, was about a court in heaven judging black urban youth. The language was terrific.' Walker also mentions Sam Shepard and Jim Cartwright: 'I acted in *Road* at college, and I love the mix of street slang and classical language'. He also sees traces of Gabriel García Márquez, Michael Ondaatje, Damon Runyon and Elmore Leonard in his work.

Been So Long was set in a tangerine-coloured Tex-Mex bar, whose window gave glimpses of the hip crowd at Jake's, the rival bar across the street. Directed by Roxana Silbert, an eloquent black and white cast embodied Walker's stylish mix of street-smart banter and literary language. Like a kind of magic realism, the writing conjured up memorable accounts of female desire and female solidarity, and threw them against images of male rivalry and male brotherhood. The friendship between Yvonne and Simone was tested when Yvonne allowed the estranged father of Simone's child to meet his little girl; the violent animosity between Gil and Raymond ended in a warm embrace. Studded with metaphors – sex is described as 'two twigs rubbing together to make a fire one night' – and full of rapture, whether quasi-poetic ('She was so beautiful, I got a nosebleed just from lookin' at her') or blatantly aggressive ('Fuck her brains out, didja? Left her dripping?'), the play felt like a flamboyant hymn to desire. As the *Financial Times* said, it has 'juicy parts' and a cast 'that sink their teeth so deep into them that the juice runs down their chins'.

When *Been So Long* was reviewed, its language was often described as 'ornate'. A typical example is Gil's: 'You'll force me to decimate your arse.' While playwright Winsome Pinnock recognized the language as 'black rhythms of speech, a kind of street argot', several theatres rejected the play because of its dialogue. 'I got one letter,' says Walker, 'which said that working-class people don't talk like this. To which I replied: first, how do you know? And second, the language is heightened because it's a play.' Walker grew up with streetwise kids who enjoy 'the sensuality of language'. 'Particularly with West Indian kids, there's a tradition of spoken poetry, church oration and the King James Bible, which influence anyone from that background.' Not to mention rap and black music. 'I'm not the only white writer who writes for black characters – look at Rebecca Prichard's *Yard Gal*. Saying people don't talk like that just means you're out of touch.' Walker's playtext doesn't specify colour, but when it came to casting, he wanted to use black actors because the play is rooted in black culture. Written in a language that tickles the ears, *Been So Long* celebrates working-class youth. 'I didn't want a middle-class audience to feel sorry for them,' says Walker. 'My experience of them is one of humour and warmth; they're full of linguistic invention and quick wit.' Young audiences certainly didn't have a problem with the play's linguistic style.

Been So Long is about erotic relationships, and especially about how past experiences affect the future. Raymond and Simone have to decide whether to part after just one sexual encounter or whether to trust each other, which includes letting the other see the worst sides of their character. Both carry baggage: Simone is a single mum with a disabled child; Raymond has been to prison. Both are capable of immense cruelty. 'Most of us are really cruel to the ones we love most,' says Walker. 'We trust them to carry it.' In the end, Raymond goes too far and says things that are unforgivable and that, 'once said, just hang in the air'. His raging speech begins:

> Well fuck this shit, since you wanna make the worst mistake of
> your life and shit shit all over me, lemme tell you about yourself, I
> know about your fucking scummy pycho cousin and his little pen-
> nychew badboy crew, and I know about your arsehole father doing
> ten on the Isle of Wight, Mrs fucking 'I know you better than you
> know yourself' fake jewellery bitch . . .

and ends by pointing out that since the father of Simone's disabled baby was a traveller – 'what kind of slag goes diving for dick among the caravan people' – 'the two of you have spawned a shitcum spastic mong for a kid'. You can see why Walker remembers critic John Peter's comment that 'here love is like a search-and-destroy mission where the rules of civilised warfare do not apply'.

In this war, both men and women break the rules. 'Raymond is a kind of peacock,' says Walker. 'A friend said: "What you want in that part is a predator, not a beast of burden." Raymond has grace as well as power. He's narcissistic, even feminine.' He has grown up in a family that doesn't make him feel wanted. 'He gets to around fifteen and suddenly he notices that women are looking at him. He realizes that this is his way of being wanted.' It takes him a while 'to realize that what they want him for is not because of who he is, but because of his broad shoulders'. Although Raymond has been to prison, he is not a hardened criminal. When Gil tracks down Raymond for seducing a woman he is infatuated with, the irony is that neither the woman nor Raymond has noticed Gil at all. The only way Gil can make emotional contact is through conflict, by challenging Raymond with a knife. But when Gil finally admits his hurt, Raymond says he is in the same boat. Their conflict is resolved. No need for a New Man, just tough love.

The two women are both brave and dangerous. They are good friends, but opposites: Simone has hauteur, an icy dignity; Yvonne is sassy, very adventurous and very confident, but she does not have got a kid to slow her down. Yvonne's sexual fantasy featured in many reviews. 'I'm at the top of Kite Hill', she says, with a 'mighty storm brewing and swelling. And I'm fucking this guy, he's a wood spirit' with

> furry cleft hooves, antlers on his forehead. And a great tree branch
> for a dick, y'get me? Even though he's so strong, I overpower him.
> I dominate him, throw him roughly to the cool wet wet grass, I pin
> him down, sink my nails into his chest. And I squat bestride his
> hirsute hips, and I'm working him down. Slowly, slowly, slowly.

The fantasy spreads itself over a page of the playtext.

Some critics picked on Yvonne's speech – 'My girl Simone love a damaged man. We all do. That's how you lot get away with it' – and saw it as the play's message. Walker disagrees: 'Don't forget the very next line, when Barney replies: "My ex-wife never let me get away with fuck all. Don't include me in that."' He wanted to articulate ideas 'without resolving them, to resist closure. I don't want to wrap the play up in a neat bow.'

In *Been So Long*, Walker confronts the emotional truth of violence, verbal and actual. A key moment is Raymond's speech about 'the maddest fight up on Holmes Road', which describes how he saw 'this pair of lovers, right, grapplin' on the pavement, hair pulling biting . . . Going at it. Rottweiler style.' To which Barney says: 'Sounds like them two was in love.' Walker says: 'This is about the mess men and women can find themselves when they love each other. For reasons they don't understand, they end up punching each other.' If you try to break up a couple who are fighting, 'they'll always turn on you'. In the play, Simone does what no man could do: she marks Raymond's face during a fight.

With its feisty language, *Been So Long* deals frankly with the emotions of the characters, from Gil's acute longing and neediness to the strong passions and suspicions of Simone and Raymond. What the language conveys are the mental and physical sensations of being in love, which are lyrical, splendid, wild. From the unease that comes from the initial fear of commitment to the final suggestion of the healing power of love, the play explores the way that psychological damage can only be overcome after open aggression and conflict.

Is the play's ending one of qualified optimism? 'Definitely,' says Walker. 'An earlier draft had a more rosy ending, but that didn't work because it didn't respect the damage that Simone and Raymond are carrying and inflicting. As a result, the damage will do damage. So I made it more ambiguous.' Walker avoids closure, but wants the audience 'to feel like they've eaten a three-course meal, not just a starter – they've got to feel satisfaction'. On the other hand, 'you want your audience to walk out with questions about their own lives'. *Been So Long* does raise questions about defensive aggression, and about how past hurt paralyses present love, but its also sings with the joys of desire and hope.

Richard Zajdlic's *Dogs Barking*

Once described as 'grit for grown-ups who aren't offended by nudity, narcotics or swearing', the BBC's trendy soap-opera *This Life* was one of the iconic television series of the nineties. When its final episode was broadcast in August 1997, some members of the audience must have wondered what would happen, now that the characters were dispersing, to the flat they once shared: who would live there now? The same question is at the heart of Richard Zajdlic's *Dogs Barking*, which opened at the Bush in May 1999. Zajdlic, who is both an actor and writer, wrote three episodes of the first series of *This Life*, before becoming its chief writer, storylining the second series and writing the opening and closing episodes. Just as *This Life* commented on relationships among twentysomethings in the run up to the millennium, so the central image of *Dogs Barking*, in which two former lovers fight ferociously over possession of the flat they once shared, says much about love, passion and materialism.

Taking place over one weekend in Alex's one-bedroom flat, *Dogs Barking* is about Neil and Alex, former lovers, who meet after some months apart. Having been dumped by his new girlfriend, Neil now wants half of the flat, even though Alex is the one who has paid the mortgage. When Alex goes out, Neil ropes in Splodge, his overweight friend, to help him clear her stuff out. Alex returns with her sister Vicky. They've been to an estate agent and tell Neil to sign a form to renounce his share of the flat. The well-healed Vicky even offers him money. Later on, the emotional temperature rises when Vicky tells Neil that Alex is pregnant and that Ben, her new boyfriend, is the father. Act II begins with Alex and Vicky quarrelling about Vicky's habit of flirting with her sister's lovers. Later, Splodge visits Alex to apologize for helping Neil. Then Neil, tormented by the idea that Alex is pregnant, bursts in and furiously demands that she transfers the flat to him. Finally, he attacks Alex, 'feels her breasts' and 'stuffs his free hand down her tracksuit pants'. He tells Splodge: 'You can fuck her.' Then he realizes she is bleeding. Grabbing his chance, he forces her to sign the permission form, giving him the flat. Horrified, Splodge takes her to hospital as Neil begins to rip the flat apart. The last scene is a flashback to when Neil and Alex first moved in, sharing a candlelit takeaway meal and making a wish on a stray eyelash.

I watched *Dogs Barking* from the front row, just inches away from the actors, so close I could smell Neil's cigarettes and Vicky's perfume. When Splodge says his wife threw him out, not because he hit her or betrayed her but because 'I just bored her', a sympathetic groan came from the audience. Later, Neil's outrageous attack on Alex happened right in front of me and, as Splodge saw the chance of raping Alex, a memorable look of opportunistic glee crossed his face. When Neil's bloodstained hand came out of Alex's pants, the revulsion rippled all around. Stunned silence; somebody knocked over a glass. One of those boundaries between the intimate and the public had been crossed, jumped even. On another night, one woman fainted during this episode and, because of the crush, had to be passed over the heads of other spectators before reaching the exit. Another time, there was an accidental onstage fire because a cigarette hadn't been put out properly.

Although some critics had doubts about Zajdlic's plot, there was well-deserved praise for his uncompromising writing. The *Telegraph*'s Charles Spencer compared the play to Patrick Marber's *Closer*, calling it 'a modern love story – raw, true, sometimes funny but more often deeply painful', while the *Sunday Times*'s John Peter compared director Mike Bradwell's production to 'an ice pick in the heart' and *What's On*'s Samantha Marlowe – in an image that recalls *Closer* – called it an 'immaculately written, devastating piece of open-heart surgery'. But what really provoked some critics was the character of Neil; *The Times*'s Benedict Nightingale wanted to 'grab' him and 'push him out of a window'. As Zajdlic points out, the Bush is a good venue for 'electrifying' theatre.

Zajdlic started writing while studying English at Southampton University, which he attended between 1980 and 1983. 'I was toying with the idea of being a journalist, but then I got sucked into theatre,' he says. Part of a group that took two musicals – *Skinned Alive* and *The Buzz* – to the Edinburgh Festival, he went on to form Ratskins Theatre Company, which wrote and performed its own material. With Richard Crowe, he put on *Cock and Bull Story* and *Cannibal*. In 1991, his first solo play, *Infidelities*, won the West London Playwriting Competition, and then, as well the play *Rage*, he also wrote episodes of the BBC's *EastEnders* and *This Life*. 'One of the attractions of *This Life* was that, because it was screened after the nine o' clock watershed, there was no censorship. After *EastEnders*, which has loads of rules, it was really liberating, a great gig.'

The starting point of *Dogs Barking*, says Zajdlic, was 'the idea of two people in the flat', one resident, the other an intruder from the past. Clearly, the people are more important than the flat. 'What I wanted to explore is the whole question of when is a relationship over.' Usually, after a couple split up, he says, 'the relationship isn't over. Most people deal with that by not seeing the other person for a long time, but you can't do that if you have something pulling you together.' In *Dogs Barking*, the flat is a device that brings Alex and Neil back together. It is a highly contemporary theme: more than ever before, relationships are mediated by property. 'I hear lots of stories about how difficult it is to buy. If you share a flat, it can be tantamount to being married.' There is no divorce until the place is sold.

The play's title is a reworking of the phrase 'a dog's bark is worse than its bite'. 'Dogs who bark a lot don't necessarily bite,' says Zajdlic. Each of the four characters 'has the capacity to really bite, but most of the time it's just bark'. Each of them 'has their moment, when they can choose to bite, and some take that opportunity'. Alex is 'a dog that bites, but she chooses not to; she's probably the strongest character'. Although she wants Neil to admit that he really loves her so that she has the pleasure of 'kicking his guts out', she never does. Neil, for all his bluster, is 'actually a dog that barks rather than bites', so 'the one time he does bite, it goes against his nature and ends disastrously'. He is not a psycho, but a normal man who has been pushed beyond endurance. A lot of people in the audience 'intensely hated Neil, especially the guys'. But why? 'Maybe they saw too much of themselves in him.' One of the play's implications is that humans behave like animals. 'Certainly, that's what we are,' says Zajdlic. 'We may have higher aspirations, but in the end we're part of the animal kingdom.'

Dogs Barking is full of canine imagery. For example, when Splodge first arrives, and Neil pretends that he is Alex's lover once more, the sexually frustrated Splodge imagines the couple 'were fucking like dogs all night'. The last time Neil and Alex had sex it was, remembers Alex, 'doggy fashion': 'We couldn't even look at each other any more.' On a different note, the last line of Act I is Vicky's 'You're not part of her life, Neil. You're just something she stepped in. Still clinging to her shoes.' As well as using such metaphors, Zajdlic also creates a naturalistic world by means of an accumulation of tiny details. For example, when Alex tells Neil she is going with Ben to a Tapas bar in Soho, he gives her a sharp look. 'Not that one,' she replies, well aware of how one couple's habits can create a sentimental urban geography.

Written with passion and verbal panache, *Dogs Barking* is a fast-moving account of a territorial skirmish in the sex war. Audiences enjoyed the heightened naturalism of Zajdlic's language, relishing its pointed jokes and put-downs, its rapid verbal thrusts. His work is both entertaining and emotionally raw. He deliberately brought *Dogs Barking* to a high pitch of emotional excitement very rapidly so that he 'could be more naked in terms of emotional directness'. 'I'm fascinated by people's struggle to communicate and how they continually tear chunks out of each other.' Examples abound: when Neil sees the dress Ben has given to Alex, he says: 'Not bad. You're sucking a better class of dick now, obviously.' Each exchange seems to heighten the aggression: when Neil tells Vicky that Alex still has his photo in her purse, she tells him that Alex is pregnant. 'Three months. It's Ben's. Hope that didn't hurt too much.' Violence is constantly in the air. Neil's solution to Splodge's marital problems is: 'You should've smashed her face in.' But although most of the arguments in *Dogs Barking* are aggressively explicit – as when Vicky mocks Neil: 'Ben is everything you're not and she [Alex] wanted to have sex with him', or when Alex reminds Vicky of how their father humiliated the mother by forcing her to have anal sex – there are also currents of emotional neediness.

The sex war is fought subtextually as well as openly. When Alex tells Vicky that Neil doesn't want the flat or the money, she is right. Neil, says Zajdlic, 'doesn't know what he wants'. He focuses on Alex, and tries to get her by means of possessing the flat, but he doesn't really know what he needs. Is this a typical male thing? 'No, one of the subtexts is that all the characters are searching for something they can't define – it's easier for them to talk about tangible things like the flat, but, in a way, the flat is the most irrelevant thing in their lives.'

When Alex and Neil argue, one of her most savage thrusts is to compare her sex life with Neil to her sex life with Ben: 'It's funny that, isn't it? You meet a certain person and suddenly you'll do things, and let him do things, that you point-blank refused to do with your other boyfriends.' But, despite this apparently mortal stab, her feelings about Neil are ambiguous. She still carries his photograph in her purse. When her sister points this out, she says she didn't realize. It is a moment of typical subtlety and ambiguity: Zajdlic allows us to half-believe and half-disbelieve her at the same time.

With Neil's attack on Alex, the play goes from a war of words to a physical battle. Although this resolves the conflict over the flat, it also seems to be a very extreme solution. But, Zajdlic points out, the outcome is 'psychologically consistent'. Neil is humiliated because no one takes him seriously; he has already suggested that Splodge should have used violence; and he is desperate because Alex's pregnancy means there is no going back. During the assault, two things are particularly disturbing. One is Splodge's reaction. 'When he gets the chance to rape, he really wants to do it. A lot of people didn't want him to do it because he's so cuddly – but he would have.' The attack on Alex

> was shocking and horrifying, but by far the nastiest moment is when Neil knows that Alex is bleeding, and could lose her baby, but forces her to sign the form. That's far more cruel than his incitement to rape.

A 'lot of people could barely watch that scene,' says Zajdlic. 'They felt that after it they could never like Neil under any circumstances, but, at the end, they did in fact feel some sympathy for him.' This paradoxical feeling comes partly from empathy with the actor and partly from the power of the play's final flashback. But what about those critics who condemned that scene as sentimental? 'I abhor sentimentality,' he says. 'The last moments are meant to show that, if those two people had actually listened to each other properly, they would have known that their relationship was doomed.' They both 'know deep down that it's not going to work, but they keep pretending because they can't face the alternative, which is splitting up'. Unwilling to 'listen to the voice in their heads that tells them something's wrong', they both 'play the game of being in love'. The scene is bitter-sweet, but because the play has been so ruthless up to that moment, and the experience of watching it so fraught, audiences needed 'some kind of affection so they accepted Neil and Alex's love as genuine, whereas actually both are pretending'.

When, in a key speech, Neil tells Splodge about the night he and Alex moved in, he says: 'I looked at her and thought . . . I wish this was enough.' Arrogantly, he imagined that he 'deserved better'. Leaving her was a 'kind of public declaration that I wasn't going to settle for second-rate'. He thought that her way of saying 'I love you' was 'whining, self-pitying', and only meant: 'Don't leave me.' Neil's comeuppance comes when his new lover leaves him, and the roles are reversed. He realizes, too late, that 'all those times when Alex said "I love you", maybe that's exactly what she meant.' That 'maybe' sums up the couple's emotional uncertainty.

Both men and women 'want to live passionately, not just sexually but with emotional intensity,' says Zajdlic. 'Everyone is looking for the one person who can rid them of all insecurity. Yet that's so rare, if not impossible.' When people are desperate to love someone, they kid themselves about their own feelings. They 'construct a convenient image of that person'. With its powerful metaphors of animal passions, the play strips back that image and reveals it as a fiction.

In the nineties, it was not just women who wanted to 'have it all'. More than ever, happiness was seen as a right and sexual relationships become a central focus of self-definition. 'Relationships shape people's perceptions of themselves. People need intimacy – they find out about themselves through other people.' Onstage, *Dogs Barking* made you feel as if you were not just a witness to, but a grown-up participant in that intimacy.

Showing sexual relationships onstage is not new, but the frankness with which it was done in the nineties helped popularize theatre with young audiences. As Zajdlic says: 'People are always interested in other people's lives – we are natural voyeurs.' Whether the plays were about emotionally confused twentysomethings or grown-ups betraying each other, and whether they tried to shrug off the pain of the past or showed people sinking their teeth into each other, what stuck in the mind were their images of bewilderment, hurt and sheer aggression. Whatever audiences thought about the differences between the sexes, each relationship came across in a starkly individual way. And if men seemed to be capable of behaving not only badly but unpardonably, the minute they made a song and dance about this, women were quick to point out that they could be equally cut-throat. In this anti-ideological decade, men were no longer simply 'the enemy', and women no longer simply victims.

The sex war plays of the nineties examined emotional extremes and came up with a sense of hurt (Grosso), accounts of irrational desire (Marber), images of delight (Walker) and metaphors of animal passion (Zajdlic). Perhaps the only thing they had in common was that they showed our capacity to be attracted to another person's damage, the baggage they haul through life. If someone else's damage brings out our compassion, our ability to forgive, emotional scars seemed to be proof not only of our toughness, but also of our vulnerability.

8 Battered and bruised

> Everybody's always killing each other and a lot of girls do have swim-
> suits. That's the best kind of programme.
>
> (Ray in Martin McDonagh's *The Beauty Queen of Leenane*)

The nineties was a jagged and violent decade. Day after day, the media
brought news of war and killing: terrorist bombs, ethnic cleansing and
mass graves left indelible images on the public imagination. The murder
of toddler Jamie Bulger by two ten-year-old boys in February 1993
became one of the key events of nineties Britain, not only because of the
intrinsic horror of the event, but also because of the impact of the grainy
security video image of the child's abduction. Elsewhere, the names Sre-
brenica, Basra and Waco became synonymous with atrocity; nearer
home, Omagh, Dunblane and Cromwell Road, Gloucester, joined the
geography of horror. As the spectres of child abuse, domestic violence
and street crime cast shadows over the idea of home as a safe haven, fear
of crime became as big a social problem as crime itself. The inquiry into
the murder of black teenager Stephen Lawrence at the hands of a gang of
white youths in April 1993 exposed not only the racism of the police but
also their incompetence. Yet such events had little impact on the public
taste for stylishly violent movies, which, although the most notorious
examples date from the early nineties (*Henry: Portrait of a Serial Killer* in
1990; *Reservoir Dogs* and *Man Bites Dog* in 1992; *Pulp Fiction* and *Natural
Born Killers* in 1994), coloured popular culture throughout the decade,
sparking widespread debates about violence. In Britain, the marriage of
an irresponsible media to a blood-thirsty public produced calls for censorship and demands for ever-more vicious retribution.

These tendencies were both reflected and contested by theatre. In the
early nineties, there was a crop of British plays about murder and prisons. As Ian Brown, artistic director of the Traverse, said in May 1992: 'I
see a lot of urban plays about people rubbing up against violent situations. There is often a violent atmosphere; there is an ongoing fascination with serial killers.' Audiences watching plays as different as Anna
Reynolds and Moira Buffini's *Jordan* (Lilian Bayliss, 1992), Rod
Williams's *No Remission* (Lyric, Hammersmith, 1992), Debbie Isitt's *The
Woman Who Cooked Her Husband* (Snarling Beasties, 1992) and Karen

Hope's *Foreign Lands* (Finborough, 1993) saw that the family was in trouble, the prisons full and that murder stalked the land. Yet such plays questioned the notion that easy answers could tackle the rise in crime, and contested John Major's dictum about the Bulger case: 'We should condemn a little more and understand a little less.'

Just as masculinity in crisis was a key theme of nineties theatre, so violence was one of its confrontational characteristics. Aggressive behaviour in small studio spaces generated powerful feelings of entrapment as serial killers, rapists and abusers became as common onstage as high-society dandies or working-class families once were. Yet the gender implications of violence remained complex. In Desperate Optimists' *Play Boy* (1998), the older woman finds violence disgusting but the younger woman is attracted by it. In such cases, ideology was less important than pessimism. Nor is what is shown necessarily as shocking as what is implied. On the subject of his excruciatingly cruel *You'll Have Had Your Hole* (West Yorkshire Playhouse, 1998), Irvine Welsh says, 'Most of the violence in this play doesn't really happen. It's psychological. The threat of violence is so much more powerful than actual violence.' While the figure of Begbie in *Trainspotting* epitomized mindless violence, Welsh's play boasted a delight in torture that was positively Jacobean. Similarly, the main emotions in Paul Tucker's black comedies – *The Last Yellow* (Chelsea Centre, 1996) and *Room to Let* (Chelsea Centre, 1999) – are extreme cruelty mixed with desperation. After a ton of humiliation, an ounce of compassion is wrung from the audience.

In this decade, theatre took on the role of reclaiming violence from the glamorization of big-budget movies. If nineties plays showed the world to be much more violent than it really was, they also contested the widespread ignorance about the reality of violence. Neilson, Kane and Ravenhill all used vividly violent images for a moral reason. Writers such as Letts and Butterworth, while claiming a similar justification, were more interested in entertainment, asking audiences to react with a dash of postmodern irony. Butterworth claims he dislikes Tarantino's 'cartoon' version of violence. 'Some people seem to think that because *Mojo* deals in violence,' he says, 'that I "approve". But I'm interested in the devastation it causes, in the ways people *experience* violence.' In *Mojo*, however, the experience felt more comic than tragic. It seemed to be a case of what newspaper columnist Julie Burchill called 'atrocitainment'.

Sometimes, comedy can make difficult subjects accessible. The debate about Hollywood's responsibility for a culture of violence was neatly articulated by Ben Elton's *Popcorn* (Nottingham/West Yorkshire Playhouse 1996; Apollo, 1997), which was also issued as a novel. In the theatre, its cartoonish vitality and crackling one-liners encouraged audiences to concentrate on the discussion and to ignore its absurd premise: a pair of psycho-killers, Wayne and Scout (the Mall Murderers, clones of *Natural Born Killers*) take a Hollywood film director and his family hostage and stage a televised debate about his role in allowing them to be 'seduced by Hollywood's pornographic imagery of sex and death'. Wayne and Scout hope that this gambit will save their necks and excuse their crimes. Despite its comic brio, and Elton's frequent use of the same sick humour he claims to be satirizing, the play does have its perceptive moments: when Wayne compares real killing with movie violence, he concludes: 'It ain't witty.' Finally, *Popcorn*'s Brechtian ending, where all the characters line up and shrug off responsibility for the play's blood bath, was an imaginative use of theatre as a public forum.

In many cases, violence was rationalized as the result of inarticulacy: when words fail, the language of physical brutality takes over. At other times, violence was shrouded in words. David Harrower's hypnotically poetic debut, *Knives in Hens* (Traverse, 1995), is set in a strange, rural past where a love triangle ends in a brutal murder as the adulterous couple crush the husband under a millstone. But the intense and sensuous language, and the production's restrained mime of the killing, distanced the audience. This was particularly apt in a play about a young woman's discovery of a language to express her feelings and whose central image is that naming things is like pushing a 'knife into the stomach of a hen'. Similarly, the crazy baby-talk of Enda Walsh's *Disco Pigs* (Corcadorca, 1996) gave the play a deliberately obscure air of unreality. Pig and Runt, born on the same day and inseparable since infancy, go to a disco to celebrate their seventeenth birthdays. But when Runt dances with another boy, Pig becomes jealous, and his furious attack on the boy mixes adult savagery with childish rage: 'You dirty liddle fuck she my girlfren bollix! Smash! Kassshhh! Open da nose da eye! Blood blood blood! An Smashhh smasshhhh smash! I am da king . . .' When, soon after, Runt feels she has outgrown Pig, she begins using ordinary speech patterns.

Showing violence explicitly can sometimes convey its terror more effectively than reporting it. Alex Jones's *Noise*, produced by the Soho Theatre Company in April 1997, was about a jobless young couple who move into a flat, only to find that their neighbour is a psycho, with a love of loud techno music. The play ended with a vicious attack by a man, armed with a Stanley knife, on a pregnant teenager. In the theatre, the disparity between the bulk of the man and the smallness of the girl was effective because, unmediated by camera angles, it was always clearly visible. Undeniably horrific, the violence was justified by Jones's conviction that poverty makes people powerless.

Some of the decade's most gruelling plays explored the emotional consequences of brutality. A good example is Zinnie Harris's *By Many Wounds* (Hampstead, 1999), which was disturbing because its account of a child who goes missing focused neither on a murderer nor on a detective, but on the victim's family and its traumatized responses. By contrast, *The Colour of Justice* (Tricycle, 1999), Richard Norton-Taylor's dramatic reconstruction of the Stephen Lawrence inquiry, showed the political consequences of a real killing. The play regularly brought audiences to their feet to bear witness, with a minute of silence, to the courage of the Lawrence family in pursuing the case. By refraining from representing the actual murder, this production showed how truth could be as powerful as fiction.

What shocks or upsets sensibilities can vary. After one performance of Anita Sullivan's savage comedy, *An Audience with the Queen* (London New Play Festival, 1996), Phil Setren, the festival's artistic director, remembers that a 'ranting man' rushed out of the play, saying that he was a vegetarian and had been disgusted by a scene in which rabbit meat was sliced onstage. Animal carcasses often have the power to revolt British audiences and metaphorically powerful images of dismembered animals were used in the staging of Julie Everton's *A Pig in a Poke* (Royal Court, 1991), Naomi Wallace's *Slaughter City* (RSC, 1996) and Kaite O'Reilly's *Yard* (Bush, 1998).

Rather than using violence 'to thrill', some writers, such as Philip Ridley, have used it to electrify sensibilities and leave the emotions open to other sensations. 'The image I've always had about the so-called shock tactics in my work,' he says, 'is that of those travelling Indian magicians who ripped the heads off live birds while – at the same time – they pulled an ace from their sleeve'. In other words, 'The shock prepares the audience for the perception of magic'. However it is used, stage violence is inherently dramatic, almost always marking a point of no return. Taking place in real time and real space, aggression seems to leap across the footlights, emotionally if not literally. So when characters onstage start pushing each other around, it is often the audience that gets battered and bruised.

Joe Penhall's *Some Voices*

In September 1994, while *Babies* – Jonathan Harvey's messy follow-up to *Beautiful Thing* – was occupying the Royal Court's main stage, Joe Penhall's *Some Voices* opened at the Theatre Upstairs. Hailed by the *Sunday Times* as 'the most thrilling playwriting debut in years', it began a momentous era in the Court's history. The opening play in Stephen Daldry's first season of new young writers, Penhall's work was soon followed by that of Nick Grosso, Judy Upton and Sarah Kane. But he doesn't see himself as part of a movement. 'Plays about perverse sexuality and extreme violence are part of our culture,' says Penhall, 'but they are also ephemeral: the nineties are obsessed with style.' But, individual as he is, Penhall's *Some Voices* is in some ways a typical example of what he himself once called a 'London crisis drama'.

Set in West London, *Some Voices* is about Ray, a schizophrenic who is released 'into the community' and the care of his brother Pete, chef of his own restaurant. Soon after his release, Ray meets the pregnant Laura, who is being threatened by her lover, Dave; Ray intervenes and gets headbutted. Later, he meets her in a pub and they start a relationship. On a trip to Southend, they find temporary bliss. But because he has stopped taking his medication, things soon start to go wrong: over a boozy meal, Pete tells Laura that his brother is a 'schizo'. In a panic, Ray turns on Laura, suggesting a 'do-it-yourself abortion'. She walks out. He starts living rough with Ives, another schizophrenic, who subsequently dies, deepening Ray's depression. Later, Ray visits Laura, and finds Dave in her bedsit. When Dave humiliates her, he attacks him with a hammer. With Dave in hospital, Laura reveals that, while he was unconscious, she also hit him. Then, during the play's climax in the restaurant kitchen, Ray covers himself with petrol and threatens to light it. Pete gradually coaxes the lighter from him, but Ray 'whips another from his pocket'. He wants, he says, to cook himself. After giving up that lighter, he whips out another. Losing that one in a struggle, he produces yet another. Interrupted by his 'voices', he gradually allows his brother to wind him down. The play ends in a hostel, with Pete teaching Ray how to cook an omelette, and telling him how Laura wants to be on her own for a while.

Critics were enthusiastic about *Some Voices* and the play won the 1995 John Whiting award. The *Guardian*'s Michael Billington summed up the main theme of the play by asking: what is 'the point of community care if the community itself is full of rage and madness?' Marked by emotional truth and the dishevelled poetry of urban life, *Some Voices* was directed by Ian Rickson with an appealing mix of savagery and tenderness. In an early exploration of the potential of the Theatre Upstairs's space, the walls were stripped right back to the brick, which was painted black, and a huge round institutional window, which opened onto the outside world, was revealed. At the beginning, when he is in the mental hospital, Ray stands next to it, complaining that Ives, another inmate, has 'shat on my window sill again'. Near the end, after the petrol scene, Ray stands by it again, and a ray of bleak light comes in. In between, the play certainly put the audience through a relentless emotional knockabout. But after all the tension, when the theatre was filled with the smell of the omelette that Pete cooks for Ray, it felt as welcome as a homecoming.

Born in 1967, Penhall grew up in Surrey. His family emigrated to Australia in 1976, and when he was twenty he returned to London. 'Half my life was in an idyllic sunny Australian suburb, the other half hemmed in by the grey inner city.' He moved house at least ten times, had about twenty different jobs, 'mostly dishwashing', and ran a pizza bar for eighteen months. After a brief stint at art school, he got a job as a news reporter on the *South London Guardian*. He'd already become involved in the Royal Court Young People's Theatre soon after returning to London, and wrote *Wild Turkey*, a one-act play put on at the 1993 London New Play Festival. Inspired and helped by actor Brian Croucher, he wrote *Some Voices*, which 'took eight months, with as many rewrites'. It was given a reading at Battersea Arts Centre in 1993. The play was then snapped up by Daldry, and Penhall quit his job as a journalist.

'*Some Voices* was inspired by an old friend of mine, a gifted musician, who was a schizophrenic,' says Penhall. At the time, Penhall didn't realize that his friend's 'confusion, hypersensitivity, depression and wild antic humour' were due to mental illness, so he was 'haunted' and 'abashed' when he discovered the truth. There were also political reasons for writing the play. At the time, the Conservative government's policy of Care in the Community was taking effect and Penhall saw it as an important issue. Working as a journalist for the *Hammersmith Guardian*, he 'felt strongly that newspaper articles couldn't convey the true misery and loneliness of schizophrenia'. In *Some Voices*, he handles a complex subject without oversimplification.

Penhall sees parallels between schizophrenia and 'the human condition'. 'Anyone who's living in a big city, as Ray is, knows that it can drive you insane.' London is a 'mad city to be in, especially if you don't have much money, or if you have problems'. Much homelessness, for example, is due to mental illness. Penhall was also fascinated by the extraordinary symptoms of schizophrenia, the compulsive forms of behaviour and wild fantasies, the sudden rushes of talk and the constant 'getting into trouble'. In *Some Voices*, Ives is given a couple of great speeches in which a torrent of words expresses his disgust with the world, his alienation. 'Anybody who's ever been deeply depressed or dead drunk has had a taste of what it's like to be mad.' But since the media is run by those who 'seem to be healthy, shiny, happy people', they 'don't understand mental illness, don't like it and don't want to invest in it'. And while 'heroin and gangsters are hip', mental illness, 'which affects many more people, is unfashionable, troublesome, taboo'. Despite all this, Penhall's thirty-five-minute film about schizophrenia, *Go Back Out*, was screened by BBC2 in April 1996.

What were Penhall's influences? While working in a bookshop, he read modernist classics and obscure books, such as Milan Füst's *The Story of My Wife*, as well as Raymond Carver, with his existential melancholy, and Charles Bukowski. In theatre, he was influenced by Mamet, Pinter, Beckett and 'any of the miserabilists'. Büchner's *Woyzeck*, 'which is about a schizophrenic and very episodic', was important. If Ray comes from Büchner crossed with Bukowski, Pete comes from Chekhov's disappointed Ivanovs and Astrovs. The brothers in Sam Shepard's *True West* are their distant cousins. Penhall also found that some films, such as Hanif Kureishi's *My Beautiful Launderette*, left their mark: 'Its Anglo-Asian outsiders struck a chord with my own peripatetic upbringing.'

All the characters in *Some Voices* are 'disenfranchised'. At the time, Penhall found that easy to relate to. More particularly, 'All my plays seem to involve a straight man and a misfit,' he says. This set up, which works so well onstage, started with Pete and Ray. They embody the conflict between freedom and responsibility, permissiveness and home-making. Pete's speech about his 'weird idea' that 'the thing to do was to go to work and do an honest day and pay a few bills and look after your family' is an early example of what became a major theme in Penhall's work.

Some Voices not only stages the violent disintegration of a schizophrenic's life, it also comments on political solutions to mental illness. The legislators, says Ives, 'profess to be in the business of caring', which is like 'a butcher professing to know how to operate on the brain'. Ray, whose medication is chlorpromazine, likens the drug to 'Lithium times ten. Or a smack on the head with a claw hammer', a vivid image that pre-figures his attack on Dave. 'The legislative viewpoint,' says Penhall, 'tends to be cut and dried; I was pointing out the fuzzy edges.' While politicians emptied mental hospitals 'indiscriminately, as a cost-cutting exercise', Penhall showed how reforms ignore individual needs. A sufferer such as Ives would probably be better off in hospital, but, having coined the phrase 'Care in the Community', the legislators are more concerned with treating 'care' as a business than in dealing with individuals.

The most moving moment in the play is when Ray says he is haunted by a memory of seeing his father 'filthy' and 'unshaven', the implication being that he was an alcoholic or mentally ill. Ray's 'voices' started when he first noticed his father's grubbiness, but his problems are chemical as well as psychological: he has stopped taking his pills. Ray, says Penhall, is 'desperately haunted, and you never know whether he's haunted because he's ill or ill because he's haunted'. He is also a bit of an anarchist: at one point he fantasizes gunning down Pete's noisy neighbours, with their 'fancy cars' and 'party frocks'. He wants to be with Laura because he thinks she understands him, and Laura, even though she only has an inkling of what is wrong with him, likes Ray the way he is, as did most audiences here. By contrast, in New York, American audiences 'just thought Ray was a bum – they had trouble understanding how anyone would want to know him'.

When Laura and Ray discuss Dave's violence, Ray, having picked up some psychobabble about inarticulacy, says: 'Maybe he couldn't . . . couldn't express himself or something.' To which Laura replies: 'Maybe he just likes hitting people.' They also talk about the dependency that violent men induce in their female victims. Penhall's account of violence is undogmatic and rooted in experience. 'There are people who do little else than commit violence; they practice; they become really good at fighting, at hurting people.' But Dave's 'violent élan' is also partly based on a desire to be understood, and, however justified, Ray and Laura's hammer attack on him remains a vicious act that cannot solve their problems.

After this overt brutality, the mere threat of a petrol explosion when Ray confronts Pete in his kitchen packs a strong theatrical punch. 'The idea of using five lighters in that scene was a way of playing with audi-ence expectations,' says Penhall. A question of pace. 'If Ray disintegrates too early, you know something terrible is going to happen.' *Some Voices* also had an experiential side:

I was conscious of having two or three violent climaxes, three very emotional climaxes, so the audience were absolutely exhausted at the end. I wanted them to be absolutely exhausted because that's what schizophrenia does to you. The tension always lasted several beats longer than you expected. I was dragging people beyond their sense of endurance.

Because he'd given his audience 'reasons for an emotional commitment to the characters', he knew that 'people would listen as long as I wanted'.

Being Penhall's first play, *Some Voices* 'was loaded with a real kick'. 'I didn't censor myself,' he says. 'Because it was my big shot, I threw everything I had at it.' Afterwards, he started writing in a more minimalist way, more technically controlled, with fewer stream-of-consciousness speeches. His second play was *Pale Horse* (Royal Court, 1995). In *Some Voices* and *Pale Horse*, the subjects were 'macro things that are easy to grasp', then he moved on to 'little things', more subtle situations, in the hilarious *Love and Understanding* (Bush, 1997) and the less satisfying, slight play, *The Bullet* (Donmar, 1998). In both, he subverted fashionable notions of being cool, arguing that it is morally better to work hard than to 'do heroin and shag lots of birds'. 'As a young playwright,' he says, 'you're encouraged to write dangerous, desperate paeans to depravity.' However unevenly, his recent plays contest the notion that 'deprivation and desperation is some kind of spiritual release', and are a quieter theatrical experience than his first two.

More explicitly political than many of his contemporaries, Penhall has a dialectical imagination. He talks about 'dichotomy' and 'contradiction'; his plays dramatize the two sides of every story. In a postmodern culture where values are seen as relative, this attitude risks seeming old-fashioned, as traditionally lefty as the conservative structure of his plays. Yet Penhall's stance is precisely a critique of postmodern culture's attitude that 'anything goes'. And as *Some Voices* demonstrates, his writing is cogent and his imagination humanistic, with an ability to explore a social issue while suggesting wider truths. But although his characters are deeply alone, they also constantly attempt to make contact. For Penhall, schizophrenia is not only a complex result of nature and nurture, often hindered by government policy, but also a potent symbol of urban alienation. Life, Penhall is saying, looks clean and dandy, but the darkness is always just an accidental slip away. And because his desperate characters, his baffled losers and lonesome oddballs, find solutions elusive, their violent lives implicitly question the cheery optimism of mainstream society.

Judy Upton's *Ashes and Sand* and *Bruises*

Although Judy Upton's early work was seen at the same venues as Pen-hall's (the 1992 London New Play Festival and in Daldry's 1994 Royal Court season), it offers a different take on violence. In two plays at the Court – *Ashes and Sand* (December 1994) and *Bruises* (November 1995) – she took audiences on garishly lit tours of quiet seaside towns, where violence seemed to be a means of communication and suffering a way of life. Her writing touched a chord and, in 1994, Upton won both the George Devine and the Verity Bargate awards. Her work has appeared at many fringe venues and on BBC Radio 4. She has also written for film and one of her dramas, *Pig in the Middle* (Y Touring), about xeno-trans-plantation, was given a reading at the House of Commons in 1998. Yet, despite her success, Upton refuses to give interviews, and stories about her eccentricities abound. In 1995, after a commission by the Red Room, she wrote *Sunspots* for no money, says Lisa Goldman, the company's cofounder. 'She told me she would do it in return for a chocolate bar.'

Set in Brighton, *Ashes and Sand* begins with a quick scene in which a teenage girl gang mugs a man on the pier. The plot then follows fifteen-year-old Hayley and her gang through their attempts to steal enough money to escape to Bali, and focuses on her infatuation with Daniel, a local plainclothes cop who dreams of a job in Gibraltar. Hayley's aggres-sion is always getting her into trouble, but Daniel – who shoplifts women's shoes and wears make-up – is equally accident-prone. Although their dreams are shattered, both snatch temporary solace with each other, until Hayley leads her gang in a dreadful humiliation of Daniel, stripping and abusing him. With a stiletto-healed shoe on its cover, the play's programme highlighted Daniel's fetishism, and onstage the fetish scenes were bathed in a lurid red light. But the play's ninety minutes were fast-moving, the set's maze of mirrors allowing telling jux-tapositions and rapid changes of scene. 'This was a story that needed many changes of location,' says Upton in a note to the playtext, 'lots of "scenelets".' Hayley and Daniel 'aren't people who stay conveniently in one room'. Instead, 'they rush around Brighton chasing their obsessions and dreams of escape'.

Born in 1966, and brought up in Shoreham-by-Sea, Upton was encouraged to write for the stage when the Royal Court Young Writers' Festival visited Sussex in 1990. 'I was angry in the spring of 1994 when I wrote *Ashes and Sand*,' she writes. 'The play just poured out.' What was she angry about? 'I was angry for myself and my friends, dragged kicking and screaming through a hell-hole of a comprehensive school, to end up living lives that fell short of our dreams.' In *Ashes and Sand*, says Ian Rickson, the play's director, 'Her anger is the impacted aggression of people from a socially deprived area.' The play 'builds up to a violent release of energy that is upsetting but also purging'. But Upton's work is more an individual vision than a documentary. The play's background, she says, 'includes newspaper reports about girl muggers on the Palace Pier' but also 'experiences from my own teenage years'. While some papers hyped up the play – the *Independent* calling it a 'vicious hand grenade' – it was left to the *Financial Times*'s David Murray to sum up the broader picture: with its theme of 'children of a demoralised working class behaving badly', the Court 'has been here often before, as far back as Edward Bond's *Saved*'.

With its muggings, fights, Daniel's account of being shot and stabbed on duty, its images of a dartboard covered with a pin-up of a woman ('the bull's-eye is her cunt') or of a decapitated car-crash victim, the first production of *Ashes and Sand* suggested that aggression is a law of nature. Rushing around in a frenzy of desire and wilfulness, Upton's characters never pause long enough to reflect on what they're doing. So while her writing is almost anorexically thin, her anger burns so brightly it tends to dazzle. The violence of the play is never explained, except in the most general way: the culture of unemployment has created an enraged youth. But if aggression is a law of nature, the implication is that nothing can be done to change it. And, without the hope of change, the temptation is simply to glamorize it, as Upton does when she writes: 'Seaside girls are fighters – we don't give up easily.'

Yet *Ashes and Sand* is more than just a shocker. It is hard to forget the scene in which Hayley and Daniel, separated by a closed front door, entwine their hands in a ballet of touching that sums up both their need for affection and their separation. Short as it is, it is one of the tenderest scenes of alienated love in nineties drama. And by giving Daniel a characteristic unwillingness to smile, Upton makes him an unexpectedly symbolic figure in such a naturalistic piece. She also refuses to be drawn into easy moral judgements. 'The few audience members and the odd critic who suggested that Daniel deserves his [violent] fate for flirting with the girls are,' she writes, 'suffering from a madness of our age. I'm sure that they, quite rightly, wouldn't dream of bringing the same judgement to bear on a woman.' She adds: 'Personally, I think the world would be a sorry place without people who smile.' Whether deserved or not, Upton's Daniel does seem masochistically self-destructive, his need for violence matching the girls' desire to inflict it.

The programme for *Bruises* – Upton's next Court play – carried an acknowledgement to G. M. Kits for supplying 'bruising gels'; they were used to good effect. The subject is domestic violence, and Upton shows how brutality breeds more of the same. Set in Worthing, the play follows Kate, who visits her divorced mother and falls for Jay, the son of Dave, who runs a bed-and-breakfast hostel. Dave has a relationship with Phoebe, another lodger, and so does Jay. Dave beats her up, and so does Jay. When Jay gets frustrated with Kate, he lashes out. Here violence has become a language, complete with grunts and moans. In this atmosphere of bewilderment and rage, Upton's postcard from the seaside superimposes an issue play onto a sketch of the culture of unemployment. Switching between tenderness and viciousness, Upton shows both the violence and the recriminations and self-pity that follow it. But one horrific incident, in which Dave, after finding out about Jay and Phoebe, forces the two of them to have sex in front of him, is effective because it is reported rather than shown.

Despite some uncertain direction from Jane Howell, the play did have the power to disturb. Kate fell for Jay almost instantly. The minute he touched her, you just knew he was bad news. Jay is narcissistic and ferocious, a young man whose idea of 'earning respect' is to beat up his girlfriend. Despite her protestations, she puts up with it. This suggests that she is attracted to an abuser, that bruising is what she is looking for. Same old story. But even if it had little new to say about domestic violence, *Bruises* was forcefully written, grimly humorous and, onstage, was presented with stark images: piles of deck chairs suggested an empty, off-season resort; a single bed summed up the loneliness of the characters. The play ends with Jay clinging to Kate, who looks worn out by being treated 'like a punchbag'. Interestingly, several critics complained that the play's violence seemed too stagy, too unreal.

As well as painting a picture of violent behaviour, *Ashes and Sand* and *Bruises* offer a troubling glimpse of sexual desire, wild and dark, and often completely self-destructive. Hayley's infatuation feels like the emotional equivalent of running into a brick wall, while Jay and Kate's attraction seems to scream 'damage'. In her other plays, especially *Sunspots* (BAC (Battersea Arts Centre) 1996), *The Girlz* (Orange Tree,

1998) and *Confidence* (Birmingham, 1998), Upton developed her particular vision of bruised intimacy and raw pain, a world of forbidden desire, split loyalties and malicious jealousies, full of inner voids and dark twists. Her London New Play Festival piece, *Everlasting Rose* (Old Red Lion, 1992) was revived in 1998 (Riverside Studios). Critic Benedict Nightingale sums up her achievement: 'Her characters might shock doctrinaire feminists, since she recognises what's destructive and self-destructive in women and men alike.' Upton's characters 'seem baffled by their own awful behaviour, but they have the vitality to incite us to ask plenty of questions'. True enough, but praising a playwright who raises questions without answering them may just be a way of refusing to face uncomfortable facts about society. After all, most people can agree that unemployment breeds angry and disaffected youth or that violent behaviour is often handed down from father to son, but it is much harder to dramatize ways of changing this situation. In the absence of such an attempt, however, drama becomes mere reportage.

The trouble with Upton is that the vitality of her writing is more evident on the stage than on the page. *Bruises*, for example, is so dreary that it is difficult to read more than once. But while it is wrong to dismiss Upton's style as 'televisual', it is true that her writing has been influenced by what Soho Theatre Company's Paul Sirett calls the 'Tarantino effect', which has made plays 'faster, edgier, more brutal, written with anger and verve'. What she offers is a series of jump cuts: flashes of insight rather than analysis of motive; glimpses of relationships rather than an exploration of feelings; shots of savage emotion rather than sustained argument.

What makes Upton's work so timely is that it fiercely illustrates the culture of victimhood. Not only does she represent victims accurately, she also has the dramatic intelligence to argue that winners don't exist: both the perpetrators of violence and their victims are equally messed up. The problem is that her work often lacks any sense of the possibility of empowerment or of change. There is neither tragic destiny nor social rehabilitation, but instead a series of cycles of deprivation. In *Ashes and Sand*, the girls are vulnerable victims of dysfunctional families and Daniel is a victim of female violence (he has been stabbed three times by women). Worse, the gang is riddled with jealousies and betrayals. In *Bruises*, I was reminded of the debates about domestic violence: why are some women attracted to violent men? Are those complicit in violence equally to blame, or is a culture of blame just a way of hiding from uncomfortable truths? Upton's importance lies in the fact that she raises these questions; her chief limitation is that she is unwilling to hazard an answer.

At the time when *Bruises* was about to open, reviewer Sarah Hemming was looking for candidates to take on the angry young man image once sported by the late John Osborne. She named Sarah Kane and Judy Upton as writers who 'both left their audiences reeling, suggesting that perhaps the true inheritor of John Osborne's mantle is an angry young woman'. Unlike Osborne, who at first gloried in the Angry Young Man label and unleashed a stream of articulate provocations in the media, neither Kane nor Upton rose to the bait. Nor did they share the same critical reception. After *Blasted* was panned, a spokeswoman for the Court pointed out that *Ashes and Sand* 'was about a gang of teenage muggers and it was running at the time Elizabeth Hurley was mugged, but we didn't have a single phone call about that'. Perhaps Upton avoided Kane's fate because her style – naturalistic, documentary, linear – is less provocative than Kane's. Or was it because the horrors she describes are such a daily occurrence that the media prefers to ignore them?

Martin McDonagh's *The Beauty Queen of Leenane*

If the anger in Upton's work was a regular theme, pessimism about humanity, exemplified in the work of Martin McDonagh, was equally common. When McDonagh's debut opened at the Royal Court's Theatre Upstairs in March 1996, the *Evening Standard* observed that while new writing seemed 'unusually healthy', the 'world it describes does not'. Hailing McDonagh as the latest in a 'gang' of 'twentysomethings who take a bleak view of human nature and like their humour served black, strong and bitter', the review called him 'precocious' and 'promising'. He soon lived up to his promise: *The Beauty of Leenane* was originally put on in Galway, where it opened the new Town Hall theatre, and then transferred to the Theatre Upstairs. After that, it successfully toured Ireland before returning to London and the Duke of York's theatre. In 1996, it won three major awards: the George Devine, the Evening Standard most promising newcomer and the Writer's Guild best fringe play. It was also nominated for a Laurence Olivier award. At one ceremony, a reportedly drunken McDonagh hit the headlines after harsh words with Sean Connery almost resulted in a fight. When *The Beauty Queen of Leenane* won four Tony awards (although not the one for best play) in New York in 1998, Mary McAleese, the Irish President, commended the playwright.

By the end of the decade, his play had been translated into twenty-eight languages.

Set mainly in the kitchen of a cottage in the west of Ireland, *The Beauty Queen of Leenane* is about forty-year-old spinster Maureen's rancorous relationship with her clinging mother, Mag. When Maureen finds out that Mag hasn't told her about an invitation to a leaving party, she makes her drink lumpy Complan and eat dry Kimberley biscuits. After the party, Maureen brings Pato back home. He calls her the 'Beauty Queen of Leenane' and stays the night. The next morning, Mag is shocked to find him there, and tries to put him off by telling him that Maureen once suffered a nervous breakdown and ended up in a 'nuthouse'. Soon after, Pato (now working in London) writes to Maureen, asking her to come with him to Boston. He sends the letter to Ray – his younger brother – with instructions to hand it to Maureen, but the youth leaves it with Mag. She reads and burns it, but makes a verbal slip, and Maureen tortures her with boiling fat until she reveals the letter's contents. In the next scene, Maureen recalls how she saw Pato off at the station, promising to join him in America. Mag is rocking back and forth, then suddenly slumps forward to reveal a 'red chunk of skull'. A few weeks later, Maureen, having got away with murder, plans to leave. Ray visits her and it emerges that her memory of seeing Pato off is a delusion. After telling her that his brother is engaged to another woman, Ray leaves with Maureen's message to him: 'The Beauty Queen of Leenane says goodbye.' Maureen then sinks into her mother's rocking-chair.

The bare bones of the plot can convey neither the dramatic impact of the story nor the sheer exuberance of McDonagh's language, which critic Fintan O'Toole calls a 'strangely beautiful hybrid', drawn from 'the edgy street-talk of English cities and the lyricism of rural Irish speech'. The result is not a dull naturalistic speech but an eloquent, artificial, highly accentuated style that carries McDonagh's characteristic mix of savage irony and surreal humour. The world of the play is held together by a series of running jokes: from the brutal ambivalence of its title to domestic details such as Complan and Kimberley biscuits; from the uncertain name of the local priest (who is known as 'Welsh – Walsh – Welsh') to the constant rain; from Mag's habit of emptying her chamber pot in the kitchen sink to her irritating tendency to call Ray 'Pato'.

But the most assured aspect of *The Beauty Queen of Leenane* is that it is a well-plotted thriller, so tightly spun that almost every exchange is significant. When a poker is admired in an early scene, you can be sure it will be used in a later one. At the start, Maureen's two absent sisters are mentioned because they promised to send in a radio request for their mother's birthday. In the final stage image, Maureen takes Mag's place, listening to the radio: her sisters' request is belatedly broadcast. On paper, it is a corny device; in the theatre, it illustrates the suffocating hopelessness of the family as well as Maureen's inability to escape.

A well-made play, *The Beauty Queen of Leenane* toys with audience expectations. Although at first glance the setting could be Ireland in the thirties or fifties, the play mixes this traditional rural ambience with nineties references: when, for example, Mag tells Ray that 'There was a priest [in] the news Wednesday had a babby with a Yank!', London audiences recognized the reference to contemporary scandals, even if they didn't know – as Irish spectators surely did – that McDonagh was thinking of Eamonn Casey, the bishop of Galway, in whose diocese the real Leenane is situated. But if, in McDonaghland, 'You can't kick a cow' without 'some bastard holding a grudge twenty year', the place is also part of the global village: Australian soap operas and American cop shows on the television, references to Spiderman comics and Cadillacs, constant travelling to London and Boston. Ireland is a country redefining itself, a place where Delia Murphy shares the airwaves with the Chieftains.

Most critics hailed McDonagh's London debut as a triumph. In the Court's studio space, the play's naturalistic set drew audiences into a mythical Irish past. Waiting for the play to start, there was time to examine the details of the kitchen, from the photos of the Kennedys to the crucifix. Whereas most in-yer-face shockers have urban or futuristic locations, McDonagh's play looked as rural as a cow pat. You couldn't smell the urine in the sink of Garry Hynes's Druid Theatre Company production, but the dampness in the air gave a sense of chronic claustrophobia. At the climax of the plot, when Mag pitches forward, dead, there were gasps. But even more effective was the play's dramatic tension: the mislaid letter may be a hackneyed device, but here its delivery had audiences curling up with tension. And, at the end, as Maureen – maddened because Ray has called her a 'loon' – approaches him from behind with the poker, you felt another atrocity was imminent, until McDonagh reversed the situation with a deft touch of comedy: Ray jumps up because he discovers a slingball set that Maureen confiscated from him years ago.

Son of a Sligo mother and a Galway father, McDonagh was born in south London. Growing up at Elephant and Castle and Camberwell, he usually visited Ireland only for summer holidays. After leaving school, he lived with John, his elder brother (also a writer) in south London while his parents moved back to Ireland. 'I was unemployed for a long time, with the odd spell in an office and a supermarket,' he says. Described by Jack Bradley, the National Theatre's literary manager, as an 'archetypal garret poet', McDonagh spent several years writing short stories, films and radio plays before finally trying his hand at stage plays. Talking to journalists in 1996, he said he'd written twenty-two radio plays, all rejected by the BBC. His prolific output shows the time he has devoted to writing, which is also evident in the perfectionism of his craft.

But McDonagh claims to know little about theatre. 'I doubt I've seen twenty plays in my life,' he says. 'I prefer films.' He says he 'only started writing for theatre when all else failed. It was a way of avoiding work and earning a bit of money.' However typical of youthful arrogance, such flip comments can't disguise the fact that, as he says, 'I used to read lots.' Judging from his plays, he is certainly familiar with most Irish play-wrights from Boucicault to John B. Keane, from Synge to Tom Murphy. You only have to read the opening scene of Keane's *Sive* to see its influence on McDonagh. What are his inspirations? 'I quite like some early Pinter stuff, but I admire filmmakers such as Scorsese, Leone and Keaton. My aim is to get as much John Woo into the theatre as possible.' The reference to Woo, whose films use highly stylized violence, is typically ironic. 'The plays I have written are the kind of plays I'd like to see.'

McDonagh boasts that he wrote *The Beauty Queen of Leenane* in eight days, 'a scene a day; it isn't all that hard'. In one session, he rewrote it, adding the 'biscuit jokes'. However fast the writing, the play has clearly been carefully worked out. Starting with an image of the two women – 'I just had this mother–daughter sniping relationship in my head' – McDonagh built up the seething resentments and sly, poisonous humanity of the household. The focus on petty grievances and cruel recriminations is deliberate, with McDonagh claiming indifference to larger political issues: 'Why should anyone pay ten or twenty pounds to be lectured at for two hours?'

McDonagh's style is based on the experience of Irish uprootedness. His use of language employs Gaelic patois – for example, 'gasur' (boy) – as well as devices such as repetition and odd sentence structures. Aptly enough, the word 'ould' is a universal adjective. 'I guess it has something to do with the language I absorbed subconsciously as a child,' he says. 'My father's first language was Gaelic, and there is something about that stylized way of talking that appeals to me.' He also drew on memories of Ireland. 'In Connemara and Galway,' he says, 'the natural dialogue style is to invert sentences and use strange inflections.' His dialogue is a 'heightening of that, but there is a core strangeness of speech, certainly in Galway'. Of course, McDonagh no more reports the true speech of Galway than Synge actually reproduced, as he once claimed, the language he heard while listening to servant girls through 'a chink in the floor of the old Wicklow house'. Whatever his inspiration, McDonagh prefers writing about Ireland to writing about London: 'That's too close to home.'

The violence of *The Beauty Queen of Leenane* feels like a cross between a Coen brothers film and an 'olde' Irish play. On one level, the violence expresses real family hatreds, with the mistrust and malevolence of people trapped in a hopeless life bursting out in blatant aggression. In the play, McDonagh uses everyday objects, such as Complan, cooking oil and a heavy poker, as instruments of torture and murder. At one point, Maureen tells Pato that the 'only' reason she buys the 'horrible' Kimberleys is 'to torment me mother'. But the violence is not only domestic; there are references to the wider world, whether the unjust imprisonment of the Birmingham Six or the war in Bosnia. Even the nostalgic details of the set carry hints of sudden death: the photos are of John and Robert Kennedy, both victims of political assassination, and the embroidered tea towel reads: 'May you be half an hour in heaven afore the Devil knows you're dead.' Nor is violence a stranger to Maureen and Mag's bickering: when her mother is aghast that a Dublin man strangled an old woman and 'didn't even know her', Maureen wishes that he'd 'clobbered you with a big axe or something and took your oul head off and spat in your neck'. Even the jokes involve social comment: Ray tells Mag that while young priests seldom use violence, 'It's usually only the older priests go punching you in the head. I don't know why. I suppose it's the way they were brought up.'

But the play's violence is not just a comment on domestic life in a suffocating backwater; it also creates a world drenched in a nineties sensibility. Instead of directly showing modern Ireland (which owes more to America than to Europe and which has a higher proportion of computer-literate young people than Britain), McDonagh prefers pastiche. Instead of following other writers – Declan Hughes, Dermot Bolger, Conor McPherson – into urban settings, he parodies the tradition of bog, blarney and poteen. McDonagh's Ireland is postmodern in its grotesque exaggeration, in its isolation in a globalized world, and in its knowing nods and winks at Irish culture. The fragmentation of modern society, implies McDonagh, encourages violence: people lash out because they no longer control their lives. McDonagh also takes a stock theatrical form – the country melodrama – and turns it upside-down: the wise old woman becomes an ignorant toad and the sad spinster a psychopath; in this grim fairy tale, the spinster daughter is transformed not into a princess but into her own ugly mother. A mythical place – the West of Ireland – is deconstructed with meticulous attention to detail. Scenic beauty becomes constant rain, folksy charm is really inbred ignorance, the old-fashioned village is isolated and full of hatred, and the family a nest of vipers. This postmodern irony is not only entertaining, it also delivers a stinging criticism of nostalgia.

In *The Beauty Queen of Leenane*, the violence is also a dramatic device. Like Hitchcock, McDonagh uses both shock (when Mag unexpectedly pitches forward and reveals her battered skull) and suspense (when Maureen, clutching the poker, approaches Ray from behind) to engage the audience. He says he wants to bring sensation back into theatre: 'I think people should leave a theatre with the same feeling you get after a really good rock concert. A play should be a thrill.' In *The Beauty Queen of Leenane*, he uses humour to distract the audience while he prepares another morsel of cruelty to force down its throat. Maureen's hopes of marrying and getting away from her mother are raised and then smashed. Here, matricide and madness are less an exploration of uncomfortable feelings than a grim joke: in the end, the murder doesn't free her, but only imprisons her more. As Ray says, she has become the 'exact fecking image' of her mother. And the violence ends up being less disturbing than McDonagh's evident relish in writing it.

After its success, *The Beauty Queen of Leenane* was revived in July 1997, at the Duke of York's, with two other plays, which make up the Leenane trilogy. *A Skull in Connemara* – praised for its 'gruesome exhilaration' – was about a gravedigger's discovery that his buried wife's corpse was missing, while *The Lonesome West* – lauded for 'manic energy and physical violence' – featured two brothers closeted together in undying hostility. While neither of these plays has the same taut perfection of the first, watching all three together on a large stage gave audiences the chance to linger in McDonaghland, with its heady language, disregard for political correctness and satirical punch. At its best, the trilogy threw audience emotions into a wild swing between gleeful laughter and moments of bleak self-awareness. Theatrical references abounded: *A Skull in Connemara* is a line from Beckett's *Waiting for Godot* and the play features a bloodstained entrance straight out of Synge's *Playboy of the Western World*; *The Lonesome West* is a macabre rerun of Shepard's *True West*. The sick jokes were provocations: in *A Skull in Connemara*, Mick Dowd, the gravedigger, explains the absence of 'willies' on corpses by claiming they're cut off and given to tinkers 'as dog food'. During the Famine, he continues, tinkers ate them.

If the shock of McDonagh's disrespect for Irish traditions, verbal inventiveness and confident theatricality was seductive when *The Beauty Queen of Leenane* first appeared, the trilogy revealed his limitations. While Mag and Maureen are deep enough to engage our interest, neither of the other plays has comparably rounded characters. However hilarious, they seemed to be repeating the same postmodern trick. And while they don't prefer style over content – their style carries the content – they do lack compassion. If this does not matter too much in one play, its absence in a trilogy leads to a sense of depressing futility.

But although McDonagh's plays do not cultivate compassion, his work can still be intellectually exciting, because he offers a method of attacking nostalgia that applies not just to Ireland but to any nation's culture. A country, he implies, can only prepare for the twenty-first century by breaking with the cultural myths of its past. To do so, it is not enough to shrug off the whimsy of nostalgia; you have to pummel the past. As surely as Mick Dowd pulverizes the bones to skitter in *A Skull in Connemara*, McDonagh attacks the cultural images of a quaint 'old country'. In other words, the essential violence of his work is a question not of murders but of a writer's attitude, an intellectual stance that scorns respect and vents its fury on all things sentimental. This intellectual aggression could be applied to any culture, including that of mainland Britain. Compared to the plethora of nostalgic adaptations of Eng Lit classics that clogged up many a stage in the nineties, McDonagh's writing is refreshing bold.

But only at its best. When the National Theatre put on his *The Cripple of Inishmaan* in January 1997, it seemed that nothing could stop McDonagh. But the comparative weakness of that play – especially its cruelly manipulative attitude to the characters – was the first sign that his meteoric rise had slowed, and the two subsequent plays of his Aran Islands trilogy have yet to be staged. After he compared himself to the young Orson Welles, claiming to be 'the greatest' and attacking older playwrights for being 'so ugly' and 'really badly dressed', his sudden decline seemed like a comeuppance.

Rebecca Prichard's *Yard Gal*

Compared to the superficial flashiness of McDonagh, the work of Rebecca Prichard offers a real insight not only into the social roots of violence but also into the feelings of those involved in perpetrating it. Born in 1971, Prichard was brought up near Billericay, Essex, and studied drama at Exeter University. 'Theatre was seen as something you should experience as well as study,' she says. Her first play, *Essex Girls*, was written just after she left university in 1993, while she was a part-time youth drama worker in Grays, Essex, where she set up an all-women drama group 'because the absence of men made everybody much less self-conscious'. Working at Ruth House, a hostel for young single mothers, increased her awareness of women's issues. Prichard then got in touch with the Royal Court's Young People's Theatre and developed her play there and at the National Studio. Directed by Roxana Silbert, it had its premiere at the Court's 'Coming On Strong' festival of new writing in November 1994.

The two acts of *Essex Girls* are like a pair of snapshots, one 'before' and the other 'after', of the lives of young teenagers. Act I, The Party, is set in the toilet of a comprehensive school. Fourteen-year-old Diane, Hayley and Kelly skive off lessons and chat about sex, school and boys with a foul-mouthed ignorance that is both funny and disturbing: 'Iss bad luck to piss on a tampon, anyway.' 'Is it?' 'Yeah. Makes you go sterile in later life.' Act II, The Holiday, shows Kelly's sister Kim, a seventeen-year-old single mum, visited in her council flat by her friend, Karen. While Kim is depressed and tired out by her baby, Karen is ebullient and regales her friend with tales of sex and shopping. Despite the constant crying of Kim's baby on the intercom, giving a sense of a cycle of neglect, there is a small note of hope in the girls' resilience: 'Our messes are ours, Kim. We gotta get ourselves out of them.' Without preaching or hectoring, Prichard makes connections between fantasy and reality, cause and effect.

One obvious influence was Caryl Churchill. 'Her work made me aware of theatrical possibilities,' says Prichard, who is drawn to experimenting with form. 'You can say a lot through the structure of the play without weighing down your characters with messages – it frees you to stay with your characters without getting bogged down in didactic dialogue.' Both halves of *Essex Girls* do talk to each other, in an allusive but powerful way, suggesting that ignorance and immature fantasies lead to desperation and impoverished life choices.

After her debut, Prichard's next major work ran straight into a media storm, with its author labelled as Sarah Kane's 'successor as the Court's hard-hitting female playwright'. In August 1997, *Fair Game*, her loose adaptation of *Games in the Backyard*, a 1991 play by Israeli writer Edna Mazya, was attacked not because it was about a rape but because the Court planned to cast young teenagers in the main roles. The concern of various children's organizations that sixteen-year-olds might be damaged by playing aggressive teenagers was clearly exaggerated. Neither do-gooders nor journalists seemed to have read the play. In fact, Prichard had taken an early draft of *Fair Game* into schools and found that most youngsters were all too familiar with the subject of peer pressure, moral irresponsibility, even rape. The scandal about the play was not its content but that it dramatized real problems that many prefer to ignore.

In 1997, Clean Break Theatre Company – set up by and for female prisoners – asked Prichard to write a play to be produced the following year. She became the company's creative writing tutor and visited Bull-wood Hall prison in Hockley, Essex, for a three-month project (later extended by nine months). While teaching, Prichard listened to the women's stories and helped them produce their own writing (examples of which appeared in the published playtext of *Yard Gal*). Among the women, she found a 'real hunger for self-expression'. In August 1997, Clean Break gave a rehearsed reading of *Yard Gal*, and the play was put on at the Court in May 1998, before touring theatres and prisons. Stagings in prisons were followed by workshops in which prisoners discussed the issues raised and tried out various drama techniques (such as Augusto Boal's forum theatre).

Prichard learnt a lot from visiting prison. 'I had assumed that prisoners were either victims or saw themselves as victims, but in fact they didn't. They took responsibility for their lives.' White women and black women often shared the 'same rich slang' and 'created their own culture with both black and white elements in it'. She not only responded 'to rhythm of speech' but also immersed herself in jungle music, listening to pirate radio stations. Despite initial misgivings about writing in Jamaican patois, the stories that young offenders told about girl gangs gave her the idea of 'bringing alive a whole world'.

Yard Gal is a good example of nineties poor theatre: the props are simple and the piece needs only two actors. At first, Boo (black) and

Marie (white) avoid looking at the audience and 'psych each other out as to who will begin'. After some banter, Boo starts: 'This is a story about me and Marie and the posse that we used to move with. It's about chatting shit, getting fucked, getting high and doing our crimes and the shit that be going down in the yard innit.' Then Marie introduces the rest of the posse: Threse, Deanne, Sabrina and Deniz – all fifteen-year-old Hackney girls.

In a heady narrative, Boo and Marie spraypaint a rough guide to their lives: drink, drugs, going dancing; children's home, police station, Trenz nightclub; prostitution; shoplifting; selling drugs. Some of the stories are really 'low': hanging around with a policeman and biting his penis while fellating him. Others are horrific: when Deanne, high on drugs, shows off on a balcony, she loses her footing and falls to her death. Gradually, the posse's rivalry with Wendy's crew leads to savage stabbings and an ambiguous ending. Boo takes the blame for Marie's attack on Wendy and goes to prison; Marie has a baby, and names it after her friend. But prison divides them: although both understand that the other 'stays inside you a bit', they are no longer best friends. Realizing this, they wind down with a Beckettian valediction: 'Can we go now?'

The Court's version of this ninety-minute story of female friendship was exciting, partly because of the vigour of the writing, with its slangy directness and racy metaphors, and partly because of the energy of the cast, Sharon Duncan-Brewster (Boo) and newcomer Amelia Lowdell (Marie), smartly directed by Gemma Bodinetz. On a bare stage at the Ambassadors venue, with its steep seating, the audience looked down on what felt like a sporting event, with words bouncing around like basketballs. Duncan-Brewster and Lowdell's rapport had the pulse of a genuine relationship, with each girl echoing the other, taking up phrases like refrains and shooting the breeze. At some performances, people in the audience called out, shouting advice to Boo or Marie. Unusually for the West End, there were many black people in the audience. As the narrative picked up speed, the girls hurtled uncontrollably towards disaster; when Marie finds out she is pregnant, or when both girls realize they've drifted apart, the rawness of emotion was desperately moving.

Despite a few gripes, most critics praised the show. One or two took a personal tone. For example, the *Telegraph*'s Charles Spencer said that 'if you met these two kids on the bus, you'd pray they didn't notice you, because they are absolutely full of lip and bad attitude'. While Prichard was praised for the 'utter lack of self-pity in the writing', some critics wished that the play 'showed more and told less'. This attitude, which forms the critical bedrock of the study of Eng Lit, misunderstands *Yard Gal*'s genre. The use of spoken narrative onstage is a deliberate, and highly stylized, means of dramatizing relationships and events, and has been used to good effect by writers such as Conor McPherson. In *Yard Gal*, directly spoken narrative not only solicits audience sympathies, it also allows the pace of the play to accelerate in a way that perfectly matches the drug-fuelled intensity of the story.

Boo and Marie's friendship pervades the whole play and is articulated in many different ways, from Marie's affectionate 'You just nutty in fights man' to Boo's sacrifice in going to prison in place of her friend. When the gang runs into trouble, and shots are heard, Boo keeps 'me eye out for Marie in case we was gonna see a dead man because she has fits sometimes, don't ya, and it's only me that knows what to do'. That 'don't ya' both expresses her affection and allows the actors to react to each other onstage. Behind the sassy dialogue, *Yard Gal* explores constant shifts of feeling. What makes Deanne's accidental death more painful is the atmosphere of larking around that precedes it: when she gets on the ledge, her mates chant: 'We can see your knickers.' Throughout the play, emotions are precisely charted, whether it is Boo's wonder that, during a fight, 'I don't feel nothing. I think it's the speed. All the fear makes me go out of meself', or when Marie says that Sabrina has a 'split personality' because 'she act totally different with the men than she did the women innit', to which Boo replies with a shrug: 'We all did man.' Despite the self-aggrandizing slang and aggressive rhetoric, Prichard's account of the girl gang is less about violence than about female friendship.

'I chose friendship,' says Prichard, 'because I wanted a contrast with some of the other themes in the play which are quite alienating: drugs, abuse, violence.' Much of the play 'is about alienation but I didn't want people to feel alienated from it'. Why does it have a sad ending? 'I wanted the audience to feel the waste of young life and also my sense of anger about it.' At the same time, 'there's a lot there about survival and I wanted to celebrate that too'. In the end, Boo and Marie do emerge tougher if sadder: 'Life gets harder.' It is a small kernel of hope, but a significant one, hinting that to share experience between equals can result in individual change. In prison, it also worked as a way of using drama to explore personal feelings and suppressed emotions.

Some of the sex and violence in *Yard Gal* is pretty blatant. 'It's really only in the theatre that you can reflect how shocking life is,' says

Prichard. 'There's a reality out there that you never see on television.' Two months after the play opened, girl gangs once again barged into the media. A report by Antoinette Hardy of Loughborough University found that 80 per cent of a sample of forty teenage girls from the Midlands had been involved in fights. After interviewing them, Hardy concluded that they 'do not want to be males, but they are imitating some male behaviour to forge a new identity'. No longer passive, they were proving their equality with their fists. Girls had stopped pulling hair, preferring to punch, kick, headbutt and stab. Popular culture, with its images of Tank Girl and the female lead in *Terminator 2*, encouraged this version of Girl Power.

So is the violence in *Yard Gal* a means of female self-assertion? 'I don't think so,' says Prichard. 'Violence is fucked up whether it comes from women or men. Women should be able to develop their own forms of strength, without trying to behave like men.' Often, female violence 'is a product of desperation rather than a quest for identity'. Violence is a way of life 'in a world where you have to be violent just to survive, to front out a situation'. At other times, violence comes from being paranoid and 'completely wired' on drugs. Even when you're not taking them, 'the emotional effects of drugs can be savage; you built up the world into a totally attacking place. Violence is an illness.'

None of the girls in *Yard Gal* is meant to be a psycho, though they're all capable of extreme behaviour. And although each of them eggs on the others, individually the girls are afraid. When people equate female violence with Girl Power, says Prichard, 'They're usually trying to make a difficult subject more easily digestible.' The central paradox is that 'violence is the opposite of assertiveness; it comes from a sense of feeling completely helpless'. In the play, for example, Boo says that, when she is paranoid, 'it ain't like I'm scared it's like a feel I might do anything.'

The play's climax is Marie's violent attack on Wendy. Her violence comes out of an intense personal conflict: she is desperate because she doesn't know who the father of her child is. But once again, the climax explores the emotions of friendship. Boo goes to prison partly because she has to get off the street, but also as a way of helping Marie, who has enough problems of her own. The act of taking the blame for a friend 'stirred up a lot of emotion during shows in prison,' says Prichard; 'people would walk out crying.'

How did other prisoners react? 'Sometimes the audience went very quiet, very intent on following the action,' says Prichard. At other times, people 'wanted to answer back, so it really opened up discussions'. Often women prisoners treated Boo and Marie as if they were real people, and offered them suggestions about how to live their lives. 'We did some exercises to find different endings to the play – the results were very moving.' Clean Break has a lot of experience in handling the powerful feelings generated by such work, but while the writer and actors are free to leave after the event, the prisoners remain locked up. 'I'm very ambivalent: on the one hand, I'm glad to have worked with some really great women; on the other, it always feels bad to leave them.'

What makes *Yard Gal* so compelling is its sheer theatrical verve. The ending, during which Boo and Marie tell two stories simultaneously, perfectly captures the escalation of their situation. Prichard enjoyed playing with the relationship of the actors to the audience, using direct address and storytelling 'to give a sense of what it was like to be close to the characters, but at the same time to be distant, which is how I felt'. Without a trace of sentimentality or ideology, Prichard shows how female friendship can get you into trouble as well as how it can help you pull through; her empathetic approach is characterized by some bold and brassy writing, and a deep sympathy with her characters.

One of the defining changes in nineties theatre was the demise of politically correct 'victim drama', where perpetrators were bad and victims good. According to Dominic Dromgoole, it was the Bush theatre's policy to put the aggressor onstage instead of 'asking the audience to spend its time being sympathetic' to victims. By emphasizing such troubling notions as the complicity of victims in their victimization, provocative drama became more complex, less ideological. Instead of a morally black and white world, theatre offered grey areas and ambiguous situations. New writing was characterized, says the *Independent*'s Paul Taylor, by

> an unindignant wit and a sharp eye for quirks and contradictions. Characters who would once have been presented as straightforward victims are shown as being complicit in their oppression. The protagonists peer with a kind of existential puzzlement at their own affectless, morally disconnected behaviour.

In *Some Voices*, at first it seems as if Laura is a classic victim of Dave's violence, then Penhall shows that she has the strength to leave both Dave and Ray. By contrast, in plays such as *Ashes and Sand* and *Bruises*, everyone seems to be victimized. In *The Beauty Queen of Leenane*, Maureen kills her mother but ends up more a victim than a victimizer. while *Yard Gal*'s Boo and Marie are shown as both criminals and victims.

In December 1995, the *Evening Standard*'s Nicholas de Jongh pointed out that this 'was the year in which theatre caught up with the increasingly violent, alienated Britain of the closing years of the century'. He not only defended *Blasted* and *Mojo*, but also argued that 'no theatre should flinch' from 'presenting serious plays which may incite revulsion and dismay'. It is the writer's 'best business to stir sleepy consciences'. Although theatre journalists tend to hype up theatre, and violence often makes good copy, De Jongh put his finger on the experiential aspect of drama, which offered audiences a taste of what it is like to be in a violent situation, as well as a glimmer of hope about how such situations might be changed.

Conclusion

> I got taken along to see a play in Chelsea and I was quite shocked. All
> eye-gouging and buggery and not five minutes from the King's Road.
>
> (Nicholas in David Eldridge's *A Week with Tony*)

The new in-yer-face sensibility in nineties British theatre was not just a
product of the Royal Court, Traverse or Bush stages, but could be found
all over the scene. Sometimes, unbearable pain was summed up in one
unforgettable image. For example, in February 1996, at the Bird's Nest
pub theatre in Deptford, Anna Reading's *Falling* had an excruciating
incident in which Ket, a fifteen-year-old, had to remove a tampon after
having been raped. As she struggles to do it, she imagines dying, 'And
then they'll cut me open and find maggots and stinking dead flesh.' In
the bar after the show, I asked Reading why she wrote about such horrors. 'Because life is like that,' she said. It was a phrase I was to hear over
and over again when talking to young writers – and it was a response
that signalled the shift in sensibility where what seems shocking to the
mainstream is seen as normal by the new wave. Young writers felt com-
pelled to tell unwelcome and distressing truths in the most unmediated
way possible. Using such images of violated intimacy, extremism
became the new norm.

The story of nineties theatre begins with a crisis in new writing. But
while statistics show that fewer and fewer new plays were being put on
in the late eighties, this was compounded, says Jonathan Meth of Writernet, by the myth that new writing was a box office risk. When subsidies
were cut, many artistic directors shied away from new plays. So did
many theatre critics, says Soho Theatre Company's Paul Sirett. To him,
the early nineties 'did feel a bit sterile': new writing companies were
doing good work, 'but there was nothing happening to make you think
it was a particularly vibrant culture'. The perception that new writing
was a ghetto also led some young directors to avoid it. Jack Bradley, literary manager of the National Theatre, says that the crisis was 'not a
reflection of writing, but of the economic situation'. Writers are drawn
to where the action is. 'If you have a moribund film industry, writers of
dialogue are more likely to try their hand at writing stage plays.' When
television abandoned the single drama, says Meth, 'theatre became a

place where young writers could express themselves', and Bradley suggests that 'while in the mid-eighties, many writers wrote novels; in the mid-nineties they wrote plays'.

Because the writer is central to British theatre, the crisis that arose in the late eighties and early nineties – as government cutbacks in subsidy imposed all kinds of constraints on creativity – was expressed as a crisis in new writing. Playwrights and theatre people, journalists and pundits, audiences and academics, all complained that there were not enough new writers and that their work was not being put on often enough. New plays were widely seen as predictable in content and dull in production. Many young directors refused to work with new writers; many artistic directors declined to put on new plays. Regional reps began to panic about the lack of 'bums on seats'; the West End was thought to be moribund. A general malaise in British theatre, characterized by defeatism and despair, was seen as a crisis in new writing.

Then came the resolution. The turning point in the nineties was the advent of in-yer-face provocation at the Royal Court in 1994–5. As Sue Higginson, head of the National Studio, which co-produced Daldry's first season, says: 'We did a season with the Royal Court that was a seminal moment. That was when people started to say: "Oh I see, new writing is sexy", and jumped on the bandwagon.' Director Ian Rickson says that when he first arrived at the Court, 'the Theatre Upstairs had been closed, there were only six new plays a year – and playwriting was in a depressing state'. The energy 'was with the classics and with directors as *auteurs*'. But as the Court began to put on more new plays in the mid-nineties, 'playwriting moved into a position of centrality in the culture'. The key moment was Daldry's first season of new writing, which included Joe Penhall, Judy Upton and Nick Grosso, and the key play was Sarah Kane's *Blasted*.

The most symbolic career in nineties British theatre was that of Stephen Daldry. Brought up in the West Country, he went from grammar school to study English and drama at Sheffield University (regional not metropolitan, redbrick not Oxbridge). After university, he worked in an Italian circus (European physical theatre), before directing plays in the Sheffield and York (regional freelance). Appointed artistic director of London's Gate theatre, he specialized in directing German Expressionist and Spanish Golden Age plays (director's theatre on the fringe). Appointed artistic director of the Royal Court in 1992, he directed two spectacular revivals – J. B. Priestley's *An Inspector Calls* and Sophie Treadwell's *Machinal* (postmodern stylization) – for the National Theatre, and began his work at the Court with a revival of Wesker's *The Kitchen* (a Court classic), for which he tore out half the seating (remodelling theatrical space). In 1993, his mission statement was: 'Why is our audience so fucking middle-aged? We have to listen to the kids.' Early productions included shocking plays by DV8 (dance theatre) and Neil Bartlett (gay theatre), followed by the 1994–5 season of young unknowns (new writing). After redefining the Court's style by promoting provocative young writers, he secured lottery funding to rebuild the Court and took up residence in the West End (creative economics). In 1998, he quit the Court and went into filmmaking (cross-media mobility).

Daldry's move from revivals to in-yer-face new work was conscious, but it also depended on chance. His first Court season was an experiment; he wasn't sure what he was doing, which explains his shyness in promoting the event. But when Kane's *Blasted* caused a massive media rumpus, with philistine calls for censorship and attacks on the Court's artistic direction, Daldry realized that he'd found a new role. When he defended her, he was also defending himself and rediscovering the Court's mission. The noise of controversy told him that provocation was the right method: as well as bringing in new audiences, it renewed his sense of identity. As the Court rediscovered its roots as a controversial theatre, Daldry became the impresario of in-yer-face drama.

But if new writing made a big splash with the arrival of Joe Penhall, Judy Upton, Nick Grosso and Sarah Kane, the two plays that consolidated the new wave were Mark Ravenhill's *Shopping and Fucking* and Jez Butterworth's *Mojo*, which both opened within a month of each other in autumn 1996. By the following year, both were being revived and other provocative plays – such as Patrick Marber's *Closer* – were being transferred to commercial West End venues. At one point in 1998, *Shopping and Fucking*, *Closer* and *Popcorn* were running next to each other on Shaftesbury Avenue, a situation that disproved the notion that new writing was uncommercial. So if the battle for a new aesthetic was fought and won over the issue of Kane's *Blasted*, the immediate beneficiaries were writers such as Ravenhill, Butterworth and Martin McDonagh.

By 1998, playwright David Hare could rightly claim, in a newspaper interview, that while 'the habit of theatregoing as a social ritual is more or less dead', there is 'an enormous appetite for plays'. 'After all those years of being fashionably beaten, theatre is suddenly healthy again,' he said. 'I've recently encountered the best audiences I've seen for years.'

When he saw *Closer* and Conor McPherson's *The Weir*, 'they were playing to young audiences'. Certainly, the number of new plays circulating
between theatres reached a dizzy figure: according to a report by the
New Playwrights Trust (now Writernet), at any one time during the
mid-nineties there were something like 25,000 plays in circulation. Of
course, this figure is inflated because several copies of each new play cir-
culate simultaneously, but even so it does suggest the existence of an
enormous reservoir of new work.

Were the new writers hyped up beyond their talent? In a decade
obsessed by spin doctors and the role of the media, and when arts journalism was often more interested in who writers were sleeping with than
in what they were writing, it is scarcely surprising that theatres
rethought the 'marketing' of their 'product'. When theatres grew more
businesslike, hype became part of their repertoire. A master of public
relations, Daldry held regular lunches with the major critics, informing
them about new developments and making them feel part of his project.
Two examples of hype are revealing. When Butterworth's *Mojo* opened
at the Court, it was widely advertised as being the first time since
Osborne's *Look Back in Anger* that a writer had made his or her debut on
the main stage. The point was that Daldry was breaking one of his theatre's rules, which was to introduce writers in small studio spaces and
then let them 'graduate' onto the main stage. But the claim that *Mojo*
was the first main-stage debut since 1956 was not based on research, but
simply on the fact that no one at a script meeting could think of any previous instance. Similarly, in the case of Ayub Khan-Din's *East Is East*,
which was hyped when it was revived at the Court in 1997 as 'seen by
more people than any play in our history', this was not a judgement
reached after comparing its final sales, but was solely based on the fact
that all the preview shows had been sold out, which (considering that it
had just played to sell-out audiences at the Theatre Royal, Stratford
East) was hardly surprising. Yet, despite such cases of reckless hype, the
fact remains that what sells plays is more often word of mouth than
publicity handouts. What filled theatres in the nineties was the quality of
new writing.

While the Royal Court rediscovered the spirit of 1956, the Year Zero
of postwar British theatre, the explosion of confrontational drama
didn't happen in a vacuum; it was part of an increasingly diverse new
writing scene. Within this diversity, there was also an element of fashion:
one year, theatres would receive dozens of plays about heroin; the next,

there would be a heap of gangster stories. But despite such copycat dramas, the nineties saw a great liberation of the imagination of British dramatists. More and more, the rules taught in playwriting courses were broken. As the Finborough's Phil Willmott says, 'At the start of the nineties, if you asked someone to write a play about Jack the Ripper, you'd get a naturalistic three-hander. Now, in 1999, you're more likely to get an amazing, huge, cinematic, fantastical play.' If young writers hadn't grabbed so enthusiastically at the possibilities offered, British theatre would have stagnated in a morass of obscure seventeenth-century classics or highly stylized versions of modern warhorses. Its energy would have been dissipated between the cults of director's theatre, physical theatre and live art. Ghettoized in obscure fringe venues, new writing might have found its creativity strangled by the demands of ideologically correct edicts or the pressure to produce work that, for financial reasons, was only allowed a cast of three and no scene changes. In short, young writers saved theatre at a time when it risked becoming wholly irrelevant to the wider culture, hermetically sealed from life.

One way of understanding the point of view of a young writer is to do a thought experiment. Imagine being born in 1970. You're nine years old when Margaret Thatcher comes to power; for the next eighteen years – just as you're growing up intellectually and emotionally – the only people you see in power in Britain are Tories. Nothing changes; politics stagnate. Then, some time in the late eighties, you discover Ecstasy and dance culture. Sexually, you're less hung up about differences between gays and straights than your older brothers and sisters. You also realize that if you want to protest, or make music, shoot a film or put on an exhibition, you have to do it yourself. In 1989, the Berlin Wall falls and the old ideological certainties disappear into the dustbin of history. And you're still not even twenty. In the nineties, media images of Iraq, Bosnia and Rwanda haunt your mind. Political idealism – you remember Tiananmen Square and know people who are roads protesters – is mixed with cynicism – your friends don't vote and you think all politicians are corrupt. This is the world you write about.

Such writers were Thatcher's Children, and their view of the world came from being brought up in the eighties. In the fierceness of its attack on market economics, in-yer-face theatre was a reaction against the idea that 'there is no such thing as society'; with its images of violent men and rude girls, it stemmed from two decades of growing feminist sensibility; in its ready acceptance of street slang and exuberant bad language, it reflected the importance of 'yoof' culture; in its obsession with laddish behaviour, it mirrored the crisis of masculinity; and in turning its back on the state-of-the-nation and issue play, it suggested a crisis of the liberal imagination. It would, however, be wrong to be too dogmatic about what makes a 'typical' young writer. Although many share similar tendencies, they are all highly individual, as the diversity of their plays shows. Some, like Sarah Kane and Mark Ravenhill, may have been Thatcher's Children, but their political awareness also put them in a direct line with the powerful leftist tradition in British theatre.

In the nineties, state-of-the-nation plays fell out of favour, but most young writers did paint a vivid picture of contemporary life. Accepted pieties about what it meant to be British were not merely questioned, they were interrogated. Britain was seen as a bleak place where families were dysfunctional, individuals rootless and relationships acutely problematic, a place where loners drifted from bedsits to shabby flats. Here, you were more likely to bump into a rent boy than a factory worker, a girl gang than a suburban birthday party, a group of petty thieves than a couple buying their first house. Foul-mouthed and irreverent, wildly gleeful and often hip, these were also troubled people. Despite their bravado, there was helplessness and anxiety: sexual, moral, existential. Such vividly drawn characters inhabited episodic stories rather than three-act plots, metaphor-rich situations rather than well-made plays. But amid the confusion, the nihilism and the pain, there were often faint rays of hope shining through the dark of the urban jungle.

No one suggests that the majority of the British people were rent boys, smack addicts or abuse victims; social surveys showed that most young people wanted a job and a stable family. But many young writers used extreme characters to redefine the image of Britain. No more cosy suburban life, no more country nostalgia. Instead, as dramatist John Mortimer put it, new writing reflected the 'strident, anarchic, aimless world of England today, not in anger, or even bitterness, but with humour and a kind of love'. This imaginary Britain was a far darker place than that experienced on a daily basis by most of its audiences. And while it could be read as an example of the 'young country' that New Labour – with its attempts to rebrand Britain – tried to promote, it was much more raw, savage and critical than the platitudinous ideas thrown up by the Cool Britannia phenomenon. New writing's Britain was a netherscape that forcefully reminded audiences that not everything in the garden was rosy.

The metaphors typical of nineties drama – summed up by stage images of abuse, anal rape and addiction – could be criticized for being literal images of horror, but their context often represented an advance on eighties drama because it saw the world in a more complex light. The best plays of the decade were most provocative when they viewed terrible acts as psychological states, usually characterized by complicity and collusion. Although the urgency of in-yer-face drama, with its compelling new aesthetic of experiential theatre, reached out and dragged audiences through ugly scenes and deeply disturbing situations, its motives were not to titillate but to spread the knowledge of what humans are capable of. Experiential theatre aimed to wake up audiences and tell them about extreme experiences, often in order to immunize them to those events in real life. As Sarah Kane once said, 'It is important to commit to memory events which have never happened – so that they never happen. I'd rather risk overdose in the theatre than in life.'

In December 1996, critic James Christopher used his review of Jim Cartwright's *I Licked a Slag's Deodorant* to announce the arrival of a 'new brutalism' which influenced theatrical sensibilities in the same way as Damien Hirst had changed ideas about conceptual art. The style of new writing was informed by 'the realms of the senses – sex, drugs, casual violence and fantasy', and 'these plays are valid because they violate' complacency. As Christopher suggests, theatre did not operate in isolation from other art forms. Attacks on audience sensibilities came from many directions in the nineties: from the Royal Academy's *Sensation* exhibition of Young British Artists to the adverts, featuring a bloody newborn baby or a man dying of AIDS, used by the Benetton clothing company. Whether it was violent films or provocative soap operas, the 'heroin chic' of the fashion industry or Channel Four's *The Word*, everywhere complacency seemed to come under fire. The role of in-yer-face theatre was precisely to question received ideas in such a way as to make audiences uncomfortable. The experience of watching harrowing plays – however physically safe the theatre – imprinted indelible images of human suffering.

This vision of Britain, as shown on countless stages, had a homogeneous feel because often the same actors appeared in different plays. Kate Ashfield played Cate in *Blasted*, Lulu in *Shopping and Fucking*, and Alice in *Closer* (as well as being in Kane's *Woyzeck* and Grosso's *Peaches*); Ewen Bremner and Susan Vidler appeared in *Trainspotting* and Nick Ward's *The Present*, as well as countless British films. More than once, you would come across Kacey Ainsworth as a cockney (*Serving It Up*, *Pale Horse*, *Attempts on Her Life*), Faith Flint as an underclass girl (*Essex Girls*, *Handbag* and Kevin Coyle's *Corner Boys*), Neil Stuke as a lad (*Mojo*, *Not a Game for Boys*, *Goldhawk Road*), Patrick O'Kane as a hard man (*The Life of Stuff*, *Popcorn*, *Trust*) and Ray Winstone as a man on the edge (*Some Voices*, *Pale Horse*, *Dealer's Choice*). Casting could also affect a play's meaning: when Tony Curran appeared in *Dogs Barking*, audiences thought he was a psycho because they'd seen him as one in Rebecca Gilman's *The Glory of Living* and Tony Marchant's television version of *Great Expectations*. James Cunningham used to joke about being cast in plays that involved anal sex (*Penetrator*, *Cleansed*) while Robin Soans seemed to relish his smarmy bossman roles (*Search and Destroy*, *Shopping and Fucking*). But while Pip Donaghy was emotionally true as Ian in *Blasted*, he seemed less comfortable as Henri in *Never Land*. Typecasting is nothing new, but seeing the same faces gave these plays a similarity not necessarily evident in the writing.

Apart from their emphasis on masculinity, what were the politics of cutting-edge new plays? It is symptomatic of the nineties that traditional categories of left and right politics didn't seem to fit any more. While in-yer-face theatre was certainly anti-middle class – in the sense of affronting social conventions and being sceptical about the values of Middle England – it is much harder to argue that it was pro-working class. Behind the violence of these plays, lies anger and confusion – a typical response to the difficulties of living in a post-Christian, post-Marxist, postfeminist and postmodern society. For most writers, both the politics of consumer society and the traditional leftist opposition were equally suspect. But if the proletariat was no longer God, commodity capitalism was still Satanic.

Political plays, as writer David Greig points out, must contain a suggestion that change is possible. In a sense, they have to inspire audiences. But even 'the most visceral, popular plays of today,' argued Michael Billington in 1998, 'imply that there is little hope of change: in Patrick Marber's *Closer* the characters end up acknowledging their inviolable solitude, in Mark Ravenhill's *Shopping and Fucking* the "money is civilisation" ethos murkily prevails, in Phyllis Nagy's *Never Land* the hero is quite clearly the victim of fate.' In Britain, Billington concluded, 'We are living in an aggressively post-ideological age.' Other critics agreed. Ian Herbert compared the concern of David Hare's generation with 'mass violence' to that of today's young writers with 'more personal acts of violence, such as rape or abuse'. Although Daldry once described himself as 'an old politico', he also said that the plays that came to the Court were invariably 'explorations of private values rather than society's morals'. Confrontational theatre's political edge came not from scrawling on large political canvasses but from intensive examination of private pain. Not for the first time, young writers discovered that the personal was political, that small stories could resonate as widely as grand narratives.

While nineties drama often evidenced an acute moral disquiet with the world, did it deliver any metaphors of change? Well, the stage images of *Blasted* are as humanistic as anything in British postwar drama, but they inspire feelings of endurance rather than hopes of change; the thematic coherence of *Shopping and Fucking* offers only glimmers of optimism; and the searing experience of sitting through *Penetrator* turned the banal brutalities of army life into a powerful critique of masculinity, without suggesting what could be done about it. Typical of the decade was the outright refusal of many young dramatists to give answers to the urgent questions they raised. For example, in the programme of *Car* (Theatre Absolute, 1999) – a play that showed how both thieves and their victims could behave with equal violence – Chris O'Connell wrote: 'There are numerous questions I've asked myself whilst writing *Car*, and there aren't any easy answers.' Writers were sceptical of easy solutions to complex problems, refrained from telling people what to do and were aware that ideological plays with big messages were old-fashioned. This attitude came less from an inability to think than from a conscious decision not to preach to audiences. If at times this felt like an abdication of moral responsibility, more often it reflected *fin-de-siècle* uncertainty. On the other hand, if you judge a culture by its interest in personal emotions, in how humans feel when they are at their most intimate, vulnerable or extreme, then cutting-edge theatre oozes good health.

But this kind of drama has always been a contested territory. On television, veteran critic Milton Shulman denounced *Shopping and Fucking* as 'a psychotic babble written by someone with an anal fetish who sees life through an arse-hole darkly'; more reasonably, he also pointed out that 'some critics reinforced their reputations as liberal observers by supporting any form of explicit sexual activity on the stage as a dramatic advance'. David Hare has agreed with this point, saying that critics belatedly acknowledged past mistakes 'by clapping their hands at every new laddish loudmouth who comes along on the fringe'. Director Matthew Warchus called plays about drugs and violence 'reactionary and really uninteresting', while as late as May 1998, the *Spectator*'s Harry Eyres regretted how 'sensation and nihilism stalk the stages' of London theatre, strutting their stuff in imitation of Tarantino and artist Jeff Koons. 'Sensationalism is predicated on insensitivity. The idea is that dulled audience response must be jerked into life by whatever violent means are necessary.' But, he argued, 'sensation merely entrenches the insensitivity it is supposed to challenge'. Attacking the 'chilling lack of compassion' of Martin McDonagh's *The Cripple of Inishmaan*, Eyres said that the idea that audiences' attention 'can only be held by acts of ever grosser lewdness' leads to densensitization and loss of humanity.

Lack of heart is the central criticism of in-yer-face theatre. One of the reasons for this is the paradox that an era that flattered itself as being 'the caring decade' – as opposed to the 'greed is good' eighties – produced a drama that often lacked compassion. Compassion is an important quality because it grounds a play in the humanist tradition, emphasizes a naturalistic aesthetic, and often works dramatically: audiences identify more readily with characters they feel are fully rounded human beings. Watching plays that are deficient in compassion often feels alienating. In the final scene of *Mojo*, Skinny is shot in the head, but Butterworth has scripted his death as a series of grim jokes: Skinny worries about getting 'blood on my new trousers' and about his teeth going 'wiggly'. Because of this, it is easy to remain unmoved. In *Closer*, the relentless rush for a punch line often compromises the humanity of the protagonists. In McDonagh's case, the writer disposes of people and their aspirations with a carelessness that eventually irritates. On the other hand, in *Shopping and Fucking*, audiences could identify with the characters despite the fact that Ravenhill has written them as cartoons. A good production can bring out the latent compassion of a piece, even when the writer has not developed it fully. The challenge of such plays for future directors is to cultivate the inherent humanity that is often obscured behind the glitzy dialogue.

Not all the critics of in-yer-face theatre can be dismissed as rightwing reactionaries. Appalled by the way that the marketing of boys' plays marginalized other voices, Phyllis Nagy pointed out that women writers were often more experimental than men – and tackled subjects with more emotional depth. She attacked the timidity of much of nineties drama and said that the real subject of serious writing should be 'the collapse of our daring, of our collective bravery'. Criticizing the 'zeal for the literal', Nagy argued that 'plays that deal with violent sex are often topical but rarely radical'. Others saw many new plays as frankly nostalgic. Writer Matthew Dunster argues that nineties new writing, 'like Britpop' music, is essentially backward-looking. What are the young Turks of today doing? 'They are rewriting old plays,' he says. 'I think it's no accident that the two writers who have most excited the establishment are Jez Butterworth, whose play *Mojo* is set in fifties, gangland Soho, and Martin McDonagh, whose plays are set in an Ireland that smacks of times forgotten.' Even more powerfully, Harry Gibson argues that new waves are first greeted and then condemned: 'In their first hot flush, critics loved rawness and uncompromising vision; but the morning after, they wish it had been properly cooked, served with an explanatory salad and a garnish of redemption.' He sees in-yer-face theatre as part of a culture that includes 'readers' wives' pornography and the ritual humiliations of *The Jerry Springer Show*: 'the excess of the wild folk becomes a spectacle for the tame folk', a form of cultural tourism that ignores the real problems that are its subject matter. After all, the 'street kids' so admired onstage are in reality either hapless addicts or vicious thugs.

In-yer-face theatre pioneered a new aesthetic. One of the reasons for the heated debate about some of its more extreme manifestations was that people were not quite ready for it. However conscious of theatrical tradition, writers such as Neilson, Kane and Ravenhill were making a conscious break with previous ways of writing. Each was committed to making theatre act directly on the senses – in much the same way as physical theatre and live art often do. One result of the new aesthetic was a change in critical criteria, in the way critics value new work. The problem with judging nineties new writing in terms of naturalism or social realism is that this tries to impose the conventions of a previous era onto the present. The problem is compounded by the influence of postmodernism, which not only undermined established critical categories but also promoted a pervasive cultural relativism that weakened the very idea that work could and should be judged. Despite this, anyone who has sat through a badly written or ineptly constructed play can tell the difference between good writing and bad. Like all new waves, in-yer-face theatre has its own conventions. The standards of the well-made play or Eng Lit criteria cannot do it justice. If a well-made play has to have a good plot, much provocative drama prefers to have a strong sense of experiential confrontation; if a well-made play has to have complex characters, much new drama has types rather than individuals; if a well-made play has to have long theatrical speeches, nineties drama usually has curt televisual dialogue; if a well-made play must have a naturalistic context, in-yer-face drama often creates worlds beyond mere realism; if a good well-made play has to have moral ambiguity, in-yer-face drama often prefers unresolved contradictions.

If you compare a play by a good nineties writer with what was written in previous decades, the strengths of new writing are immediately apparent. What strikes the reader about nineties writing is its vitality and immediacy, both of which recall and mimic real speech, but without being either documentary or realistic. Compared to previous new waves, the dialogue is faster, the exchanges sharper, the expressions of emotion more direct and extreme, and the language more highly coloured. Plays have rarely been so thrillingly alive. By contrast, much political theatre and the issue plays of the seventies and eighties are – with a few exceptions – wordy, worthy and woolly. In them, people speak as if they were broadcasting; their language is middle-classless and bookish; their speeches large and baggy and rhetorical.

In terms of ideas, nineties theatre also makes a notable break with previous new waves. Unencumbered by ideology, today's theatre doesn't debate issues. Unlike political and feminist drama, it doesn't show you who is guilty and who is innocent. It avoids simplification. Typically, it present ideas within individual lives and grounds them firmly in the contradictions of character. For example, in *Blasted*, Ian is not simply an abuser, nor is Cate simply a victim. Ian is both a likeable character and a repulsive bundle of prejudices; Cate is both a naive young woman and complicit victim. As Kane said, 'I don't think that the world is neatly divided into perpetrators and victims.' Those kinds of divisions result 'in very poor, one-dimensional writing'. In *Blasted*, the play's ideas about masculinity, warfare and the media at first arise solely out of rapid and spare exchanges of dialogue. Finally, the ideas are emphatically underlined by the play's structure.

The question of structure reflects a crisis in how we see reality. While the world seems increasingly fragmented and dislocated, some writers react by emphasizing its chaos; at the same time, many audiences yearn for narrative cohesion and dramatic resolution. Much of nineties new writing was uninterested in well-made plays or in what some writers called 'plotting by numbers'. Although many stuck to a naturalistic linear structure, their attitude to form could be both experimental and playful. The challenge of questioning form was taken up most enthusiastically and radically by women, often inspired by the example of Caryl

Churchill. Nagy, Wallace and Kane have used shifting timescales and open-ended structures to question our ideas of reality and to subvert received notions of what a play should be. By contrast, Ravenhill's *Handbag* was a less successful attempt to juxtapose different timescales. But if nineties new writing stressed stories, conflict and character, it was suspicious of plots with clear beginnings, middles and ends, and avoided the closure implied by a neat ending. Most plays ended on a note of uncertainty and irresolution.

Although moral panics and controversy tended to warp our view of the most provocative plays of the decade, it is possible to distinguish between them. As writers, Ridley, Nagy and Wallace are well established and it is not difficult to see that their work will stand the test of time. As theatre, *Blasted*, *Shopping and Fucking*, *Mojo*, *Closer* and *The Beauty Queen of Leenane* are already contemporary classics and part of the canon of nineties drama. On the page, Kane's work has a density and depth that clearly proclaim her talent. However idiosyncratic, her *Cleansed*, *Crave* and *4.48 Psychosis* will repay further exploration by different directors. Neilson's *Normal*, *Penetrator* and *The Censor* will be revived as long as people want to create experiential theatre. However, it is not clear that future productions of Ravenhill's *Faust Is Dead* or *Handbag* will yield more shades of meaning that their original versions. Similarly, plays such as Prichard's *Yard Gal* are so tied to the circumstances of their original productions that future revivals, however useful in their context, may not yield more riches. But Prichard's *Essex Girls* is already a minor classic, and as a writer she goes from strength to strength, as does Zajdlic. The same can't be said for Upton, whose work is uneven and sometimes bizarrely idiosyncratic, but her *Ashes and Sand* at least is troubling enough to be worth reviving. In their different ways, Block and Walker, the one appealingly sensitive, the other entertainingly ornate, could also develop and progress. By contrast, Penhall, Grosso and Eldridge – after making blazing debuts – have produced work that raises unresolved questions about form and content. Penhall's explorations of the quiet side of life are traditionally plotted but lack the punch of his first two plays. Both Grosso and Eldridge refuse to use traditional plot structures which deliver onstage climaxes, preferring to concentrate on subtext and fine character shading. Whether the loss of dramatic impact will continue to be compensated for by their humane and witty attitude remains to be seen. Even if some of their plays are unsatisfactory, most of these writers have achieved a maturity of craft –

however narrowly focused – at a comparatively early age, which raises hopes for their continued development.

The story of nineties theatre is one of turning weakness into strength. At a time of cuts in subsidy, there was a paradoxical explosion of creativity. Despite lack of funding, many young writers learn their craft while working for little money; the new wave was a part of Do-It-Yourself culture. Phil Willmott at the tiny Finborough deliberately encouraged writers to write 'big plays on big subjects' because, since no one was getting paid, there was no need to be bound by restrictions on how many cast members you could afford. Here, Eldridge's second play, *A Week with Tony*, had a cast of thirteen. The ability of young writers to take advantage of the insecurity of being a playwright in an era of cutbacks can also be seen in the way they move freely from theatre to radio to television to film. Such cross-media creativity is a cultural strength. Much of their best work also turns the disadvantage of being confined to small studio spaces – which are easier than large venues to fill with new plays – to an advantage in terms of pioneering a much more intense theatrical experience. This capitalizes on theatre's innate strength. As the Court's Ian Rickson says,

> There's something so powerful about the eloquence of the live human event. You find yourself in a cauldron, a crucible in which something is happening physically. Even metaphorical violence or offstage violence can be incredibly powerful because you are implicated and involved. Since the Greeks, one of theatre's jobs is to take us into some of the darkest areas of life so that we should leave the theatre crying out for change.

Experiential theatre was the new aesthetic of the nineties.

One evidence of its quality is the immense appeal of in-yer-face drama on foreign stages. A log of overseas productions kept by the Court shows that plays by Neilson, Kane, Ravenhill, Butterworth, McDonagh, McPherson, Nagy, Penhall, Prichard, Walker – mounted all over Europe, as well as in north America and Australia – numbered about fifty by 1999. In Europe, Germany had the most productions, followed by Austria, Sweden, the Netherlands and Denmark. Other popular plays include Crimp's *Attempts on Her Life* and Cartwright's *I Licked a Slag's Deodorant*. Over the period 1995 to 1999, there were more than 400 productions worldwide of plays premiered at the Court. Inspired by such imports, a group of German writers set up the short-lived TNT

(Theatre of a New Type) in 1997 with the aim of creating a writer's theatre in Berlin. Two years later, the Taormina theatre festival awarded the Court a major prize for 'its efforts in recent years to discover and promote the work of young British dramatists' and for 'encouraging the spread of the phenomenon in other countries'. The programme for the festival stressed the theatre's role in giving a 'voice to a new generation of young writers whose moral anger, urban despair and political disillusion have sent shockwaves throughout the whole of Europe'. In New York, in the first six months of 1999, there were eight Court shows on Broadway, including Pinter's *Ashes to Ashes* and Caryl Churchill's *Blue Heart* as well as plays by Ravenhill, McDonagh and McPherson. Ridley's *The Pitchfork Disney* and Marber's *Closer* also made United States debuts. But while some of the shows were direct transfers of British originals, many of the productions in Europe were newly translated versions. And, although a few were directed by big-name directors such as Peter Zadek (*Cleansed*) and Claude Regie (*Knives in Hens*), the advent of British new writing encouraged a questioning of the European assumption that the director is God. Being led by writers, the British presence encouraged European writers to emulate them, and to value the word rather than the image. It is hard to disagree with theatre agent Mel Kenyon when she says: 'We are stimulating a new writing culture abroad.'

Nor has the film industry been slow in seeing the potential of the rebirth of new writing. So far, the fortunes of film versions of stage plays have been mixed. If Welsh's *Trainspotting* (Danny Boyle, 1995) was one of the high points of recent British film-making, the film of *The Life of Stuff* (Simon Donald, 1997) was a commercial and critical disaster. Butterworth's own film of *Mojo* boasted a strong cast, but the film cruelly revealed the shallowness of the play's plot. By 2000, several other plays were being developed as films: Wallace's *The War Boys*, Penhall's *Some Voices*, Eldridge's *Serving It Up*, Grosso's *Peaches* and Upton's *Ashes and Sand*. Such examples show the versatility of today's young writers, but the main problem is that film versions, while reaching a wider audience, can rarely capture the intensity of a stage experience. As writer Simon Burke says, 'I cannot see the purpose of theatre unless it is to plunge down the U-bend where television and film cannot go without losing their shirts.'

The renewal of confidence in blatant or disturbing writing did not leave older writers unaffected. Would David Hare have begun *The Judas Kiss* (Almeida, 1998), his play about Oscar Wilde, with an act of onstage cunnilingus, if younger writers had not used similar images? Older writers certainly enjoyed the same freedoms as the twentysomething generation. For example, even in a comedy such as Terry Johnson's *Dead Funny*, marital conflict was staged in a gobsmackingly vicious way – Eleanor confronts her apparently impotent husband with his infidelity: 'It's not all bodies you find repellent? Just mine? These particular breasts, these particular legs, this particular cunt?' Likewise, sexuality had never been so open or so problematic. In Nick Ward's *The Present* (Bush, 1995), Danny is seduced by Becky, who tries to strangle him while they're having sex. In Doug Lucie's *Love You, Too* (Bush, 1998), Shelley is shown as a sexual predator, using a man to get pregnant and then discarding him like a used condom. At the time, the play felt like a response to *Closer*. One year later, Hugh Whitemore's *Disposing of the Body* (Hampstead, 1999) was surprisingly frank in its portrayal of middle-aged sexuality. But sometimes, explicit sex acts provoked an unexpected reaction. In Hanif Kureishi's *Sleep with Me* (National, 1999) a man performs cunnilingus on his lover and then comments, 'The mouth of the world.' The remark was greeted with derisive laughter.

By 1999, in-yer-face theatre had become a new orthodoxy. Audiences were no longer surprised by unnaturalistic devices such as the insistent use of words such as 'cunt', nor by scenes of anal rape or drug injection. Rawness, pain and degradation became common means of representing the world. Narratives were told in new ways. Ultimately, in-yer-face theatre has redefined our notion of beauty, our ideas of what can or can't be said, of what can or can't be shown. It also was a powerful reminder that culture is a place of half-truths, contradictions and ambiguity. Those searching for absolute truths and simple answers didn't find them in theatre, which is more a place in which tentative understandings are created. If most of the news that came from British stages seemed to be bad, there was also a sense of hope that by confronting such extremes we might all grow more able to bear the real world of which they were a lurid reflection.

At the same time, several writers – from Neilson to Penhall – who once relished extreme emotions have shown themselves capable of exploring quieter feelings. In-yer-face theatre is less a school of writing or a movement than series of networks, in which individuals such as Neilson, Ravenhill and Kane formed temporary milieus. Perhaps the best metaphor for in-yer-face writing is that of an arena, an imaginary place that can be visited or passed through, a spot where a writer can grow up, or where they can return to after other adventures. A few writers have taken possession of this space; others have passed by quickly. But the developments in this arena meant that new writing at the start of the millennium was characterized by increased diversity, by greater willingness to experiment, by a variety of dissonant voices and by the breakdown of many of the old divisions that were part of our traditional idea of British theatre: subsidized/commercial; fringe/mainstream; theatre/film; high/low. Thanks to the provocations and innovations of a handful of writers, theatre left the nineties in a more fluid and complex state than when it began.

By 2000, there were signs that the heady days of outrage were numbered: the death of Sarah Kane, the failure of Irvine Welsh's shock-fest *You'll Have Had Your Hole* and the enormous success of Conor McPherson's *The Weir* all suggested that the tide was turning and that an era of confrontation had come to an end. 'This could be the end of one particular cycle,' Neilson said in 1999. 'How much further can you take it? *The Weir* wouldn't have been so successful if it hadn't been for in-yer-face theatre, but its success is also a sign that people have had enough.' By January 2000, the *Guardian* and the *Evening Standard* were already printing the obituaries of new writing, with Simon Reade, the Royal Shakespeare Company's literary manager, arguing that the *succès de scandale* of *Blasted* had resulted in a widespread misunderstanding of the new wave of what critic John Lahr dubbed 'nihilistic urban chic'. On this reading, Sarah Kane had more in common with other poetic writers of the nineties – such as Biyi Bandele, David Harrower and Marina Carr – than with the 'loud-mouthed aggression' and 'self-loathing' that characterized much youth culture in that decade. While Kane was certainly much more than just a shocker, it was the experiential quality of her work and that of some of her contemporaries that did the most to wake up audiences. There has always been plenty of poetry in British theatre – but rarely has that been enough to revive new writing. Whether or not the current new wave really has broken, it has certainly done its work, restoring the writer to the centre of the theatrical process, and reminding society at large that living writers are not only symbols of theatre's vitality but also a crucial resource for the whole culture.

John Russell Taylor ends his classic book, *Anger and After*, first published in 1962, by wondering whether new writers were 'fated by their beginnings never to break out of the original charmed circle' of being the 'over-praised, under-talented' darlings of a 'precious clique'. Since in-yer-face theatre had a similar role in the nineties to that performed by the first new wave of Royal Court dramatists in the late fifties and early sixties, the future of British theatre once again lay in the hands of its dramatists. The final judgement on them will not be literary or political, but theatrical and cultural. Only future revivals will show whether the issues they addressed so urgently have outlived their sell-by date – or whether they've become an established part of theatre's vocabulary of social criticism. As Shaw once said, on the subject of Ibsen's *A Doll's House*, its real strength will be what it does in the world.

Bibliography

Place of publication is London unless otherwise stated.

1 What is in-yer-face theatre?

Alfreds, Mike, 'Dramatic moments', *Guardian*, 12 June 1996.

Aston, Elaine, *An Introduction to Feminism and Theatre*, Routledge, 1995.

Barker, Howard, *Arguments for a Theatre*, 2nd edn, Manchester: Manchester University Press, 1993.

Barnes, Peter, 'Introduction', *Plays: 1 – The Ruling Class; Leonardo's Last Supper; Noonday Demons; The Bewitched; Laughter!; Barnes' People: Eight Monologues*, Methuen, 1989.

Berkoff, Steven, *Free Association: An Autobiography*, Faber, 1996.

Berkoff, Steven, *Plays 1 – East; West; Greek; Sink the Belgrano!, Massage; Lunch*, Faber 1994.

Billington, Michael, *One Night Stands: A Critic's View of Modern British Theatre*, Nick Hern, 1993.

Boireau, Nicole (ed.), 'Beyond taboos: images of outrageousness in recent English-speaking drama', *Contemporary Theatre Review*, vol. 5, part 1 (1996).

Bradwell, Mike (ed.), *The Bush Theatre Book*, Methuen, 1997.

Brenton, Howard, 'Preface', *Plays: 2 – The Romans in Britain; Thirteenth Night; The Genius; Bloody Poetry; Greenland*, Methuen, 1989.

Chambers, Colin, *Peggy: The Life of Peggy Ramsay, Play Agent*, Methuen, 1998.

Chambers, Colin, and Mike Prior, *Playwrights' Progress: Patterns of Postwar British Drama*, Oxford: Amber Lane, 1987.

Coveney, Michael, *The Aisle Is Full of Noises: A Vivisection of Live Theatre*, Nick Hern, 1994.

Craig, Sandy (ed.) *Dreams and Deconstructions: Alternative Theatre in Britain*, Ambergate: Amber Lane Press, 1980.

De Jongh, Nicholas, *Not in Front of the Audience: Homosexuality on Stage*, Routledge, 1992.

Dowie, Claire, interview with author, 23 July 1998.

Edgar, David (ed.), *State of Play: Playwrights on Playwriting*, Faber, 1999.

Edwardes, Pamela (ed.), *Frontline Intelligence 3: New Plays for the Nineties*, Methuen, 1995.

Elsom, John, *Erotic Theatre*, Secker & Warburg, 1973.

Elsom, John, *Post-War British Theatre*, Routledge & Kegan Paul, 1979.

Hare, David, *The Blue Room: Freely Adapted from Arthur Schnitzler's La Ronde*,

Faber, 1998.

Hewison, Robert, *Too Much: Art and Society in the Sixties, 1960–75*, Methuen, 1986.

Holroyd, Michael, *Bernard Shaw: The One-Volume Definitive Edition*, Vintage, 1998.

Innes, Christopher, *Modern British Drama 1890–1990*, Cambridge: Cambridge University Press, 1992.

Itzin, Catherine, *Stages in the Revolution: Political Theatre in Britain Since 1968*, Eyre Methuen, 1980.

Johnston, John, *The Lord Chamberlain's Blue Pencil*, Hodder & Stoughton, 1990.

Lahr, John, *Prick Up Your Ears: The Biography of Joe Orton*, Allen Lane. 1978.

Lloyd Evans, Gareth and Barbara, *Plays in Review 1956–80: British Drama and the Critics*, Batsford, 1985.

O'Toole, Fintan, 'Introduction' to Tom Murphy, *Plays: 4 – A Whistle in the Dark; A Crucial Week in the Life of a Grocer's Assistant; On the Outside; On the Inside*, Methuen, 1989.

Rebellato, Dan, *1956 and All That: The Making of Modern British Drama*, Routledge, 1999.

Rose, Peter, interview with author, 19 November 1998.

Salgādo, Gāmini (ed.), 'Introduction' to *Three Jacobean Tragedies*, Harmondsworth: Penguin, 1969.

Stanford, W. B., *Greek Tragedy and the Emotions: An Introductory Study*, Routledge & Kegan Paul, 1983.

Tushingham, David (ed.), *Live 3: Critical Mass*, Methuen, 1996.

Tynan, Kathleen, *The Life of Kenneth Tynan*, Methuen, 1988.

Wandor, Michelene, *Look Back in Gender: Sexuality and the Family in Post-War British Drama*, Methuen, 1987.

Wardle, Irving, *The Theatres of George Devine*, Eyre Methuen, 1979.

2 Come to the shock-fest

Billington, Michael, *One Night Stands: A Critic's View of Modern British Theatre*, Nick Hern, 1993.

Billington, Michael, 'Fabulous five', *Guardian*, 13 March 1996.

Bradwell, Mike (ed.) *The Bush Theatre Book*, Methuen, 1997.

Brown, Ian, interview with author, 1 July 1999.

Daldry, Stephen, 'Writing the future', *Guardian*, 7 September 1994.

Daldry, Stephen, interview with author, 7 January 2000.

Dromgoole, Dominic, interview with author, 10 May 1999.

Edgar, David, 'Eighth Birmingham Theatre Conference Paper', in *Studies in Theatre Production* 15, June 1997.

Hemming, Sarah, 'Look forward with anger', *Financial Times*, 18/19 November 1995.

Meth, Jonathan, interview with author, 7 July 1999.

Nightingale, Benedict, 'Ten with the playwright stuff', *The Times*, 1 May 1996.
Nightingale, Benedict, *The Future of Theatre*, Phoenix, 1998.
Rickson, Ian, interview with author, 25 May 1999.
Ward, Nick, 'Introduction' to *Plays: 1 – The Present; Apart from George; The Strangeness of Others; Trouble Sleeping*, Faber, 1995.
Whybrow, Graham, interview with Emma Freud, *Theatreland*, ITV, 9 March 1997.

Philip Ridley
Billington, Michael, 'A little blood goes a long way', *Guardian*, 20 April 1994.
Black, Ian, 'A chainsaw reaction to non-violence', *Sunday Times*, 28 March 1993.
Grove, Valerie, 'Gentle East End son who penned a cinema portrait of gangland evil', *Sunday Times*, 29 April 1990.
Hannan, Chris, 'Introduction', *The Evil Doers & The Baby*, Nick Hern, 1991.
Lloyd, Matthew, 'The cost of cruelty', *Guardian*, 23 April 1994.
Ridley, Philip, *Ghost from a Perfect Place*, Methuen, 1994.
Ridley, Philip, *Plays: 1 – The Pitchfork Disney; The Fastest Clock in the Universe; Ghost from a Perfect Place*, Methuen, 1997.
Ridley, Philip, 'My best teacher: Cecil Collins', *Times Educational Supplement*, 13 March 1998.
Ridley, Philip, interview with author, 25 January 1999.
Ridley, Philip, interview with author, 23 March 1999.
Topper, Jenny, 'Pushing the barrier', *Guardian*, 23 April 1994.
Topper, Jenny, interview with author, 8 February 1999.
Woddis, Carole, review of *The Fastest Clock in the Universe*, *Plays and Players*, July 1992.
Reviews of *The Pitchfork Disney*, *Theatre Record*, vol. XI, no. 1 (1991).
Reviews of *The Fastest Clock in the Universe*, *Theatre Record*, vol. XII, no. 10 (1992).
Reviews of *Ghost from a Perfect Place*, *Theatre Record*, vol. XIV, no. 8 (1994).

Phyllis Nagy
Bayley, Clare, 'Playwrights unplugged', *Independent*, 24 February 1995.
Benedict, David, 'Music to murder by', programme note for *Butterfly Kiss*, Almeida Theatre, April 1994.
McAuley, Tilly, 'Playing unhappy families', *Evening Standard*, 7 April 1994.
Freeman, Sandra, *Putting Your Daughters on the Stage: Lesbian Theatre from the 1970s to the 1990s*, Cassell, 1997.
Nagy, Phyllis, 'Foreword' to *Weldon Rising* in Annie Castledine (ed.), *Plays by Women: Ten*, Methuen, 1994.
Nagy, Phyllis, *Butterfly Kiss*, Nick Hern, 1994.
Nagy, Phyllis, interview in Heidi Stephenson and Natasha Langridge, *Rage and Reason: Women Playwrights on Playwriting*, Methuen, 1997.
Nagy, Phyllis, *Plays: 1 – Weldon Rising; Butterfly Kiss; Disappeared; The Strip*, Methuen, 1998.

Nagy, Phyllis, *Never Land*, Methuen, 1998.

Nagy, Phyllis, interview with author, 30 March 1999.

Nagy, Phyllis, interview with author, 2 June 1999.

Nagy, Phyllis, 'Hold your nerve: notes for a young playwright', in David Edgar (ed.), *State of Play: Playwrights on Playwriting*, Faber, 1999.

Reviews of *Weldon Rising*, *Theatre Record*, vol. XII, no. 25–26 (1992).

Reviews of *Butterfly Kiss*, *Theatre Record*, vol. XIV, no 8. (1994).

Reviews of *Disappeared*, *Theatre Record*, vol. XV, nos 3 and 13 (1995).

Reviews of *The Strip*, *Theatre Record*, vol. XV, no. 5 (1995).

Reviews of *Never Land*, *Theatre Record*, vol. XVIII, no. 1–2 (1998).

Tracy Letts

Bayley, Clare, 'Texan trailer-park blues', *Independent*, 18 January 1995.

Curtis, Nick, 'Stand by for more blood on the walls', *Evening Standard*, 24 September 1996.

Christopher, James, 'Doing the dirty', *Time Out*, 18–25 January 1995.

Dromgoole, Dominic, interview with author, 10 May 1999.

Letts, Tracy, *Bug*, programme for the Gate Theatre production, September 1996.

Letts, Tracy, *Killer Joe*, unpublished script, William Morris Agency, January 1999.

Letts, Tracy, interview with author, 8 March 1999.

Llewellyn Smith, Julia, 'Connoisseur of white trash, sex and violence', *The Times*, 24 February 1995.

Morris, Tom, 'Foul deeds, fair play', *Guardian*, 25 January 1995.

Reviews of *Killer Joe*, *Theatre Record*, vol. XIV, no. 19 (1994), vol. XV, no. 1–2 (1995) and vol. XV, no. 4 (1995).

Harry Gibson

Appleyard, Bryan, 'We failed the acid test', *Sunday Times*, 2 August 1998.

Gibson, Harry, interview with author, 30 January 1999.

Gibson, Harry, letter to author, 9 April 1999.

Lezard, Nicholas, 'Escape into a dirtier world', *Sunday Times*, 23 February 1996.

Poole, Steven, 'Mad, but ah'd love tae gie it a go', *Times Literary Supplement*, 29 December 1995.

Smith, Andrew, 'Irvine changes trains', *Sunday Times*, 1 February 1998.

Tonkin, Boyd, 'Mainline connections', *New Statesman & Society*, 27 May 1994.

Welsh, Irvine, *Trainspotting*, Minerva Paperback edn, 1994.

Welsh, Irvine, *Trainspotting & Headstate*, Minerva, 1996.

Reviews of *Trainspotting*, *Theatre Record*, vol. XIV, no. 10 (1994); vol. XV, no. 7 (1995) and vol. XV, no. 25–26 (1995).

3 Anthony Neilson

Basset, Kate, 'Good, bad and ugly', *The Times*, 10 September 1996.

Christopher, James, 'Inside story', *Time Out*, 5–12 January 1994.

Kelly, Jane, 'Britain saved this boy from Hitler, now he wants to save us from our own vulgarity', *Daily Mail*, 2 February 1998.

Morris, Tom, 'Foul deeds, fair play', *Guardian*, 25 January 1995.

Neilson, Anthony, *Heredity*, unpublished script, 1995.

Neilson, Anthony, 'Dramatic moments', *Guardian*, 11 September 1996.

Neilson, Anthony, 'Manifesto', *Time Out*, 14–21 August 1996.

Neilson, Anthony, *The Censor*, Methuen, 1997.

Neilson, Anthony, *Plays: 1 – Normal; Penetrator; The Year of the Family; The Night Before Christmas; The Censor*, Methuen, 1998.

Neilson, Anthony, interview with author, 23 February 1999.

Neilson, Anthony, interview with author, 2 March 1999.

Neilson, Anthony, interview with author, 15 March 1999.

Neilson, Anthony, interview with author, 13 April 1999.

Neilson, Anthony, fax to author, 25 September 1999.

Reynolds, Nigel, 'Enthusiast puts up £1 million to combat theatre "filth"', *Telegraph*, 29 January 1998.

Senter, Al, 'Curtain call: Anthony Neilson', *What's On*, 26 April 1995.

Senter, Al, 'Class of '99: Anthony Neilson', *The London Magazine*, January 1999.

Stratton, Kate, 'Censor sensibility', *Time Out*, 4–11 June 1997.

Stringer, Robin, 'The Young Vic hands out heart monitors to test horror drama', *Evening Standard*, 2 September 1996.

Reviews of *Normal: The Düsseldorf Ripper*, *Theatre Record*, vol. XI, no. 20 (1991).

Reviews of *Penetrator*, *Theatre Record*, vol. XIII, no. 21 (1993) and vol. XIV, no. 1 (1994).

Reviews of *The Year of the Family*, *Theatre Record*, vol. XIV, no. 7 (1994).

Reviews of *The Censor*, *Theatre Record*, vol. XVII, nos 7, 12 and 18 (1997).

4 Sarah Kane

Armitstead, Claire, 'No pain, no Kane', *Guardian*, 29 April 1998.

Benedict, David, 'Disgusting violence? Actually it's quite a peaceful play', *Independent*, 22 January 1995.

Benedict, David, 'What Sarah did next', *Independent*, 15 May 1996.

Bond, Edward, 'A blast at our smug theatre', *Guardian*, 28 January 1995.

Ellison, Mike and Alex Bellos, 'Blasted: a deeply moral and compassionate piece of theatre or simply a disgusting feast of filth?', *Guardian*, 20 January 1995.

Fanshawe, Simon, 'Given to extremes', *Sunday Times*, 26 April 1998.

Farr, David, 'Phaedra and Hippolytus', programme note to Sarah Kane's *Phaedra's Love*, Gate Theatre, May 1996.

Hemming, Sarah, 'Look forward with anger', *Financial Times*, 18/19 November 1995.

Inverne, James, *Jack Tinker: A Life in Review*, Oberon, 1997.

Kane, Sarah, *Blasted* in *Frontline Intelligence 2: New Plays for the Nineties*,

Methuen, 1994.

Kane, Sarah, *Skin*, unpublished script, Casarotto Ramsay, 1995.

Kane, Sarah, *Blasted & Phaedra's Love*, Methuen, 1996.

Kane, Sarah, interview in Heidi Stephenson and Natasha Langridge, *Rage and Reason: Women Playwrights on Playwriting*, Methuen, 1997.

Kane, Sarah, *Cleansed*, Methuen, 1998.

Kane, Sarah, *Crave*, Methuen, 1998.

Kane, Sarah, interview with author, 14 September 1998.

Kane, Sarah, in conversation with Dan Rebellato, Royal Holloway, University of London, 3 November 1998.

Kane, Sarah, letter to author, 4 January 1999.

Kane, Sarah, letter to author, 18 January 1999.

Kane, Simon, interview with author, 24 June 1999.

Kane, Simon, press release about *4:48 Psychosis*, 21 September 1999.

Macdonald, James, 'Blasting back at the critics', *Observer*, 22 January 1995.

Macdonald, James, 'Sarah Kane returns to the Royal Court', Royal Court *Newsletter*, March-June 1998.

Mayer, Anne, interview with author, 12 October 1998.

Morris, Tom, 'Foul deeds, fair play', *Guardian*, 25 January 1995.

Morris, Tom, 'Damned and blasted?' *Sunday Times*, 29 January 1995.

Neilson, Anthony, letter to the *Guardian*, 25 February 1999.

Ravenhill, Mark, Sarah Kane obituary, *Independent*, 23 February 1999.

Rebellato, Dan, 'Sarah Kane: an appreciation', *New Theatre Quarterly* 60, November 1999.

Stratton, Kate, 'Extreme measures', *Time Out*, 25 March–1 April 1998.

Tabert, Nils, interview with Sarah Kane (8 February 1998) in *Playspotting: Die Londoner Theaterszene der 90er*, Hamburg, Germany, 1998.

Tushingham, David, 'There's only now', programme note for the Stuttgart State Theatre production of *Cleansed*, Stuttgart, July 1999.

Wilson, Snoo, 'Blasted metaphors', *New Statesman*, 3 February 1995.

Reviews of *Blasted*, *Theatre Record*, vol. XV, no. 1–2 (1995).

Reviews of *Phaedra's Love*, *Theatre Record*, vol. XVI, no. 11 (1996).

Reviews of *Cleansed*, *Theatre Record*, vol. XVIII, no. 9 (1998).

Reviews of *Crave*, *Theatre Record*, vol. XVIII, no. 18 (1998).

5 Mark Ravenhill

Actors Touring Company, programme for *Handbag*, 1998.

Billington, Michael, 'Would you like your children to be brought up by a rich, kindly old pervert?', *Guardian*, 16 September 1998.

Christopher, James, *et al.*, programme note to *Shopping and F***ing*, Gielgud Theatre, 1997.

Edgar, David, 'Plays for today', *Sunday Times*, Culture essay, 7 September 1997.

Fannin, Hilary, Stephen Greenhorn, Abi Morgan and Mark Ravenhill, *Sleeping*

Around, Methuen, 1998.

Freud, Emma, *Theatreland*, London Weekend Television, 9 March 1997.

Gibbons, Fiachra, 'Angry Young Men under fire from gay writer', *Guardian*, 8 November 1999.

Hare, David and Mark Ravenhill, 'The success of new writing in the commercial theatre', London New Play Festival platform, Apollo Theatre, 21 May 1998.

Miller, Carl, 'Shocking and fussing', http://www.royal-court.org.uk, July 1997.

Philippou, Nick, interview with author, 12 January 1999.

Ravenhill, Mark, Max Stafford-Clark and Stephen Daldry, 'Do new writers have hearts?' *New Sceptics*, session 1, Theatre Museum, 15 October 1996.

Ravenhill, Mark, *Shopping and Fucking*, 1st edn, Methuen, 1996.

Ravenhill, Mark, interview in *Theatreland*, London Weekend Television, 9 March 1997.

Ravenhill, Mark, 'Dramatic moments', *Guardian*, 9 April 1997.

Ravenhill, Mark, *Shopping and Fucking*, 2nd edn, Methuen, 1997.

Ravenhill, Mark, *Faust (Faust Is Dead)*, 1st edn, Methuen, 1997.

Ravenhill, Mark *et al.*, programme note to *Faust*, Actors Touring Company, 1997.

Ravenhill, Mark, 'The difference a day made', *Guardian*, 19 January 1998.

Ravenhill, Mark, 'My life was a voyage with Dr Who. Then the Tardis turned to cardboard', *Independent*, 27 January 1998.

Ravenhill, Mark, *Faust Is Dead*, revised edn, unpublished script, Casarotto Ramsay, April 1998.

Ravenhill, Mark, in conversation with Maria Delgado, People's Palace, Queen Mary and Westfield College, London, 3 November 1998.

Ravenhill, Mark, interview with author, 11 November 1998.

Ravenhill, Mark, interview with author, 3 December 1998.

Ravenhill, Mark, *Handbag*, Methuen, 1998.

Ravenhill, Mark, interview with author, 19 January 1999.

Ravenhill, Mark, *Some Explicit Polaroids*, Methuen, 1999.

Ravenhill, Mark, interview with author, 14 January 2000.

Robson, Cheryl, 'Bonner Biennale: new plays from Europe', *New Playwrights Trust News*, no 119, July 1998.

Stafford-Clark, Max, interviewed by Malcolm Jones, 'Royal Court Modern Classics', Theatre Museum study day, 20 July 1997.

Stokes, John, 'Look back at anger', *Times Literary Supplement*, 29 October 1999.

Taylor, Paul, 'Damned if he does, damned if he don't', *Independent*, 26 February 1997.

Thornton, Michael, 'A shop window for outrage', *Punch*, 21–27 September 1996.

Whitley, John, 'The importance of being shocking', *Telegraph*, 4 September 1998.

Reviews of *Shopping and Fucking*, *Theatre Record*, vol. XVI, no. 20 (1996); vol. XVII, no. 13 (1997); vol. XVIII, no. 1–2 (1998).

IN-YER-FACE THEATRE

Reviews of *Faust, Theatre Record*, vol. XVII, no. 5 (1997).
Reviews of *Sleeping Around, Theatre Record*, vol. XVIII, no. 6 (1998).
Reviews of *Handbag, Theatre Record*, vol. XVIII, no. 19 (1998).
Reviews of *Some Explicit Polaroids, Theatre Record*, vol. XIX, no. 21 (1999).

6 Boys together

Edgar, David, 'Eighth Birmingham Theatre Conference Paper', in *Studies in Theatre Production* 15, June 1997.
Gibbons, Fiachra, 'You'll never walk again', *Guardian*, 7 November 1998.
Lewis, Jonathan, interview with the author, 25 April 1999.
Lukowiak, Ken and Lyn Gardner, 'Tinker, tailor, soldier . . . lie?' *Guardian*, 1 September 1998.
Nightingale, Benedict, 'Ten with the playwright stuff', *The Times*, 1 May 1996.
O'Rowe, Mark, *From Both Hips: Two Plays*, Nick Hern, 1999.
Rickson, Ian, interviewed by Emma Freud, *Theatreland*, London Weekend Television, 8/9 March 1998.
Stephenson, Heidi and Natasha Langridge, *Rage and Reason: Women Playwrights on Playwriting*, Methuen, 1997.
Topper, Jenny, interview with author, 8 February 1999.

Naomi Wallace

Basset, Kate, 'A woman behind the lines', *The Times*, 2 August 1994.
Bayley, Clare, 'Make love, not war', *Independent*, 3 August 1994.
Pile, Stephen, 'An American wonder in Yorkshire', *Telegraph*, 17 July 1999.
Wallace, Naomi, *The War Boys*, unpublished script, Rod Hall, 1992.
Wallace, Naomi, *One Flea Spare* in *Bush Theatre Plays*, Faber, 1996.
Wallace, Naomi, *Slaughter City*, Faber, 1996.
Wallace, Naomi, *Birdy*, Faber, 1997.
Wallace, Naomi, interview in Heidi Stephenson and Natasha Langridge, *Rage and Reason: Women Playwrights on Playwriting*, Methuen, 1997.
Wallace, Naomi, interview with author, 9 January 1999.
Wallace, Naomi, letter to author, 14 April 1999.
Reviews of *The War Boys, Theatre Record*, vol. XIII, no. 3 (1993).
Reviews of *In the Heart of America, Theatre Record*, vol. XIV, no. 16 (1994).
Reviews of *One Flea Spare, Theatre Record*, vol. XV, no. 21 (1995).
Reviews of *Slaughter City, Theatre Record*, vol. XVI, no. 2 (1996).
Reviews of *Birdy, Theatre Record*, vol. XVII, no. 5 (1997).

Jez Butterworth

Anon, 'Jez Butterworth, writer,' *Guardian*, 26 July 1995.
Butterworth, Jez, *Mojo*, 1st edn, Nick Hern, 1995.
Butterworth, Jez, *Mojo*, 2nd edn, Nick Hern, 1996.
Butterworth, Jez, 'Getting *Mojo* working', *Sunday Telegraph*, 28 June 1998.
Butterworth, Jez, *Mojo & a Film-Maker's Diary*, Faber, 1998.

Reynolds, Anna, 'Uncool for cats', *The Big Issue*, 10–16 March 1997.

Poole, Steven, 'Raddled, but no Keith Richard', *Times Literary Supplement*, 4 August 1995.

Rickson, Ian, interview with author, 25 May 1999.

Shelley, Jim, 'The idler', *Guardian Weekend*, 4 July 1998.

Wolf, Matt, 'Great British hopes: Jez Butterworth', *The Times*, 15 June 1995.

Wright, Michael, 'Jez scoops £5,000 for a slice of Soho life', *Telegraph*, 8 July 1995.

Yates, Robert, 'I'm interested in violence. But that doesn't make me Tarantino', *Observer*, 2 November 1997.

Reviews of *Mojo*, *Theatre Record*, vol. XV, no. 15 (1995) and vol. XVI, no. 21 (1996).

Simon Block

Block, Simon, *Not a Game for Boys*, Nick Hern, 1995.

Block, Simon, 'Personally speaking: theatre is irrelevant to anyone under 20. Discuss', *Independent*, 18 February 1999.

Block, Simon, programme note for *No Exp. Req'd*, Hampstead Theatre, March 1999.

Block, Simon, interview with author, 29 April 1999.

Block, Simon, fax to author, 23 June 1999.

Block, Simon, interview with author, 24 June 1999.

Freud, Clement, 'Ping-pong ain't the game it used to be', *The Times*, 22 September 1995.

Reviews of *Not a Game for Boys*, *Theatre Record*, vol. XV, no. 18 (1995).

Reviews of *Chimps*, *Theatre Record*, vol. XVII, no. 15 (1997).

David Eldridge

Eldridge, David, *Serving It Up*, 1st edn, Bush Theatre, 1996.

Eldridge, David, *Serving It Up & A Week with Tony*, Methuen, 1997.

Eldridge, David, 'Looking back', in Mike Bradwell (ed.), *The Bush Theatre Book*, Methuen, 1997.

Eldridge, David, 'Time travels', panel discussion, at *Losing the plot? Tenth Birmingham Theatre Conference*, 31 March 1999.

Eldridge, David, interview with author, 12 April 1999.

Eldridge, David, 'Back to the future', in David Edgar (ed.), *State of Play: Playwrights on Playwriting*, Faber, 1999.

Jensen, Hal, 'Cashing in on the state of the nation', *Times Literary Supplement*, 5 July 1996.

Rosenthal, Daniel, 'Great British hopes: David Eldridge', *The Times*, 2 April 1997.

Ryder, Tanya, interview with author about her 1999 production of *Serving It Up* at Liverpool John Moores University, 31 March 1999.

Senter, Al, 'Curtain call: David Eldridge', *What's On*, 26 March 1997.

Reviews of *Serving It Up*, *Theatre Record*, vol. XVI, no. 4 (1996).

Reviews of *A Week with Tony*, *Theatre Record*, vol. XVI, no. 13 (1996).
Reviews of *Summer Begins*, *Theatre Record*, vol. XVII, no. 7 (1997).
Reviews of *Falling*, *Theatre Record*, vol. XIX, no. 4 (1999).

7 Sex wars

Bent, Simon, *Three Plays: Goldhawk Road; Wasted; Bad Company*, Oberon, 1997.
Bhula, Mo, 'Joe Nineties: a look at urban life in the last decade of the millennium', programme note to Murray Gold's *50 Revolutions*, Whitehall Theatre, September 1999.
Greig, David, *Europe & The Architect*, Methuen, 1996.
McPherson, Conor, *Four Plays: Rum and Vodka; The Good Thief; This Lime Tree Bower; St Nicholas*, Nick Hern, 1999.
Penhall, Joe, *Plays: 1 – Some Voices; Pale Horse; Love and Understanding; The Bullet*, Methuen, 1998.
Ravenhill, Mark, 'Plays about men', in David Edgar (ed.), *State of Play: Playwrights on Playwriting*, Faber, 1999.
Welsh, Irvine, *Trainspotting & Headstate*, Minerva, 1996.

Nick Grosso
Bassett, Kate, 'Great British hopes: Nick Grosso', *The Times*, 27 January 1996.
Edwards-Jones, Imogen, 'The boys can't help it', *The Times*, 24 October 1998.
Edwards-Jones, Imogen, 'Future famous five', *The Times*, 2 January 1999.
Grosso, Nick, *Peaches*, in *Coming On Strong: New Writing from the Royal Court*, Faber, 1995.
Grosso, Nick, *Sweetheart*, 1st edn, Faber, 1996.
Grosso, Nick, interview with author, 6 October 1998.
Grosso, Nick, public platform, Offstage Bookshop, London, 11 November 1998.
Grosso, Nick, interview with author, 20 November 1998.
Grosso, Nick, *Sweetheart*, 2nd edn, Faber, 1998.
Grosso, Nick, *Real Classy Affair*, Faber, 1998.
Grosso, Nick, letter to author, 12 April 1999.
Reviews of *Peaches*, *Theatre Record*, vol. XIV, no. 23 (1994).
Reviews of *Sweetheart*, *Theatre Record*, vol. XVI, no. 3 (1996).
Reviews of *Real Classy Affair*, *Theatre Record*, vol. XVIII, no. 21 (1998).

Patrick Marber
Chunn, Louise and Neil Norman, 'Not in front of your lover', *Evening Standard*, 2 April 1998.
Forrest, Emma, 'The upper hand', *Guardian*, 1 December 1997.
Gardner, Lyn, 'Sex in a chilling climate', *Guardian*, 3 January 1998.
Garner, Lesley, 'Closer to the truth?', *Sunday Times*, 19 July 1998.
Jenkins, Amy, 'The human condition: women can behave badly too', *Independent on Sunday*, 19 July 1998.
Kellaway, Kate, review of *Closer*, *New Statesman*, 1 May 1998.

Marber, Patrick, *Dealer's Choice*, Methuen, 1995.

Marber, Patrick, interview with Nicholas Wright, in *Platform Papers 8: Playwrights*, National Theatre, 1995.

Marber, Patrick, 'Dramatic moments', *Guardian*, 14 February 1996.

Marber, Patrick, interview with Richard Eyre (April 1997), programme for *Closer*, National Theatre, May 1997.

Marber, Patrick, interview with Emma Freud, in *Theatreland*, London Weekend Television, 30 November 1997.

Marber, Patrick, *Closer*, 1st edn, Methuen, 1997.

Marber, Patrick, 'On *Closer*', *Evening Standard Hot Tickets* magazine, 26 March 1998.

Marber, Patrick, interview with Jack Bradley, programme for *Closer*, Lyric Theatre, March 1998.

Marber, Patrick, live conversation on Internet website, http://www.closer.co.uk, 25 June 1998.

Marber, Patrick, letter to author, 24 June 1999.

Marber, Patrick, 'NT2000: 100 plays of the century – *Closer*', National Theatre public platform, 15 December 1999.

Marber, Patrick, *Closer*, 2nd edn, Methuen, 1999.

Miller, Andrew, 'A lunatic algebra of love', *The Times*, 4 April 1998.

Shone, Tom, 'Close and personal', *Sunday Times*, 26 October 1997.

Smith, Ben, 'Why we hate women', *Independent on Sunday*, 12 July 1998.

Taylor, Paul, Review of *Closer*, *Independent*, 25 October 1997.

Reviews of *Closer*, *Theatre Record*, vol. XVII, no. 11 (1997) and vol. XVIII, no 7. (1998).

Che Walker

Christopher, James, 'Great British hopes: Che Walker', *The Times*, 25 March 1998.

Pinnock, Winsome, 'Breaking down the door', in Vera Gottlieb and Colin Chambers (eds), *Theatre in a Cool Climate*, Oxford: Amber Lane, 1999.

Walker, Che, public platform, Offstage Bookshop, London, 25 November 1998.

Walker, Che, interview with author, 9 December 1998.

Walker, Che, *Been So Long*, Faber, 1998.

Walker, Che, interview with author, 26 March 1999.

Reviews of *Been So Long*, *Theatre Record*, vol. XVIII, no. 7 (1998).

Richard Zajdlic

Allfree, Claire, 'Breaking up is really hard to do', *Metro London*, 4 May 1999.

Anon, 'Londoner's Diary', *Evening Standard*, 13 May 1999.

Bond, Matthew, 'An accent on achievement', *Sunday Times*, 11 April 1999.

Daley, Janet, 'This is life', *Telegraph*, 8 August 1997.

Grant, Brigit, 'Give us all a new lease of life', *Mirror*, 8 August 1997.

Zajdlic, Richard, 'Looking back', in Mike Bradwell (ed.), *The Bush Theatre Book*, Methuen, 1997.

Zajdlic, Richard, *Infidelities*, in Matthew Lloyd (ed.) *First Run 3: New Plays by*

New Writers, Nick Hern, 1991.

Zajdlic, Richard, interview with author, 6 July 1999.

Zajdlic, Richard, interview with author, 12 August 1999.

Zajdlic, Richard, *Dogs Barking*, Faber, 1999.

Reviews of *Dogs Barking*, *Theatre Record*, vol. XIX, no. 10 (1999).

8 Battered and bruised

Christopher, James, 'Fairytales with a streak of violence', *The Times*,
     27 January 1998.

De Jongh, Nicholas, 'The year of living violently', *Evening Standard*,
     21 December 1995.

Elton, Ben, *Plays: 1 – Gasping; Silly Cow; Popcorn*, Methuen, 1998.

Hemming, Sarah, 'Tomorrow is another play', *Independent*, 13 May 1992.

Setren, Phil, 'Introduction' to *Best of the Fest: A Collection of New Plays
     Celebrating 10 Years of London New Play Festival*, Aurora Metro, 1998.

Smith, Andrew, 'Irvine changes trains', *Sunday Times*, 1 February 1998.

Taylor, Paul, 'Ten years in the arts', *Independent*, 11 October 1996.

Walsh, Enda, *Disco Pigs* in John Farleigh (ed.), *Far from the Land:
     Contemporary Irish Plays*, Methuen, 1998.

Yates, Robert, 'I'm interested in violence. But that doesn't make me Tarantino',
     Observer, 2 November 1997.

Joe Penhall

Fanshawe, Simon, 'Aiming high', *Sunday Times*, 5 April 1998.

Kingston, Jeremy, 'Fair to the middling', *The Times*, 30 April 1997.

Logan, Brian, 'A life more ordinary', *Time Out*, 25 March–1 April 1998.

Penhall, Joe, *Some Voices* in *Frontline Intelligence 3: New Plays for the Nineties*,
     Methuen, 1995.

Penhall, Joe, *Some Voices & Pale Horse*, Methuen, 1996.

Penhall, Joe, *Wild Turkey* in Phil Setren (ed.) *Best of the Fest: A Collection of New
     Plays Celebrating 10 Years of London New Play Festival*, Aurora Metro, 1998.

Penhall, Joe, *Plays: 1 – Some Voices; Pale Horse; Love and Understanding; The
     Bullet*, Methuen, 1998.

Penhall, Joe, interview with author, 14 July 1999.

Penhall, Joe, email to author, 17 August 1999.

Penhall, Joe, letter to author, 17 August 1999.

Reviews of *Some Voices*, *Theatre Record*, vol. XIV, no. 19 (1994).

Reviews of *Pale Horse*, *Theatre Record*, vol. XV, no. 21 (1995).

Reviews of *Love and Understanding*, *Theatre Record*, vol. XVII, no. 9 (1997).

Reviews of *The Bullet*, *Theatre Record*, vol. XVIII, no. 7 (1998).

Judy Upton

Hemming, Sarah, 'Look forward with anger', *Financial Times*, 18/19 November
     1998.

Nightingale, Benedict, 'Ten with the playwright stuff', *The Times*, 1 May 1996.

Rosenthal, Daniel, 'Small-beer venues get champagne treatment', *The Times*, 31 January 1996.

Rose, Guy, 'Judy Upton: brief cv', email to author, 2 August 1999.

Rose, Guy, email to author, 8 October 1999.

Upton, Judy, *Ashes and Sand*, in *Frontline Intelligence 3: New Plays for the Nineties*, Methuen, 1995.

Upton, Judy, *Bruises*, Methuen, 1995.

Upton, Judy, *Bruises & The Shorewatcher's House*, Methuen, 1996.

Upton, Judy, *Everlasting Rose* in Phil Setren (ed.) *Best of the Fest: A Collection of New Plays Celebrating 10 Years of London New Play Festival*, Aurora Metro, 1998.

Reviews of *Ashes and Sand*, *Theatre Record*, vol. XIV, no. 25–26 (1994).

Reviews of *Bruises*, *Theatre Record*, vol. XV, no. 24 (1995).

Martin McDonagh

Anon, 'Bond star shaken by award stir', *Mirror*, 30 November 1996.

Bradley, Jack, 'Making playwrights', programme note to Martin McDonagh's *The Cripple of Inishmaan*, National Theatre, January 1997.

Christiansen, Rupert, 'If you're the greatest you must prove it', *Telegraph*, 6 January 1997.

Coveney, Michael, 'He compares himself with the young Orson Welles. Oh dear. . .', *Observer*, 1 December 1996.

Dallat, C. L., 'A last chance for love', *Times Literary Supplement*, 15 March 1996.

Hemming, Sarah, 'Gift of the gab', *Independent*, 2 December 1996.

McDonagh, Martin, *The Beauty Queen of Leenane*, Methuen, 1996.

McDonagh, Martin, *Plays: 1 – The Beauty Queen of Leenane; A Skull in Connemara; The Lonesome West*, Methuen, 1999.

O'Toole, Fintan, 'Martin McDonagh is famous for telling Sean Connery to f*** off. He also happens to be a brilliant playwright', *Guardian*, 2 December 1996.

Owen, Michael, 'Success comes in threes', *Evening Standard*, 29 November 1996.

Reynolds, Oliver, 'Pressure cooking', *Times Literary Supplement*, 8 August 1997.

Walters, Guy, 'Great British hopes: Martin McDonagh', *The Times*, 5 October 1996.

Weston, Alannah, 'Martin McDonagh: the playwright injecting a rock 'n' roll buzz into the theatre', *Daily Telegraph* magazine, 12 July 1997.

Reviews of *The Beauty Queen of Leenane*, *Theatre Record*, vol. XVI, nos 5 and 25–26 (1996).

Reviews of *The Leenane Trilogy: The Beauty Queen of Leenane, A Skull in Connemara* and *The Lonesome West*, *Theatre Record*, vol. XVII, no. 15 (1997).

Reviews of *The Cripple of Inishmaan*, *Theatre Record*, vol. XVII, no. 1–2 (1997).

Rebecca Prichard

Alberge, Dalya, 'Charities alarmed at casting of children in "gang rape" play', *The Times*, 26 August 1997.

Basset, Kate, 'Atrocities on the fringe', *Telegraph*, 30 October 1997.

Benedict, David, '"Essex Girl" writes play shock horror', *Independent*, 22 October 1997.

Carroll, Rory, 'Gangs put boot into old ideas of femininity', *Guardian*, 22 July 1998.

Cavendish, Dominic, 'Girls 'n the hood', *The Big Issue*, 4 May 1998.

Curtis, Nick, 'Rising star: Rebecca Prichard', *Evening Standard Hot Tickets* magazine, 7 May 1998.

Kraft, Susannah, 'Yard Gal', *Royal Court Newsletter*, July–October 1998.

Prichard, Rebecca, *Essex Girls* in *Coming On Strong: New Writing from the Royal Court Theatre*, Faber, 1995.

Prichard, Rebecca, *Fair Game*, Faber, 1997.

Prichard, Rebecca, *Yard Gal*, Faber, 1998.

Prichard, Rebecca, interview with author, 30 May 1999.

Prichard, Rebecca, interview with author, 18 July 1999.

Prichard, Rebecca, 'Plays by women', in David Edgar (ed.), *State of Play: Playwrights on Playwriting*, Faber, 1999.

Reviews of *Essex Girls*, *Theatre Record*, vol. XIV, no. 21 (1994).

Reviews of *Fair Game*, *Theatre Record*, vol. XVII, no. 22 (1997).

Reviews of *Yard Gal*, *Theatre Record*, vol. XVIII, no. 10 (1998).

Conclusion

Billington, Michael, discussion of Sarah Kane's *Blasted* on *The Late Show*, BBC2, 23 January 1995.

Billington, Michael, 'A knight at the theatre', *Guardian*, 4 September 1998.

Billington, Michael, 'The other Marx brother', *Guardian*, 10 February 1998.

Bradley, Jack, interview with author, 22 July 1999.

Christopher, James, 'Life pulses at Court', *Sunday Express*, 8 December 1996.

Coveney, Michael, 'His last play was full of sodomy and vomiting. This time the mood is a bit darker', *Observer*, 9 February 1997.

De Jongh, Nicholas, 'The London stage: it's like a neutered old tomcat', *Evening Standard*, 5 January 2000.

Dunster, Matthew, 'There are no contemporary playwrights', typescript, 1998.

Edwardes, Jane, 'Israelite touch', *Time Out*, 9–16 September 1998.

Eyres, Harry, 'Sensation stalks the stage', *Spectator*, 9 May 1998.

Fanshawe, Simon, 'Staging an invasion', *Sunday Times*, 13 December 1998.

Gardner, Lyn, 'The end of the word', *Guardian*, 5 January 2000.

Gibson, Harry, 'Rant', letter to author, 9 April 1999.

Hemke, Rolf C., 'The old history of new German drama', undated typescript, [August 1999].

Hemming, Sarah, 'Upstairs, downstairs', *Independent*, 18 February 1998.

Herbert, Ian, 'Prompt corner', *Theatre Record*, vol. XVIII, no. 6 (March 1994).

Higginson, Sue, interview with author, 1 September 1999.

Kane, Sarah, interview with author, 14 September 1998.

Meth, Jonathan, interview with author, 7 July 1999.

Mortimer, John, 'Why stage beats TV every time', *Evening Standard*, 20 April 1995.

Nagy, Phyllis, 'Hold your nerve: notes for a young playwright', in David Edgar (ed.), *State of Play: Playwrights on Playwriting*, Faber, 1999.

Neilson, Anthony, interview with author, 13 April 1999.

Reade, Simon, 'Poetry please', *Guardian*, 12 January 2000.

Reading, Anna, *Falling*, unpublished script, 1996.

Setren, Phil, interview with author, 1 September 1999.

Shulman, Milton, *Marilyn, Hitler and Me*, Andre Deutsch, 1998.

Sirett, Paul, interview with author, 13 July 1999.

Stratton, Kate, 'Art act to follow', *Time Out*, 15–22 April 1998.

Taormina Arte, 'Europe theatre prize', programme, Taormina, Italy, May 1999.

Taylor, John Russell, *Anger and After: A Guide to the New British Drama*, 2nd edn, Methuen, 1969.

David Tushingham (ed.) *Live 3: Critical Mass*, Methuen, 1996.

Whybrow, Graham, interview with author, 7 July 1999.

Willmott, Phil, interview with author, 5 July 1999.

Index